COLLECTING EARLY CHRISTIAN LETTERS

From the Apostle Paul to Late Antiquity

Letter-collections in late antiquity give witness to the flourishing of letter-writing, with the development of the mostly formulaic exchanges between elites of the Graeco-Roman world to a more wide-ranging correspondence by bishops and monks, as well as emperors and Gothic kings. The contributors study individual collections from the first to sixth centuries CE, ranging from the Pauline and deutero-Pauline letters through monastic letters from Egypt, bishops' letter-collections and early papal collections compiled for various purposes. This is the first multi-authored study of New Testament and late-antique letter-collections, crossing the traditional divide between these disciplines by focusing on Latin, Greek, Coptic and Syriac epistolary sources. It draws together leading scholars in the field of late-antique epistolography from Australasia, Sweden, the United Kingdom and the United States.

BRONWEN NEIL is the Burke Senior Lecturer in Ecclesiastical Latin in the Faculty of Theology and Philosophy and associate director of the Centre for Early Christian Studies at Australian Catholic University (ACU). Her publications include Latin and Greek text editions of Maximus Confessor and Pope Martin I, and the Routledge Early Church Fathers volume on Leo the Great. Her most recent books, both co-authored with Pauline Allen, are *Crisis Management in Late Antiquity (410–590 CE): The Evidence of Episcopal Letters* (2013), and a translation of Gelasius I's letters as evidence for the late-antique papacy. She and Pauline Allen are currently co-editing the *Oxford Handbook of Maximus the Confessor*.

PAULINE ALLEN is director of the Centre for Early Christian Studies at ACU, and an honorary research fellow at the University of Pretoria. She has written extensively on the christological controversies of the fifth, sixth and seventh centuries, with recent translation volumes of the letters and other writings of Severus of Antioch and Sophronius of Jerusalem. Apart from two volumes co-authored with Bronwen Neil (see above), her most recent work, co-authored with Wendy Mayer, is *The Churches of Syrian Antioch (300–638 CE)* (2012).

COLLECTING EARLY CHRISTIAN LETTERS

From the Apostle Paul to Late Antiquity

EDITED BY

BRONWEN NEIL AND PAULINE ALLEN

CAMBRIDGE
UNIVERSITY PRESS

CAMBRIDGE
UNIVERSITY PRESS

University Printing House, Cambridge CB2 8BS, United Kingdom

Cambridge University Press is part of the University of Cambridge.

It furthers the University's mission by disseminating knowledge in the pursuit of education, learning and research at the highest international levels of excellence.

www.cambridge.org
Information on this title: www.cambridge.org/9781107091863

© Cambridge University Press 2015

First published 2015

Printed in the United States of America by Sheridan Books, Inc.

A catalogue record for this publication is available from the British Library

Library of Congress Cataloguing in Publication data
Collecting early Christian letters: from the apostle Paul to late
antiquity / edited by Bronwen Neil, Pauline Allen.
pages   cm
Includes bibliographical references and index.
ISBN 978-1-107-09186-3 (hardback)
1. Letter writing–History.   2. Letter writing–Religious aspects.
I. Neil, Bronwen, editor.   II. Allen, Pauline, 1948– editor.
PN4400.C43 2015
809.6–dc23
2014043073

ISBN 978-1-107-09186-3 Hardback

Contents

List of figures and tables   *page* vii
List of contributors   viii
Acknowledgements   xi
Abbreviations   xii

PART I INTRODUCING EARLY CHRISTIAN LETTERS   I

1   Continuities and changes in the practice of letter-collecting
    from Cicero to late antiquity   3
    Bronwen Neil

2   Rationales for episcopal letter-collections in late antiquity   18
    Pauline Allen

PART II COLLECTING NEW TESTAMENT AND EARLY
MONASTIC LETTERS   35

3   The Pauline letters as community documents   37
    Ian J. Elmer

4   *2 Corinthians* and possible material evidence for composite
    letters in antiquity   54
    Brent Nongbri

5   The letter-collections of Anthony and Ammonas: shaping a
    community   68
    Samuel Rubenson

6   From letter to letter-collection: monastic epistolography in
    late-antique Egypt   80
    Malcolm Choat

v

129739

PART III COLLECTING EARLY BISHOPS' LETTERS   95

7   Letters of Ambrose of Milan (374–397), Books I–IX   97
    J. H. W. G. Liebeschuetz

8   The letters of Basil of Caesarea and the role of
    letter-collections in their transmission   113
    Anna Silvas

9   The ins and outs of the Chrysostom letter-collection:
    new ways of looking at a limited corpus   129
    Wendy Mayer

10 The letters of Theodoret of Cyrrhus: personal collections,
    multi-author archives and historical interpretation   154
    Adam M. Schor

PART IV   COLLECTING EARLY PAPAL LETTERS   173

11 *Collectio Corbeiensis, Collectio Pithouensis* and the earliest
    collections of papal letters   175
    Geoffrey D. Dunn

12 *De profundis*: the letters and archives of Pelagius I of
    Rome (556–561)   206
    Bronwen Neil

Bibliography   221
Index of people, places and things   251
Index of biblical citations   259

Figures and tables

Figures

4.1   *P.Sarap.* 87–9. Letters from Heliodorus copied on a roll in the same hand (90–133 CE; possibly 117 CE)   *page* 60

4.2   *BGU* 4.1206–7. Letters from Isidora to Asclepiades in different hands glued together (28 BCE)   61

4.3   *P.Lille* 1.3 (Inv.Sorb. 3), column 3. Collection of letters of an official, possibly with marginal dates (216–215 BCE).   63

Tables

9.1   Sequence of *Epp.* 1–17 to Olympias   148

9.2   Chronological order of authentic letters written by John Chrysostom   148

11.1   Contents of Paris, BnF, lat. 12097 (fol. 1 to fol. 139v) with emphasis on papal letters   190

11.2   Contents of Paris, BnF, lat. 1564 with emphasis on papal letters   200

Contributors

PAULINE ALLEN is director of the Centre for Early Christian Studies at Australian Catholic University (ACU), and an honorary research fellow at the University of Pretoria and the Sydney College of Divinity. Allen has written extensively on the christological controversies of the fifth, sixth and seventh centuries, with recent translation volumes of the letters and other writings of Severus of Antioch, Sophronius of Jerusalem and Gelasius of Rome. She and Bronwen Neil are co-editors of the *Oxford Handbook to Maximus the Confessor* (forthcoming). Allen is an elected Fellow of the Australian Academy of the Humanities, and a Fellow of the Alexander von Humboldt-Stiftung. She and Bronwen Neil are chief investigators on the ARC Discovery Project *Negotiating Religious Conflict: Letters between Rome and Constantinople in the Seventh Century, An Era of Crisis* (2014–2016).

MALCOLM CHOAT is associate professor in Ancient History and director of the Ancient Cultures Research Centre at Macquarie University. He has published widely on monastic literature communities in late-antique Egypt, including his recent volume in the Brepols series Studia Antiqua Australiensia. His research project, 'Communication networks in Upper Egyptian monastic communities in the sixth to eighth centuries CE', was funded by the Australian Research Council (2008–10).

GEOFFREY D. DUNN is senior lecturer in the Faculty of Theology and Philosophy and a member of the Centre for Early Christian Studies at ACU. He has published two books on Tertullian and one on Cyprian, and is now working on an edition and translation of the letters of Innocent I for Corpus Christianorum Series Latina, partially funded by an Australian Research Council Fellowship (2007–11). He is an honorary research associate at the University of Pretoria.

IAN J. ELMER is lecturer in New Testament Studies at ACU and a member of the Centre for Early Christian Studies. He has recently published a book, *Paul, Jerusalem and the Judaisers: The Galatian Crisis in Its Broadest Historical Context*, as well as several book chapters.

J. H. W. G. LIEBESCHUETZ is honorary research fellow in the Department of Archaeology at the University of Nottingham. He is one of the most senior figures in the field of late antiquity and has published extensively on many subjects, including a collected studies volume, *Decline and Change in Late Antiquity: Religion, Barbarians and Their Historiography*, and a study of Ambrose of Milan's *Letters*, Book 10, as *Ambrose of Milan: Political Letters and Speeches* in the TTH series.

WENDY MAYER is a research fellow in the Centre for Early Christian Studies at ACU. Her books include the Routledge Early Church Fathers volume on John Chrysostom (with Pauline Allen) and a comprehensive study of Chrysostom's sermons, as well as a monograph, *Churches of Antioch*, co-authored with Pauline Allen. Mayer is a former Queen Elizabeth II Research Fellow of the Australian Research Council, and has held fellowships at Dumbarton Oaks in Washington, DC, and at the University of South Africa.

BRONWEN NEIL is associate professor in Ecclesiastical Latin in the Faculty of Theology and Philosophy and associate director of the Centre for Early Christian Studies at ACU. Her publications include editions and translations of Latin and Greek texts relating to Maximus Confessor and Pope Martin I in Corpus Christianorum Series Graeca (with Pauline Allen), Oxford Early Christian Texts (with Pauline Allen) and Studia Antiqua Australiensia. Her volume on Leo the Great in the Routledge series The Early Church Fathers appeared in 2009. With Pauline Allen, she has recently co-authored *Crisis Management in Late Antiquity (410–590 CE): The Evidence of Episcopal Letters*, and a forthcoming translation of Gelasius I's letters as evidence for the late-antique papacy. Neil is a Future Fellow of the Australian Research Council (2014–2018), a Fellow of the Alexander von Humboldt-Stiftung and an elected Fellow of the Australian Academy of the Humanities.

BRENT NONGBRI is an Australian Research Council post-doctoral research fellow in the Department of Ancient History at Macquarie University. He is the recipient of an Australian Research Council Early Career Researcher Award (2014–16) for his project on the earliest texts of the New Testament preserved on ancient Greek papyri from Egypt. His interests centre on method and theory in the study of religion and the material culture of the ancient Mediterranean world. In the sphere

of material culture and archaeology, Dr Nongbri specialises in papyrology and early Christian manuscripts.

SAMUEL RUBENSON is professor in the Centre for Theology and
Religious Studies at Lund University, and *preses* of Collegium
Patristicum Lundendse. His research has mainly dealt with emerging
Christianity, the oriental churches and early Christian literature in
Greek and oriental translations. His main publications deal with the
emergence of monasticism and include the second, revised edition of
Letters of St Antony: Monasticism and the Making of a Saint, and he is
the director of a research programme on early monasticism and classical
paideia.

ADAM M. SCHOR teaches Mediterranean history at the University of
South Carolina. His book, *Theodoret's People: Social Networks and
Religious Conflict in Late Antiquity*, is the best-known study of the
epistolary and social networks of Theodoret of Cyrrhus.

ANNA SILVAS is an honorary research fellow at University of New
England. Her books include studies of the letters of Gregory of Nyssa
(Cambridge University Press), Gregory Nazianzen and the *Rule* of
Basil of Caesarea. Silvas is a Fellow of the Australian Academy of the
Humanities, and a former Australian Research Council Fellow.

Acknowledgements

The current volume draws together work from four Discovery Projects funded by the Australian Research Council.

We are grateful to Australian Catholic University (ACU) and Macquarie University for the funding that allowed Andrew Gillett and Bronwen Neil to convene a three-part symposium, *Epistolary Conversations in Classical and Late Antiquity*, in Sydney. The first two sessions were hosted by Macquarie University's Ancient Cultures Research Centre in 2010 and by the Centre for Early Christian Studies at ACU in 2011. The third session was presented at the 34th Conference of the Australasian Society for Classical Studies, hosted by Macquarie University in January 2013. We are grateful to the organisers of this conference, Blanche Menadier and Ken Sheedy, for accommodating our panel in the programme. Thanks to all the participating scholars and students from ACU, Macquarie, University of Sydney, University of New England, Monash University, University of Queensland and University of Adelaide. Selected papers have been amplified by contributions from four leading scholars from the United Kingdom, Sweden and the United States in the field of late-antique epistolography.

Many thanks to Trish Darcy and Amanda Thorley for their help with the bibliography and indices, and to Michael Sharp and his assistants at Cambridge University Press for their expert assistance and encouragement. The three images of papyri in Brent Nongbri's chapter are used by permission.

Bronwen Neil and Pauline Allen

Abbreviations

ACO	Schwartz, E. (ed.) (1914–40) Acta Conciliorum Oecumenicorum. Series prima. Berlin and Leipzig
CCSG	Corpus Christianorum Series Graeca
CCSL	Corpus Christianorum Series Latina
CPG	Geerard, M. (ed.) (1974–87) *Clavis Patrum Graecorum*, Corpus Christianorum (5 vols.). Turnhout
	Geerard, M. and Noret, J. (eds.) (1998) *Clavis Patrum Graecorum. Supplementum*, Corpus Christianorum. Turnhout
CPL	Dekkers, E. (ed.) (1995) *Clavis Patrum Latinorum*, CCSL. 3rd edn. Turnhout
CSCO	Corpus Scriptorum Christianorum Orientalium
CSCO, Scr. Syr.	Corpus Scriptorum Christianorum Orientalium Scriptores Syri.
CSEL	Corpus Scriptorum Ecclesiasticorum Latinorum
DM	Chabot, J.-B. (ed.) (1908) *Documenta ad origines monophysitarum illustrandas.* CSCO 17. Scr. Syr. 37. Louvain.
	(tr.) (1933) *Documenta ad origines monophysitarum illustrandas.* CSCO 103. Scr. Syr. 52. Louvain.
Ep./Epp.	*Epistola/Epistolae*
GCS NF	Die Griechischen Christlichen Schriftsteller. Neue Folgung.
JBL	*Journal of Biblical Literature*
JECS	*Journal of Early Christian Studies*
JK	Jaffé, P. and Kaltenbrunner, F. (eds.) (1885) *Regesta pontificum Romanorum ab condita ecclesia ad annum post Christum natum MCXCVIII*, 2nd edn. (2 vols.). Leipzig

JTS	*Journal of Theological Studies*
LCL	Loeb Classical Library
LP	*Liber Pontificalis*
MGH	Monumenta Germaniae Historica
MGH AA	Monumenta Germaniae Historica Auctores Antiquissimi
MGH Epp	Monumenta Germaniae Historica Epistolae
MS, MSS	manuscript, manuscripts
ns	new series
NTS	*New Testament Studies*
PG	Migne, J.-P. (ed.) (1857–66) *Patrologiae cursus completus. Series Graeca*, 161 vols. Paris
PL	Migne, J.-P. (ed.) (1844–64) *Patrologiae cursus completus. Series Latina*, 221 vols. Paris
PLRE I	Jones, A. H. M., Martindale, J. R., and Morris, J. (eds.) (1971) *The Prosopography of the Later Roman Empire, AD 260–395*, vol. I. Cambridge
SC	*Sources chrétiennes* (Paris, 1943–)
SP	*Studia Patristica* (Berlin, Leuven, 1957–)
TTH	Translated Texts for Historians (Liverpool, 1988–)
VC	*Vigiliae Christianae*
VCS	Vigiliae Christianae Supplements (Leiden, 1987–)

PART I

Introducing early Christian letters

CHAPTER I

Continuities and changes in the practice of letter-collecting from Cicero to late antiquity

Bronwen Neil

Letter-collections in classical and late antiquity give witness to the flourishing of letter-writing, from the formulaic exchanges between the elites of the Graeco-Roman empire to more wide-ranging correspondence by Roman, Gallic and eastern bishops and the monks of Egypt. While in classical antiquity only the elites could afford to write and send letters, due to the expense of the materials and limited access to postal services, in late antiquity the letter and the letter-collection became democratised, and their purpose broadened far beyond the original scope of Graeco-Roman letters. This volume is the first multi-authored study of classical, New Testament and late-antique letter-collections, crossing the traditional divide between these disciplines by focusing on Latin and Greek epistolary sources. Its authors attend to various aspects of the mechanics of making and transmitting letter-collections, whether in the ancient author's lifetime or in the following centuries.

Any attempt to identify the rationale behind most compilations of letters from classical and Christian antiquity is difficult, not least because poor survival rates make pronouncements on letter-collections hazardous.[1] Nevertheless, through careful study of compilation techniques and distribution strategies, we may assess and compare the epistolary outputs of classical and early Christian writers, both individually and collectively.

Epistolary theory has been the focus of much excellent scholarship in recent decades, especially in the fields of classical and New Testament studies.[2] Until recently, however, scholarship on letter-collections mostly focused on individual authors and their collections,[3] and did not seek to emphasise

---

[1] On some of the hazards assailing late-antique letter-writing and distribution, see Allen 2013a, and Allen in this volume.

[2] E.g. Stowers 1986; White 1986; Aune 1987: 158–82; White 1988: 85–105, with annotated bibliography; Malherbe 1988; Klauck, 2006; Morello and Morrison 2007.

[3] E.g. Paulinus of Nola: Mratschek 2002; Synesius of Cyrene: Roques 1989; Augustine of Hippo: Morgenstern 1993; Allen 2006a, 2006b; Jerome: Cain 2009; Leo I, bishop of Rome: Pietrini 2002, Neil 2009; Sidonius Apollinaris: Harries 1994, van Waarden 2010; Theodoret of Cyrrhus: Wagner 1948, Schor 2011; Severus of Antioch: Allen and Hayward 2004.

the ways in which late-antique letter-collections were similar to or distinct from Graeco-Roman epistolography.

The shift in focus on letter-collections as a literary unit in their own right is signalled by Roy Gibson's groundbreaking 2012 article, in which he argued that there was considerable continuity of purpose other than biographical or historical narration in the rationales of those who collated non-fictional classical and late-antique letters.[4] A new volume of studies of the collections of some thirty letter-writers, both pagan and Christian, of the fourth and fifth centuries, is now in preparation.[5] The current volume focuses on the trajectory of letter-writing, and the act of collecting it, over the course of 700 years, from classical Graeco-Roman epistolography to the sixth century. In this introductory chapter, I will assess Gibson's claims for continuity by looking at classical Latin letter-collections, New Testament letters, and late-antique letter-collections. My aim is to provide a methodological framework for the individual studies of New Testament and late-antique letter-collections that follow, addressing questions of collation practices, survival rates, intended audience and usage of letters generally in letter-collections of classical and late antiquity.

Classical letter-collections

Classical antiquity produced few letter-collections of any size that have survived, when compared with late antiquity, the western Middle Ages and the Byzantine era.[6] Those collections from ancient Greece and Rome that have survived have passed through numerous redactions in the process of their selection and reproduction. Surviving fictional letter-collections include the corpus of Greek letters of Chion of Heraclea, Themistocles and Euripides, as well as lesser-known authors such as the Greek sophist Philostratus (*c.* 170–*c.* 250), the author of a collection of love letters directed toward anonymous addressees, both male and female. One might also include the epistolary poems from exile (*Epistolae ex Ponto*) by the exiled Roman poet Ovid, and his fictive love letters, the *Heroides*, also written in poetic metre. Collections from authors of the early Christian era who self-consciously adopted classical, pagan models, such as the emperor Julian (361–63), the Roman senator Symmachus (370–84) and

---

[4] Gibson 2012.   [5] Watts *et al.* forthcoming.

[6] Constable 1976 remains the only systematic treatment of mediaeval epistolary sources across the whole of western Europe. Studies of epistolographic production in northern Italy from the fifth to the fifteenth centuries are collected in Gioanni and Cammarosano 2013. Mullett 1997 provides a good model of a treatment of a collection from a single author of the middle Byzantine period.

the orator Libanius, will be considered in the forthcoming volume of Watts *et al.*, and thus have not been dealt with here.

The surviving evidence of non-fictional letter-collections from the first century BCE to the second century is amazingly sparse. Only four such collections survive from this period, and all are in Latin: those of Cicero (106–43 BCE), Seneca (*c.* 1–65), Pliny the Younger (*c.* 61–112) and Fronto (*c.* 95–166). In keeping with Graeco-Roman epistolographical practice, all of these authors hail from the intellectual elite, and write only to elite friends or acquaintances. In keeping with the lasting literary importance of these four authors, we will consider them individually, giving a brief summary of recent scholarship on the rationales behind their collections.

Cicero penned several collections divided, after his death, according to addressee: those addressed to his close friend Atticus (*Ad Atticum*); to his brother Quintus (*Ad Quintum*, three books), to his friend Brutus (*Ad Brutum*, two books), and the major collection of letters addressed to a range of friends and acquaintances, including P. Lentulus, C. Curio and the consul A. Claudius Pulcher (*Ad familiares*, sixteen books).[7] The sixteen books of letters *Ad Atticum* did not enter circulation until the time of Nero.[8] While modern editors from the seventeenth century have endeavoured to place these in chronological order, this was not a concern of Cicero's. Rather he grouped them first by addressee and then by theme.

Seneca seems to have collected and distributed his letters in a number of discrete books for distribution within his lifetime. Twenty books survive, comprising 124 letters. The subject matter of all of Seneca's *Epistulae morales* is his friend Lucilius' progress in the philosophical life, specifically in the Stoic life. The fact that his corpus remains the best evidence of Stoic philosophy makes it of particular interest in this context because of the affinities between early Christianity and Stoicism.[9] As Mark Davies and others have argued, Seneca was concerned to paint a picture of himself in his letters to Lucilius as a moral example and mentor, and to this end may have invented his purported correspondent.[10] Certainly Lucilius does not exist in any other literary sources. In this letter-corpus, written for posterity and intended for publication, Seneca may have been making a deliberate attempt to rival Cicero's epistolary output. Indeed, he points out on several occasions that his subject matter is more serious than that of Cicero's letters. Three of Seneca's letters illustrate the *consolatio* genre (*Epp.*

---

[7] On Cicero's letters and their arrangement in ancient sources and modern editions, see White 2010; Beard 2002.

[8] Gibson 2012: 57 and n. 5.   [9] See Ross 1974: 124.

[10] Davies forthcoming; with secondary literature.

63, 93 and 99), to which we return in the next section on New Testament letters.

Pliny the Younger carefully crafted his letter-collection in a way that displayed his skills as a politician, husband, lawyer and rhetor. Like Seneca, he also used his forebears as models, namely Cicero and Seneca himself.[11] In a recent doctoral thesis, Michelle Borg shows how Pliny was concerned to align himself with the newly ascended house of Trajan, leading him to elide details of his previous support for the Flavian dynasty.[12] Pliny's works have recently been made the subject of a number of studies, of which we must single out Roy Gibson and Ruth Morello's excellent introduction to the letters.[13] With the possible exception of Book 10, his correspondence with the emperor Trajan,[14] Pliny's correspondence was – like that of Seneca – meant to be circulated in his own lifetime. Several late-antique collections mirror the structure of nine books of private correspondence and one book of public or business correspondence, including those of the Roman senator Symmachus, author of some 900 letters; Ambrose of Milan, whose epistolary oeuvre is the subject of Wolf Liebeschuetz's chapter in this volume, and the Gallic bishop of Clermont, Sidonius Apollinaris.[15]

Marcus Cornelius Fronto's collection survives in a single palimpsest manuscript, discovered in the Ambrosiana library by Angelo Mai and first edited by him in 1815,[16] and again in 1823 with the inclusion of several single folia found in the Vatican library, then by Samuel Naber in 1867,[17] and more recently by M. P. J. van den Hout.[18] Fronto's numerous correspondents included the emperors Marcus Aurelius, Antoninus Pius and Lucius Verus, other members of the imperial household and various friends, all members of the senatorial class. In a letter to his friends, Fronto famously complained that he hated writing letters (*Ad amicos* 1.19). The problem was that Aulus Gellius was hounding him for copies of his works for publication. Recent literary scholars have moved away from the theory that Fronto collected and distributed the books of his correspondence himself, toward a more nuanced view that the books could have been published after the author's death by his friends and correspondents.[19]

---

[11] Gibson and Morello 2012: 74–103.   [12] See Borg forthcoming.
[13] Gibson and Morello 2012.   [14] Gibson 2012: 59.
[15] On Sidonius' letter-collection, preserved in some ninety codices, see van Waarden 2010: 30–55; Gibson 2013b.
[16] Mai 1815; 1823. See discussion in Gibson 2013a: 408–9; and Reynolds 1983: 173–4.
[17] Naber 1867.
[18] van den Hout 1988.
[19] Gibson 2012: 60, citing Champlin 1974. More recently see van den Hout 1999.

Roy Gibson notes that classical, non-fictional Latin and Greek letters were not arranged chronologically by their ancient collectors, although modern editors have seen this as a shortcoming and sought to rectify it.[20] Instead they were divided up according to theme and/or addressee. Seneca's letters were all undated, and addressed to a single addressee. Fronto's letters were also not arranged in any chronological order. Gibson has plausibly argued that editorial rearranging of letters in a strictly chronological order changes their genre from that of epistolography to history or biography or even autobiography in the case of collections organised by the author himself.[21]

In his 2012 article, Gibson considered the rationales behind eleven classical and late-antique collections, asserting at the outset: '[D]espite fundamental changes in belief (and preferred narrative patterns) between the first and fourth centuries AD, methods of arranging letter-collections display not only some consistency of practice, but even continuity.'[22] Was there also a substantial similarity in the *types* of letters, as Gibson suggests?[23] Certainly the four types he identifies are constants across his sample of Latin collections from Cicero to Jerome: namely, consolation, recommendation, praise and exhortation. However, it seems that several other types developed, which were new to episcopal letter-writers of late antiquity, and reflected the new uses to which letters were being put. These were: (1) polemical letters; (2) dogmatic letters; (3) pastoral letters; (4) disciplinary letters; (5) administrative letters; (6) letters of advice; (7) letters of admonition; (8) decrees; and (9) judgements.[24]

That is not to say that Christian bishops abandoned their classical training in rhetoric when they took up the mitre. The letters of Synesius of Cyrene, bishop of Ptolemais, are ample evidence against such a fatuous notion. Even Augustine, champion of plain speech that the faithful can understand in his homilies, and in *De doctrina Christiana*, returned to his oratorical training when writing to his peers and patrons of the aristocracy. Certainly, the late fifth-century bishop of Clermont, Sidonius Apollinaris, offers a striking example in the parallels he made between the structure of Pliny's collection in ten books, and that of his own nine books, some four centuries later.[25] One wonders, therefore, whether literary tropes

---

[20] Gibson 2012; Gibson 2013a: 407–8; a prime example is the editions of Cicero's letters by Shackleton Bailey 1977, 1980 and 1988.
[21] Gibson 2013a: 392. [22] Gibson 2012: 59. [23] Gibson 2012: 59.
[24] These nine types, together with the four mentioned by Gibson, were identified by Allen and Neil 2013: 16–17.
[25] Gibson 2013b.

were stronger than the 'beliefs' and 'preferred narrative patterns' to which Gibson referred in the quotation above. The rules of these tropes were strictly observed by Christian writers and redactors, down to the proper arrangement by theme and/or addressee. As Gibson observes, chronological organisation was not favoured at all (and not adopted in papal letter-collections until the innovation of the Scythian monk Dionysius Exiguus, in his early sixth-century collection of decretals and canons).[26] Nor was there any sense of historical or biographical narrative in Christian letter-collections, which would seem to privilege the identity of the author as an individual, rather than a servant of God. If one leaves aside ordering by addressee (of increasing irrelevance over the passage of time, and especially in letters of the bishops of Rome in their grand push for universal application of their decretals), what other principles of organisation remained to collators of late-antique letters?

By contrast to the non-fictional collections, the fictional collections of Chion of Heraclea, Themistocles and Euripides, written in Greek, were arranged chronologically. Gibson confesses himself unsure as to why this should be so.[27] Perhaps the reason is a banal one: it is much easier to date letters that are invented, than it is in the case of non-fictional letters whose dates might be missing, wrong or falsified. Seneca's letters to Lucilius perhaps fall between the two types: they bear no dates, and are possibly addressed to a fictitious correspondent.

New Testament letters

Only a few New Testament letters can be confidently ascribed to a particular author. The six disputed or 'deutero-Pauline' letters, of uncertain authorship (2 Thessalonians, Colossians, Ephesians and the pastoral letters: Titus, 1 and 2 Timothy), also date to the first and second centuries. These canonical 'forgeries' have been studied in great detail, along with 1 and 2 Peter, and extra-canonical letters, such as Paul's letters to and from his contemporary Seneca,[28] and Jesus' purported correspondence with the Ethiopian king Abgar. This is a Syrian forgery documenting the conversion of the people of Edessa, along with their king Abgar IX (179–214), by the disciple Addai, purportedly one of the seventy-two sent out by Christ. Abgar made a reply in the form of a verbal message or, according

---

[26] On this very early collection of papal letters, see further Neil 2013a.
[27] Gibson 2012: 58 n. 9.   [28] Sevenster 1961.

to Eusebius (*HE* 1.13), a letter. Only a fifth-century Armenian version of the letter from ps-Abgar survives.[29]

Continuities of subgenres of letter found in ancient Greek and Latin letters, such as the *consolatio* or letter of consolation, have been noted by some scholars, including David Luckensmeyer and Bronwen Neil in their study of 1 Thessalonians, the apostle Paul's earliest letter. This letter, with its strong eschatological elements, should be read as a letter of consolation to the community to which it was addressed.[30] In the same way as three of Seneca's letters (*Epp.* 63, 93 and 99) offer consolation to his friend Lucilius (whether or not that friend was a fictional character),[31] so the first letter to the Thessalonians offers consolation to a community facing difficult challenges and signs of the end times. That Seneca's letter-corpus was intentionally structured for a wider audience is clear from *Ep.* 1.36–39 and *Ep.* 8.1–3.[32] Paul wrote his first letter to the community in Thessalonica in either 50 or 51, probably with the aid of Silvanus (i.e., Silas), and Timothy.[33] Malherbe described 1 Thessalonians as 'the first Christian pastoral letter',[34] a curious turn of phrase, since it could well be argued that pastoral letters, that is, letters of spiritual direction from a spiritual leader to a group or community, are indigenous to early Christianity. While the letter has also been called a 'friendship' letter, from the founders of the nascent church of Thessalonica to the community from whom they are unwillingly separated, this does not adequately account for its repeated references to afflictions and suffering.[35] Instead, the letter should be read as a classical consolation, from one absent friend to another, in the face of real adversity and possible death for their faith.[36] The reason that scholars have been reluctant to interpret 1 Thessalonians in this way lies in a basic misunderstanding of the nature of ancient epistolary and rhetorical handbooks. These handbooks, dating from the third century BCE to the sixth century CE, include two unrelated handbooks of ps-Demetrius,[37]

---

[29] Ed. Alishan 1868. See discussion of all of these works in Ehrman 2013.

[30] Luckensmeyer and Neil, forthcoming.

[31] Cancik 1967; Maurach 1970; Russell 1974: 70–95; Klauck 2006: 170–1.

[32] Luckensmeyer and Neil, forthcoming, n. 13.

[33] For the literature on Paul's authorship see Luckensmeyer 2009: 51–3.

[34] Malherbe 2000: 211.

[35] Luckensmeyer and Neil, forthcoming, n. 16, reject the assertion to the contrary of Schoon-Janßen 2000: 189–90.

[36] That consolation was part of the hortatory purpose of 1 Thessalonians, see also Malherbe 2000: 81–6 and 279–80; Chapa 1994; and a brief statement by Donfried 1993: 5. See the discussion of these sources by Luckensmeyer and Neil forthcoming, nn. 28, 29 and 31.

[37] Ps-Demetrius, περὶ ἑρμ. or *De elocutione* 223–35, Roberts 1932, repr. in Malherbe 1988: 16, 18; ps-Demetrius, τύποι ἐπιστολικοί, Weichert 1910: 1–12; see the discussion of authorship at xvii–xviii.

as well as those of ps-Libanius,[38] Aelius Theon,[39] Menander Rhetor[40] and Julius Victor.[41] These texts need to be read as descriptive rather than pre-scriptive: no single letter contains all the stock elements indicated by ps-Demetrius, ps-Libanius or other rhetorical handbooks.

By using three letters of Seneca (*Epp.* 63, 93 and 99) as a test case, Luckensmeyer and Neil showed that contemporaries of the antique world did not necessarily follow generic structures, but rather adapted those structures to suit their occasional purposes.[42] This caveat, against read-ing ancient epistolary handbooks prescriptively, is apposite in our con-sideration of how the genre of letter-writing changed with the advent of Christianity.

Papal letters

Papal letter-collections are in a class of their own, largely because most have been preserved in canon law-collections made from the sixth century into the mediaeval period.[43] Thus they have a relatively narrow focus on dogmatic issues and matters of clerical discipline or territorial disputes. Gregory the Great's *Register* of 854 letters is an exception, being collected and distributed as a whole even before his death (604). The next largest papal letter-collections that have been preserved from late antiquity are those of Pope Leo I (440–61) and the lesser-known, yet sizeable, col-lections of Popes Innocent I (401–19), Gelasius I (492–6) and Pelagius I (556–61). Papal letters went by various names: a wide range of words could designate letter-types of a canonical status, for example *constitutum*, *epistula decretalis* or *epistula encyclica*.[44] Other, more general terms used by all bishops were *libellus*, which could be a document, communication or report; *relatio* (narration or recital of events); *suggestio* (points for con-sideration) and *commonitorium* (reminder, instruction). Synodical letters (*epistulae synodicae*) were those disseminated by an incoming bishop to demonstrate where he stood on matters of faith; synodal letters (*epistulae synodales*), on the other hand, communicated the decisions of synods. The

---

[38] Ps-Libanius (sometimes falsely attributed to Proclus in manuscripts), ἐπιστολιμαῖοι χαρακτῆρες, Weichert 1910: 13–34, and discussion of authorship at xxv–xxix.

[39] Ael. Theon, *Progymnasmata*, 8. *Prosopopoeia*, Kennedy 2003: 47–9.

[40] Menander Rhetor, *Treatise* 2.9: *The Consolatory Speech*, Russell and Wilson 1981: 160–5; and Menander Rhetor, *Treatise* 2.11: *The Funeral Speech*, Russell and Wilson 1981: 171–9.

[41] Julius Victor, *Ars Rhetorica* 27 (*De epistolis*), Halm 1863: 447–8; Trapp 2003: 185–9.

[42] Luckensmeyer and Neil forthcoming, n. 44. On Christian consolation letters more generally, see Gregg 1975: 53–8.

[43] See Maassen 1870; more recently Moreau 2010: 487–506.

[44] See Moreau 2010: 489–92; Allen and Neil 2013: 17.

chapters of Dunn and Neil will analyse the common themes and different organising principles of these collections, drawing attention to the ways in which the authors and collators sought to enhance the bishop of Rome's authority, and to the revolution in preservation practices in the Roman *scrinium* from the fourth to sixth centuries.[45]

Methodological challenges

Perhaps the most important point to make at the outset is that there is no single, commonly accepted, definition of a letter in classical and late antiquity.[46] The presuppositions behind an ancient letter may be summed up as follows: it is one half of a dialogue or takes the place of a dialogue;[47] it is a communication with somebody absent as if he or she were present; it is speech written down; it reflects the personality of the letter-writer.[48] Similarly, there is no simple division to be made between 'classical' and 'late-antique' letters. There are extant *c.* thirty Latin and Greek collections surviving from the fourth to sixth centuries.[49] Their authors are bishops, priests, monks, emperors, statesmen and orators – several held a combination of two or more of these offices, and they might be Christian or notoriously pagan. Pagan letter-writers of note from the Christian era included Julian the Apostate, Libanius of Antioch and the Roman senator Symmachus. Letters could be used for various purposes of communication, for dissemination of ideas, for polemical ends, for consolation and for pastoral or political instruction.

The public nature of ancient and late-antique letters[50]

Cicero famously described two types of letter: the private and the public, surely an over-simplification of divisions in the genre. There was no such thing as a 'private' letter in the modern sense, in classical or late antiquity. Letters were meant to be read aloud, in front of other people. This naturally had an effect on the sorts of topics that could be discussed, and secret codes were sometimes adopted between correspondents 'as Caesar and Augustus and Cicero and many others did', as Julius Victor

---

[45] See also Neil forthcoming a.
[46] See Gibson and Morrison 2007: 1–16, where the concept of 'family resemblances' is employed.
[47] Attributed to Aristotle by Artemon, according to Demetrios, *De elocutione* 223, Trapp 2003: 180–1.
[48] Zelzer 1980.
[49] These thirty authors are the subjects of the essays in Watts, Storin and Sogno forthcoming.
[50] This section is an abbreviated form of Allen and Neil 2013: 18–21.

reports.[51] Personal messages were often deliberately kept out of letters, to be conveyed verbally by the messenger upon delivery of the letter. The letters themselves make oblique references to such verbal messages. Other epistolary theorists divide letters into as many as twenty-one types (ps-Demetrius) or forty-one types (ps-Libanius). This indicates that there was a great flexibility in the deployment of the letter-writing genre and that it could be used at will for various purposes of communication. Cicero's remark that few can carry a letter without lightening the weight by reading it,[52] or Libanius' assertion that 'any letter you get is immediately known to people here',[53] holds true for late antiquity too. Thus while we have both public and private letters from many fourth- to sixth-century bishops, there is sometimes little to choose between the two points.[54]

The public nature of the letter in late antiquity is exemplified by two extant letters, the first by the pagan orator Libanius, in which he describes the arrival of Basil's letter to the pagan orator. When the letter-bearers arrived, several official men were sitting with Libanius. Libanius read the piece through in silence, then exclaimed aloud, prompting the others to want it to be read to them too. The reader read it aloud and went out, probably to show it to others too, and only reluctantly gave it back.[55] The letter was regarded as public property. Here apparently the reader was not one of the bearers.[56]

Similarly, Gregory of Nyssa speaks of a friend who handed him, 'as a feast day present', a letter from Libanius addressed to himself, and Gregory went on to share the letter with other friends.[57] Libanius himself pressured the recipients of letters from his friend to show them to him, in the absence of any direct address.[58] The wide dissemination of letters had the added advantage of guaranteeing freedom of speech (*parrhesia*).[59]

---

[51] Julius Victor, *Ars Rhetorica* 27, Halm 1863: 447–8; Trapp 2003: 187. Julius here (Halm 1863: 447, Trapp 2003: 185) distinguishes 'official' from 'private' letters.

[52] Cicero, *Ep.* 13.1 to Atticus, Shackleton Bailey 1912/1: 60–1.

[53] Libanius, *Ep.* 16, Norman 1992/1: 401.

[54] As pointed out by Paoli-Lafaye 2002: 235.

[55] Basil, *Ep.* 338, ed. Courtonne 2003/III: 205–6.

[56] On the role of letter-bearers, see Allen 2013a: 481–91, with a list of Latin and Greek terminology for letter-bearers at 490–1.

[57] Gregory of Nyssa, *Ep.* 14.3–4 to Libanius, Maraval 1990: 202–4, 17–26; Silvas 2007: 157.

[58] *Ep.* 86, Norman 1992/11: 109: 'Well, even if you do not write to me, I feast on your letters, for whenever I find out that anyone has received one, I present myself forthwith, and either by persuasion or by overpowering his reluctance I get to read it.'

[59] On *parrhesia* in letters, see Allen forthcoming, where she cites Severus of Antioch: 'How can it not be right that we should also proclaim openly in words the things that we in actual practice think and do?' (Severus, *Ep.* 1.55, Brooks 1903: 166–7), and Emperor Julian's *Ep.* 29.

Augustine of Hippo laments that his writings cannot be kept from those who, because they are not too bright, could misconstrue them.[60]

While the majority of episcopal 'personal' letters were addressed to male readers, there are a number of surviving letters to women. Female addressees were most commonly recipients of consolation letters (*consolationes*), as for instance Fulgentius of Ruspe's *Letter* 2 to the widow Galla on the death of her husband.[61] Many of John Chrysostom's 240 letters from exile offer consolation to female members of the church in Constantinople, which was thrown into disarray by his second sudden deposition and relegation to Cucusus.[62] As the above-mentioned Pauline letter to the Thessalonians demonstrates, the classical letter of consolation to an exile typically used the principles of Stoic philosophy to advocate patient endurance in adverse circumstances.[63] At the same time, such letters functioned as self-consolation, through the exile's application of the lessons of Stoic philosophy to his own situation. John's many surviving letters from exile include pleas for women as well as men to write to him and let him know that his advice has been taken.[64] In a letter to Karteria, John expresses his fear of being left out of the information loop regarding parish affairs in Constantinople and missionary activities further afield.[65] John's *Letter* 117 to Theodora is a good example of his attempts to exercise influence in exile in order to extract consolation for himself.[66] In this letter, he bemoans his reduced capacity to send letters because he rarely met with people to convey them.[67] In two letters to his deaconess Olympias, he accuses the bishop Pharetrios of Caesarea of betrayal, in refusing to let his wealthy parishioner Seleucia accommodate John at her house when he was being transferred under guard to Cucusus.[68]

Simple friendship letters abound, such as Ruricius of Limoges' letter to Ceraunia,[69] as do letters of spiritual instruction. Bishops frequently corresponded with women with whom they seemed to be in patron–client relationships, for example the letters to Hormisdas from Anastasia (*Ep.* 70) and Juliana Anicia (*Epp.* 71 and 119). The papal letter-corpus

---

[60] Augustine, *Ep.* 162.1, Nuova Biblioteca Agostiniana 22: 670.
[61] Fulgentius, *Ep.* 2, ed. Fraipont 1968/1: 197–211.
[62] See Mayer in this volume.   [63] See further Claassen 1999.
[64] *Ep.* 75 to Harmatius (PG 52: 649); *Ep.* 117 to Theodora (PG 52: 672–3); *Ep.* 197 to Stoudius, the urban prefect (PG 52: 721–2); *Ep.* 217 to Valentinus (PG 52: 730–1).
[65] *Ep.* 34 to Karteria (PG 52: 629–30)
[66] *Ep.* 117 to Theodora (PG 52: 673).
[67] *Ep.* 117 to Theodora (PG 52: 672–3).
[68] *Ep.* 204 (PG 52: 724–6); *Ep.* 14.3 to Olympias (PG 52: 615–16).
[69] Ruricius, *Ep.* 2.15 to Ceraunia, ed. Krusch 1887: 323–6 (*c.* 495/500 CE). On the development of the subgenre of friendship letters in late antiquity see Mews and Chiavaroli 2009.

includes several petitions to female members of the imperial family, such as Gelasius of Rome's letters to Hereleuva, mother of the Gothic king Theodoric,[70] and Leo I's petitions to Theodosius II's sister Pulcheria, and Valentinian III's mother and regent, Galla Placidia.

The hybridisation of late-antique letters

According to the rules of ancient epistolography the letter was theoretically limited in length and was also supposedly confined to one subject, but in late-antique practice the genre became much more flexible,[71] and the crossover from letter to treatise, for example, was frequently made. Such hybrid texts were letters in the technical sense but in terms of their nature, content and function had in fact crossed over into the realm of homilies or theological treatises, two new genres appearing in early Christian literature. Among the surviving letter-collections there are huge variations in length, with some communications from Pope Innocent I, Synesius of Cyrene and Theodoret of Cyrrhus, for example, containing only a few lines, whereas others, among which are Pope Leo I's *Tome* (*Ep.* 28) and *Second Tome* (*Ep.* 165, containing about twelve pages of text and thirteen pages of *testimonia*), are the length of a tractate. Two long letters of Augustine (*Epp.* 140 and 157), are cases in point: were these pieces originally letters which subsequently exceeded the epistolary norm, or were they intentionally written in letter-form with some ulterior motive?[72] On the basis of these two compositions, Johannes Divjak branded such 'letter-tractates' as 'false letters', while affirming that the criterion for what is and is not a letter for Augustine appears in other cases to be fulfilled by the formula *quis ad quem scribat* (that is, dependent upon to whom he was writing).[73]

Finally, questions of authenticity plague the epistolographer. Forgery was considered a valid way of supporting an argument, and the use of some older authority's name on one's correspondence was considered to be the highest compliment that one could pay to a revered figure of the past. By the early third century, pseudo-apostolic forgeries were already appearing. The first and second letters attributed to Clement I, bishop

---

[70] Gelasius, *Frag.* 36, ed. Thiel 1867 [2004]: 502; *Ep.* 46, ed. Ewald 1880: 521–2.

[71] Basil of Caesarea, for example, wrote to his correspondent Philagrius: 'send plenty of letters, as long as you can [make them], for shortness is not a virtue in a letter, any more than it is in a man.' *Ep.* 323, ed. Courtonne 2003/III: 195, 12–14. Basil's letters are the subject of Silvas in this volume.

[72] For a more extensive treatment of these two letters see Allen, Neil and Mayer 2009: 51–2.

[73] Divjak 1983: 21.

of Rome (d. *c.* 98), are a case in point, as is the lesser-known second- or third-century Greek letter supposedly written by the same Clement to James, the brother of the Lord, and translated into Latin by Rufinus of Aquileia in the fifth century.[74] Attributions found in the rubrics of ancient or even some modern editions may also be inventions of the editor or redactor. In spite of these pitfalls for the researcher, letters remain an unparalleled and largely untapped source for the social historian.

Themes and structure of the volume

The following chapters concentrate on significant moments in the development of the epistolary genre from the first century to the sixth century, taking in various types of letter-collection: encyclical letters, papal decretals, episcopal letters conserved in the acts of church councils, monastic correspondence, and other novel contexts for letter-writing that emerged in late antiquity. The inclusion of Pauline and deutero-Pauline letters allows us to bridge the gap between pagan letter-collections and early Christian ones. We are also concerned with continuities and discontinuities (both in the genre of letter-writing and in the use and organisation of letter-collections) from the pre-Christian period to the end of late antiquity. Our contributors seek to generalise from a single letter-collection to points which might affect our readings of many others. We are primarily interested in making connections between disparate letter-collections, and in the influences of an individual collection upon the formation and reading of other collections diachronically.

In the second part of our introduction, Pauline Allen instantiates the issues raised here in her examination of individual letter-collections from or pertaining to late-antique bishops in an attempt to establish some guidelines for assessing compilation techniques. Allen will also consider two multi-authored collections and the uses to which they were put (Chapter 2). The remaining chapters are divided into three sections, arranged chronologically.

Part II, 'Collecting New Testament and early monastic letters', comprises four chapters, focusing on the use of letter-collections in early Christian lay and monastic communities. The use made of the canonical letters of the apostle Paul and the deutero-Pauline letters of the New Testament to build a Christian community is the focus of Ian Elmer's chapter (Chapter 3). The value of the deutero-Pauline letters rested not so

---

[74] See further Neil 2003.

much on the genuine identification of their author with the first apostle, but on their use by a nascent faith community in search of cohesion. The preservation of these letters on papyri and their apparent use in Pachomian monastic communities have led Brent Nongbri (Chapter 4) to consider the way single, composite letters could be formed by piecing together smaller letters, and challenges the theory that 2 Corinthians is a composite letter, using papyrological evidence. Samuel Rubenson (Chapter 5) shows how the writing and sending of letters was crucial for shaping a sense of community in spite of the distance between early Egyptian monastic centres, but also how letters were signs of authority within the community sharing them, and thus essential for shaping the community. He focuses on some of the earliest extant monastic letters, the collections attributed to Antony and to his disciple Ammonas, which belong to a period before the monastic movement was consolidated and clearly integrated into the institutionalised church. This contribution analyses the formative function of the collections and looks at how the collections developed in different contexts. Malcolm Choat, using documentary sources on papyri and ostraca, as well as collections of letters in deluxe codices (Chapter 6), shows how the letters of Pachomius were both foundational and critical to the articulation of the monastic movement in Egypt.

The four chapters in Part III, 'Collecting early bishops' letters', will address common themes, generic constraints and reception questions regarding the rationale of the collector or collectors. One of the most influential collections by a bishop from late antiquity was that of Ambrose of Milan, in ten books. Wolf Liebeschuetz (Chapter 7) studies the content and arrangement of Books I–IX, in an effort to discern a rationale for their selection and organisation, ending with a brief comparison with Book X. Anna Silvas (Chapter 8) studies the methodological issues arising from the letter-collections of Basil of Caesarea, comparing that collection with that of his brother, Gregory of Nyssa, another famous Cappadocian. The two latter chapters focus on how letters were used to develop and reinforce social networks. John Chrysostom's letters and two pseudo-Chrysostomic letters are the focus of Wendy Mayer's chapter (Chapter 9). Building on Delmaire's analysis of the order in which the letters have been transmitted in the manuscripts, Mayer attempts to further our knowledge of the rationale for this one-sided and severely limited collection by including consideration of the few extraneous letters that survive. Adam Schor's survey (Chapter 10) of Theodoret of Cyrrhus' letters on church-political matters from 430–5 focuses on historical and methodological questions: what a single author collection could be used for in late antiquity; what can be gained from following one author within a multi-author conciliar document collection (in this case, in a Latin translation); how letters in these collections (while reshaped by editors) reflect, albeit imperfectly, real social exchanges, and can be treated as rhetorical works within the matrices of historical relationships.

The final part ('Collecting early papal letters') focuses our attention on one of the most significant but complex epistolary products of late antiquity, early papal letter-collections. Geoffrey Dunn (Chapter 11) examines the *Collectio Pithouensis*, particularly its transmission of the letters of Popes Innocent I, Zosimus, Celestine I and Leo I, and compares it with the *Collectio Corbeiensis* and other similar collections to offer new insight into the redactional stages of its compilation, especially the formation of the earliest core material. Bronwen Neil (Chapter 12) examines the transmission of the single-author collection(s) of Pelagius I, bishop of Rome, and weighs up the evidence for new preservation practices adopted by the papal *scrinium* in the mid-sixth century.

CHAPTER 2

Rationales for episcopal letter-collections in late antiquity

Pauline Allen

The rationale behind letter-collections surviving from pagan and Christian antiquity is complex and varied, if it exists at all. Here I wish to examine various episcopal letter-collections from late antiquity in an attempt to establish some guidelines for assessing compilation techniques. I begin by proposing some types of letter-collections that may assist in determining the rationales, although these types are by no means exhaustive and are meant only to signal the problem behind late-antique letter-collections.

Types of letter-collections

Four broad types of letter-collection can be identified among those surviving from late antiquity. These are listed below and then discussed in more detail:

1 Something put together by the authors themselves, with varying degrees of deliberation and revision. To this category we can assign, among others, Gregory of Nazianzus, Sidonius Apollinaris, Avitus of Vienne and the author of the *Documenta Monophysitica*.
2 Intentional collections made by later compilers for specific purposes, often rhetorical or polemical. A good example of a rhetorical collection is Firmus of Caesarea, discussed in what follows. The letters of Hormisdas of Rome and some other bishops of the same city owe their preservation to their inclusion in the *Collectio Avellana*, a collection with a polemical purpose. Compliers may be contemporaries, near-contemporaries or Byzantine/mediaeval scribes or scholars. Their purpose may also be canonical, political or hagiographical, which can result in a skewed collection: for example, the letters of John Chrysostom (only from exile), conciliar *acta* including the bulk of the correspondence of Cyril of Alexandria and John of Antioch, Ennodius of Pavia (none from his episcopate) and Severus of Antioch.

3 'Collections' with mixed transmission, for example, Theodoret of Cyrrhus, Severus of Antioch and Augustine of Hippo. However, the transmission of many other 'collections' is also mixed.

4 'Collections' that have been made by post-enlightenment editors trying to group usefully letters of particular authors that have survived in various collections, for example, parts of those of Severus of Antioch (miscellaneous letters) and Hormisdas, as grouped in Thiel's edition.

Deliberate and/or authorial collections

As a selection, here we shall consider the letters of Sidonius Apollinaris and the so-called *Documenta Monophysitica*.

The letters of Sidonius Apollinaris, bishop of Clermont-Ferrand from 469/72–87,[1] constitute a very deliberate collection, about whose genesis we are well informed by the author himself. As they have come down to us, Sidonius' 147 letters are divided into nine books of unequal length, each book comprising between eleven and twenty-five pieces. At the beginning of Book 1 the author writes to his friend, the priest Constantius of Lyons, who supposedly had pressed Sidonius to collect and revise his letters for publication. The bishop professes his art to be inferior to that of Symmachus, Cicero, Pliny, Julius Titianus and Fronto (in that non-chronological order), but nevertheless undertakes to send Constantius letters 'for purging ... and polishing', 'roll after roll gushing with exuberant garrulity'.[2] This was the genesis of the collection described by its reluctant English translator, W. B. Anderson, as follows: 'It is impossible here to give any adequate idea of the ostentatious combination of stylistic elaboration with sesquipedalian verbiage, Frontonian archaisms, weird neologisms, and verbal jingles which makes the correspondence such a nerve-wracking conglomeration.'[3] At any rate, the letters appeared in instalments, and the last letter of what was ostensibly to be the seventh and last book is addressed to Constantius. However, Sidonius was prevailed on by Petronius, a *vir inlustris* and eminent lawyer, to add an eighth book, the last letter of which is also addressed to Constantius. Here Sidonius says he has run out of material because he has lost his copies of certain letters. Whether this was true or not, he was able to add a ninth book at the insistence of the *savant* Firminus of Arles, who pointed out

[1] On Sidonius in general see Harries 1994; van Waarden 2010.
[2] *Ep.* 1.1.3, 4, Anderson 1936: 332–5.   [3] Anderson 1936: lxii.

that Pliny the Younger had published nine books of letters.[4] Firminus, to whom the book is dedicated,[5] could equally have cited the example of Symmachus.[6] In revising his letters, Sidonius generally restricted their scope to one theme, in the manner of Pliny, and limited the number of insulting remarks that could normally be expected in communications of a personal nature.[7] He was also careful to include letters to a wide range of well-placed contemporaries, thus ensuring the popularity of his collection. Sidonius' intentional letter-collection directly inspired his younger relatives, Bishops Avitus of Vienne[8] and Ruricius of Limoges,[9] as well as Bishop Ferriolus of Uzès (d. 581),[10] in their epistolary endeavours. An obvious parallel with the intentionality and focus on relationships in Sidonius' collection is Gregory Nazianzen's epistolary construction of his relationship with Basil of Caesarea, unmasked a decade or so ago by McLynn.[11] McLynn argues that at least five or six of Basil's letters to Gregory were originally included in the latter's collection, such that 'when related letters are read in conjunction they present a dialogue, which in each case shows Gregory up to advantage'.[12]

In 1908 Jean-Baptiste Chabot published the Syriac text of what he called *Documenta ad origines monophysitarum illustrandas* (*DM*), but it was not until 1933 that he was able to translate this dossier into Latin. It is a deliberate collection of forty-five pieces, mostly letters written by and to sixth-century anti-Chalcedonian bishops of Syria, Arabia and Egypt, individually or collectively, and embodies at least five different letter-types. Insofar as the *DM* has been used in modern scholarship, it has mostly been to outline the career of the divisive patriarch of Antioch, Paul the Black, which resulted in a schism between the sees of Antioch and Alexandria in 575CE.[13] Before the publication of Chabot's dossier, these events had been known only from the *Ecclesiastical History* of the sixth-century anti-Chalcedonian bishop, John of Ephesus,[14] which contains lacunae,

---

[4] *Ep.* IX.1, Anderson 1936: 500–5. Cf. *Ep.* IX.16.1, Anderson 1936: 596–7. Both Firminus and Sidonius conveniently omit from their tally Pliny's tenth book, which deals with the emperor Trajan.
[5] *Ep.* IX.1, Anderson 1936: 500–5.   [6] See Wood 1993: 29–43.
[7] See further Anderson 1936: lxii.
[8] Peiper 1961, Schanzer and Wood 2002 with intro.
[9] Luetjohann 1897: 299–350; Neri 2009; tr. Mathisen 1999.
[10] Although Ferreolus' letter-collection does not survive, it is attested to by Gregory of Tours in his *Decem libri historiarum* II.34, Krusch and Levison 1951.
[11] McLynn 2001: 178–93 (183–93); cf. Macé 2006: 144.
[12] McLynn 2001: 191.
[13] See Hermann 1928, corrected and supplemented by Brooks 1930; Honigmann 1951: 195–205; Van Roey and Allen 1994. On the longevity of the schism, which lasted well into the seventh century, see Allen 2009: 3–33.
[14] Brooks 1935: 191; 194–7, 202–2, 205–6, 207; Brooks 1936: 134, 143, 147, 151, 155.

and from the twelfth-century Jacobite chronicler, Michael the Syrian.[15] Apart from the usual letters between priests, bishops, monks and imperial officials, in Chabot's collection we find five synodical letters, that is, letters written by new bishops or patriarchs in which they publish their confession of faith to other bishops;[16] one widely disseminated encyclical letter which accompanied a theological discourse;[17] one canonical letter (so called, obviously, because it had canons appended to it);[18] two *entolika* or *mandata* of a hortatory nature in letter-form;[19] and four letters designated as *syndoktika* or *edicta*, which encompass agreed statements of a theological or disciplinary nature.[20] While in themselves these various letter-types are of interest, my aim here once again is to discern as far as possible the rationale and method behind the collection.

The Syriac manuscript in which the collection survives can be dated probably to the end of the sixth or the beginning of the seventh century, thus shortly after the redaction of numbers 42 and 43 in 580/1.[21] Most of the documents date from *c.* 560 to 568 and most are also in chronological order, making this 'a truly remarkable dossier'.[22] There are four main concentrations in the collection: (1) the *Theological Discourse* composed by the patriarch Theodosius in *c.* 560 to settle the controversy around tritheism, or the supposed heresy that posited three gods, godheads, substances or natures in the Trinity;[23] (2) the consecration of the Alexandrian archimandrite, Paul the Black, in 564 as patriarch of Antioch;[24] (3) the sending of Paul to the Alexandrian church in 565; and (4) the tritheist dispute from Theodosius' death in 566 until the excommunication of the tritheist leaders, Conon of Tarsus and Eugenius of Seleucia, in 569.

It is clear that the dossier is the work of supporters or a supporter of Paul, whose turbulent and colourful career certainly needed much defence.[25] An Alexandrian *syncellus*, Paul was consecrated patriarch of Antioch by Patriarch Theodosius of Alexandria in 564 against the wishes of the influential Syrian, Jacob Baradaeus, head of the eastern churches, and against the will of the Syrian bishops, who had not been consulted. On Theodosius' death on 22 June 566, which left Paul as the heir of

---

[15] Chabot 1899–1901, II: 381–94.
[16] *DM*, nos. 1, 2, 14, 14 and 44. On this epistolographical subgenre see Allen 2009: 47–51. These letter-types are also discussed in Allen and Neil 2013: 137–8.
[17] *DM*, no. 3.   [18] *DM*, no. 6.
[19] *DM*, nos. 18 and 19.   [20] *DM*, nos. 26, 27, 29 and 31.
[21] Dating established by Van Roey and Allen 1994: 267.
[22] Van Roey and Allen 1994: 270.
[23] On tritheism see Martin 1960; Van Roey 1985; Ebied, Wickham and Van Roey 1981; Van Roey and Allen 1994: 105–263; Grillmeier 2002: 279–91.
[24] On which see Allen 2011: 32–3, 2013b: 187–99.
[25] On the career of Paul the Black see Allen and Neil 2013: 139–40.

the property of the deceased, Paul used his legacy to try to buy his way into the position of patriarch of Alexandria. When this was unsuccessful, Paul retired to Syria, then to the Arabian camp of his protector, the anti-Chalcedonian Arab sheik al-Harith. In 570, we find him debating with the tritheites in Constantinople, where he subsequently accepted the edict of union designed by Emperor Justin II and communicated with the Chalcedonians (571). With other bishops Paul withdrew from communion and was incarcerated as a result, upon which the group communicated again. Since by now Paul was regarded as a security risk by the imperial government, he was kept in prison, and the eastern synod broke off relations with him, but he was able to escape to the camp of al-Moundhir, the successor of al-Harith, from where he went to Egypt, disguised as a soldier (574). After further misadventures, Paul was deposed as bishop by the new patriarch of Alexandria, Peter.

Eventually Paul returned to Constantinople and lived in hiding until his death in 581. He was buried in a convent under cover of darkness with a false name and no funeral.

While it is easy enough to establish that the dossier was compiled by contemporary or near-contemporary supporter(s) of Paul, it is more difficult to identify the compiler(s) more precisely. Suffice it to say that the gathering, ordering and editing of these forty-five documents required access to a number of archives, as well as meticulous care; it also involved translation of various Greek documents into Syriac. We may not be far off the mark in thinking this was all the work of an anti-Chalcedonian person (or persons) in Syria whose defence of Paul was both scholarly and wholehearted.

Later, intentional collections

Under consideration in this section are the letters of John Chrysostom; letters preserved in conciliar *acta* such as those of Cyril of Alexandria and John of Antioch; the correspondence of Ennodius of Pavia; the letters of Hormisdas; and those of Firmus of Caesarea.

The public career of John Chrysostom included on-and-off service as lector in the church of Antioch (*c.* 371–86), and a twelve-year presbyterate in the same city (386–97), before his elevation to the patriarchate of Constantinople in 398. Since he died in 407, the bulk of his writing may be presumed to stem from his work in Antioch, rather than from his shorter episcopate. However, while the other writings from his Antiochene phase are copious, no letters survive, and, with one exception preserved outside the collection,[26] the same holds true for the years 398–403, after which time John suffered two bouts of exile. Paradoxically, with that one exception, the letters which survive from or to him derive from his second exile, more precisely from June 404 to the beginning of 407. These amount to 242 pieces, of which five are from the Antiochene priest Constantius (*Epp.* 237–41) and another two are to be considered spurious (*Epp.* 125 and 233).[27] This is indeed a meagre harvest from a prominent and productive churchman over a period of more than thirty years.

Since Wendy Mayer deals in detail with Chrysostom's 'letter-collection' in this volume, here I am not even going to attempt an explanation of this phenomenon, since those more expert than I, like Roland Delmaire, have not sought to do so. Rather I shall focus on the arrangement in the 'collection', of which only *Letters* 1–7 to Olympias have received a modern edition so far,[28] although a new edition is well advanced in the series Sources chrétiennes. As with several groups of the surviving letters of Augustine,[29] as illustrated by Divjak, those of Chrysostom are grouped in the manuscripts in 'packets', destined for the same person(s) or the same destination. John himself was mostly not accustomed to date his letters. When they were first published by Sir Henry Savile in his monumental edition of 1613, the letters were organised according to the alphabetical order of the names of the addressees; later editors rearranged this already arbitrary classification also in an arbitrary manner, relying neither on chronological order nor on the sequence of the letters in the manuscripts.[30] If we return to my five points on letter-collection above, we see that in the case of Chrysostom's letters we are dealing with a collection that has been put together unhelpfully and now has to be unravelled by the twenty-first-century editors on the basis of the manuscript tradition and prosopographical induction.[31]

The greater part of the letters of Cyril, patriarch of Alexandria from 412 to 444,[32] survive thanks to their inclusion in the *acta* of the Council of Ephesus (431), which were edited mostly in the various fascicules of ACO 1. A good number of these survive also in the Latin translation made by Rusticus during the reign of Justinian I (527–65), arranged in various collections.[33] These letters, which were contained in the minutes of

---

[26] Malingrey 1988: 11, 68–95 = PG 52: 529–36.
[27] See further Delmaire 1991: 72.   [28] Ed. Malingrey 1968.
[29] See Divjak 1996–2002: 893–1057 (912–13). Some of Augustine's 'packets', however, also circulated separately.
[30] See further Delmaire 1991: 71–3.
[31] A *modus operandi* dealt with in detail by Delmaire 1991.
[32] On Cyril see *CPG* 5301–411; Russell 2000; McGuckin 2003, 2004; Wessel 2004.
[33] On these see Wickham 1983: xliv–xlvi.

the council, were collected for propaganda purposes, as were those too of Cyril's opponent, John of Ephesus. Other works in letter form, which are not a collection but are transmitted individually, are the *Answers to Tiberius, Doctrinal Questions and Answers* and the *Letter to Calosirius*, which survive outside the conciliar collections. Their Greek text is incomplete and has to be supplemented from Syriac and Armenian translations.[34] Apart from these two sets of Cyril's letters, we also have seventeen of the patriarch's *Festal Letters* (*CPG* 5240), influential pieces composed on an annual basis by the patriarchs of Alexandria to announce the forthcoming dates of Lent, Easter and Pentecost and disseminated through Egypt and even beyond.[35] While these are couched in letter-form, they are more akin to pastoral and dogmatic treatises and thus constitute a hybrid genre, which could explain their separate transmission as a traditionally recognised group – the Alexandrian patriarchs published their *Festal Letters* from the second half of the third century onwards, and in particular many of those of Athanasius and Cyril's uncle Theophilus have survived whole or in part.[36] The manuscript tradition of Cyril's *Festal Letters* is quite straightforward compared with other groups of letters: of the fifteen manuscripts which transmit the pieces whole or in part, thirteen contain all the letters in their entirety, thus evincing a relatively homogenous transmission.[37] Accordingly, although we owe the great bulk of Cyril's doctrinal and polemical correspondence to conciliar *acta*, we are fortunate to have a mixed transmission of the totality of his oeuvre because in the *Festal Letters* we are given glimpses of Cyril in a more pastoral mode.[38]

Like those of Cyril, many of the letters of John of Antioch (*CPG* 6301–60), who died in 441, have come down to us in conciliar collections, where not only those pieces composed by John himself but also those written collectively by the Syrian bishops under his leadership are preserved. Similarly many letters of Theodoret of Cyrrhus and Severus of Antioch (see further below on both) are extant because of their inclusion in *acta*. With the correspondence of these last two episcopal authors too we are dealing with mixed 'collections'.

Ennodius began as deacon in Milan (*c.* 502) before being consecrated bishop of Pavia in 513/14. He died in 521. As bishop he was expected to represent papal interests in the region, and indeed in 515 and 517 he participated in two unsuccessful embassies to Emperor Anastasius I in

---

[34] On which see further Wickham 1983: xlvii–xlix.
[35] Ed. Evieux *et al.* 1991–8; tr. Amidon and O'Keeffe 2009; cf. Allen 2010: 195–202.
[36] See Allen 2010: 195–202.   [37] See Evieux *et al.* 1991: 119.
[38] For considerations of Cyril as pastor see McGuckin 2003: 208; Allen 2014b.

Constantinople that were concerned with the resolution of the Acacian schism between the western and eastern parts of the empire.[39] From Ennodius we have some 297 letters,[40] almost all of which appear to date from his diaconate. This is the reverse of the case of John Chrysostom, whose surviving letter-collection dates from the last years of his episcopate. As an intriguing addendum here I mention the case of Epiphanius, who became bishop of Pavia in 466 and remained in his office until his death in 496. He mediated on numerous occasions with the Germanic kings, as related in his biography, written by his successor as bishop, Ennodius.[41] According to the biography, about which there are caveats,[42] Epiphanius was actively engaged in the well-being of his city and was regarded by the Ostrogothic king Theodoric as impressive enough to negotiate the release of some 6,000 prisoners held by the Burgundian king Gundobald. Whatever the favourable bias in Ennodius' account of his predecessor, what concerns us here is that from such a long and eventful episcopate we do not have a letter-collection, let alone a single surviving letter from this bishop, although it is unthinkable that someone of Epiphanius' stature did not compose many of them. Another consideration is that not *all* of them would have perished because they were politically sensitive or confidential. The lack of material evidence points to the finger of fate.

From Hormisdas, bishop of Rome from 514 to 523,[43] we have ninety-three letters, but also preserved are thirty-one pieces addressed to him, and a further twenty-six which are neither written by nor addressed to him. These letters are collected by Andreas Thiel,[44] and all except ten of them are transmitted in the *Collectio Avellana*.[45] To elucidate the background of these letters, a word needs to be said here on the politico-ecclesiastical activities of Hormisdas during his episcopate, for they were multi-faceted and included negotiations with the Gothic King Theoderic, Emperor Anastasius, various dignitaries in Constantinople, and bishops in both the East and the West. Not only was he embroiled in the schism involving Acacius, the deposed patriarch of Constantinople, which lasted from 484 to 519,[46] but he also lived to witness the death of Emperor Anastasius in 518 and the subsequent

---

[39] See Gioanni 2006: VII–XCV.　　[40] Ed. Gioanni 2006.
[41] Ed. Vogel 1885: 84–109; tr. Ferrari 1952: 301–51; see Gillett 2003: 148–71, 169.
[42] Issued by Gillett 2003: 169.
[43] Menze 2008: 58–105; Sardella 2000: 426–82.
[44] Thiel 1867 [2004]: 739–1006.
[45] Guenther 1895: 495–742. *Epp.* 9, 24, 25, 26, 88, 125, 142, 148, 149 and 150 are not contained in this collection.
[46] Frend 1972: 181–99, 232–3, 235–8; Blaudeau 2007: 65–98.

Chalcedonian restoration under Justin I and Justinian from that year until his death in 523. Indeed, Hormisdas' *Libellus*, which like many *libelli* could technically be classed as a letter but in the tradition bears the title *Fides Hormisdae papae* (*CPL* 1684), was an important instrument in the aim of the new imperial policy to unite eastern and western Christians.[47] Thus, unlike, for example, Firmus of Caesarea or Sidonius Apollinaris, as a letter-writer (and, significantly, as bishop of Rome) Hormisdas played a crucial role in directing the politico-ecclesiastical policies of his time. Like Severus of Antioch (on whom see below), in his day Hormisdas was what we would now call a big name.

The letters of Bishop Firmus of Caesarea (d. *c.* 439)[48] are transmitted in the beautiful tenth-century minuscule manuscript Ambrosianus B 4 sup. (gr. 81),[49] which at the beginning transmits the treatises attributed to Demetrius and Libanius on letter-writing. There follows a collection of letters of eighteen authors, both pagan and Christian, authentic and pseudonymous, arranged by the compiler in the following, non-chronological, order. Represented are Isidore of Pelusium, Firmus of Caesarea, Theophylact Simocatta, Emperor Julian, Basil of Caesarea, Libanius, Aelian, Aeneas of Gaza, Heraclitus, Iunius Brutus, Procopius of Gaza, Dionysius of Antioch, Apollonius of Tyana, Philostratus, Diogenes, Crates, Phalaris and Photius, the ninth-century patriarch of Constantinople and teacher of Arethas of Caesarea. It has been suggested that the manuscript belonged in fact to Arethas, the great collector (d. 935), who as archbishop of Caesarea in Cappadocia would have had easy access to the works of his predecessor Firmus.[50] Given the inclusion of the two treatises on the art of letter-writing at the beginning of the manuscript, it is clear in any case that the compiler wished to transmit pieces of letter-writing that he considered models worthy of imitation. Grünbart informs us that as far as Byzantine letter-collections are concerned, two methods are discernible: that of authors who produced or arranged collections, and that of friends, acquaintances or others interested in rhetoric.[51] This collection, whether attributable to Arethas or not, clearly belongs to the second group.

---

[47] On the significance of Hormisdas in these developments see the groundbreaking account of Menze 2008: 58–105. For other studies on the *Libellus* see Haacke 1939; Fortescue 1955.

[48] There is little secondary literature on Firmus, apart from the text of his letters, with introduction and notes, ed. Calvet-Sebasti and Gatier 1989, we have Gatier 2009: 115–23.

[49] Described by Martini and Bassi 1906: 92–4 and Calvet-Sebasti and Gatier 1989: 9–10.

[50] See Laourdas 1951: 370–2; Calvet-Sebasti and Gatier 1989: 10 n. 8.

[51] Grünbart 2006: 144–5.

So it is that forty-six letters of Firmus have come down to us, apparently arranged in the manuscript not according to the rank of their addressees, their contents, chronology or genre, and most of them composed in the spring and summer of the year 432.[52] Most letters are short, and those pertaining to friendship predominate. Although Firmus participated in the Council of Ephesus in 431 and belonged to the group of bishops that deposed Nestorius, there is little in the letters about the christological conflicts of his time, although *Letters* 37 and 38 refer to possible reconciliation between the Cyrillian party and their opponents. However, it would be dangerous to assume that the forty-six surviving letters are the sum total of Firmus' epistolographical output during his episcopate, which must have lasted at least eight years, if we calculate his participation at Ephesus and the probable election of his successor as bishop of Caesarea in 439.

'Collections' with mixed transmission

Here I discuss three extremely important 'collections', those of the controversial bishop-theologians Theodoret of Cyrrhus and Severus of Antioch and of the influential Augustine of Hippo.

Born in Antioch *c.* 393, Theodoret became bishop of the Syrian city of Cyrrhus in 423. An elegantly erudite writer in various genres, he was deeply embroiled in the church politics of his time due to his association with Nestorius, and was declared *persona non grata* by the second Council of Ephesus in 449. Rehabilitated at the Council of Chalcedon in 451, he died *c.* 460, perhaps in 466.[53] In the fourteenth century Nicephorus Callistus had access to over 500 of Theodoret's letters,[54] whereas today we have only 232. We can assume, too, that the corpus available to Nicephorus was not the total epistolographical output of an active bishop, pastor and theologian like Theodoret. Adam Schor discusses Theodoret's epistolary corpus in greater detail in this volume in terms of his epistolary networks. What, then, has survived, and how?

Almost all Theodoret's surviving letters date from the years 431–37 or from 444–51,[55] meaning that we have little evidence from 437 to 444, and only fragments of one letter from the period between the Council

---

[52] Discussed in Calvet-Sebasti and Gatier 1989: 24–6 and 46.
[53] On the career of Theodoret see most recently Urbainczyk 2002: 10–28; Pásztori-Kupán 2006: 3–27. On Theodoret as a letter-writer see Wagner 1948; Spadavecchia 1985: 249–52; Tompkins 1993; Tompkins 1995; Allen 2006c (on which I draw on 6–7 in what follows); Schor 2011.
[54] *Historia ecclesiastica* 14.54; PG 146: 1257A.
[55] As pointed out by Richard 1941–2: 415 (= no. 48 in Richard 1977a).

of Chalcedon and Theodoret's death.[56] While this imbalance compares favourably with the more extreme case of the surviving letters of Firmus of Caesarea, which date to just a period of a few months, the spread is nonetheless disappointing. There are three main collections in which Theodoret's letters are transmitted:[57]

1 The *Collectio Patmensis*, also known as the *Collectio Sakkelionis* (*CPG* 6239), edited by Iohannes Sakellion in 1885 from a *codex unicus* deriving from the island of Patmos and comprising forty-seven letters. One of these letters (no. 16) also appears in the next collection (as no. 58).

2 The *Collectio Sirmondiana* (*CPG* 6240), named after its first editor, Jean Sirmond (1642), containing 147 letters.

3 *Acta* from the Council of Ephesus (*CPG* 6241–78), containing thirty-two letters in Latin translation, and four in Greek.

The letters in the *Collectio Patmensis/Sakkelionis* range in all probability from 423/9,[58] to about April 448 (*Ep.* 16). On some occasions consecutive letters are addressed to the same person, but cannot be dated, for example *Letters* 8 and 9 to the magistrates at Zeugma, and *Letters* 27 and 28 to the sophist Isocacius. In other cases, for example, to Aërius the sophist (*Epp.* 7, 10, 23, 50), or again to Isocasius the sophist (*Epp.* 27–8, 38, 44, 52), they are spread through the collection. The letters in the *Collectio Sirmondiana* range from possibly before 431 (*Epp.* 66 and 67) to the end of 448. In this collection, festal letters (that is, those communications sent on special occasions like Easter) tend to be grouped together according to years.[59] On the other hand, *Letter* 8 to Eugraphia is posterior to *Letter* 104 to her, and *Letter* 11 to Flavian is posterior to *Letter* 104 to him. The rationale for letters in this collection dating from the end of 448 to 451, when Theodoret was embroiled in conciliar controversies, is easier to perceive because of his increasing self-involvement.[60] As for the letters preserved in the conciliar *acta*, the rationale is even more easily discerned again: many of these pieces, written by others, were included either to discredit or, to a lesser extent, rehabilitate Theodoret's christological and canonical position. We are speaking here about multi-faceted and complicated rationales behind the survival of the correspondence of the bishop of Cyrrhus.

[56] See Richard 1941–2: 415–23.
[57] Azéma 1982 (vol. I), 1964 (vol. II), 1965 (vol. III) and 1998 (vol. IV).
[58] *Epp.* 32 and 45 to Theodotus, bishop of Antioch (423–9).
[59] *Epp.* 4–6, 25–6, 38–9, 54–6, 63–4.   [60] *Epp.* 21, 83, 85, 101, 104, 131, 146.

The second 'collection' under the microscope here is that of Severus, anti-Chalcedonian patriarch of Antioch from 512 to 518.[61] Because of the imperial condemnation of his person and works in 536, for the most part Severus' letters survive in early Syriac translations and not in the original Greek. Otherwise they are extant in catenae or fragments, principally in Greek and Coptic. Severus' letters have come down to us in several groups. Originally they were divided into three classes: those before his patriarchate when he was a monk-lobbyist, those during his patriarchate and those after his expulsion from his see in 518 until his death in Egypt in 538. These contained four, ten and nine books respectively. In addition there were letters outside these twenty-three books that were transmitted separately. The total number of Severus' letters must have been between 3,759 and 3,824, of which fewer than 300 survive, thus less than one-fifteenth of the total.[62]

1   In the first collection we have 123 letters translated into Syriac by the priest Athanasius of Nisibis in 669.[63] These deal solely with ecclesiastical/canonical matters and are not in chronological order. However, at the beginning of each letter its place in the original collection of twenty-three books is stated.

2   The second collection is an artificial one containing 117 scattered letters, again in Syriac translation, brought together randomly from twenty-eight manuscripts by an early twentieth-century editor, the indefatigable E. W. Brooks.[64] In only twenty-six of these do we find any indication of what book the letter originally belonged to, and consequently dating is mostly speculative. The subject matter is doctrinal, exegetical, pastoral and personal in turn.

   From a collation of both these 'collections' it appears that the ten books containing letters from Severus' patriarchate are much longer than the others.[65]

3   Next we have another six letters preserved in the *Ecclesiastical History* of ps-Zachariah Scholasticus.[66] These pieces are important sources for Emperor Justinian's ecclesiastical policies and the part that Severus was expected to play in them, hence their interest to a church historian. They were, however, obviously of no interest at all to Athanasius of

---

[61] On the life, times and writings of Severus see Lebon 1909; Lebon 1951; Chesnut 1976: 9–56; Grillmeier 1995: 17–173; Allen and Hayward 2004; Alpi 2009a.

[62] See further Brooks 1902–33: ii/ix–x; Allen 1999: 388–9.

[63] Brooks 1902–3.   [64] Brooks 1915 and 1920.   [65] See Brooks 1915: 167–70.

[66] Book ix: 11, 13, 16, 20, 22, 23; ed., tr. Brooks 1920: 103–4, 106–13, 124–31, 139–40; 147–58; Greatrex, Phenix and Horn 2011: 355–6, 337–43, 354–61, 372–3, 378–87.

Nisibis, the compiler of the first collection, or to the scribes of the various letters in the artificial collection.

4 Three so-called letters of Severus to Sergius the Grammarian survive in an early Syriac translation made by Paul of Edessa after 519.[67] These compositions are really theological tractates couched in letter-form and constitute a self-contained corpus, making it understandable that they were transmitted separately. Hence we may speak of a rationale behind this collection, although the pieces are not letters *sensu stricto* but rather resemble tractates.

5 The *Synodical Letter* (*Epistula Synodica*), composed by Severus in exile on 26 July 535 on the accession of the anti-Chalcedonian Theodosius to the patriarchate of Alexandria and his subsequent role as leader of the anti-Chalcedonian party, is preserved in Syriac in the *DM*, a collection of documents intended to defend the cause of the controversial patriarch of Antioch, Paul the Black,[68] which has been treated at some length above. It is inexplicable that this letter, a document of such importance for the biography of Severus and the history of the anti-Chalcedonian church, survives only in a collection dedicated to the exoneration of somebody other than the condemned Severus himself. Add to that the fact that Theodosius himself was an extremely influential sixth-century ecclesiastical leader and theologian and the puzzle of transmission becomes even more baffling.

In addition to these five groups of Severus' letters there are individual pieces surviving in different ways and letters in Coptic and Arabic translations, thus making this important corpus of letters one of truly mixed transmission.

From the treatments above of the letters of Theodoret and Severus it will have become clear that groups of letters could be transmitted in a variety of ways: only some of these groups can responsibly be called 'collections' and some of them, like those of Severus, are completely artificial, having been put together by a modern editor and translator from various manuscripts.

In this section I have left until last the important number of over 300 letters that has come down to us from Augustine of Hippo (d. 430), a number, however, that falls far short of what the bishop must really have

---

[67] See the study and translation by Torrance 1998: 19; 2011: xxiii.
[68] On the *DM* see Chabot (ed., tr.) 1908: 12–24, 1933: 6–22. See also Allen and Neil 2013: 139–45; Allen 2013b: 187–99.

composed over his long episcopate. Here, although, as stated above, part of the genesis of what has survived appears to be attributable to the incorporation of 'packets' of his letters either to an individual or on a topic, of the 4,000 or so manuscripts containing Augustine's correspondence whole or in part only about 100 transmit the bulk of his work, whereas the other manuscripts preserve single letters, small groups with no visible rationale behind them, and letters arranged according to addressees or topics.[69] In addition to this somewhat haphazard transmission, we have the famous group of thirty-one letters that came to light in the 1970s, contained in two manuscripts dating from the twelfth and fifteenth centuries, which can be assigned to between 417 and 430, thus towards the latter part of the bishop's life. Nor can this group in reality be called a collection, although a number of the pieces shed new light on social and other practices in Augustine's sphere of influence that were hitherto unknown to us, such as people-trafficking, the indentured labour of children and the onerous duties involved in the *audientia episcopalis* or bishop's court.[70] While twenty-eight of these letters are from Augustine himself, two are from his correspondent Consentius[71] and one from Jerome to Aurelius, bishop of Carthage.[72] Although it is not unusual for extraneous materials to infiltrate 'collections' – indeed the large group of Augustine's other letters contains such pieces, as does the group from Hormisdas of Rome – it does seem strange that a small and otherwise reasonably homogeneous group should have accommodated three letters unconnected with the rest of the dossier.

'Collections' made by post-enlightenment editors

Here I draw attention briefly to two examples of post-enlightenment 'collections', namely parts of those of Severus of Antioch (miscellaneous letters) and of Hormisdas, as grouped in Thiel's edition. The tactics of these editors have been mentioned above in the general discussions of these two authors; these tactics serve to remind us of our dependence on what modern editors of texts present to us. We recall that in the 'collection' of Hormisdas, bishop of Rome, we have ninety-three letters composed by him, but also thirty-one pieces addressed to him, and a further twenty-six which are neither written by nor addressed to him.

---

[69] See in detail Divjak 1996–2002: 907–14.
[70] See most recently Allen and Neil 2013: 180–6.
[71] See Wankenne 1983: 225–42.   [72] Divjak 1996–2002: 919–20.

In the nineteenth century these letters were collected by Andreas Thiel,[73] and all except ten of them are transmitted in the *Collectio Avellana*.[74] Thus to describe Thiel's compilation as a 'collection' would be quite misleading. Similarly for Severus we have an artificial collection containing 117 scattered letters in Syriac translation, which were brought together randomly from twenty-eight manuscripts by an early twentieth-century editor, E. W. Brooks.[75] In only twenty-six of these do we find any indication of which of the twenty-three books of the patriarch's letters each piece originally belonged to, and consequently the dating is mostly speculative.

Concluding remarks

From the preceding exposition it will have become clear that whatever of late-antique correspondence has been transmitted to us in whatever ways, we must take account of serious gaps in the extant materials. This in itself should give us pause in the present volume, where we examine letter-collections and their transmission. I gave the telling example of the letters of Severus of Antioch, for which we have incontrovertible ancient evidence that only 7.5 per cent has come down to us – a figure, I suggest, that may be representative across the board. Even from such a prominent figure as Cyril of Alexandria we have really no personal and only a few pastoral letters, if we except the *Festal Letters* which are a hybrid genre anyway. Likewise we lament the loss of what must have been a significant number of missing letters from Augustine's epistolary corpus, as well as from that of Firmus of Caesarea. However, the same probably holds true for other late-antique letter-writers in general.

With John Chrysostom and Ennodius of Pavia we have observed reverse cases of transmission, Chrysostom's surviving letters deriving only from the last years of his life and those of Ennodius deriving in large part only from his diaconate. Firmus' letters survived through being found worthy of inclusion in a letter-writing codex by a scholar 400 years later, but most of them cover only a period of a few months. The case of Epiphanius is extreme, there being no collection under his name and not a single surviving letter from a long episcopate. We might compare him with Caesarius of Arles, from whom we also have no collection per se and only a few letters preserved otherwise, or with numerous high-profile sixth-century

---

[73] Thiel 1867 [2004]: 739–1006.
[74] Guenther 1895: 495–742.   [75] Brooks 1915 and 1920.

Chalcedonian and anti-Chalcedonian bishops in the East from whom we have not a single surviving letter.[76] No obvious explanation springs to mind for any of these phenomena.

Sidonius' letters survived by his own efforts and particularly by his self-publicity. Hormisdas' letters present another problem in that while we can attribute the survival of ninety-three letters probably to the activity of the *scrinium* or papal archive, other pieces concerned not only with him but also with the Acacian schism have come down to us as well, preserved by other processes. Against the vagaries of fate in many other collections, the anonymous compilation of the *DM* is a stand-out – a deliberate, well-organised and well-researched entity with the obvious aim of defending a controversial bishop whose career spanned sixth-century Alexandria, Antioch, Constantinople and places in between.

The survival of Theodoret's letters in three main collections is a much more complex affair, owing much to that bishop's literary activity on the one hand, and to his involvement in christological and canonical crises on the other. In the preservation of his letters dealing with ecclesiastical debates, conciliar *acta* and their own complicated transmission played a significant role. With regard to the complexity of the letter-collections in which Theodoret's letters have come down to us, it is instructive as a comparison to look at those of Severus of Antioch, from whom we have four collections, as well as an individual, significant letter not subsumed in any of them. The intricacy and obscurity of the transmission of the letters of both Theodoret and Severus may be closely linked with the condemnation that both incurred for their christological stances. In the case of Severus we have no fewer than five collections of letters, each one transmitted in a completely different way, such that we are speaking of a very complex tradition that is possibly due to both his condemnation and the varying ecclesio-political fortunes of the anti-Chalcedonian party after his death.

While we can do little with the random or skewed elements in letter-compilations except to note, as in the case of Firmus' letters, that four centuries after their composition they were considered elegant pieces, the intentionality and even archival obsession of other collections may legitimately invite suspicion: not all compilers were as upfront, if vain, as Sidonius or the bishops of Rome in ensuring that a particular

---

[76] As examples we could cite the patriarchs of Antioch, Ephrem (527–45), Anastasius (559–70, 593–8) and Gregory (570–93).

collection was preserved for posterity, and the motives of later compilers can sometimes only be guessed at. I suggest, then, that our only recourse is to take early Christian letter 'collections' and their transmission on an individual basis in order to assess how deliberate or random each was, and what motivation or accident lay behind the transmission of what we have today.

PART II

Collecting New Testament and early monastic letters

CHAPTER 3

The Pauline letters as community documents

Ian J. Elmer

A cursory survey of Paul's letters within the context of the New Testament canon reveals the following conclusions: thirteen letters are attributed to Paul, nine of which were occasional in nature, written to named local communities for specific purposes (e.g. Rome, Corinth, Philippi, Thessalonica, Colossae, Ephesus, Galatia), and four of which were written to individuals (Philemon, Timothy and Titus). Despite the occasional or personal nature of Paul's letters it seems that they were read publicly in the church, probably in the context of worship,[1] including those addressed to individuals (Phlm. 1–2).[2] Some were intended to be circulated to other churches (Col. 4:16; Gal. 1:1). Furthermore, the collection is not complete and there are some notable gaps and anomalies. Colossians (4:6) mentions an otherwise unknown letter to the Laodiceans. In his Corinthian correspondence, Paul refers to a letter that pre-dates the two Corinthian letters we do have (1 Cor. 5:9) and one that was probably written between these two, the so-called 'letter with tears' (2 Cor. 2:4). Some scholars have argued that fragments of these two letters have been preserved in 2 Corinthians, and that 2 Corinthians is a composite creation containing between three and six letter fragments.[3]

Of the canonical letters attributed to Paul, several were most likely written after his death by close associates and former co-workers: Ephesians, Colossians, 1 and 2 Timothy, Titus and possibly 2 Thessalonians. A couple of these 'deutero-Pauline' texts refer to even more letters attributed to Paul that are likely to have been counterfeit (2 Thess. 2:2; 2 Tim. 2:16–18). In addition to this list, we must add the letter to the Hebrews, which appears in earliest collections of Paul's letters and, as a consequence, was included

---

[1] 1 Thess. 4:13; 5:27; Col. 4:16. [2] Stirewalt 2003: 13–18.
[3] Bieringer has conveniently outlined and analysed the various theories concerning the integrity of 2 Corinthians in a series of articles, which have been reprinted in Bieringer and Lambrecht 1994: 67–179.

in the canon of the New Testament.[4] So, it seems that we have less than what Paul wrote and, of those letters we do have, Paul wrote less than what is attributed to him. This observation alone testifies to the communal nature of the enterprise focused on the preservation, redaction and collection of Paul's letters. What remains unclear, however, is how, when and why that process occurred in the first place. Sources for reconstructing the development of the Pauline corpus are either non-existent or subject to a variety of interpretations. There is very little scholarly consensus as to what could and did in fact happen. Hypotheses abound, but in many cases we are left with a bewildering number of probabilities.[5] The story of the emergence of the Pauline corpus is a complex one that stretches back to Paul and his intimate circle of co-workers and missionaries.[6] A short study such as this cannot hope to chart the processes that led to the formation of the Pauline letter-collection. Rather, this chapter offers a brief survey of current theories only by way of seeking to demonstrate that the letters of Paul were always considered community documents and their collection not a mere happenstance of history.

The emergence of the Pauline corpus

It can be reasonably assumed that Paul's letters would have been valued and preserved by the churches to which they were written, although, as we have noted, there may have been exceptions, such as those now lost letters to Corinth (1 Cor. 5:9; 2 Cor. 2:4) and Laodicea (Col. 4:16). The present state of the Pauline corpus with its several variants in the manuscript record indicates that, after his death, Paul's disciples and co-workers preserved, copied, augmented and passed on the extant letters, sometimes combining various fragments into a single piece, as may be the case with 2 Corinthians and possibly also Philippians.[7] In a few places we can detect interpolations and glosses (e.g. 1 Thess. 2:14–16; 1 Cor. 14:33b–36), which appear to have been added to the original text by early scribes. Some of

---

[4] Trobisch 1994: 11.

[5] See recent discussion in Porter 2011: 12–42; Porter 2009: 95–128; Reicke 1951: 23–61.

[6] A very strong and cogent argument for Paul's role in the editing and collection of his own letters has been made by Trobisch 1989: 56–62, who is followed by Porter 2011: 30–5. Other commentators who have suggested that the collection may have begun with Paul are Guthrie 1990: 657 and Richards 2004: 218–23.

[7] On partition theories and Philippians, see R.P. Martin 1994: 37–41 and more fully Jewett 1970: 40–53. See also Alexander 1989: 87–101, who has analysed Philippians in the light of contemporary Hellenistic letters and argued that the inconsistencies in Philippians are compatible with the conventions of Hellenistic letter-forms.

the canonical letters exist in variant forms in different early manuscripts. We have manuscripts of Romans, for example, that do not have the final chapter, which contains Paul's greetings to members of the Roman community. The debate over the originality of Romans 16 has raised questions about the later utility of Paul's letters in edited form.[8]

At some point, Paul's correspondence was acknowledged to have a wider or more universal application. Other communities, recognising the enduring apostolic and pastoral value of Paul's letters, acquired copies of letters from neighbouring congregations. As a consequence of such sharing, the collection probably grew incrementally. Commonly called the 'snowball' or 'gradual-collection' theory, this approach to understanding the development of the Pauline corpus was championed widely in the late nineteenth and early twentieth centuries.[9] Proponents of this approach argue that each letter of Paul, which would have been read and reread by the original addressees, gradually found its way to other communities. The assumption is that Paul's letters had been carried and circulated by significant church leaders in the same way that Paul had his letters delivered by such messengers as Timothy and others (see 1 Thess. 5:27). But it was not until the second century that collections of Paul's letters emerged.[10]

Following this line of argument, it is usually posited that the circulation of the letters and their limited collection may have begun in those regional areas where Pauline communities flourished, such as Asia Minor (Colossae, Ephesus, Hierapolis and Laodicea), Macedonia (Thessalonica and Philippi) and Achaia (Corinth). Proponents of the 'gradual-collection' theory point to the manner in which groups of three Pauline letters appear to be associated with different regions: 1 and 2 Thessalonians with Philippians from Macedonia, Philemon, Colossians and Ephesians from Asia Minor and the Corinthian correspondence from Achaia.[11] To this list one must also add the Pastoral Epistles, which appear to have been composed and to have circulated as a three-letter codex.[12] Similar three-letter sets found places in the canon of the New Testament, such as 1 and 2 Peter with Jude and the Johannine epistles.[13] In the first decades of the second century the regional collections of Paul's letters became part of a larger and definitive Pauline corpus. Our three earliest surviving canons of Pauline letters, the Marcionite canon, Muratorian canon and P46, all

[8] See, for example, Byrne 1996: 29; Dunn 1988: 9–16, 884–5; Morris 1988: 9–11, 21–31.
[9] Reicke 1951: 55–6. See also Gamble 1985: 36. The two most notable proponents of the 'gradual-collection' theory were Zahn 1975: 811–39; von Harnack 1926: 6–27.
[10] Porter 2011: 23.   [11] So Mowry 1944: 73–86; Zuntz 1953: 278–9.
[12] Barnett 1941: 251.   [13] Neunhaus 2007: 82–3.

date from the middle to late second century – although between the three there remain variations in the order and the number of Paul's letters.[14]

Despite the inherent plausibility of the 'gradual-collection' proposition, there is no evidence that such small collections existed.[15] The earliest definitive evidence we have for a possible small collection of Pauline letters comes from *1 Clement*, a late first-century letter from Rome addressed to the Christian communities in Corinth.[16] The author of *1 Clement* (5:2–7) places Paul alongside Peter as one of two apostolic pillars of the church, whose 'outstanding model of endurance' won him a place in heaven.[17] A close reading of *1 Clement* suggests that the author knew and alluded to 1 Corinthians, Romans, Galatians, Philippians, Ephesians and possibly Hebrews.[18] Certainly the author is aware of 1 Corinthians, which he explicitly mentions in chapter 47 of his own epistle when he exhorts the Corinthians to avoid factionalism (*1 Clement* 47.3). Clement cites Paul as one who wrote 'with true inspiration' when he warned against factionalism in his letter to the same Corinthian churches to which Clement was now writing (*1 Clement* 47.1–5; cf. 1 Cor. 1:10–12). Clement's point is that 'even then you were given to faction' (*1 Clement* 47.3), but that it was worse now because the Corinthians had become partisans not of apostles or of those of noble reputation, like Paul, Cephas or Apollos (as in 1 Cor. 1:12), but of far lesser figures (*1 Clement* 47.4).[19]

Remarkably, despite his extensive use of 1 Corinthians the author of *1 Clement* seems unaware of 2 Corinthians, the content of which would have served his argument better.[20] While his silence vis-à-vis 2 Corinthians may indicate that the author of *1 Clement* has only partial access to Paul's letters, the absence of 2 Corinthians from a collection containing 1 Corinthians tells against arguments in favour of regional collections. Hence, the real significance of Clement's letter lies not so much in the number of letters that it referred to as in the fact that his letter of the Church of Rome 'to the Church of God in pilgrimage at Corinth' (*1 Clement* pref.) reflects an acquaintance with two letters that are unrelated geographically.[21] Of course, it is also possible that Clement was cognisant of more letters than

---

[14] Trobisch 1994: 5–26; Porter 2011: 20–21.

[15] Pervo 2010: 55 makes the telling point that while the advocates of the 'snowball' hypothesis rightly recognise 'the value [placed on] Paul's letters after his death and the perceived drive towards collecting them', they fail to account for the obvious neglect suffered by some key Pauline letters, such as the lost letters to Corinth and Laodicea.

[16] Gamble 1985: 282. The text of *1 Clement* is translated in Glimm 1947a: 9–58.

[17] Glimm 1947a: 14. See also Polycarp, *Letter to the Philippians* 9.1–2, Glimm 1947b: 140.

[18] Grant 1971: 81–3.   [19] Glimm 1947a: 46.

[20] Pervo 2010: 130.   [21] Glimm 1947a: 9.

he utilised in his correspondence. Moreover, we cannot be sure if Clement actually had access to the letters or even a letter-collection. It is entirely possible that he is quoting or paraphrasing passages from various Pauline texts from memory.[22]

Perhaps the most obvious flaw with the 'gradual-collection' theory is the difficulty in seeing this early circulation and assembly of Paul's letters occurring without the guidance of some significant individual or group. The editorial and redactional activity in the Corinthian correspondence, and possibly Philippians and Romans, confirms that someone was working on the letters, and that this redactional activity occurred very early on in the process.

The process of collecting and editing Paul's letters may have been performed by a 'school' of Paul.[23] This envisions a process whereby, after Paul's death, a group of his disciples or co-workers met together to study his theology in order to pass on the theological traditions that they had inherited from their master. It is suggested that the deutero-Pauline letters were attempts of the school, or certain individuals within the Pauline circle, and under the name of Paul, to interpret, reinterpret and apply Paul's theology to later generations by appealing to Paul's apostolic authority. Indeed, when we look at the deutero-Pauline texts, it seems clear that from the very earliest years after Paul's death, his disciples in the late first-century church attempted to press-gang the departed apostle into the service of their causes. This is apparent with the Pastoral Epistles, 1 and 2 Timothy and Titus, the language and stylistic features of which are more characteristic of a later generation, and the opposition confronted in the Pastorals seems to reflect developments that led to the Gnostic systems of the second century (e.g. 1 Tim. 1:4; 6:20).[24] The structure envisaged for the churches in view seems to demonstrate the sort of institutionalising tendencies (overseers, deacons and elders) that are characteristic of the second and third generations of charismatic movements.

Colossians and Ephesians similarly present a clear case of the development of Paul's legacy by later disciples. While some debate remains on the Pauline authorship of Colossians, most scholars accept that Ephesians is clearly dependent upon Colossians, but represents a significant theological

---

[22] Martin 1986: 277.

[23] The idea that a 'Pauline school' stands behind the Pauline corpus was first suggested, although not fully fleshed out, by Goodspeed 1927: 218. See more recently and in greater detail Pervo 2010: 26–7, 55–61, 286 n. 36.

[24] Recent commentary has begun to raise questions about the deutero-Pauline status of the Pastorals: see Johnson 2008: 55–97; Towner 2006: 9–26. On Gnosticism and the opponents in the Pastorals, see Schmithals 1972: 239–74.

departure from traditional Pauline themes.[25] Ephesians looks like a conscious attempt by a disciple of Paul to preserve Paul's heritage in a form that was of general rather than specific use, that was easy to incorporate within congregational worship and that maintained the earlier Pauline emphases regarded as of greatest continuing value. This would explain its general character. Ephesians is probably a circular letter, which was not directed to a particular church – the words 'in Ephesus' (Eph. 1:1) are not present in the earliest and best manuscripts (e.g. P46). Marcion apparently knew the letter under the heading 'to the Laodiceans', which might support the argument for the letter being a circular rather than an occasional letter.[26] Ephesians is not addressed to particular issues, which would explain the absence of many of the specific features of the genuine Pauline letters. Ephesians is written in a richly resonant style, which is uncharacteristic of either Colossians or Paul's genuine letters. So, for example, the first three chapters take the form of a lengthy thanksgiving prayer, full of what might be called 'liturgical redundancies',[27] elaborating the body imagery in Ephesians 4:7–16, the marriage imagery in Ephesians 5:21–33 and the warfare imagery in Ephesians 6:10–17, respectively. All of this was probably intended to nurture a Pauline congregation's devotion and dedication more effectively than Paul's more typically epigrammatic exhortation.

The appeal to Paul's name and authority would have been especially significant as the church confronted new forms of false teaching and needed to establish 'sound doctrine and practice'. From these deutero-Pauline letters emerges what Victor Furnish called a 'Paulusbild', a new exalted 'view' of Paul as apostle and martyr, whose sufferings 'are said to have completed Christ's afflictions, and to have been, like Christ's own, on behalf of the whole church'.[28] However, there are also apparent in this emerging 'Paulusbild' attempts to 'put Paul in his place', to domesticate him and render his words harmless.[29]

Putting Paul in his place

Paul's legacy to Christian literature is unarguably one of the most significant in church history, and probably also one of the most ambiguous. Several decades after Paul's death, the author of 2 Peter warns his readers that Paul's letters 'contain some things that are hard to understand, which

---

[25] See discussion with specific reference to the concept of a Pauline school in Pervo 2010: 64–77.
[26] Pervo 2010: 29, 109.   [27] Eph. 1:17–19; 2:13–18; 3:14–19.
[28] Furnish 1994: 5. E.g. Col. 1:23–5; 4:10; Eph. 3:1; 4:1.
[29] Reicke 1969: 5–16.

ignorant and unstable people distort, as they do the other scriptures' (2 Pet. 3:16).

Sometimes it was Paul's own disciples who misrepresented him, most likely out of good intentions. The Pastorals, for example, hail Paul as the pre-eminent apostle, whose faithful endurance and righteous way of life are the model for all Christian living.[30] This is a far cry from Paul's own self-abasement as 'the least of the apostles' (1 Cor. 15:9–11), and his gospel proclamation of radical freedom in the Spirit.[31] In the Pastorals, Paul's gospel is rendered down to mere appeals for strict adherence to 'sound doctrine' (1 Tim. 1:10–11) and 'godly living' (1 Tim. 6:3). 'Paul is himself reduced to the guarantor of apostolic doctrine (1 Tim. 1:11; Titus 1:3) and the prototypical Christian man (e.g. Titus 1:1)'.[32]

Perhaps one of the most obvious expressions of the emerging 'Paulusbild' in the late first century is the Lukan Acts of the Apostles. Acts presents Paul as God's 'chosen instrument' who strives laboriously, risking his own life (Acts 9:23–9; 20:19), to proclaim the gospel 'before Gentiles, kings and the whole people of Israel' (Acts 9:15–16). Like Jesus, Paul heals the sick (Acts 19:11–12) and raises the dead (Acts 20:10), is falsely accused of apostasy and blasphemy by a Jerusalem mob (Acts 20:21, 27–9),[33] is arrested and tried before the Sanhedrin (Acts 22:30–23:10), the Roman governor (Acts 24:1–25:12) and Herod Agrippa (Acts 25:23–26:29). The Paul of Acts is a good Law-observant Jew (Acts 16:3), who is falsely accused of being a libertine (Acts 21:17–26). Yet Paul clearly tells us in his letters that he no longer observed the Law.[34] Furthermore, Luke plays down all instances of conflict between Paul and other factional leaders of the early church (cf. Acts 15:1–29; 21:17–19), the very debates that are a central concern in Paul's letters.[35] Perhaps this is why Luke does not even tell us the one thing that is most obvious about Paul, that Paul wrote letters. In summary, the Paul of Acts looks and sounds very little like the Paul who emerges from his own authentic letters, namely Romans, 1 and 2 Corinthians, Galatians, Philippians, Philemon and 1 Thessalonians.[36]

---

[30] 1 Tim. 6:11; 2 Tim. 2:10–12; 3:10; Titus 2:2, 12.

[31] 1 Cor. 1:18–2:16; Gal. 3:1–5; 5:16–26; cf. Rom. 12:1–2.

[32] Furnish 1994: 6–7.   [33] Cf. Acts 18:12–13.

[34] E.g. Rom. 6:1–23; 7:6; 10:4; 1 Cor. 9:20–1; Gal. 2:19; 5:11, 18; Phil. 3:8.

[35] E.g. Gal. 2:1–14; 1 Cor. 1:10–17; 9:5; 15:8–11; 2 Cor. 3:1–6; 10:1–33; Rom. 3:8; 15:25–33.

[36] Elmer 2009: 35–8. See also Haenchen 1966. In the same volume, a similar view has been expressed by Vielhauer 1966. See more recent discussion of Haenchen and Vielhauer in Porter 1999: 187–206. Porter, by contrast, does not see 'any significant or sustainable contradictions' between the Paul of Acts and the Paul of the letters (1999: 205). However, he does admit that there are 'differences in emphasis and focus' that can be explained by the specific 'theological issues' raised by Acts (1999: 206).

Recent scholarship has been willing to view Luke in more positive terms. For example, I. H. Marshall, while acknowledging Luke's unique theological perspective, insists that Luke is a careful and accurate historian, at least by the standards of first century historiography.[37] Similarly, M. Hengel, a prominent proponent of the historical veracity of Acts, concurs that 'Luke is no less trustworthy than other historians of antiquity' and, hence, Luke's 'account remains within the limits of what was considered reliable by the standards of antiquity'.[38] Still, there remain a number of very real questions as to Luke's knowledge and/or use of Paul's letters. It may be true that Luke made no use of Paul's letters, but that does not substantiate the claim that he did not know them.

Like the author of 2 Peter, Luke may have considered some things in Paul's letters 'hard to understand'. More likely, however, Luke had an apologetic agenda – he says as much to his patron, Theophilus (Luke 1:4; cf. Acts 1:1). Luke wanted to 'set the record straight' (Luke 1:3), but in so doing he glossed over Paul's conflicts with other church authorities, straightened out the ambiguities of Paul's story and ignored the differences inherent in the early church, thereby 'putting Paul in his place'.

Some commentators argue that the publication and dissemination of Acts may have proved a watershed in the production of the Pauline corpus.[39] So, for example, E. J. Goodspeed, in response to the 'gradual-collection' theory, argued that Paul's letters were widely ignored, even relatively unknown, until after the arrival of Acts.[40] Goodspeed posited that Acts' lack of dependence upon the Pauline letters, contrary to what we find in later Christian literature, signals a rapid growth in interest in Paul only late in the first century. So, rather than arguing for a sustained and growing appreciation of Paul, Goodspeed maintained that, because Paul's letters were occasional, they had little value for anyone else and were simply stored in church chests and gradually fell into obscurity.[41] Only after the publication of Acts of the Apostles (c. 85) was awareness of Paul, and particularly his role in the Gentile mission, revived. The underlying assumption here is that anyone reading Luke's history of the early church would be fascinated with Paul and undoubtedly ask questions about the apostle's literary activity.

Godspeed is very specific in his reconstruction of events. Taking his lead from the fact that Acts makes no mention of Colossae, Goodspeed

---

[37] Marshall 1980: 75. Similarly, Barrett 1961: 24–5 characterises Luke's work as giving the 'impression of a screen upon which two pictures are being projected at the same time – a picture of the church of the first period, and, superimposed upon it, a picture of Luke's own times'.

[38] Hengel 1979: 60–1.   [39] Porter 2011: 24–6; Guthrie 1990: 647.

[40] Goodspeed 1927: 1–103; 1937: 210–21.   [41] Goodspeed 1927: 21.

singles out Colossians and Philemon as the kernel around which the rest of the Pauline corpus was built. Since Ephesians is non-specific in its focus and because it relies heavily on Colossians, Goodspeed suggests that this later letter was penned as a circular letter of introduction to the corpus. According to Goodspeed's reconstruction, Ephesus emerged in the later decades as the second most important centre of Christianity and, hence, many of the later canonical texts, the Johannine Gospel, letters and Revelation, as well as the letters of Ignatius, were composed in that city.[42] References and allusions to most of Paul's letters can be found in Ignatius of Antioch and also in his contemporary Polycarp of Smyrna, a near neighbour to the Ephesian community.[43] Like Clement, Ignatius knew 1 Corinthians.[44] In his *Letter to the Ephesians* Ignatius also makes it clear that he knew that Paul had written several letters.[45] Polycarp alludes to most of Paul's letters. 1 Corinthians is best demonstrated, but also well attested are Romans, 2 Corinthians, Galatians, Ephesians, Philippians, the Thessalonian letters and the Pastorals. Polycarp, in addition to his own collection, is aware of a similar collection in the Philippian church – 'when he was absent, [Paul] wrote you letters. By the careful perusal of his letters you will be able to strengthen yourselves in the faith given to you.'[46]

To pursue this thesis further, Goodspeed and other proponents of this school of thought, commonly called the 'lapsed interest' or 'big bang' theory, argue that a single, prominent individual must be credited with the primary role in bringing the first collection of Paul's letters together into a single codex.[47] Goodspeed identified Onesimus who appears in both Philemon (Phlm. 10) and Colossians (Col. 4:9) as the one who initially collected and published Paul's letters as a corpus. Onesimus is later named as bishop of Ephesus by Ignatius.[48] Similarly, J. Knox, following Goodspeed, argued for Onesimus on the basis of the inclusion of Philemon in the Pauline canon, an inclusion that would seem inexplicable on the basis of the letter content alone.[49]

While Goodspeed appears to present a fairly solid argument, it must be admitted that it depends on a high degree of speculation.[50] The evidence,

---

[42] Goodspeed 1927: 52–61, followed by Mitton 1951: 45–54 and Knox 1959: 67–78. More recently, and already noted, Pervo 2010: 66.

[43] Gamble 1985: 282.

[44] Ignatius, *Letter to the Ephesians* 16.1; 18.1, Walsh 1947: 94; *Letter to the Romans* 5.1; 9.2, Walsh 1947: 110, 112.

[45] Ignatius, *Letter to the Ephesians* 12.2, Walsh 1947: 92.

[46] Polycarp, *Letter to the Philippians* 3.2, Glimm 1947b: 137.

[47] Pervo 2010: 56–7; Porter 2011: 24–6; Richards 2004: 210–11.

[48] Ignatius, *Letter to the Ephesians* 1.3; 6.2, Walsh 1947: 87, 89.

[49] Knox 1959: 67–78.   [50] So, rightly, Martin 1986: 278.

such as it is, is open to multiple interpretations. For instance, there is no doubt that Ephesus was an important centre for the Pauline mission, even in Paul's own lifetime. Of the several letters written by Paul, the Corinthian correspondence was written here shortly after his arrival in Ephesus, probably in the autumn of 52 (1 Cor. 16:8). The fact that Paul sent greetings to the Corinthians from the 'churches of Asia' (1 Cor. 16:19) further indicates that Ephesus was the location of his writing this correspondence.[51] Depending on the location of Paul's imprisonment at the time, Philemon may have been written at Ephesus, as the Pastorals were later. But there were additional places of prominence for Paul and his immediate heirs. An argument in favour of Corinth has been offered by W. Schmithals, who also concludes that the anti-Gnostic flavour of the Pastorals seems to be an extension of earlier problems Paul encountered at Corinth, especially at the time of writing 2 Corinthians.[52] Others have thought Alexandria more likely, based primarily upon the nature of scholarship behind the collection of sacred texts.[53] Rome may be equally possible, given recent arguments in favour of a Roman provenance for both Colossians and Ephesians.[54]

The first Pauline collection

A similar variety of theses exists when it comes to naming the editor behind the first Pauline collection. The concept of a major editor working in a single locale has merit, and should be preferred over that of the haphazard approach underlying the 'gradual-collection' theory. The problem, once again, is the difficulty in narrowing the field of candidates down to a single probable identity. In the past, Marcion has often been proposed primarily on the basis of the extant Marcionite canon

---

[51] I have argued previously that Paul may have been imprisoned at Ephesus for some time and that it was for this reason that many of his early letters were written from Ephesus. See Elmer 2009: 189–91.

[52] Schmithals 1972: 88, 262.

[53] Grant 1971: 121–4; Zuntz 1953: 14; Bruce 1988: 129–30.

[54] See Dunn 1996: 307–9. Dunn has argued that while Colossians differs linguistically from the authentic Pauline letters, the close overlap with Philemon as well as the detailed personal requests made in Colossians 4:7–17 and the concluding autograph (Col. 4:18) make it hard to doubt that Paul himself stood behind the letter in some personal capacity. Dunn (1996: 309) argues that the best solution is probably that the letter was composed in Rome by Timothy (named as co-author in Col. 1:1) but approved by Paul with the addition of his own name at the end. Dunn concludes: 'If Colossians was written on Paul's behalf during his final imprisonment (from which he was never released) and if the points of overlap between the two are to be understood as indicating one letter (Colossians) written shortly after the other, then Philemon is presumably tied with Colossians into a Roman imprisonment.'

and the use of that list by the later Muratorian canon.[55] However, as we noted above, there is sufficient evidence to suggest that collections or, at least multiples, of Paul's letters were known to earlier authors, such as Clement, Ignatius and Polycarp. It could just as easily have been one of these three early church Fathers, although it is not entirely clear if they actually possessed a collection of Paul's letters. By contrast, R. P. Martin suggested Luke, but one might wonder then why the picture of Paul presented in Acts is so at odds with that of the Pauline letters.[56] Perhaps Timothy would be a better candidate, especially given his prominence as co-author of two of the deutero-Pauline letters, Colossians (4:18) and 2 Thessalonians (1:1), as well as the addressee of two of the Pastorals (1 Tim. 1:2; 2 Tim. 1:2).[57] Ultimately, however, the possibilities are as numerous as the number of those named as Paul's co-workers and co-authors in the greetings and postscripts of Paul's letters. Of course, that observation may be the key to unlocking the mystery. Is it not possible that the collection, redaction and augmentation of the Pauline letters began much earlier than the late first- or early second-century dates espoused by previous theories? Maybe it began with Paul and his original circle of co-workers.

Paul and his companions

Returning again to the author of 2 Peter, it is remarkable to note how quickly 'all Paul's letters' became identified as 'scripture' and, like all scripture, the subject of misunderstanding and misinterpretation (2 Pet. 3:16). The most likely explanation for this development is that a collection of Paul's letters had been in wide circulation for quite some time prior to the writing of 2 Peter. Paul always had his detractors and opponents, and his letters attracted numerous negative responses, even in his own lifetime. Similarly, Paul probably also had his collectors, and may even have contributed to the process himself.

One of the assumptions that underpin much of the commentary on Paul's letters is that Paul was the sole author of his letters, and that such compositions were in the nature of personal correspondence between Paul and his communities. Of course this does not mean that Paul physically wrote his own letters; we have good evidence to the contrary. On three occasions we find Paul appending a hand-written 'signature' to letter

[55] Bruce 1988: 163–4.   [56] Martin 1986: 278–80.
[57] Guthrie 1990: 655–7.

conclusions,[58] the purpose of which was to establish the authenticity of the letter. Moreover, these examples of hand-written signatures indicate that the body of the letter was written in another hand, probably that of a professional secretary or co-worker – assuming that one or other of Paul's companions had the necessary training and the requisite equipment. Most commentators presume Paul used secretaries to write the letters down, but few consider that such secretaries played any significant role in the composition of the letters. In Graeco-Roman literary circles, professional secretaries played a far greater role in the composition of letters than we would normally assume. On one level, a secretary's contribution could mean simply ensuring that the grammar and spelling were correct. More commonly, however, the secretary fulfilled the role of writing partner or final editor.

Many of Paul's letters are prefaced by greetings, not just from Paul, but from various co-workers who were with him at the time, and who may have had some role in composing or writing down the letters – Silvanus/Silas and Timothy for the Thessalonian letters,[59] Sosthenes for 1 Corinthians (1:1; cf. 16:21–4), Timothy for 2 Corinthians (1:1), Philippians (1:1) and Colossians (1:1; cf. Col. 4:18). Most scholars assume that, whatever their contribution, those named team members should not be considered genuine authors. It may simply be that the named individuals were with Paul when he wrote, one or two of whom may have functioned as Paul's secretary as the need arose. In the first century, however, secretaries were neither mere note-takers nor stenographers, and letter-writers rarely directly dictated their letters to them, and this is probably true of Paul's co-workers too.[60]

It is notable that in those letters where co-workers are named at the outset, Paul writes in the third person or first person plural, thereby indicating that the letter is from him and his team.[61] Paul's letters were not merely private correspondence. Pauline Christianity was a collaborative effort; it was a movement, not simply the sole work of a single individual. Paul probably spent very little time in any one place – except Corinth and Ephesus where he seems to have spent about eighteen months and two or three years respectively. For the most part, his communities were run and administered by fellow workers. The network of communities and

---

[58] Gal. 6:1; 1 Cor. 16:21; Phlm. 19; cf. 2 Thess. 3:17; Col. 4:18.
[59] 1 Thess. 1:1; 2 Thess. 1:1; cf. 1 Thess. 2:18.
[60] See discussion in Elmer 2008. Also Richards 2004: 59–80; 1991: 189–94; Murphy-O'Connor 1995; Longenecker 1974; more fully, Stowers 1986: 36–52.
[61] Murphy-O'Connor 1995: 16–33.

communications between these churches and Paul were maintained by travelling emissaries. Hence, the composition of all the Pauline letters was probably also the product of a collaborative enterprise.

It is interesting that most commentators have little problem in accepting that the Gospels were the product of community traditions and careful redaction, yet seldom view the Pauline letters in the same way. Paul wrote not only for specific communities, but from within a community, which shared common scriptures, beliefs and liturgical practices.[62] A close examination of Paul's letters demonstrates that he was as dependent upon community traditions as were the evangelists. Scholars have regularly recognised that Paul incorporates into his letters a good deal of pre-existing material, scriptural texts, liturgical prayers and hymns, credal formulae, traditional vice lists and, no doubt, passages and aspects of his favourite speeches and arguments. Several of the letters, most notably 2 Corinthians and Philippians, bear clear signs of editorial activity and appear to be composite compositions of pre-existing letter fragments, which may have been the work of later disciples of Paul, but may just as easily date from Paul's own lifetime. It is noteworthy that no manuscripts of either 2 Corinthians or Philippians exist that diverge significantly from the canonical letters. If, indeed, both letters are composites, then their creation must have occurred very early in the history of the Pauline churches.

Given the complexities of the Pauline network, where the exchange of letters played a central role, we would expect that such letters or fragments of letters would be retained, copied and circulated to other communities. As was the custom in antiquity, Paul most likely retained a copy of his letters both for subsequent reference[63] and because of the danger of loss or damage in transit. It is also likely that he allowed the church where he was writing to make a copy of the letter for its own use and that he permitted or instructed the recipients to make copies for themselves or for neighbouring congregations.[64] So it is not surprising that, even in his own lifetime, Paul was forced to fend off the accusation that 'his letters are weighty and strong, but his bodily presence is weak, and his speech contemptible'.[65] Some in the early church presumed to spread prophetic messages, reports

---

[62] This point is made by Stirewalt 2003: 9–10 and Ellis 1971: 439–40.

[63] Cf. 1 Cor. 5:9–10; 2 Cor. 7:8; 2 Thess. 2:15.

[64] Cf. 2 Cor. 1:1, Gal. 1:2; Col. 4:16.

[65] 2 Cor. 10:10; cf. 1 Cor. 1:17–31; 2:1–16; 2 Cor. 11:16. It is noteworthy that in his defence Paul explicitly admits that he was 'untrained in speech' (2 Cor. 11:16), which might indicate that he was not a trained orator or a skilful communicator. If we are to take such comments seriously, it would suggest that Paul must a priori have employed the services of others, and especially trained secretaries, to compose, correct and polish his letters. A posteriori, the criticism retailed by Paul in 2 Cor. 10:10

and letters, which they falsely attributed to Paul (2 Thess. 2:2). Others lied outright, claiming that Paul still taught circumcision (Gal. 5:11), or that he misrepresented his dealings with the Jerusalem apostles (Gal. 1:19) or that the story of his conversion experience was a fantasy (1 Cor. 9:1; cf. Gal. 1:10–12). Such 'slander' even found its way to Rome, a community that Paul had never visited prior to the time of writing to the Christians in the imperial capital (Rom. 3:8). Perhaps this makes Paul the first theologian to be reported to Rome. All of this testifies to the very strong possibility that Paul's letters were circulated and read among many Christian communities even before his death. In this way the apostle himself initiated, virtually at the outset, different textual traditions with inevitable variations in the wording of his correspondence.[66] There is an interesting passage in 2 Timothy where the author, writing in Paul's name, requests Timothy to 'bring the cloak that [he] left with Carpus at Troas, also the books, and above all the parchments' (4:13). While we cannot determine the exact nature of the 'books' and 'parchments', it would not be a huge stretch of the imagination to suggest that these may be copies of Paul's letters. It seems that it was quite 'fashionable' at the time of Paul for letter-writers to retain parchment copies of their correspondence in codices.[67]

One of the few commentators to take this suggestion seriously is D. Trobisch who, based upon an exhaustive survey of letter-collections from several centuries adjacent to the Pauline period on either side (300 BCE to 400 CE), argued that in many cases an initial collection of an author's letters was made by the author himself. Trobisch suggested that a close examination of the existing Pauline canons and early codex manuscripts of the New Testament pointed to an early 'authorised recension' of four of the authentic Pauline letters addressed to church communities (Romans, 1 and 2 Corinthians and Galatians), the so-called *Hauptbriefe*, and a later posthumous 'expanded edition' with Paul's 'personal' letters and additional deutero-Pauline texts.[68]

Trobisch calls attention to the fact that, with very few exceptions, the ancient manuscripts arranged Paul's letters in order of length, longer to shorter, except for Ephesians, which headed a second set of texts including the deutero-Pauline texts and Paul's personal letters to Philemon, Timothy and Titus. There are one or two small variations in the canons

---

further suggests a disparity between Paul's written communiqués and his spoken performances, which might be explained by his recourse to the input of co-workers and co-authors in the composition of his letters. See Reicke 2001: 39–102.

[66] Guthrie 1990: 657; Richards 2004: 218–23.   [67] Richards 2004: 219.

[68] Trobisch 2000: 38–41; 1994: 5–24; 1989: 56–62.

and manuscripts, particularly with regard to the placement of Ephesians, but Trobisch accepts in part Goodspeed's view that Ephesians may have functioned as a later introductory letter to either the appended texts or to the whole expanded edition.[69] Trobisch and others have noted that the collection of thirteen letters is formed by two distinct sections, each arranged by length: the first constituted by letters to church communities and grouped according to common destinations, that is, 1 and 2 Corinthians, Ephesians, Philippians and Colossians, 1 and 2 Thessalonians; the second containing letters to individuals – 1 and 2 Timothy, Titus and Philemon.[70] Only Hebrews appears to defy this arrangement, appearing only once in the canonical lists and manuscripts (P46) after the church letters and before the personal letters. In all other instances of its appearance it is placed after the thirteen letters attributed to Paul. This organisation and order are remarkably stable and appear at all strata of the traditions. There is no reason to imagine and, more importantly, no hard evidence to support the claim that this arrangement was a second-century phenomenon that resulted from a gradual process or a later 'big bang' event occasioned by the advent of the Acts of the Apostles. Similarly, there is no need to identify a specific place with a Pauline 'school' or to credit a specific individual with the accomplishment of gathering the letters into a single corpus.

According to this 'Pauline involvement' theory, proponents quite credibly posit that Paul would have composed his assortment of church and personal correspondence from numerous places to be sent to different destinations, while he or his companions retained copies as they travelled on their various missionary enterprises.[71] The assemblage of Paul's letters would not have been the result of an afterthought, nor would it have required any effort of Paul's companions after Paul's death to gather the disparate letters or smaller, regional letter-collections together. Rather, because these were important documents that were subject to reuse and revision, copies of all the letters would have been kept initially by Paul, his companions and his co-authors. Perhaps those letters that failed to survive, such as the missing Corinthian letters, were either not deemed worthy of retention or were superseded by other letters into which they were incorporated (e.g. 2 Corinthians or Philippians).[72] This theory also provides scope to account for the variant versions of Romans and Ephesians that appear in some manuscripts stripped of any specific indications of the addressees. If it was the custom of Paul and his companions to reuse materials, such letters could have served as introductory or ambassadorial letters sent to multiple recipients.

Such an approach also blurs the distinction between Pauline and deutero-Pauline letters and raises questions about supposed interpolations and glosses (e.g. 1 Thess. 2:14–16; 1 Cor. 14:33b–36). The letters of Paul are community products that were collaboratively produced, edited, copied, retained and collected by Paul and his companions both during and after his death. In that case it may be possible to challenge any attempt to distinguish 'authentic' letters from later pseudepigraphal creations on the basis of style alone. The best examples here are Colossians and 2 Timothy, which seem to stand on the cusp between Paul and 'post-Paul' and in which it is difficult to isolate the genuine voice of Paul from that of his secretary, his editor or his imitator. Similarly, interpolations and glosses may as easily be the result of pre-dispatch editorial work as of the reconfiguring of an early version of the letter.[73] Given the communal nature of Paul's letters, the presence of interpolations and glosses should be assumed as a working principle. Paul permitted and even instructed the recipients of some of his letters to make copies for themselves or for neighbouring communities.[74] In this way Paul himself effectively initiated different textual traditions with inevitable variations in the wording of his correspondence.

Conclusion

In this chapter I have tried to chart the process by which Paul's letters came to be collected. Along the way I surveyed three of the most popular theories, briefly testing the veracity of each. We cannot now be certain of the precise details of the events that led to the Pauline letter-collection; most of what I have considered here is hypothetical and highly speculative. Nevertheless, on the basis of the evidence presented, it seems unlikely that the route that led to the assembly of Paul's letters would have been via either a gradual accumulation or an aggregation of disparate individual letters and/or small regional collections. Similarly, there is no real evidence to link the formation of a Pauline canon to the publication of Acts. Indeed any link between Acts and Paul's letters appears difficult to

---

[73] So Murphy-O'Connor 1995: 16.   [74] Cf. 2 Cor. 1:1; Gal. 1:2; Col. 4:16.

maintain, given the disparity between the Paul presented in Acts and the Paul derived from the letters.

Imagine, then, how much poorer we would be if Paul's letters had not survived, and how little we would know of events in the early church. His letters would later be considered 'scripture' (2 Pet. 3:13) and his insights would continue to inspire the growth and development of the church as an entirely new religious movement independent of its Jewish roots. Yet, if the proponents of the 'snowball' or 'big bang' theories are to be believed, the survival of Paul's letters was a mere accident of history. It seems an incredible stretch of the imagination to argue that Paul's letters would not have continued to exert a considerable influence upon the life and theology of the early church, and especially within those communities founded by Paul. Similarly, it would seem difficult to believe that Paul's companions, if not Paul himself, would not have retained copies of the letters.

A much more likely scenario, therefore, is one that credits Paul and his companions with initiating the development of the collection. Paul would have kept duplicates of his letters; that, after all, was common practice amongst contemporary letter-writers. More important, however, is the fact that the letters of Paul were not merely personal letters, but the products and the property of the network of Pauline communities from within which Paul and his companions wrote their correspondence. Paul wrote as part of a team. Paul expected the letters to be read publicly, most likely in worship services. Paul encouraged the copying and sharing of letters between neighbouring communities. It should come as no surprise that, from the very first and in the years after his death, Paul's 'books' and 'parchments' were treasured, copied and passed between communities (cf. 2 Tim. 4:13), nor that by the end of the first century 'all his letters' would be the subject of misunderstanding and misrepresentation (2 Pet. 3:16). Furnish (1994) is probably correct in suggesting that many in the early church would seek to 'put Paul in his place', but it would seem that via the preservation of his letters both Paul and his immediate circle of co-workers secured Paul's place firmly at the centre of the early church and at the centre of its emerging canon of sacred scripture.

CHAPTER 4

2 Corinthians *and possible material evidence for composite letters in antiquity*

Brent Nongbri

The tradition of Christian letter-collections begins with the letters of the apostle Paul, and, according to many scholars, the collection of Paul's letters involved the combination of fragments of discrete letters to form so-called composite letters. While nearly all of the letters attributed to Paul have, at one time or another, been subject to such partition hypotheses, it is the composite nature of 2 Corinthians that enjoys the widest agreement among scholars of the New Testament. It is no overstatement to say that the majority of critical scholars of ancient Christianity are convinced that the letter now known as 2 Corinthians actually contains parts of multiple different letters.[1] Partition theories generally divide 2 Corinthians into between two and six letters.[2] The arguments for the composite nature of 2 Corinthians are usually described as 'internal'; that is to say, they are based on perceived inconsistencies in the rhetoric and content of the composition and apparent 'literary seams'. Yet, all of our surviving manuscripts of Paul's letters present 2 Corinthians as a seamless whole, which would mean that any compilation of letters to assemble 2 Corinthians must have taken place before the archetype(s) of our surviving manuscripts came into being.[3] In other words, partition theories posit

---

Abbreviations for corpora of papyri follow the conventions laid out in the *Checklist of Editions of Greek, Latin, Demotic, and Coptic Papyri, Ostraca, and Tablets* available online at http://scriptorium. lib.duke.edu/papyrus/texts/clist.html. For literary papyri, the identification numbers of the Leuven Database of Ancient Books (LDAB) are provided. This chapter benefited from feedback provided by the participants in the Epistolary Conversations symposium at Australian Catholic University, North Sydney, in 2011. Cavan Concannon, Edwin Judge, Dale Martin, Michael Peppard, Stanley Stowers and Larry Welborn also read an earlier version of this chapter and offered several helpful suggestions. Remaining infelicities are, of course, my own responsibility.

[1] Such a viewpoint is standard in the most frequently used introductory textbooks. See, for example, Ehrman 2004: 326–31. The prestigious Hermeneia commentary series is producing separate commentaries on the purported letter fragments thought to make up canonical 2 Corinthians.

[2] Betz 1992, a standard reference work in the field of biblical studies, treats 2 Corinthians as six distinct letters (or letter fragments).

[3] The date of the collection (or perhaps better, collections) of Paul's letters is itself open to some question, but multiple collections were certainly circulating by the time of Marcion, that is,

that several shorter letters were (either intentionally or unintentionally) blended into one longer letter at some point not long after the sending and receiving of the hypothetical 'original' shorter letters.

The present chapter sets out some ancient material evidence relevant to the question of how letters were collected and archived in the decades immediately after their sending and receipt. I begin by examining recent attention dedicated to the letters of Cicero in regard to the question of composite letters before moving to what I see as a potentially even more fruitful area of investigation – namely, two bodies of ancient material evidence, the letters of Pachomius and collections of documentary papyrus letters. I briefly explore how these corpora might bear on the question of the alleged composite nature of 2 Corinthians.

Composite letters in the correspondence of Cicero

Before discussing the Pachomian and documentary materials, it will be useful to review the (rather short) history of the use of ancient evidence for the phenomenon of composite letters.[4] Parallels from antiquity have in fact seldom played a role in justifying partition theories for 2 Corinthians.[5] For instance, Hans Dieter Betz's Hermeneia commentary on 2 Corinthians 8 and 9, which appeared in 1985, provided the most systematic argument to date that these two chapters were originally independent letters.[6] In a generally positive review of that volume, Stanley Stowers levelled the following criticism:

> One thing which Betz has not done is to make sense of why some ancient editor would have omitted the epistolary prescripts and postscripts, and tried to fuse the two fragments, together with others, into what is now 2 Corinthians. It was not unusual for editors of collected letters to omit prescript and postscript, but I know of no case where ancient editors fused

well before the time our earliest surviving manuscripts of Paul's letters. See Lovering 1988 and Clabeaux 1989.

[4] While there is a dearth of literature on ancient composite letters, the phenomena of interpolation of passages and the addition of entire letters into ancient letter-collections is well known. A classic example is the collection of letters attributed to Ignatius, which exists in three quite different forms (see Lightfoot 1885–90: IV). These phenomena, however, are distinct from the hypothesis of composite letters – multiple letters by a single author fused into a single letter.

[5] One clear exception is Stewart-Sykes 1996. Stewart-Sykes painted an almost comical portrait of a bumbling editor or scribe trying in vain to handle multiple papyrus rolls in order to produce a composite letter. His account, however, probably underestimates the dexterity of ancient users accustomed to the technology of the papyrus roll. See the discussions of Skeat 1981 and 1990. Both pieces are reprinted in Skeat 2004: 60–4 and 71–2. See further the comments of Mitchell 2005: 323–4, n. 62.

[6] Betz 1985.

letters into a new work. Even where beginnings and endings are omitted, the writings are allowed to stand as independent letters. Betz usually displays his enormous erudition by producing ancient analogies. In this case he does not.[7]

The lack of discussion of ancient analogies persisted for about fifteen years after Stowers' observation until Hans-Josef Klauck produced a groundbreaking and illuminating study of Cicero's epistles with this issue of composite letters in mind.[8] Using the Oxford edition of Cicero's letters produced by W. S. Watt and the Teubner edition by Shackleton Bailey, Klauck provided a list of Cicero's letters that have been sub-divided by modern editors. He found about sixty instances of allegedly composite letters in the Ciceronian corpus but noted that this number is probably too low because the earliest modern editors of Cicero's letters, who established the canonical numbering system, themselves introduced divisions that were not present in the manuscripts.[9] Klauck noted the presence of epistolary postscripts and evidence for the composition of single letters over extended periods of time. He carefully concluded that, while 'it no longer suffices to assert … that there are no analogies in ancient epistolary literature' for the composite letter, the presence of composite letters in modern editions of Cicero 'does not necessarily prove that partition theories [of the Pauline letters] are correct'.[10]

Just a year after Klauck's chapter appeared, Thomas Schmeller produced an article that built upon (and complicated) Klauck's observations, especially in regard to 2 Corinthians.[11] Schmeller explored different ways of detecting composite letters in the Ciceronian corpus and speculated on different reasons why certain letters might have been truncated and brought together to form composite letters, before reassessing what can be learned about Paul's letters from those of Cicero. Schmeller found that quite different circumstances brought these two collections into being (professional editing of a large number of letters in the case of Cicero versus a smaller number of letters gathered in a non-professional setting in the case of the Corinthian correspondence). Nevertheless, he concluded that the types of composite letters found in Cicero's correspondence render it at least plausible that originally separate letters in the Pauline corpus might be combined – in proper chronological sequence – into a single letter.[12]

---

[7] Stowers 1987: 728.
[8] Klauck 2003a, also published in Klauck 2003b: 317–37.
[9] Klauck 2003a: 139–40.   [10] Klauck 2003a: 153.
[11] Schmeller 2004.
[12] Schmeller 2004: 207–8 concludes, 'Die Kompilationen, die wir in den Briefkorpora Ciceros finden, lassen allenfalls (!) eine *addierende* Verschmelzung *chronologisch geordneter* Paulusbriefe zu

To be clear, the studies by Klauck and Schmeller mark a quantum leap in our thinking about the possibility of the presence of composite letters in the Pauline corpus.[13] Yet, it is good to bear in mind two caveats when comparing the letters of Cicero with those of Paul. First, as Klauck notes, the majority of instances of allegedly composite letters in Cicero's correspondence are the result of the ingenuity of modern editors. That is to say, in few cases is there any manuscript support for the proposed divisions.[14] Second, we would do well to remember that the earliest surviving substantial manuscripts for Cicero's letters are much later than the earliest manuscripts of Paul's Corinthian correspondence. The earliest relatively complete manuscript of Cicero's *Ad familiares* is dated to the ninth or tenth century, while the surviving copies of *Ad Atticum* and other named collections date from no earlier than the fourteenth century.[15] Again, Klauck is well aware of this fact and its implications for the question of letter compilations, noting that:

> it is not clear at which stage of this process compilations were made. They may have been produced by scribes through the centuries, they may result from mechanical accidents like the damage and loss of pages or the displacement of pages in a codex. But the possibility remains that at least in a few instances we have to go back to the moment when the collections were produced, or even to the archives, though we can no longer prove this.[16]

With Cicero's corpus, allegedly composite letters could have been created at any point in the nearly thousand-year stretch between the sending and receiving of the letters and the time of our earliest extensive manuscripts.

2Kor plausibel erscheinen. Allerdings sind die Umstände, Gründe und Motive, die in den ciceronianischen Korpora zu Briefkompilationen geführt haben, für 2Kor kaum relevant.'

[13] As both Klauck and Schmeller have noted, a careful inspection of the manuscripts of Cicero's letters with questions such as these in view is clearly needed. Such a project is rapidly becoming more feasible in both practical and theoretical terms. On the practical side, digital images of some of the most important manuscripts of Cicero's letters are becoming available online. For example, the most important manuscript of *Ad familiares* (Plut.49.09) and a key witness of *Ad Atticum* and the other collections (Plut.49.19) are digitised and can be viewed at the website of the Biblioteca Medicea Laurenziana. On the theoretical side, we are now seeing serious reflection on the problems involved in using modern editions of Cicero's letters for purposes other than providing a linear historical narrative of political events of the late Republic. See, for example, Beard 2002.

[14] Klauck 2003a: 137. Strictly speaking, then, what Klauck most clearly demonstrates is evidence for the practice of modern editors partitioning the letters of a classical author (with no manuscript support) in much the same way that some New Testament scholars treat some Pauline letters. This phenomenon in itself should be noted by scholars of the New Testament.

[15] For the discussion of the manuscripts of Cicero's letters, see Shackleton Bailey 1977: 3–26 and 1965–71/I: 77–101.

[16] Klauck 2003a: 140. The point is also noted by Schmeller 2004: 204–5, though, in general, he seems more willing to entertain that combinations of originally independent letters in Cicero's collection happened early in the transmission history of the corpus.

In the case of the Corinthian correspondence, any compilations would have taken place most likely within only a few decades after the letters were composed and sent.[17]

These caveats in the comparison of Cicero's letters and the Corinthian correspondence do, however, point us in the direction of the kinds of ancient evidence that might more securely ground an argument for the plausibility of 2 Corinthians being a composite letter. What we should ideally like to have is evidence *in an ancient manuscript tradition itself* for the combination of originally independent letters and/or more material evidence showing the different ways in which ancient letters were collected.[18]

The letters of Pachomius

One example of the former phenomenon is the collection of letters attributed to the monk Pachomius. Until the middle of the twentieth century, the letters of Pachomius were known to us only through a Latin translation produced by Jerome early in the fifth century.[19] In recent decades, however, manuscripts of the letters in Coptic (the language of composition) and Greek, some of which were likely copied at roughly the time Jerome was making his translation, have been discovered.[20] These witnesses provide us with a glimpse of the formation and transmission of a Christian letter-collection perhaps within a century of when the letters were composed.[21]

The critical edition of Jerome's Latin translation of Pachomiana includes eleven 'letters'.[22] The first seven items carry titles beginning *epistula patris nostri Pachomii*, and the eighth item *epistula patris Pachomii*. The last three items, however, have titles of a rather different format: number 9: *verba per litteras patris nostri Pachomii*, number 10: *verba quae locutus est pater noster Pachomius*, and number 11: *verba patris nostri Pachomii*. The contents of the letters are a blend of fairly typical epistolary hortatory materials ('We were at your place but because we were in too much of a hurry,

---

[17] See n. 3 above.
[18] Arzt-Grabner 2014, unavailable to me while preparing this chapter, promises to shed much light on these questions from the standpoint of ancient material evidence.
[19] A critical edition of Jerome's text of the letters can be found in Boon 1932.
[20] For texts and introductions to the Greek and Coptic materials, see Quecke 1975. An English translation of the letters is available in Veilleux 1980–2/III.
[21] Caution is always in order in the dating of literary papyri. The Greek parchment roll in the Chester Beatty Library that I will discuss (W 145; LDAB 3513) has been assigned to the fourth century, and the leaves from the Coptic codex (Ac. 2556; LDAB 108078) have been assigned to the sixth century.
[22] Boon's chart (1932: xxi) and apparatus indicate that a number of the letters are not present in different manuscripts, and in some manuscripts the letters appear in different orders.

we could not have a spiritual talk with you; therefore we talk to you now in a letter') and cryptic discussions of secret meanings of various letters of the Greek alphabet ('Watch yourself so as not to write δ over φ, lest your days grow old and your waters diminish').[23]

In the more recently discovered manuscripts of the letters of Pachomius, some of these letters are divided differently. A Greek parchment roll of Pachomius' letters in the Chester Beatty Library (W 145) places no division between Jerome's letters 1 and 2, and includes additionally only letters 3, 7, 10, and, as a 'stand alone' letter, the first half of Jerome's letter 11 (now generally referred to as 11a).[24] In another Coptic papyrus codex at the Chester Beatty Library (Ac. 2556), we find (in this order): the second half of Jerome's letter 11 (now generally designated 11b), letter 10, the first half of Jerome's letter 11 (11a), the first half of Jerome's letter 9 (9a), and finally the second half of Jerome's letter 9 (9b) clearly marked as a separate letter.[25] It seems that either Jerome or his exemplar (or one of its ancestors) combined the originally separate 9a and 9b and 11a and 11b to form longer, composite 'letters' within the collection.[26] Similarly, either letters 1 and 2 were originally a single letter that was later divided, or (more likely) the two were originally independent and later combined to form a composite letter in some manuscripts.

Thus, although some of this Pachomian material is not what we might typically identify as epistolary and although some of the items are not precisely labelled as *epistulae*, this material was explicitly transmitted as a collection of letters in at least three languages probably within a century of the composition of the material. With the letters of Pachomius, then, we have reasonably solid evidence of letters being combined to form composite letters in antiquity.

Ancient collection of papyrus letters

The second type of evidence I wish to bring to bear on the question of the composite nature of 2 Corinthians is a particular sub-section of letter-collections preserved on papyrus.[27] There is a great deal of data for

---

[23] Occasionally, this odd mixture occurs even within a single sentence. At the conclusion of *Letter* 1, the typical imperative 'Greet so-and-so' becomes 'Greet the head, the feet, the hands, the eyes and all the rest of your spirit, which is α'.

[24] In this manuscript, divisions between letters are marked by a line, a hook, or a *verschnörkelter Winkel*. See Quecke's introduction to his edition of the manuscript, 1975: 81–2.

[25] See the edition of Quecke 1974. In this manuscript, individual epistles are marked off by dividing lines made of various combinations of symbols: > > > and/or >————.

[26] Whether the initial conflation was accidental or intentional is difficult to say with any certainty.

[27] In this line of inquiry, I am indebted to the pioneering work of Deissmann 1910. Some of the material I treat in this section was already noted by Deissmann (1910: 227–8) in relation to the

Figure 4.1 *P.Sarap.* 87–9. Letters from Heliodorus copied on a roll in the same hand
(90–133 CE; possibly 117 CE).
Image © Institut für Papyrologie, Heidelberg.

collections of papyrus documents (archives and dossiers).[28] I focus here especially on the placement of multiple letters onto a single roll.[29]

The first example is from the early second-century archive of Eutychides son of Sarapion.[30] Here we have the remains of a single papyrus roll containing three short letters from Heliodorus to different recipients, all copied in the same hand (see Figure 4.1).

Each of the three visible columns begins a new letter. This piece provides an example of the practice of a sender of letters keeping a personal copy of sent letters. The practice is known in the literary tradition from one of Cicero's speeches against Verres.[31] Cicero claims to have found a copy of an

theory that Romans 16 was originally a separate letter sent to Ephesus. More recently, some of this material has been treated with reference to the Pastoral letters in Luttenberger 2012: 362–5. I am grateful to Andrea Jördens for the latter reference.

[28] See Vandorpe 2009.

[29] Harry Gamble has suggested that the collection of the Pauline letters may have provided the impulse for Christian adoption of the codex (see Gamble 1990). This conjecture has not found a great deal of support among scholars. My working assumption is that Paul's letters were first gathered together on papyrus rolls. This assumption seems reasonable given the reference in the *Acts of the Scillitan Martyrs* (likely written in the late second century) to the *epistolae Pauli* being carried in a *capsa* (a cylindrical case for holding rolls). It appears that Paul's letters were still being copied in roll format well into the late second century.

[30] *P.Sarap.* 87–9. *P.Sarap.* 85–6 and 89a–89b are fragments of similar rolls of letters sent. See Schwartz 1961. For further bibliography, see the entry at the Leuven Homepage of Papyrus Collections at www.trismegistos.org/arch/detail.php?tm=87.

[31] *Against Verres* II 3.71.167. See the edition of Peterson 1916.

Figure 4.2 *BGU* 4.1206–7. Letters from Isidora to Asclepiades in different hands glued together (28 BCE).
Image courtesy of the Staatliche Museen zu Berlin – Preußischer Kulturbesitz, Ägyptisches Museum und Papyrussammlung, Berliner Papyrusdatenbank.

incriminating letter among a sender's 'rolls of sent letters' (*libris litterarum missarum*) in Rome. Interestingly, Cicero also asserts that he discovered a second copy of the letter among the recipient's collection of received letters (*litterarum adlatarum libris*) in Sicily. This latter practice, the archiving of received letters in a roll format, is also attested in the papyrological record.

An example comes from the archive of Asklepiades, which consists of multiple letters he received between 29 and 23 BCE.[32] Figure 4.2 shows two of these letters, which Asklepiades had received from one Isidora. As the image makes clear, these letters are in different hands, *BGU* 4.1206 (on the left) likely the hand of Isidora herself and 4.1207 that of a scribe. These are original copies of letters received (the addresses are visible on the versos) that have simply been pasted together to form a roll for record-keeping.

The production of this kind of pasted roll, a *tomos synkollēsimos* in papyrological terminology, was more common for official correspondence,

[32] For further discussion of this archive and images of some of the other pieces, see Bagnall and Cribiore 2006: A3.2–A3.5, *Letters* 16–20; the e-book has plates which the print edition lacks. For further bibliography, see the entry at the Leuven Homepage of Papyrus Collections at www.trismegistos.org/arch/archives/pdf/111.pdf.

but *tomoi synkollēsimoi* are sometimes found in private contexts, as in the present case.[33] Some of the letters in the roll are marked (in a different hand, likely that of Asklepiades) with the date that they were received, which allows us to see that 4.1207 was sent before 4.1206, but 4.1207 arrived later. We thus have evidence for collections of letters to a single recipient that have been pasted together out of their proper (or, more precisely, compositional) chronological sequence.

These pasted rolls of received letters were sometimes copied onto fresh papyrus. We can see an example of this step in the archiving process in *P.Oxy.* 60.4060, a papyrus roll preserving copies of letters received by an official in Oxyrhynchus in the year 161. Remains of five columns of text are preserved, and they provide evidence for an interesting method of collection. In the editor's words, the original *tomos synkollēsimos* 'was assembled with each new entry being glued on to the left of the previous entry. The date that this was done was recorded in an annotation at the head of each entry, and later on item numbers were assigned starting from the left ... item numbers preserved are 35 to 40 with no entry number 37 in our copy.'[34] Thus, again, the order in which the letters have been received seems, at least in part, to have determined the order of the assembled collection. The missing item (number 37) is also of interest. The editor offers two possible reasons for its absence: 'the number [was] inadvertently omitted when the original *tomos* was "paginated", or item 37 was present in the original *tomos* but was omitted when making the present copy.'[35] In the case of *P.Oxy.* 60.4060, then, we have evidence for a collection of letters placed into a single roll format out of their compositional chronological order, possibly with at least one letter having fallen out of the collection.

The final two examples I wish to highlight also come from collections of official correspondence and span a broad period from the Ptolemaic period to the turn of the fourth century. The first example is *P.Lille* 1.3, a collection of letters of an official from the years 216–215 BCE.[36] Figure 4.3 illustrates one of the partially surviving columns.

[33] See Clarysse 2003.

[34] All quotations here are drawn from the editor's introduction and notes to *P.Oxy.* 60.4060. With the addition of the dates of gluing, we can determine the length of time between the composition of the letters and their inclusion in the roll (these range between seven days and at least thirty-one days).

[35] Also relevant is the editor's comment regarding an unusually long temporal gap between two of the entries: 'This can hardly indicate that no correspondence was received in this period; what came in must have been attached to a different roll or rolls.'

[36] See Jouguet 1928: 26–36.

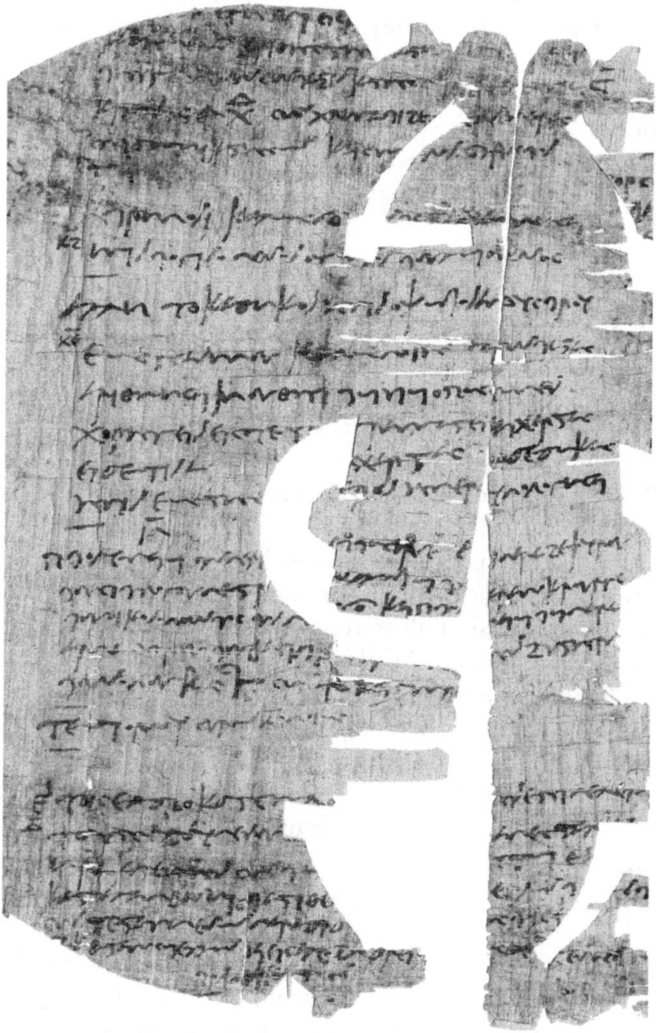

Figure 4.3 *P.Lille* 1.3 (Inv.Sorb. 3), column 3. Collection of letters of an official, possibly with marginal dates (216–215 BCE).
Image courtesy of the Institut de Papyrologie, Université Paris-Sorbonne (Paris IV).

For the purpose of the present investigation, there are two especially noteworthy features of this piece. The first item to point out is the treatment of the epistolary openings. The openings consist of the name of the recipient in the dative case, but when two successive letters have the same recipient, the salutation is abbreviated to simply αλλη ('to the same').[37] The second feature is the numbers in the left margin (such as κζ and κε visible in the upper half of the image in Figure 4.3). The original editors of this piece suggested these numbers were dates and noted that they were in reverse order, 27 and then 25 (and then later on in the column ια, or 11). If the editors are correct, we have another example of a collection of letters gathered in something other than the chronological order of their dates of composition.

A final example comes from one of the rolls used to construct the Chester Beatty tax codex.[38] This 'book' was constructed by pasting together the written sides of two rolls to produce a length of papyrus of double thickness that was blank on both sides. This thickened papyrus roll was then cut into sheets that stacked upon one another and then folded over to form a single-quire codex. The two papyrus rolls used to construct the codex were in fact copies of official correspondence.[39] The earlier roll (*P. Panop.Beatty* 1 of 298 CE) was a collection of letters sent by a *strategus* of the Panopolite nome, and the second roll (*P.Panop.Beatty* 2 of 300 CE) contained copies of correspondence received by a *strategus* (Apolinarius) from a procurator. It is the latter roll that is of interest for the present discussion.

I draw attention first of all to the epistolary closings of the letters preserved in *P.Panop.Beatty* 2. Of the more than forty letters preserved on this roll, all but three end with the closing statement ἐρρῶσθαί σε εὔχομαι πολλοῖς χρόνοις. It seems that either the scribe of the procurator's letters simply left off the closing on only those three occasions, or the clerk making the copy for the archive of the *strategus* sometimes failed to copy the closings. So again, we see an example of the loss (or omission) of epistolary closings.

It should also be noted that dates of reception are recorded in this papyrus. On some occasions, more than one letter was received on a given day. In such situations, we can observe a chronological displacement similar to what we have seen in some of the preceding examples. For instance, among the letters received on a single day in the month of Phamenoth, we find (in this order) letters composed on Phamenoth 3, Phamenoth 5, Phamenoth 4 and Phamenoth 3. Again, then, chronology of composition is not necessarily reflected in collections of received letters. Even letters

---

[37] Abbreviation or omission of epistolary closings (and openings) is quite common in ancient letter-collections. See Stowers 1986: 20–1.

[38] See the edition of Skeat 1964.

[39] For a discussion of similarly constructed codices, see Bagnall 2002; repr. in Bagnall 2006: XIX.

composed on the same day and received on the same day may not end up in compositional chronological order in the archive.

Before leaving this material, I should briefly address what I imagine could be a fairly obvious objection to the idea that papyri like these are relevant for thinking about the Pauline letters. Most of the papyrus correspondence examined here is personal business correspondence or official correspondence, which may not make them the best comparanda for the letters of Paul. Two responses are in order. First, much of what is going on in Paul's letters, *especially* in 2 Corinthians, has to do with financial transactions with his addressees – thanks given for money received and flattering appeals for additional money. It is conceivable that either Paul or the recipients of his letters in Corinth (or both) would keep a record of the correspondence in something like the formats described above. Second, some aspects of Paul's letters do in fact match up well with official correspondence (Paul did, after all, address his letters to assemblies, ἐκκλησίαι).[40]

Furthermore, a similar method of archiving non-official and non-business related letters seems to have been employed by Cicero and his associates. In the letter to Atticus designated *Ep.* 9.10, Cicero indicates directly that he has kept a roll of letters received from Atticus: *evolvi volumen epistularum tuarum*, rather misleadingly translated in E. O. Winstedt's old Loeb edition as 'I opened the packet of your letters' (the verb *evolvere* generally means 'to unroll'). Cicero kept copies of letters received from Atticus in a roll, either pasted originals or freshly written copies produced from the originals he had received. It seems that Atticus made a similar collection of the letters he received from Cicero. Cornelius Nepos, a contemporary of Cicero and Atticus, describes in his *Life of Atticus* 'eleven rolls of letters' sent by Cicero to Atticus (*xi volumina epistularum ... ad Atticum missarum*).[41] The papyrological evidence surveyed here does, then, seem relevant for thinking about the process of collecting Paul's letters.

Conclusions

At the outset of the chapter, I gestured toward the notion of intention: some partition theories posit that 2 Corinthians came into being in a mechanistic fashion, unintentionally, as the result of simple mistakes

---

[40] For Paul's letters as 'official' correspondence, see Stirewalt 2003, though Stirewalt perhaps pushes the evidence too far.

[41] *Life of Atticus* 25.16. In the Loeb, Budé and Oxford editions of Cornelius Nepos, the numeral *xi* in this passage has been emended to *xvi* to correspond to the extant sixteen books of letters to Atticus.

on the part of compilers or copyists, while other theories imagine a careful editor intentionally assembled the fragments to produce canonical 2 Corinthians.[42] My impression is that most scholars who believe 2 Corinthians is a composite letter assume that it was an intentional creation. That is to say, in spite of the perceived 'literary seams', the assumption is that canonical 2 Corinthians was not an accident – someone tried to shape these hypothetical letter fragments into the larger letter. This assumption, however, is only rarely made explicit, and even less frequently are the possible motivations of the hypothetical editor explored.[43]

The archiving and copying practices surveyed in this chapter are suggestive for thinking about the alleged composite nature of 2 Corinthians considered as both an intentional and an unintentional creation. The Pachomian letter-collection shows that conflation of originally independent letters into composite letters could in fact happen quite early in the manuscript transmission process.[44] Whether the composite letters in the Pachomian corpus are intentional or unintentional creations is an open question, but it is difficult to imagine that *Letters* 1, 9, and 11 all happened to lose epistolary openings and closings in the short period of time between the earliest extant manuscript and Jerome's Latin translation. It seems most likely that an editor was involved, who perhaps combined the shorter letters in order to create a collection of letters more nearly equal in length to one another.[45]

---

[42] For bibliography and an excellent discussion of the problem of 'intention' in the collection of Paul's letters, see Lovering 1988: 88–104. Lovering's discussion uses a slightly different organisational scheme, 'seriatim connecting' (generally accidental) and 'splicing' (involving editorial intent).

[43] Lovering 1988: 88 identified this problem some time ago: 'To the extent that one breaks apart the various, supposed pieces of a puzzle because they do not fit well, it is important that one be able to show how they came, in the first place, to be put together into their poorly fitting form.' There are, of course, exceptions to this generalisation. Walter Schmithals famously argued that an editor assembled canonical 1 and 2 Corinthians out of several originally distinct letter fragments in order to combat Gnostics (Schmithals 1971: 88–90). More recently, David Trobisch has argued that Paul himself was responsible for assembling 2 Corinthians from parts of his own correspondence with Corinth for the benefit of 'friends in Ephesus' (Trobisch 1989: 123–31 and 1994: 55–96). Both these proposals strike me as dubious, but authors such as these should be given credit for at least presenting a theory of why a document like 2 Corinthians would be compiled. See further n. 45 below and Kurz 1996.

[44] Thus, we might imagine a brief period when some of the hypothetical fragments thought to make up 2 Corinthians circulated independently. Michael Peppard has drawn my attention to an interesting datum that may constitute a piece of external evidence for such independent circulation of smaller units of Corinthian material. Codex Claromontanus, usually assigned to the fifth or sixth century, contains a stichometrical list of biblical books that is thought to have been created at a rather earlier period (see Metzger 1987: 310–11). In this list, the number of *versus* in 2 Corinthians is recorded as LXX, a number that is far too low for a document as long as canonical 2 Corinthians. The number is thus generally taken to be an error. Yet, given the other sums in the list, seventy would be a reasonable sum for *a portion* of canonical 2 Corinthians such as 2 Cor. 8–9.

[45] Indeed, Lucetta Mowry offered a similar explanation for the particular shape of canonical 2 Corinthians (Mowry 1944: 81).

Similarly, the documentary papyrus letter-collections reviewed here demonstrate that some of the events that scholars have imagined were necessary to produce 2 Corinthians unintentionally did indeed happen – letters were attached or copied out of their compositional chronological sequence, and epistolary openings and closings were altered or removed. Yet, in the case of 2 Corinthians, we would have to imagine several of these processes all happening to a single collection, perhaps multiple times, depending on which particular partition hypothesis of 2 Corinthians is in view. From the standpoint of probability, then, the most likely hypotheses of the unintentional production of 2 Corinthians would be those which propose the fewest divisions (for instance, hypotheses that imagine a single division after 2 Cor. 9). The papyrological evidence is perhaps less supportive of partition theories that posit the splitting up and repositioning of parts of a single letter.[46] Such theories would likely need to invoke the intentional activity of an editor and then to explain why that editor would shuffle and fuse the fragments in that particular way.

To conclude, neither the evidence for the collection of the letters of Pachomius nor any single one of these papyrological examples of letter-collections provides a precise parallel for the hypothesised assembly of 2 Corinthians from originally independent letters, but as we continue to ponder the puzzling features of 2 Corinthians, it is a good idea to keep one eye on the ancient material evidence for letter-collecting.

---

[46] Elegant literary arguments have been made for this type of partitioning of 2 Corinthians; see, for example, Welborn 1996. While I am unaware of any direct papyrological evidence for this kind of proposal, given the types of collecting and archiving practices we have observed, it is not impossible that such dislocations could occur with a pasted sheet coming loose from a roll and being reattached out of sequence.

CHAPTER 5

The letter-collections of Antony and Ammonas
Shaping a community

Samuel Rubenson

Letters make up the majority of early monastic texts, that is, the texts written by the monks themselves. This may seem surprising given the traditional image of the first generations of monks as illiterate, and the impression that early monastic literature is mainly anecdotal and hagiographic, transmitting sayings and stories about holy men and women, or educational and regulative texts, transmitting the instructions and rules of the early monastic leaders. The first generations of monks of Egypt are not supposed to have written large amounts of letters to one another, and the sources used to depict their lives have been the accounts by bishops and travellers, the anecdotes and sayings attributed to them, and the preserved rules and ascetic treatises of the founders of communities. This lack of concern for the letters is not only due to a greater scholarly interest in other genres and authors, as well as a certain scholarly prejudice, but also to the fact that many of the collections of letters have a much more complicated history of transmission. As a result early monastic correspondence through letters has not received much scholarly attention and has thus made little impact on the study of early monasticism.[1]

As pointed out by Malcolm Choat, there are two major difficulties in any attempt to achieve a comprehensive view of early Egyptian monastic

---

[1] Except for the letters of Antony, letters are conspicuously absent in the general surveys of early monasticism and its literature. See for example Dunn 2000, Caner 2002, Harmless 2004. Except for McNary-Zak 2000, who only and rather briefly discusses the letters attributed to Antony, Ammonas and Pachomius and his followers, and Choat 2013a, who raises some basic issues on monastic epistolography, there is no survey of early monastic letter-collections. Several collections have been edited and analysed, but without reference to monastic epistolography in general. The letters of Antony are treated in detail in Rubenson 1995. The message of the letters of Ammonas is presented in McNary-Zak 2011. For an analysis of their relation see Rubenson 2011a. The interpretation of the letters of Pachomius has been discussed in detail by Quecke 1975, Joest 1996 and 2002 and most recently Kalvesmaki 2013. The letters of Evagrius are translated with a major introduction in Bunge 2006. There is still no major study of the letters of Shenoute. For an edition of the letters of his successor see Kuhn 1956 and for the voluminous correspondence of Isidore of Pelusium see Evieux 1997, 2000.

letter-writing.[2] Firstly, the epistolographic evidence is divided between manuscript studies as part of the history of monastic literature, and the study of papyri and ostraca as part of archaeology and history. The study of the letters preserved as monastic literature has been done without any consideration of the letters preserved on papyri and ostraca, and the latter has been done without much attention to the transmission of letters in manuscripts. Secondly, letters are often, and especially in papyrological records, classified as something else, for example legal or economic transactions. Thus we are still in an early phase of the study of early monastic written communication, and a number of questions, such as the reasons for sending letters, the characteristics of the authors, the models used, the types of addressees, the means of transmission and the purpose of creating collections and archival dossiers, are still unanswered.

If we limit ourselves to the issue of *collections* of early monastic letters, I suggest that we ought to distinguish between three types of collections: the archival collections related to specific monasteries, the collections of letters of monastic founders and of leaders of monastic communities created by their disciples and successors, and finally the collections of scattered letters attributed to a monastic author. The first type is exemplified by the letter-collections of the monastic archives of Nephoros, Paphnutius and Johannes.[3] In the second type I count, for example, the collection of letters by Pachomius, Shenoute, Isidore of Pelusium, Barsanuphius and John.[4] In both these cases the rationale behind and the process of making the collections seem to be fairly clear. The collections are part of the collective memory of the community and at least in the second case preserve the authoritative voice of the past. The third type of collection is made up by the collections attributed to famous monastic authors, but not part of the tradition of a specific community. To this type belong the collections attributed to famous monastic figures like Antony, Ammonas, Macarius, Arsenius and Evagrius.[5] Here the rationale behind and the process of shaping the collections are much more obscure. In contrast to the other two types of collections where the collection is authorised by the sender, whether the author or the community of the author, I suggest that we should look at these collections as having been created

---

[2] Choat 2013a: 227, 235.

[3] See Bell 1924: 38–99; Karmer and Shelton 1987: 11–20.

[4] See n. 1 above. The letters of Barsanuphius and John are easily accessible with a solid introduction in Chryssavgis 2006–7.

[5] The letters attributed to Antony and Ammonas will be discussed in detail below. For Evagrius see above, n. 1. A letter of Arsenius preserved in Georgian was edited by Garitte 1955a. See also Outtier 1985.

on the side of the recipients, including not only the first recipients, but a long chain of recipients, accounting for great variation in content and order of the collections.

Confining myself to the collections of letters attributed to Antony and Ammonas, after an introduction to the collections and their characteristics I will discuss some of the problems related to the creation of collections such as these, and compare them with other collections of early monastic texts, suggesting that the preservation of these letters shares important characteristics with the preservation of sayings, edifying stories and monastic teachings in the tradition of monastic florilegia. In doing this I will try to address some of the issues pointed out by Choat and thus reflect also on the relations between these literary collections and the epistolographic evidence of the papyri and ostraca.

The collection attributed to St Antony

The collection of seven letters attributed to Antony has been the subject of intensive debate for the last twenty years. The letters were first printed in 1516 in a Latin version later reprinted in PG.[6] As Peter Tóth has shown, this Latin version was not the result of a fifteenth-century translation, as has been commonly stated, but a much older, probably sixth-century translation of a Greek version.[7] The same letters, albeit in a different sequence, are also found in several Georgian manuscripts from the monastery of St Catherine in Sinai.[8] The first of the letters in both these versions is also preserved in a large number of Syriac manuscripts, without any trace of its being part of a collection.[9] A fragment of a Coptic parchment codex, of which no other parts have yet been identified, contains one letter, with the end of the previous and the beginning of the next, again in a sequence different from both the Latin and the Georgian.[10] An Arabic version of all seven letters is preserved in a large number of Arabic manuscripts where they are the first seven of a collection of twenty letters attributed to Antony.[11] Of the remaining thirteen letters in this Arabic collection,

---

[6] Champerius 1516; PG 40: 977–1000.   [7] Tóth 2013.
[8] The text was edited by Garitte 1995b, on the basis of Sin. geo. 25 and Sin. geo. 35.
[9] For the Syriac MSS see Nau 1906 and the critical comments in Rubenson 1995: 16–17.
[10] The Coptic fragment was first edited by G. Zoega in his catalogue of the Coptic MSS at Naples, and later by Winstedt 1906, and Garitte 1955b.
[11] The Arabic text has never been edited critically, but all twenty letters were first printed in Cairo in 1899 from a MS of the Coptic patriarchate, and again in 2001 from a MS of the monastery of St Macarius. A Latin translation was published by A. Ecchellensis in Paris in 1641 and reprinted in PG 40: 999–1066. For MSS and discussion see Rubenson 1995: 20–1 and Farag 2012: 81–3.

the majority are closely related to the collection of letters attributed to Ammonas, and I will return to them. Strangely enough no trace of the Greek version that must have been the model for the Latin and Georgian, and most probably also the Syriac, has yet been found.[12] The collection is available in several modern translations.[13]

Although the Antonian authorship for the letters, or at least for the majority of them, has been questioned, the arguments have not received much support.[14] In view of the strong attestation of Antony's authorship in the entire manuscript tradition as well as in early references by Jerome and Besa, the arguments against authenticity based on differences between the letters and the image of Antony derived from other texts, primarily the *Life of Antony* and the sayings attributed to him in the *Sayings of the Desert Fathers*, are not sufficient, taking the tendencies and objectives of these texts into consideration.[15] The claim that the Alexandrian philosophical and theological tradition of Clement and Origen, clearly attested in the letters, was alien to early fourth-century Egyptian monasticism is an unproven assumption, as is the suggestion that the letters deviate from the original spirituality of early Egyptian monasticism.[16]

On the basis of the considerable differences between the first letter and the other six of the collection, Dimitrij Bumazhnov has argued that they cannot have the same author. According to his analysis the first letter differs from the others not only in style, but also in fundamental theological ideas about the human body.[17] Not denying these differences, we must, however, ask if an author of letters that might have been written at very different times and to different audiences for different purposes need have a consistent theology. This might be true for a collection arranged and revised for publication by an author, but not necessarily so for letters collected from different places, perhaps decades after the death of the author.[18]

Except for the first letter, which looks more like an instruction than a proper letter, with only a very brief greeting in the beginning and no epistolary ending, the remaining letters all have epistolographic traits such

---

[12] Part of the first letter is, however, excerpted into a saying preserved in the Greek alphabetic collection of sayings, *Apophthegmata Patrum*/G Antony 22 (PG 65: 84).

[13] Rubenson 1995: 197–231 has a translation based on a comparison of the different versions. The translations into French, Italian and Dutch are listed on p. 236.

[14] For an in-depth discussion and criticism see Bumazhnov 2009: 1–18.

[15] For a detailed discussion see Rubenson 1995: 35–42.

[16] For this claim see Williams 2002. A reply is found in Rubenson 2011a.

[17] Bumazhnov 2009: 83–8.

[18] Several sources refer to Antony writing letters to different recipients at different periods in his life. See Rubenson 1995: 37–8, 165–72 and 183, and for the letters also mentioned in the *Life of Antony*, Rubenson 2011b.

as introductions marking the relations between the author and recipients, repeated references to shared experiences, and extensive concluding greetings referring to the limits of communication by letters. There can be little doubt that these six letters are real letters. In their epistolary form and style they are, moreover, clearly influenced by the Pauline letters of the New Testament.

A strange fact variously interpreted by scholars is that *Letters* 2–7 are partly parallel in structure, in several cases even using exactly the same phrases and terminology to the extent that they at least partly look like different versions of basically the same letter.[19] Thus previous scholars regarded the letters as repetitive, limited in scope and lacking the dynamic one would have expected, a fact explained variously as a sign of old age on the part of the author or as a sign of the letters being a falsification.[20] The repetitions and the same emphasis can, however, also be the result of these letters having been written at approximately the same time, conveying the same message to different but in essence similar monastic groups. In this case they were not intended for circulation between the different recipients but as one message adapted for six different recipients.

Thus the question of authorship and unity of the Antonian collection is closely related to our understanding of various types of monastic letter-collections. We have to ask new questions about where, why, how and by whom collections were made. In his analysis of a perceived disorder in the letter-collection Richard Shaw makes a first attempt in this direction.[21] This is not the place to discuss the arguments for a disorder in the collection or Shaw's reconstruction, but only to point out that we need to envisage a process from original letter documents to a collection, a process that may have been very different for different collections, and that we need to look for methods to trace the process in the material we have at our disposal.

The collection attributed to Ammonas

The letters attributed to Ammonas are much less studied, partly due to a very complex textual transmission.[22] The most widely discussed version of

---

[19] See details in Rubenson 1995: 54–8.

[20] For the views of Bardenhewer and Bardy, see Rubenson 1995: 35 and for Klejna and Khosroyev, see Bumazhnov 2009: 12–17.

[21] Shaw 2013. On the basis of the repetition of a common structure not only between the letters, but also within two of them (*Epp.* 6 and 7), as well as the fact that some introductory and final greetings occur in the wrong places, he argues for the division of the longest letter (*Ep.* 6) into two, and the combination of one of the shortest (*Ep.* 4) with the latter part of another (*Ep.* 7), keeping the same total number.

[22] A French translation of the fourteen letters considered genuine, reconstructed with the help of the various versions and provided with a solid introduction, is found in Outtier 1985. The English

the letters is the Syriac. Here a total number of sixteen letters is attributed to Ammonas. These are found in different numbers and sequences in a dozen manuscripts. Of these the fourteen found in the oldest manuscript, dated 534, have generally been considered genuine, although there is some debate about the identity of the author.[23] The variations in numbers and sequence between the manuscripts are, however, great, and the precise delineations of the letters is somewhat obscure. In Greek only eight letters have yet been identified, five in a seventeenth-century ascetic manuscript of Sinai, two in two different Greek manuscripts, and one as the seventh of a series of homilies attributed to Macarius.[24] The eight letters identified in Greek largely overlap with the Syriac, albeit that one Greek letter combines paragraphs found in three different Syriac letters. For six of the Syriac letters no Greek parallels have yet been found. In Georgian there is a collection of sixteen letters attributed to Ammonas.[25] Thirteen of these are among the fourteen regarded as genuine in Syriac, but again in a very different sequence, parallel to letters in the old Syriac collection.[26] Since the Georgian version is translated from Greek there must have existed a larger Greek corpus than in the preserved manuscripts, at the time of translation; a corpus, moreover, arranged differently.

In the large Armenian collection of monastic writings printed by the Mechitarists in 1855 there are three letters attributed to Ammonas. The first is a parallel to the main part of one of the Syriac letters and equivalent to the Greek letter transmitted as a homily by Macarius. The second consists of passages found in at least five different Syriac letters, and the third equals the major part of a letter found also in Syriac, Greek and Georgian.[27] Two of the letters are also found in an Ethiopic monastic collection, the first as part of an Ethiopic version of the sayings (Gk. *logoi*) of Abba Isaiah and parallel to the first of the Armenian letters, the second directly before sections from the *Lausiac History*, and equivalent to the third of the Armenian letters.[28] In Arabic, most of the letters attributed to

---

translation (Chitty 1979) is based solely on the Syriac. For a discussion see Rubenson 2009 and 2011a.

[23] For the Syriac material see the edition by Kmosko 1915, with a detailed introduction.

[24] For seven letters see Nau 1916: 393–401 (introduction), 432–54 (Greek text with French translation). Five letters were edited (Iordanites 1911) from a collection of five in a Sinai MS, and the others were taken from two different Paris MSS. An additional letter (Marriott 1918) is transmitted as a homily of Macarius in a Bodleian MS as well as in a MS in Moscow.

[25] Only one letter has been edited: Garitte 1976. The sixteen letters are found in the MS Sin.geo. 35, fols. 43va–73va. See Garitte 1956. Four of the letters are also found in Sin.geo. 25, fols. 503–70v, 78v–96v. A third MS of the new finds, Sin.geo.N.13, also contains some of the letters.

[26] For the different sequences of the letters see the French translation, Outtier 1985: 12.

[27] Sakissian 1855: 597–603. See Outtier 1971: 343.

[28] The Ethiopic letters are found as no. 25 and no. 47 in Arras 1963.

Ammonas are found in the latter part of the collection of twenty letters attributed to Antony.[29] No Coptic version of these letters has yet been found, but quotations from the letters by Coptic authors, here attributed to Antony, make it clear that there was a Coptic text already in the late fourth century.[30] A Coptic version of the twenty letters is, moreover, attested in mediaeval Arabic literature,[31] as well as in a colophon in a majority of the Arabic manuscripts referring to two Sahidic manuscripts used as a basis for the Arabic translation.[32] There are thus good reasons to believe that the Arabic collection represents an old Coptic collection of letters.

As shown above, it is questionable if we should talk at all about *one* collection of letters attributed to Ammonas. It is not only that, like in the Antonian collection, not all versions have all letters, that the sequencing of the letters differs, or that the division between letters may be challenged, but here we have a situation where every manuscript even has a different number and sequence, and where paragraphs of letters are combined differently in the different versions. Not even in the Syriac version, which is the only one analysed in detail, do two manuscripts agree in number and sequence.

In spite of this, it is clear that we are not dealing with fragmentary teachings freely combined into letters. In general the letters, as preserved, do present basic epistolographic elements. They are generally introduced with greetings and different ways to establish the relation between sender and addressee. They constantly refer to the relations between the author and the recipients and to their shared experiences. Moreover the author, especially towards the end of the letters, refers to his wish to meet with the recipients and regrets that the conditions of the letter restrict what he is able to transmit.

In contrast to the Antonian attribution, the attribution to Ammonas is somewhat vague, since the names Ammon, Ammonas, Ammonius, etc. were quite common in the early monastic tradition. In the *Apophthegmata Patrum* collections there are a number of sayings attributed to Ammonas and other sayings in which an Ammonas is mentioned, and in the *History of the Monks in Egypt* Antony's successor is named as Ammonas.[33] In

---

[29] For the Arabic text see n. 11 above on the Arabic collection of twenty letters attributed to Antony. For a detailed analysis of the entire corpus see Farag 2012.

[30] The quotations from the letters of Antony as well as of Ammonas were noted and discussed in Garitte 1939, and in more detail in Farag 2012: 94–102.

[31] See Rubenson 1995:16 and Farag 2012: 103.   [32] See Rubenson 1995: 20.

[33] *Apophthegmata Patrum*/G Ammonas 1–11 (PG 65: 120–4); *Historia Monachorum* XV.

view of the very early attribution of the same letters to Ammonas and to Antony (in Coptic and Arabic) it seems plausible that the letters come from a successor of Antony named Ammonas. The clear differences in style, purpose and content between the two collections have led to suggestions that the authors cannot have had the same lineage, but the letters also share some very specific features, which makes it quite likely that they come from authors related to one another.[34]

Characteristics of the letters

The letters found in the collections attributed to Antony and Ammonas are, no doubt, genuine letters written to groups of recipients. With few exceptions they all contain standard introductory greetings to the addressees, confirming the close relation between sender and addressee, as well as farewell greetings in which the author reminds the addressees of his concern for them. Due to textual disorder, these greetings are sometimes displaced or even lost, but there is reason to think that all letters originally had such greetings. An exceptional case is the first letter of the Antonian collection, which reads more like an instruction for novices, but even here there is a clear authorial voice that speaks to a specific group. In both collections several of the letters share the same themes, expressions, concerns and often even phrases, indicating that they were most probably written to similar but different groups of monks. In the case of the letters of Antony, the exact repetition of parts of the letters and series of biblical quotations in most letters seems to indicate that they were written on the same occasion and with the same purpose but to different recipients, sharing approximately the same relation to Antony himself.[35]

The letters are, as is most clearly manifest in the case of the Antonian letters, modelled upon the Pauline letters, quoting them and using their phraseology. The authors express in emotional terms a very close and special relation to the addressees, variously designated as beloved children, brothers and friends. They repeatedly stress that they pray for the recipients of the letters, sharing their difficulties and concerns. In both collections the authors lament the limitation inherent in depending on letters rather than physical encounter, and refer to their desire to see the

---

[34] In his analysis of the letters of Ammonas, Bumazhnov draws the opposite conclusion and finds clear evidence that the letters attributed to Antony and the letters attributed to Ammonas belong to completely different traditions. See Bumazhnov 2009: 209–52.

[35] For a comparative table see Rubenson 1995: 58.

recipients in person, thus indicating a certain geographical distance in where they live.[36]

A central theme in the letters is the emphasis on knowledge gained by experience, and thus the necessity of gaining this experience. The recipients are repeatedly encouraged to understand and to know, and warned about negligence in this matter. The authors, in particular in the letters of Ammonas, refer to their own experience and their willingness to share this with the recipients as a privileged group. Repeatedly the authors emphasise that they know the recipients and know what they need.

Although there are a few instances where the authors refer back to a previous letter, there is little indication that the letters are intended to be read together. The repetitions of the same matters and phrases rather indicate the opposite. Each letter stands on its own, and can be seen as an attempt to strengthen the bond between the master and a group of disciples. In contrast to the letters of Pachomius and Shenute, they are clearly not written to a fixed cenobitic community, but rather to scattered groups all related directly to the author. The letters thus are witness to attempts to create a community that does not live together, but rather shares an allegiance to the same master, the author. The bond between the author and the addressees, as between the various individuals within the group addressed, is not upheld by common living or by a common rule, but by shared experiences and privileged teaching. In the letters of Ammonas, in particular, there is an emphasis on secrecy and on mysteries that presupposes adherence to the special relationship created and maintained by the letters. In a sense the connection is more similar to the one between a famous teacher and his followers and successors than between members of a community.

Collections or not?

In view of the independence of the single letters within the collections, as well as the complex and, in the case of the letters of Ammonas, scattered and diversified transmission of the letters, we need to ask ourselves in what sense we are talking about collections here. Is any combination of two or more letters attributed to an author a collection, or part of the transmission of a collection of letters? Are all letters attributed to an author part of a collection of letters by that author, independently of their transmission? Or should we restrict the use of the word collection to letters that

[36] For a more detailed discussion see Rubenson 2004.

we can show to have been consciously compiled as a unit, which, with some exceptions, has been transmitted together in more or less the same sequence? And does it matter if the unit was created by the author, by disciples and successors, by groups of recipients or by later compilers?

Restricting ourselves to the transmission of early monastic letters, it is evident that the problems encountered in the transmission of the collections attributed to Antony and Ammonas are not different from many other early monastic letter-collections. Through manuscript catalogues and occasional publication of one version or another, we know of collections attributed to Macarius,[37] Evagrius and Arsenius, as well as to Moses and other less-known figures. These are in general even less studied than the collections discussed above, but it seems clear that the transmission is often as complicated as in the case of the Ammonas letters. The letters appear individually or in collections that differ in numbers and sequences, differences found between the languages of preservation as well as within. Actually few of them seem to have been transmitted even as coherently in content and numbers as the letters of Antony.

In order to grasp the process that has resulted in the very differentiated reception and transmission of these letters, I suggest that we should not look at letter-collections of authors who were in one way or other themselves involved with the publication of their works, or whose letters were collected deliberately as their legacy. In contrast to these, as far as I can see, there is no reason to think that Antony or Ammonas were in any way involved in the making of the collection, nor that the letters were collected by the first recipients in order to preserve a specific heritage. The repetitious character of several of Antony's letters, as well as the quite similar concerns expressed repeatedly in the letters of Ammonas, indicate rather that the letters were occasional writings to different communities, never intended to be read together. The lack of variation, of rhetorical sophistication or of consistency in doctrine cannot be judged on the presumption that the authors themselves, or their disciples, had a collection of letters in mind.

This difference between the letters attributed to monastic authors like Antony, Ammonas, Macarius and Arsenius, and monastic leaders such as Pachomius and Shenoute, is easily explained by the fact that the former never became founders of institutions. In contrast to the letters of the

---

[37] For the eight letters attributed to Macarius in a Greek collection see Géhin 1999. Several of the letters also appear in collections in other languages either as collections of various composition or as single letters.

founders of communities, their letters were not transmitted as part of the legacy of specific communities but of the larger monastic tradition. The collectors of the letters of the first group were not concerned about preserving unity, but rather were trying to include in the transmission of monastic teaching the texts they regarded as useful and authoritative. Interestingly enough the Copto-Arabic collection of Antony is a special case, somehow in between, since we can here discern an attempt to shape a tradition, absent in the other textual transmissions of the Antonian material.

Instead of comparing the collections of letters attributed to Antony, Ammonas and others with authorial or communal collections, I suggest that they should be regarded as similar in transmission to the anecdotes, instructions and sayings found in a variety of monastic florilegia, often collectively known as *Paterika*, *Lives of the Fathers* or as 'gardens' or 'paradise' of the Fathers. It is as part of such collections, including the *Sayings of the Desert Fathers*, that our letters are generally preserved, and most probably the process of collection of them has been similar and had a similar purpose.[38]

The collection and transmission of the letters may, I suggest, be compared to the chapters and paragraphs of texts such as the homilies attributed to Macarius, the *Ascetic Rule* of Abba Isaiah, or the *Lausiac History* and the *History of the Monks*. Although there are standard versions of these established in editions, the manuscript evidence for these texts gives a much less organised impression. In the case of the *Lausiac History* and the *History of the Monks*, chapters, or even parts of chapters, are transmitted independently and quite often in a different order than in the standard edition. As Britt Dahlman has demonstrated, this independent transmission may, moreover, represent earlier stages of the transmission than the standardised collection.[39] In the florilegia the stories are, moreover, linked to other texts with similar content, including letters, short homilies and series of sayings.

As has been demonstrated by Jean-Claude Guy,[40] and more recently in some detail by Chiara Faraggiana and Britt Dahlman,[41] the collection of early monastic material into florilegia has been a continuous process where at every stage decisions have been made about content, sequence and attribution. In this process, material has been divided and combined in new ways to create the product asked for or wanted. The persons

---

[38] For a discussion on the transmission of the sayings see Rubenson 2013: 5–22.
[39] See Dahlman 2013: 23–34.   [40] Guy 1962: 36–41.   [41] Faraggiana 1997; Dahlman 2013: 23–34.

involved will have had access to a variety of sources to choose from and to combine. Thus the manuscripts very seldom have the same combination of texts in the same order, and often represent a mix of material modern scholars classify as not belonging together. But the general tendency to regard pure collections as more primitive, and mixed and complex collections of material as derivative, is probably as much a result of the modern search for authenticity, clarity, unity and consistency, as it is based on the historical evidence.[42]

Conclusion

Looking back at the collections of letters attributed to Antony and Ammonas, I suggest that we have to think of these as consisting of actual letters once sent to various groups of disciples, many of them rather similar in content but with variations dependent on the precise addressees. The letters were then copied and handed on, ending up in being combined with other letters of the same author or other related authors. For the letters of Antony the name had such an importance that we can easily imagine that attempts were made rather soon to create a standard collection transmitted together, as is evidenced by Jerome already in 392 and made likely by the quotations of Shenoute and Besa in the fifth century. But for less well-known authors like Ammonas or Arsenius there was less immediate need to collect all material or adhere to a standard collection once it had been made. Unfortunately the manuscripts preserving them do not give us much information about this process. The only indication is the sequential numbering of the letters that we find in most of the manuscripts.

---

[42] An illustrative example of this is the stratification of the Greek collections of the *Apophthegmata Patrum*, in which collections that are not purely alphabetic or systematic are regarded as derivative. See Guy 1993: 23–5.

CHAPTER 6

From letter to letter-collection
Monastic epistolography in late-antique Egypt
Malcolm Choat

The phenomenon of the letter-collection is characteristic of late antiquity. Taking their cue from classical models, in particular those of Pliny the younger and Cicero, and with Christian authors inevitably looking back to Paul and other early Christian letter-writers such as Polycarp and Ignatius, late-antique authors and editors crafted collections of letters which survive in the manuscript traditions of most of the major Mediterranean languages. Religious and civic leaders from both the classical and Christian traditions collected and circulated their letters, in the process transforming them from everyday documents to part of a burgeoning literary genre. Alongside this runs the evidence of the documentary papyri, among which survive archives of letters from Roman and late-antique Egypt, which, if they were not 'published' (inasmuch as the word can be used of anything in antiquity), at least provide evidence for the letter-writing and collecting impulse which lies behind the better-known letter-collections.

It is within this framework that we must investigate letters within the monastic tradition in Egypt. From documentary papyri and ostraca to collections of letters in deluxe codices, the letter is both foundational and critical to the articulation of the monastic movement in Egypt. What I wish to do here is to reflect on the monastic letter-collection, on its path from a papyrological archive to one transmitted in a manuscript tradition, by way, I hope, of better understanding the importance of this genre to the development of monasticism in Egypt.

To address this theme, I have a set of general, and specific, questions. The general ones are part of a wider consideration currently taking place in various parts of the academic world from various perspectives on the role of the letter, and particularly, the function of the letter-collection, in late antiquity. We should certainly consider to what extent the number of letter-collections we have for late antiquity is a product of factors external to the content of the letters themselves, such as the relative proximity of that time to us, and the consequent higher rate of survival of

literature from that era; and perhaps the rise of the codex as the domin-
ant book-form, which makes larger collections more feasible. More closely
related to their content, of course, is the fact that many of them are by
enormously influential Christian leaders, or, if we extend the concept of a
letter – as I suggest we should – to an imperial rescript, collections of laws
which were foundational for European culture.

Beyond these factors, something was happening across the Roman
world in late antiquity which caused the growth and propagation of the
many letter-collections we have. And it is in this context that we should
assess monastic letter-collections; that is, they are part of a wider context,
and the impulse to collect, copy and distribute letters is not in any sense a
phenomenon unique to monasticism. However, even though monasticism
stands within a wider framework, monks *did* choose to use the epistolary
format, or, at least, texts to which they gave the title ἐπιστολή,[1] to put
forward monastic theology or ideology and to present ideas which were
written for the spiritual benefit of other monks. And whether or not these
letters were intended for a wider, or a later, audience, monks chose to
copy collections of letters and transmit them for their inherent value. The
mechanics of that process lead me to my specific question: that is, how
did monasteries, and monks, marshal the epistolary inheritance of the
monastic tradition? How did these letters pass from being part of everyday life (if that is what some of them ever were) into items in manuscripts,
with much wider circulation and more general application?

If one can easily enough ask this question, one must just as quickly
admit that most of the time we have the letters only in manuscripts, often
in languages other than those in which they were composed, preserved
far from where they were written, shorn sometimes of contextual information which might have seemed irrelevant to those transmitting them.
And at the other end of the scale, we have the personal letters to, from and
between monks, written on papyrus and ostraca, which are usually not
at all the sorts of letters which we have in the manuscripts.[2] It is between
these two bodies of information that we must look for clues; here I will
seek them in two bodies of evidence, and from two points of view: one is
provided by the letters of Pachomius, the other by papyrological monastic
epistolary assemblages. A third perspective is provided, by way of conclusion, from narrative sources on monastic letter-writing in Egypt.

---

[1] On the issues with the (somewhat liberal) use of this title in the scriptorium of the White Monastery, see Choat 2013b.
[2] On the contrast in content, see Choat 2013a.

Letters of Pachomius

Pachomius, or Pachom ('the eagle') as he was known to speakers of
Egyptian, lived in upper Egypt in the late third and first half of the fourth
century.[3] He is known as the founder of coenobitic monasticism, and while
he would have had now-nameless contemporaries who established similar
communities,[4] he was certainly one of the earliest, and undoubtedly the
most famous, to gather a group of monks around him in a κοινὸς βίος,
from which had spread by his death in 347 a monastic κοινωνία which
included nine monasteries. He is known primarily though a related series
of *Lives* in Greek and Coptic, which descend through numerous versions
and translations from the late fourth century.[5] We get closer to Pachomius
himself in various sets of Rules, which form, via translation into Latin,[6]
one of the ultimate ancestors of the great coenobitic monastic Rules of the
mediaeval West. Yet the layers of monastic injunctions – some of which
are clearly later than Pachomius' lifetime – are difficult to separate.[7]

Behind this, presumably closer to the man himself, lies a series of letters attributed to Pachomius.[8] These are described in the first Greek *Life*
of Pachomius.

> While he was still alive moreover, the father himself [*sc.* Pachomius] dic-
> tated [one recension adds 'in Egyptian'] not only the talks and ordinances
> about the edification of the community, but also many letters to the fathers
> of the monasteries. He used in them the names of the characters from A to
> Ω, expressing to those fathers of the monasteries in a secret spiritual lan-
> guage things for the governance of souls, when he had no leisure to come
> to them. And since they were spiritual men, they would answer him in the
> same manner. They understood so well that he would lead them to perfec-
> tion, guiding them in detail with characters and a language [*sic*], that he
> was asked to make a book of those spiritual writings.[9]

This 'code', which is fully visible in the letters of Pachomius which
survive,[10] has not been satisfactorily explained,[11] and the letters are thus

---

[3] See in general Rousseau 1999; on the chronology, Joest 1994.

[4] On one such contemporary competitor, the Melitians, see Goehring 1999. On Melitian monasticism in general, see Hauben 2012.

[5] On their relationship see Rousseau 1999: 38–48; Veilleux 1968: 16–107.

[6] Boon 1932: 13–74; for the surviving Coptic fragments and Greek *excerpta* see Boon 1932: 155–82. For
an English translation see Veilleux 1980–2/II: 145–83.

[7] See most recently Joest 2009, 2010, 2012; cf. Rousseau 1999: 48–53.

[8] In addition to the editions cited below, see the English translation in Veilleux 1980–2/III: 51–83.

[9] *Life of Pachomius* G¹ 99, ed. Halkin 1932: 66–7; tr. Veilleux 1980–2/I: 366–7.

[10] See the quotations from the letters below at nn. 21 and 22.

[11] See Quecke 1975: 18–40; more recently Joest 2002, 1996, but see the critique of Kalvesmaki
2013: 13–14.

somewhat less useful for reconstructing the monastic life than they might otherwise be. But as a collection, and in their manuscripts and transmission, they present a number of interesting entry-points into the circulation and transmission of letter-collections in late-antique Egypt and beyond.

We have access to the letters in several forms: a series of Greek[12] and Coptic[13] parchment rolls; a Coptic codex;[14] and the collection translated by Jerome and transmitted in the western manuscript tradition.[15] It is an interesting phenomenon that for their attribution to Pachomius we rely on the source most chronologically, geographically and linguistically distant: none of the Greek or Coptic copies gives the name of the writer or addressees, or contains any trace of the headings given to each letter in the manuscripts which transmit the translation of Jerome, of which the following is a representative example:

> Letter of our father Pachomius to the holy man Cornelius, who was father of the monastery of Mochansis [*sic*; *sc.* Thmoušons], in which he speaks a language given to both of them by an angel, and the sound of which we have heard without being able to understand the meaning.[16]

These are clearly titles, rather than epistolary addresses: while they could in part have been extrapolated from epistolary introductions, other elements are either descriptive of the contents, or indeed draw on traditions outside the letters themselves. At times regarded as possibly late inventions,[17] there are some grounds for thinking that at least the addresses are not entirely fictional,[18] and that they may go back to the time of Jerome. They could have arrived at that point either via oral tradition, or in 'the books [*libri*] sent to me [i.e. Jerome] by the man of God, the priest Silvanus, who had', Jerome says, 'received them from Alexandria that he should bid me to translate them', that is, in a Greek

---

[12] *Letters* 1–3, 7, 10 and 11a in Greek on a parchment roll: Chester Beatty Ms. W. 145 + *P. Köln* 4.174 (*P.Köln* inv. 3288), ed. Quecke 1975: 97–110; Kramer *et al.* 1982: 90–8. Papyri and ostraca (signalled by 'P.' or 'O.') are abbreviated according to J. F. Oates *et al.*, *Checklist of Editions of Greek, Latin, Demotic, and Coptic Papyri, Ostraca and Tablets*, http://scriptorium.lib.duke.edu/papyrus/texts/clist.html.

[13] *Letter* 8 on a parchment roll in Sahidic Coptic: *P.Köln Ägypt.* 8 (*P.Köln* inv. 3286 = *P.Köln Lüddeckens* 2); *Letters* 10–11a on a parchment roll in Sahidic Coptic: = *P.Köln Ägypt.* 9 (*P.Köln* inv. 3287 = *P.Köln Lüddeckens* 1), ed. Quecke 1975: 112–18, with other editions in Kurth *et al.* 1980 and Kropp *et al.* 1968. See also *Letter* 11b, on a parchment roll in Sahidic Coptic: *P.Bodmer* XXXIX, which remains unpublished.

[14] *Letters* 9a–b, 10, 11b, in a papyrus codex in Sahidic Coptic: Chester Beatty Glass Container No. 54: ac. 2556; ed. Quecke 1974, see also Quecke 1975: 111–18.

[15] Eleven letters are preserved, ed. Boon 1932: 77–101.

[16] Ed. Boon 1932: 77; tr. Veilleux 1980–22/III: 51, adjusted.

[17] See Quecke 1975: 16–17.   [18] Joest 2002: esp. 94.

exemplar in circulation in the Pachomian monastery of the Metanoia in Lower Egypt.[19] We might (to speculate) think of some sort of written index which accompanied the letters. In the earliest manuscript, both the rules and letters are found, though not sequentially;[20] it is a natural enough assumption that among the *libri* received by Jerome were codices containing all the material he translated, including the letters of Pachomius.

Despite the lack of formulaic introductions and farewells in the letters as transmitted in Greek and Coptic, the letters of Pachomius retain many telltale signs of their original genre. These come both in the form of greetings,[21] and in internal references to their character: the opening of *Letter* 2 talks of an earlier letter;[22] *Letter* 4 starts by noting that the writer will say now in a letter that which he could not say in the haste of a previous meeting;[23] *Letter* 6 opens with talk of writing and its answer[24] and refers to 'every letter which I have written to you'.[25] Nor should the titles in the Latin be given too much weight; that to *Letter* 10 carries a title in the manuscripts which makes it seem as if it may have been a record of a homily:

> Words pronounced by our father Pachomius through images teaching the brothers of the monastery of Mochansis [*sic*; *sc.* Thmoušons] about the things that were to come. By these words in the spirit the brothers were informed of what the superiors of the monastery were going to do and suffer.[26]

---

[19] From the Preface of Jerome to his translation of the Rules: *accepi libros ab homine Dei Siluano presbytero mihi directos, quos ille Alexandria missos susceperat, ut mihi iniungerat transferandos*; ed. Boon 1932: 3–4; tr. Veilleux 1980–2/II: 141.

[20] See Boon 1932: ix–xxxii.

[21] See e.g. the close of *Ep.* 1: ἀσπάζου τὴν κεφαλὴν καὶ τοὺς πόδας καὶ τὰς χεῖρας καὶ τοὺς ὀφθαλμοὺς καὶ τὸ κατάλοιπον τοῦ πν(εύματό)ς σου, ὅ ἐστιν ⲁ (ed. Quecke 1975: 100); *salute caput et pedes et manus et oculos et reliqua spiritus tui, quae sunt A* (ed. Boon 1932: 78): 'Greet the head, the feet, the hands, the eyes, and the rest of your spirit, which is A' (tr. Veilleux 1980–2/III: 52).

[22] μνημόνευε, ὅτι ἔγραψά σοι Ο ἐν τῇ ἐπιστολῇ διὰ τὸ Τ, ὅτι γέγραπται (ed. Quecke 1975: 100); *memento quod scripserim tibi U; in epistula T scriptum est* (ed. Boon 1932: 78): 'Remember that I wrote to you U in the letter because of the T, for it is written' (tr. Veilleux 1980–2/III: 52)

[23] *Transiuimis per te et non potuimus prae nimia festinatione diuinum tecum conferre sermonem; ideo nunc per epistulam loquimur* (ed. Boon 1932: 86): 'We were at your place but because we were in too much of a hurry, we could not have a spiritual talk with you; therefore we talk to you now in a letter' (tr. Veilleux 1980–2/III: 59)

[24] *Volo uos intellegere litteras quas scripsistis mihi, et quas ego rescripsi uobis* (ed. Boon 1932: 92–3): 'I want you to understand the character that you wrote to me and that I wrote to you in answer' (tr. Veilleux 1980–2/III: 67).

[25] *In omni epistula quam scripsi uobis* (ed. Boon 1932: 94; tr. Veilleux 1980–2/III: 68).

[26] Ed. Boon 1932: 99; tr. Veilleux 1980–2/III: 74.

Despite the impression this title gives, Shenoute explicitly refers to this being a 'letter' when he cites it in his sermon *The Rest of the Words*.[27] In neither this citation, nor that from *Letter* 1 in *I have heard about your wisdom*,[28] does Shenoute mention Pachomius' name; as Quecke noted, 'he introduces it both times in an almost mysterious way'.[29] Is it conceivable that Shenoute did not know who the author of these letters was? This would seem a priori surprising, and he certainly invests their author with the sort of authority which one would expect him to give someone whose identity he knew. It is possible that we glimpse here some competition between these great monastic federations,[30] but only when further study of Shenoute's citation practice has been undertaken will a fuller answer be possible.[31]

This lack of attribution by Shenoute is interesting in comparison to the earliest copies of the letters of Pachomius, the parchment roll in Greek now in the Chester Beatty library, palaeographically dated by T. C. Skeat to the fourth century.[32] Whether or not the entirety of the assemblage commonly referred to as the 'Dishna library' is the library of a Pachomian monastery, and indeed whether this Pachomian material is part of that assemblage,[33] a monastic library is a very likely provenance for this roll. And it is thus of interest to note that the letters as they appear in this roll do not contain the standard epistolary introductions and farewells which are overwhelmingly found in contemporary letters.[34]

[27] ⲚⲀⲒ ⲚⲈ ⲚⲢⲰⲘⲈ ⲈⲦⲤⲞⲞϥ ⲈⲚⲦⲀ ⲚⲈⲒⲞⲦⲈ ⲚⲈⲦⲞⲨⲀⲀⲂ ⲀⲨⲰ ⲈⲦⲚⲞⲈⲒ ϨⲚϨⲰⲂ ⲚⲒⲘ ⲤϨⲀⲒ ⲈⲦⲂⲎⲎⲦⲞⲨ ϨⲚⲚⲈⲨⲈⲠⲒⲤⲦⲞⲖⲎ, 'these are the defiled men, about whom our holy fathers, who know everything, wrote in their letters' (followed by citation from Pachomius *Ep*. 10): for the text, see *P.Ryl.Copt*. 67 (Crum 1909: 31) = MONB.GO 396 (Coptic codices are cited by codex designation and page number in the system of the *Corpus dei Manoscritti Copti Letterari* [http://cmcl.let.uniroma1.it/]).

[28] ⲀⲞⲨⲈⲒⲰⲦ ⲚⲀⲄⲀⲐⲞⲤ ⲀⲨⲰ ⲚⲤⲀⲂⲈ ⲚⲈⲨⲤⲈⲂⲎⲤ ⲚⲀⲘⲈ ϪⲞⲞⲤ ϨⲒⲦⲚ ⲚⲈϥⲤϨⲀⲒ ϨⲚ ϨⲈⲚⲈⲠⲒⲤⲦⲞⲖⲎ, 'A good and wise Father, truly pious, spoke through his writings, in letters' (then citation from Pachomius, *Ep*. 1), Shenoute, *I have heard about your Wisdom*, MONB. XH 277b.6–12; a marginal note added after the codex was written (i.e. many centuries after Shenoute's death) provides the information ⲈϪⲘ ⲠⲈⲚⲈⲒⲰⲦ ⲠⲀϨⲰⲘ ('on our father Pachom'). On these citations see Choat 2013b.

[29] Quecke 1975: 51 ('führt ihn beide Male auf geradezu geheimnisvolle Weise ein'); see also Leipoldt 1903: 86 n. 4, suggesting that Shenoute did this in the case of the citation from *The Rest of the Words* because it was in a speech before the *praeses*, who perhaps might not know of Pachom. The way *Ep*. 10 is cited not unnaturally led Crum to mention prophets and apostles in his note on the passage (Crum 1909: 31 n. 1).

[30] See Goehring 2008.

[31] See Timbie 2007. On Shenoute's citation of the letters of 'the holy messenger of the lord, Athanasius the Archbishop' as the source for some unfavourable opinions concerning the Manichaeans, which actually seem to have their origin in the *Acta Archelai*, see Choat 2013c: 60 with n. 72.

[32] On the date, see Quecke 1975: 77–8.

[33] See Robinson 2011; for further references to the debate see Choat 2013b: 86 n. 73.

[34] On these, see Choat 2010.

We can only conjecture that Pachomius' letters originally contained these elements. We might note, looking across at Shenoute's *Canons*, that these texts, which were in origin mostly letters sent from Shenoute's escarpment retreat down to the monastery below, also do not contain such elements, at least as we have them in the manuscripts. Insofar as I have been able to tell (and this will be doubtless need to be revised in the future), a ϭϩⲁⲓ ('it is who writes') opening formula – commonly used in Shenoute's letters to people outside the monastery preserved in the manuscripts of the *Discourses*, as in most contemporary Coptic letters[35] – occurs only once in the *Canons*, as opposed to the *Discourses*: namely, in *Canon* 9's *Shenoute writes to Tahom*.[36] We might wonder whether the letters which make up Shenoute's canons ever contained such epistolary formulae. If they were sent directly to, and received within, the monastery, would one need an address?

In some letters found at the monasteries of Apa Thomas at Wadi Sarga and Apa Apollo at Bala'izah, both sender and recipient are unnamed;[37] admittedly these are usually quite short affairs, and not always sent within the monastery, insofar as this can be judged. These letters date to the seventh or eighth century, in which period letters on papyrus in both Greek and Coptic commonly eschew the sort of epistolary introductions which name sender and recipient. By way of example, a pair of letters which cannot be dated more closely than the sixth to eighth century bear no introductory formulae and only a brief farewell, and the body of the letters does not identify their correspondents. Only in the addresses on the back do we learn that it is Christophoria – who seems to have been a female monastic leader – who is writing to the 'Christ-loving count [*komes*]' Mena.[38] Pachomius' letters, of course, were written in a period when such introductory formulae elements were virtually ubiquitous. If the addresses as preserved in Jerome's translation are accurate, not all of Pachomius' letters were sent within a single monastery either. They were, of course, sent within the federation, and surely would have been carried by a monk journeying between the communities.

The other possibility, of course, is that such elements have been removed: in their role as documents of the founder which contain important precepts whose application stretches well beyond their original

---

[35] See Richter 2008: 748–51, 765–6; Choat 2010: 162 n. 47.

[36] See Richter 2008: 751. For the text see Leipoldt 1908: 21–2; on its place in the Shenoutean corpus, Emmel 2004: 604–5; the historical circumstances are discussed in Krawiec 2002: 49, *et passim*.

[37] *P.Bal*. II.186, 263; *O.Sarga* 101, 110.

[38] *P.Lond.Copt*. I.1104–5; see also Bagnall and Cribiore 2006: 255–7.

purpose, such elements are superfluous. Conversely, in the context of a Pachomian monastery in Upper Egypt, presumably everybody knew the identity of the author – probably Shenoute did as well – just as the monks of the White Monastery were under no illusions about the sender of one letter which wound up in the *Canons*, certainly not when it was read to them after its arrival, nor, probably, on subsequently encountering it in the library or monastery archives or hearing it read aloud.[39]

However, outside the immediate context provided by the home monastery or federation of the writer, the user of the collection craves context: by whom was the letter written, and to whom? What we may see in the collection of Jerome is a repackaging of the letters of Pachomius into a form which Graeco-Roman readers would expect, that is, a letter-collection proper. The monks of the White Monastery who were able to connect Shenoute's citation of Pachomius' *Letter* 1 with its author may have had such a collection (or perhaps liturgical tradition had enshrined the annotation in the codices at the relevant places?). Leaving speculation aside, we can nevertheless see, in the different forms in which the letters of Pachomius survive, different responses to collecting and transmitting letters, reflecting perhaps different envisaged uses, and different types of letter-collection.

What Shenoute did, collecting his letters into a canon of rules for the White Monastery, the Pachomians may have done in an embryonic way in the collection of Pachomius' letters (except in their case, of course, they also codified an entire set, perhaps several entire sets, of free-standing rules). So the texts become something more than letters, and enter a state in which genre is rather more fluid. It might be worth noting here the final text in Schøyen MS 193, a fourth-century Coptic codex;[40] this is an untitled text, which exhorts the brethren to pray for God's mercy. Pietersma and Comstock, who recently published additional fragments of the manuscript from the Chester Beatty library,[41] suggest Pachomius himself may have been the author, in which connection it is interesting to note that no author is cited in the manuscript. The text is usually referred to as a homily, but is perhaps better, as Pietersma and Comstock note, seen as an exhortation; yet its tone and content compare well with some early monastic letters.

---

[39] For Shenoute's injunction that the federation's rules (whether the whole nine volumes of Shenoute's *Canons*, or a written rule such as that of the Pachomians), see Layton 2007: 68.
[40] Generally known as the 'Crosby-Schøyen codex', edited in Goehring 1990.
[41] Pietersma and Comstock 2011.

When we attempt to study early monastic epistolography within the manuscript tradition, then we must reckon with a situation in which genre boundaries are blurred and porous, where there are different imperatives for different sorts of collections, and different priorities in the way the letters are presented in different contexts.

Papyrological monastic epistolary assemblages

If we struggle to recreate the context, except in outline, in which many of the letters which survive in the Egyptian manuscript tradition were copied, it is only rarely that we are reliably informed on how documentary letters were stored in a monastic context. Many well-known 'archives', including fourth-century monastic archives such as those of Paieous, Nepheros and Apa Johannes,[42] come through the antiquities trade.[43] We thus have no real idea of their exact provenance, let alone how they were stored: some may have been kept in ways with which we are familiar from archives found intact, such as wrapped in cloth or placed in a jar,[44] but many such 'archives' were probably not 'stored' at all, but were rather simply discarded. The set of letters which seem to centre on a monk named Sansnos in the cartonnage of the Nag Hammadi codices may well have come from a scrap papyrus dealer.[45] Some assemblages which did come via excavation were not recovered systematically enough for us to know how they may have been stored in antiquity: one might think here of the monastery of Apa Apollo at Deir el-Bala'izah in the Lycopolite nome (south-west of modern Asyut), where we have no clear idea of the place, or the state, in which the many papyri from the site were found.[46] At times when we know the provenance more exactly, we may debate the significance of the way they were stored: in eighth-century western Thebes, the anchorite Frange kept many of the letters which he had himself sent

---

[42] Paieous: *P.Lond.* 6.1913–1922, SB Kopt. 3.1310. Nepheros: *P.Neph.* 1–42 (not all of which may have been part of the archive in antiquity but which came in the same purchase); Apa Johannes: *P.Herm.* 7–10, 17, *P.Ryl.Copt.* 268–76, SB 18.13612, *P.Amh.* 2.145.

[43] On the distinction in papyrology between an 'archive' (texts stored together in antiquity) and a 'dossier' (a group of related texts assembled in modern times) see A. Martin 1994. On papyrological archives see in general Messeri 2001; Vandorpe 2009.

[44] Vandorpe 2009: 219–20; Messeri 2001: 61–2. An example is the sixth-century Melitian papyri from Labla (*P.Dubl.* 32–4), which Flinders Petrie found wrapped in cloth and placed in a jar. The jar was buried in a church in Harawa: see McGing 1990.

[45] *P.Nag Hamm.* Gr. 68, 72, 75, 76, 77, 78; *Copt.* 5; see Wipszycka 2000: 67.

[46] See Kahle 1954/1: 1–3, esp. 3 with n. 2; Crum, in Petrie 1907: 39, speaks of 'the monastery, around the ruins of which the [manuscripts] were scattered', and says 'the manuscripts are clearly the debris of the monastic library and charter room'; but the latter merely represents Crum's opinion.

(but which he had somehow retrieved) in a fissure in the tomb which formed his cell; yet his motivation in doing so is not fully understood.[47]

Only rare cases allow us to be more definite. Several times in Theban legal documents, it is stated that a copy of a contract will be placed in the library (ΒΙΒΛΙΟⲐΗⲔⲈ) of the monastery of Apa Phoibammon.[48] Although the remains of this monastery were being progressively dismantled in the nineteenth century even before Naville lifted them off the top of the funerary temple of Hatshepsut (Deir el-Bahri) without record,[49] it is fairly certain that the location from which the majority of the documents were retrieved was a building on the north of the upper terrace, which was probably the residence of Apa Abraham and his successor abbots, and the location of the archive of the monastery.[50] Alongside the many documents which have survived from the monastery's archives (including many letters between monks) are a number of texts of more literary content, which may be useful to place on the continuum between documentary and monastic letters.

From here come a number of texts, classified by Crum as 'Homily or Epistle', some of which are written in the hand of the priest Victor,[51] Abraham's secretary before he succeeded him as abbot, who also writes documents and letters for the bishop and himself; some are in other hands.[52] The monastery of Epiphanius, which lay near to that of Phoibammon in western Thebes, was paradoxically more scientifically excavated but with less clear idea of where the central archives of the monastery may have been.[53] It also produced a variety of literary texts, a number of which are in the hand of a scribe who writes both literary and documentary texts.[54] Among these, we encounter a wide range of genres, including excerpts

---

[47] Boud'hors and Heurtel 2010/I: 9.

[48] *P.KRU* 89.35–36 (*c.* 775): ⲦⲀⲢⲈϤⲔⲀⲀϤ ⲈⲚⲦⲂⲒⲂⲗⲒⲟⲐⲎⲔⲎ ⲘⲠⲘⲀ ⲈⲦⲞⲨⲀⲀⲂ ('and he shall place it in the library of the holy place'), so too in *P.KRU* 100.51–2 (778); *P.KRU* 96.66–7 (*c.* 775): ⲦⲀⲢⲈϤⲔⲀⲀϤ ⲈⲚⲦⲂⲒⲂⲗⲒⲰⲐⲎⲔⲎ ⲘⲠⲘⲞⲚⲀⲤⲦⲎⲢⲒⲞⲚ ('and he shall place it in the library of the monastery'). See also *P.CLT* 5.85–6 (24.II.711), where the parties go to the monastery of Phoibammon to consult a 'corner [i.e. fragment] of a papyrus [document]' (ⲠⲔⲞⲞⳠ ⲚⲬⲀⲢⲦⲒⲚ).

[49] See in general Godlewski 1986.

[50] Godlewski 1986: 51–9, especially 51–2 on the ostraca found during Naville's excavations, and 53–7 on papyri such as those published in *P.KRU*, some of which also may have been found in the monastery at an earlier date; on the provenance of the latter texts see also Schiller 1971.

[51] That is, Crum's 'Hand A': see Crum 1902: xiv. It should be noted that the distinctions between these hands (and the attribution of all the texts designated as in 'Hand A' by Crum to Victor) are rather less clear cut than might be believed on the basis of Crum's discussion.

[52] *O.Crum.* 8–9, 10–11; the first two are assigned by Crum to 'Hand A'.

[53] Or even the exact provenance within the monastery of many of the texts: see Winlock *et al.* 1926/I: xxii–xxv.

[54] See the list of texts in Winlock *et al.* 1926/II: 155 (n. 1 on *P.Mon.Epiph.* 1). On the possible identity of this scribe, see below.

from the works of Shenoute,[55] Severus of Antioch[56] and the patriarch Damian of Alexandria,[57] as well as many documentary letters.[58]

From different hands there are a letter in whose fragmentary beginning can be seen an introductory ⲤϨⲀⲒ formula urging the addressees on in the monastic life (ⲠⲰⲚϨ ⲚⲦⲘⲚⲦⲘⲞⲚⲀⲬⲞⲤ), in which the writer shares (*P.Mon.Epiph.* 62); a strongly worded letter of admonition (*P.Mon. Epiph.* 64); and some further admonitions addressed to a second person addressee which could also come from an epistle (*P.Mon.Epiph.* 72). These are often preserved in too fragmentary a state to be confident of how they were presented in terms of their titles or introductions.

It has been suggested that the scribe referred to above who wrote both literary and documentary letters is the Elias who, with Jacob, led the monastery of Epiphanius in one of the subsequent generations after the latter's death.[59] It is also possible that this same Elias is the scribe of a large number of letters – now held in the Cairo and Berlin collections – from a monk of that name.[60] Among the texts in his hand is one which, lacking any epistolary formulae, and with a more hortatory and 'monastic' content than the (clearly documentary) letters from Elias, was placed by Crum with the literary ostraca.

> Gird your[61] body and become a son of the *topos* with your whole heart, for like me you have been vowed to this *topos*; and it is your duty to serve, that the angel of the *topos* may be favourable to you. [Back] If[?] you often have leisure, come in with the offerings [πρόσφορα] which you are sending [i.e. offering], and you will find rest with me, not associating with evil men, and my heart shall be satisfied with you.[62]

[55] Shenoute: *P.Mon.Epiph.* 56 (headed ⲖⲞⲄⲞⲤ ⲤⲒⲚⲞⲨⲐⲒⲞⲨ) 57, 58, 65 (from Shenoute's work *I have been reading the holy gospels*); on these, see Emmel 2004: 88–9.

[56] Severus: *P.Mon.Epiph.* 59, headed [ⲀⲠ]Ⲁ ⲤⲈⲨⲎⲢⲞⲤ ⲰⲀⲤⲰⲦⲎⲢⲒⲬⲞⲤ [ⲠⲈⲠⲒ]ⲤⲔⲞⲠⲞⲤ ⲚⲦⲔⲀⲠⲠⲀⲆⲞⲔⲒⲀ. The text is re-edited in Dijkstra and Greatrex 2009: 246–54. On Severus (*c.* 456–538), anti-Chalcedonian patriarch of Antioch from 512 to 518, see Allen and Hayward 2004.

[57] *P.Mon.Epiph.* 54 is perhaps a letter of the Damian, patriarch of Alexandria 578–607 (see Davis 2004: 108–12); cf. short extracts from his festal letters, *P.Mon.Epiph.* 53 and 55, the latter in a different hand. See also the long acephalous epistle, *P.Mon.Epiph.* 60.

[58] E.g. *P.Mon.Epiph.* 143 (which also quotes Severus of Antioch), 161, 166, 215, 260, 284, 348, 349, 403 and others.

[59] See Dekker (forthcoming). For the will of Jacob and this Elias, in which they leave the monastery and all its property to Stephen, see *P.KRU* 75 (= Winlock *et al.* 1926/II, Appendix III).

[60] For Crum's suggestion that the Elias of these texts was he of the will (see previous note), and thus of the monastery of Epiphanius, see Crum 1902: 60 (n. 1 to the translation of *O.Crum.* 227); and Winlock *et al.* 1926/ II: 344 n. 7. I thank Renate Dekker for pointing out the latter reference to me. The provenance of this group of texts is unknown, but they do not come from the monastery of Phoibammon.

[61] Singular here and in the rest of the text.   [62] *O.Crum.* 15, tr. Crum 1902: 7, adjusted.

This text, which offers advice to the novice ascetic of the sort we find in monastic letters transmitted in manuscript, could be an excerpt from a longer work, such as seems to be a text on a single sheet of papyrus from the Deir el-Bala'izah, which offers monastic advice to a second person singular addressee (*P.Bal.* 1.51) and likewise contains no epistolary formulae (as well as seeming to start and end in the middle of sentences). Alternatively, *O.Crum.* 15 could be a contemporary composition by Elias. We stand in any case on the boundary between the literary and documentary genres.

While some of these texts speak to a second person addressee,[63] as one would expect of a letter, none contains any epistolary introductory or farewell formulae, and their more hortatory and monastic content apparently led Crum to place them with the literary ostraca. It is not at all unlikely that some or all of these texts started their lives as actual letters from a monastic superior to a monk or group of monks; however, what we have in these ostraca is not the original copy, but the text once it has been recopied for its inherent value. If there was ever an epistolary introduction, or a farewell formula, they have been removed: what matters at this stage is their content; the identity of their writer is either well known, or not relevant. In this respect, they are not too far from the format in which we find the letters of Pachomius, except that the latter are preserved in full on parchment or papyrus. But we get closest here, perhaps, to glimpsing the conditions in which the letters passed from a documentary context into a manuscript tradition.

Narrative sources on monastic letter-writing in Egypt

To go beyond the context of the documents and manuscripts themselves, we must piece together testimonia from the narrative sources on letter-writing for monasticism in Egypt. In previous approaches into this topic,[64] I have discussed letters embedded in the Pachomian *Vita* tradition. I omitted to mention the reference cited above to the first Greek *Life of Pachomius* 99, which is a testimony – rare in the Egyptian tradition – to a request for a collection of letters from their writer. Even if such a request for 'a book of those spiritual writings' was formulated by the compilers of the Greek *Life* to explain a collection in their presence,[65] it is nonetheless

---

[63] E.g. *O.Crum.* 9 (second singular addressee), 11 (second plural addressee).
[64] Choat 2013a, 2013b.
[65] Note that this episode is not included in the Coptic *Lives* of Pachomius.

a rare commentary on the process of forming a letter-collection. In later testimonia, such as those on the letters of Isidore of Pelusium, we encounter already-formed collections.[66] If we seek to fill this gap, we find that testimonies to letter-writing in early Egyptian monasticism are relatively infrequent. Perhaps this is in part the nature of the sources: the *Sayings of the Desert Fathers* (*Apophthegmata Patrum*), for instance, represent (at least in their narratological framework) an oral culture, and so references to letter-writing,[67] such as Poemen writing to a famous *hesychast* (ἡσυχαστής) on the mountain of Athribis, or the mention of Arsenius' aversion to writing letters, are rare.[68] Another anecdote in the literary tradition provides a different sort of illustration. In the *History of the Monks* 13, the authors are told of John, a monk 'from another age', who moved from place to place in the desert (though he had once stood motionless for three years praying), about whom the authors are told by Apelles, a monk from Achoris, modern Tehna:[69]

> It was once revealed to him with regard to his *monasteria* that some of them did not maintain a strict observance. He wrote letters to them through the priest, saying that these were lax and those zealous for virtue. And it was found that what he said was true. He also wrote to their superiors, saying that some of them were negligent about the salvation of the brethren, while others encouraged them satisfactorily, and he declared the rewards and the punishments of each.[70]

Large sections of the *History of the Monks of Egypt* represent the oral traditions of the communities visited by the authors. Yet it is noteworthy that the story relayed through Apelles about John writing hortatory letters (the only time, in fact, that letters are mentioned in the *History of the Monks*) was enshrined in the traditions passed down within the communities under his direction.[71] Indeed, we can easily imagine that the letters in which John set forth this advice were kept, and circulated, within

---

[66] The earliest mention of a collection of Isidore's letters appears to be Severus of Antioch, *Contra impium grammaticum* 3.39; see Evieux 1995: 347–73.

[67] Something we know from the corpora of such figures as Evagrius Ponticus was not uncommon in the Lower Egyptian monastic communities, see e.g. Bunge 2006.

[68] *Apophthegmata Patrum*/ Poemen 90; *Apophthegmata Patrum*/Arsenius 42.

[69] *Historia monachorum* 13.1–2.

[70] *Historia monachorum* 13.10; ed. Festugière 1971: 100; tr. Russell 1981: 94, adjusted.

[71] Earlier in the story Apelles relates a conversation between John and the devil which must have circulated as an apophthegm (*Historia monachorum* 13.5); but in *Historia monachorum* 13.11, which follows the paragraph about letter-writing, by noting that on another occasion John 'summoned others to a more perfect way of life', and then quoting what he suggested (ὑπεμίμνησκεν) to them, can we imagine that this suggestion was also made by letter, and Apelles was quoting from it (even if from memory)?

these communities, just as the communities of Pachomius and Shenoute preserved their founders' letters on rolls and codices, and as the monastic scribes of the monasteries of Phoibammon and Epiphanius copied letters containing advice for monks onto ostraca, and filed them with everyday letters they had written. They were thus placed on the epistolographic continuum from document to hortatory epistle, on which we must seek the monastic letter.

Conclusion

Via examination of letters on different media, surviving in different forms, we may plot points on this scribal and translational continuum. Yet large sections of it remain opaque to us. In the papyri and ostraca, we are witness not only to the quotidian epistolary activity of individual monks, but to their scribal activity in copying what appear to be excepts of (or perhaps in some cases complete) letters which transmit monastic advice, and which may have been written earlier for a different specific audience. It is the latter sort of scribal activity which generates the copies of the letters of Pachomius surviving in Greek and Coptic, and which produced the collection of them which Jerome translated, that the western manuscript tradition then carried forward in a new setting. But the decision-making processes of the editorial activity are not always easily discernable: why were particular selections made? How, where and why were the opening descriptive sections which feature in the Latin translations of Pachomius' letters, but not in the Greek and Coptic versions, generated? For such context, we must turn to narrative vignettes of the sort preserved in the *Life of Pachomius* and the *History of the Monks*. These show monks, and those outside the monastic system, transmitting the letters of earlier figures, building them into hortatory models, forming them into corpora and transforming them from documentary letters into a literary genre.

PART III

Collecting early bishops' letters

CHAPTER 7

Letters of Ambrose of Milan (374–397), Books I–IX

J. H. W. G. Liebeschuetz

As readers of this volume will be aware, a number of letter-collections have survived from late antiquity. Those of Julian, Libanius and Symmachus are pagan,[1] but the majority are Christian. The collections differ greatly from each other, as they reflect not only the various personalities and lives of their authors, but also the circumstance in which a collection was assembled, whether by the writer himself or by his pupils or by later, sometimes much later, admirers. Besides, some collections seem to be complete as 'published', if that is the right word,[2] while others have survived in only a fragmentary condition.[3]

Of Ambrose's correspondence, ninety-one letters have been preserved. Of these, seventy-one have come down to us in a single collection of ten books. Sixteen additional letters have been transmitted outside the collection (*extra collectionem*)[4] in two *corpora* containing respectively ten and five letters. Two more letters have been preserved among the *Acts* of the Council of Aquileia of 381. The larger of the two *corpora* transmitted outside the collection probably originated with Paulinus, one of Ambrose's priests,[5] and his biographer. The smaller *corpus* appears to be later, dating perhaps from the late ninth or early tenth century.[6] The first printed edition of the letters was published in 1490. The second volume of the Maurist edition (M) appeared in 1690.[7]

The general character of Ambrose's collection

Was the collection composed by Ambrose himself? Though that is not absolutely certain, it has been generally agreed that it was.[8] He certainly

---

[1] See Neil's introduction to this volume.
[2] See Starr 1987; and essays in Johnson and Parker 2009.
[3] E.g. the letters of Synesius and of John Chrysostom.
[4] This is abbreviated below as *Ep. ex.*   [5] So Faller and Zelzer 1982: lxxxv–vi.
[6] See Faller and Zelzer 1982: cx and cxxii.
[7] Zelzer 1980.   [8] *Ep.* 32 (M48), 7.

kept copies of his letters, and so evidently assumed that they would one day be read by a wider public. For he could write to Sabinus, bishop of Placentia: 'I have sent you these introductory remarks (with the works I am sending you for criticism), and if you are agreeable, I will insert them in the *books of my letters*, and preserve them among their number, so that they [*sc.* the books] will be promoted by the inclusion of your name.'[9] Ambrose quotes Paul's Second Letter to the Corinthians: '*What we are by letters when absent such we are also in deeds when bodily present*', and comments: 'Paul printed the image of his presence on his letters.'[10] He clearly hoped to achieve the same effect with his own letters, and, again like Paul, not only while he was living, but for long after. As we will see, the collection has a very individual character, and it is reasonably safe to assume that this reflects the interests of its compiler, and that the compiler was Ambrose himself.

If Ambrose put together the collection himself it is almost certainly his last work.[11] The collection was certainly in existence when Paulinus wrote his *Life of Ambrose* in *c.* 412–13, for he assumed that readers of the biography would be able to find elsewhere the full text of a letter to which he only alludes, but which is included in the collection (*Ep.* v.30).[12] The collection must therefore have been in existence by that time. Book vi of the collection is introduced by a letter commenting on the decision of Paulinus of Nola and of his wife to give away their property and live an ascetic life. This was in 395.[13] Book x includes the oration on the death of Theodosius I, who died in January 395. Ambrose died in 397. So the collection was probably compiled and given to the public between 395 and 397.

Ambrose's duties as bishop and public figure must always have obliged him to write a very large number of 'business letters' to a wide range of individuals. But when he was old the letter also became his preferred literary medium, as he writes to his colleague Chromatius, bishop of Aquileia: 'I prefer to chat with you in the words of an old man, to show that I can still do it, rather than to go on in loftier style about something that befits neither my interest nor my strength.'[14] Similarly he tells Sabinus, bishop of Placentia: 'I have now chosen that which old men find easier, to write letters in ordinary and familiar language, weaving in any passages from the scriptures that happen to come to mind.'[15] So it was

---

[9] *Ep.* 32 (48), 7.   [10] 2 Cor. 10: 10–11, in *Ep.* 37 (M47), 7.

[11] *Ep.* 32 (M48), 7; also 37 (M47), 7; 28 (M50), 16; 34 (M45), 1.

[12] Paulinus, *Vita Ambr.* 19; Ambrose, *Ep.* 30 (M24) on an embassy to the usurper Maximus. Paulinus also paraphrased part of *Ep.* 74 (M40).

[13] *Ep.* 27 (M58).   [14] *Ep.* 28 (M50), 16.   [15] *Ep.* 32 (M48), 7.

only natural that he chose that his last literary work should be a collected edition of his letters.

The collection is certainly selective, including only a small proportion of the letters Ambrose wrote in the course of the twenty-three years of his episcopate. We know that Ambrose preserved copies also of some letters that he had not included in the collection, because Paulinus cites passages from two such letters in his biography.[16] He had evidently found those letters in an archive at Milan. Subsequently Paulinus offered those two letters together with eight others to a wider readership in the smaller *corpus* of ten letters which has been mentioned earlier.[17] In addition we have a few references to some letters, the texts of which have not come down to us.[18]

Ambrose sometimes deprecates his own literary efforts, but he was in fact a very careful writer. When Sabinus offered to read his writings critically, Ambrose gladly accepted the offer, and sent Sabinus a volume:[19]

> I have thought it right to take up your invitation; it is now up to you to discern clearly and examine carefully what requires correction ... Everyone is beguiled by what he himself writes and its faults escape his ear ... A writer is flattered by his own discourses however inelegant. The meaning is often expressed carelessly, or so as to arouse antagonism in the reader, or ambiguously.

Sabinus is to read the work and to correct all such faults. Subsequently Sabinus complained that a volume Ambrose has sent him is difficult to read. Ambrose explains that in his old age he is anxious to choose his words with precision, and to compose his literary works with deliberation. This he finds easier if he writes them down himself than if he dictates them to a scribe.[20]

Ambrose gives as the reason for his fastidiousness that he wants to make sure that he is disseminating 'sound faith and a sober confession'.[21] A religious opponent must not find any words which could be construed to support heretical beliefs. But almost certainly there was also another reason. In late antiquity letters were recognised as a distinct literary genre, one which offered highly educated men a medium in which they could exercise and display their education, taste and learning, irrespective of their everyday occupation and way of life. Ambrose had enjoyed a very

---

[16] Paulinus, *Vita Ambr.* 23; *Ep. ex.* 1 (M41), 25; *Ep. ex.* 10 (M57), 27.

[17] See Faller and Zelzer 1982: lxxxv–vi.

[18] See Faller and Zelzer 1990: xvi.   [19] *Ep.* 32 (M48), 2.

[20] *Ep.* 37 (M47), 2: *nobis curae est senilem sermonem familiari usu ad unguem distinguere, et lento quodam figere gradu.*

[21] *Ep.* 32 (M48), 3: *fidei sinceritas et confessionis sobrietas.*

full education in both Latin and Greek rhetoric, at a time when good knowledge of Greek was becoming rare in the West. He certainly used his letters to display his considerable literary skill, good Latin style and learning, particularly of course his knowledge of the text of the Bible, but also of Cicero, Virgil[22] and Pliny, at least when writing to a correspondent who would recognise and appreciate allusions to Latin classics.

Ambrose's collection was divided into ten books. We know this because in the manuscript the words *explicit liber* and *incipit liber* seem to have signalled the end of each book and the start of the next.[23] The books are of very different lengths, Book x being by far the longest. It is significant that there are just ten books, that is the same number of books as in the classical collection of the younger Pliny. Moreover Ambrose's tenth book, like Pliny's Book x, is concerned with high politics, and its author's relations with the secular state and successive emperors. (This book will be discussed in the final section of this chapter.) The similarities cannot be accidental. Ambrose's collection is clearly, at least in this respect, modelled on that of Pliny, as is the collection of the letters of Ambrose's contemporary, the famous pagan senator and orator Aurelius Symmachus, who too preserved copies of his letters for eventual publication. When he died in 402, it was left to his son, Memmius Symmachus, to edit his father's letters, and like Ambrose he arranged them in ten books, of which the last is once more composed of letters to emperors. Ambrose was a committed Christian and Symmachus a conservative pagan, but both had been brought up in the same literary culture. Ambrose certainly wanted his writings to be appreciated not only for their Christian message but also for their literary style. In 384 Aurelius Symmachus had addressed a speech to the emperor Valentinian II arguing for the restoration of the Altar of Victory to the senate chamber at Rome, and Ambrose had answered him in a speech refuting Symmachus' arguments, one by one. Ambrose included both speeches in his collection, and in so doing challenged readers to compare not only the religious arguments of the two men, but also their oratorical skills.

While Ambrose surely had Pliny's collection of letters in mind when he composed his own collection, his letters are very different from those of Pliny. What then are the characteristics of Ambrose's collection? First some negatives. The letters are not in chronological order. Ambrose has made no attempt to arrange the letters in the order in which he had

---

[22] List of allusions to Virgil: Faller and Zelzer 1996: 48.
[23] Faller and Zelzer 1990: xvii–xviii. The relevant phrase is missing from the end of Book ii, and the beginning of Book iv because the last letters of Book ii and the first letters of Book iv, like the whole of Book iii, have been lost.

written them. He was not concerned to produce an autobiography in letter-form. Nor did he try to provide a complete documentation even of all the sensational and controversial events in which he had been involved. Had that been his aim he would surely have included also every one of the letters which have only been preserved outside the collection.[24] While he has included a letter describing the discovery of the relics of Gervasius and Protasius in 386,[25] he has not included any document describing the discovery in 395 of relics of Nazarius.[26] Ambrose was deeply involved in the Arian controversy, but this bitter dispute figures only occasionally in the collection. Most of the letters relating to the council of Aquileia have been transmitted outside the collection.[27] The collection includes a few letters that show Ambrose acting as the leader and spokesman of the north Italian bishops,[28] but he must have written far more of such letters than he has included to construct and maintain his authority. The collection presents nothing like a complete record of Ambrose's life. What it gives us is rather selected representative glimpses of the wide range of activities that filled Ambrose's time. People ask Ambrose for advice, most often about the meaning of passages of the Bible, but also about practical matters. Letters show Ambrose as a pastor and conciliator,[29] giving instructions to his own clergy,[30] and taking an interest in the election of bishops at Vercelli[31] and at Thessalonica.[32] The letters show him exercising jurisdiction at Verona,[33] but also, and consistently in Book x, that he had been ready to intervene whenever he thought that the rights of the church were being infringed, no matter by whom, even confronting the emperor when necessary. Ambrose's letters have impressed posterity, as Ambrose no doubt hoped that they would, but the letters of, for instance, Basil and Augustine give a much fuller account of the varied business that occupied a bishop in late antiquity. The collection is not focused on Ambrose's activities as a bishop.

---

[24] To us the most surprising omission is *Ep. ex.* 11 (M51) condemning Theodosius I for the massacre of Thessalonica.

[25] *Ep.* 77 (M22).   [26] Paulinus, *Vita Ambr.* 32.2–33.4.

[27] *Epp. ex.* 4–6 (M10–12), 8–9 (M13–14).

[28] He has included in the collection two letters reporting decisions of the Council of Capua of winter 391–92: *Ep.* 70 (M56) on the Antiochene schism, and *Ep.* 71 (M56A) on the case of Bishop Bonosus who denied the virginity of Mary. He has not included any of the letters he wrote on behalf of the Council of Aquileia of 381: *Ep. ex.* 4 (M10), 5 (M11), 6 (M12), 8 (M14), 9 (M13); nor *Ep. ex.*7 on behalf of Roman council of 378, probably written by Ambrose.

[29] *Ep.* 8, a very classical *consolatio*; *Ep.* 9 on deferring baptism; *Epp.* 24 (M82), 35 (M83), 48 (M66), 58–9 (M60 and M84).

[30] *Ep.* 17 (M81).   [31] *Ep. ex.* 14 (M63).

[32] *Epp.* 51–2 (M15 and 16).   [33] *Epp.* 56–7 (M5–6).

Like Pliny, Ambrose used his collection of letters to introduce the reader to numerous acquaintances, to senators, bishops, clerics and laymen, and last but by no means least, emperors. But unlike Pliny, he was not concerned to construct an impressionist panorama of the society in which he lived. The letters contain very few personal details, and as a result many individuals figuring in his correspondence are difficult to identify with persons mentioned in other sources. The shortage of personal and circumstantial information also makes the dating of most of the letters very uncertain, and often impossible.[34] It is, however, clear that Ambrose's choice of letters for preservation was not motivated by snobbery. He was not concerned to publicise the extent of his intimate relations with magnates of the empire. Of his letters to emperors no fewer than eleven have only survived outside his collection. We can be certain that his position would have obliged him to write far more letters to senators and high officials than he has admitted into his collection. Moreover, the letters addressed to individuals whom scholars have identified as secular magnates are usually short and formal.[35] The addressees whose names recur in the collection are simple clerics and laymen. Ambrose was out to show that he has not been a respecter of persons.

Ambrose, unlike for instance Synesius, tells his correspondents little, or indeed most often nothing, about his own circumstances. He did not write letters in order to talk about what he was doing, or to explore his own feelings. This does not mean that he had no feelings. He enjoyed letter-writing as a form of companionship. So he writes to Sabinus: 'I am never less alone than when I seem to be so.[36] For then I summon at pleasure whom I will, and associate to myself those whom I love most or find most congenial, and no man interrupts or intrudes upon us.'[37] But what he enjoyed in correspondence with friends was the discussion of problems posed by the Bible, not exchanges of information about each other's business.

Here are some of the problems discussed in letters: in the first letter of the collection, Ambrose interprets a sentence from Exodus which commands that in a time of plague each Israelite should give half a drachma as a ransom for his life to the Lord.[38] How can a benevolent God say: '*I put*

---

[34] Many of the dates of the edition of the Maurist Fathers are unreliable: Palanque 1931: 480–556, as are those still cited in Beyenka 1967.

[35] E.g. in Book VIII, *Epp.* 58 (M60), 59 (M84), 60 (M90), 61 (M89).

[36] Cicero, *De off.* 3.1.1.   [37] *Ep.* 33 (M49), 1.

[38] Ex. 30:11–13. Ambrose interprets the half drachma to mean faith.

to *death and I make alive, I wound and I heal*' (Deut. 32:39)?[39] What is the underlying deeper meaning of Jeremiah's reference to a partridge which has spoken, and fostered a brood that is not hers (Jer. 17:11)?[40] What is the deeper significance of the law concerning a man who has two wives, one whom he loves and the other who is unloved (Deut. 21:16)? Why does God no longer rain down manna as he did on the Israelites in the desert?[41] Why does the Law condemn cross-dressing (Deut. 22:5)?[42] What does the prophet Haggai mean when he says: '*Is it time for you to dwell in carved houses?*' (Hag. 1:4).[43] Why was the Law promulgated if it profited nothing?[44] Sometimes the problem is a pastoral one, for instance: does it make a difference whether one has been a Christian believer since childhood, or only been converted in the course of life?[45] Or, may an official who has inflicted the death penalty receive communion?[46]

The friends to whom letters about such problems were sent were not civil grandees or bishops of prominent towns. Irenaeus, probably a layman,[47] received thirteen letters, more than anybody else. Orontianus, who received eight, was a simple cleric. Among bishops, Sabinus received most letters, eight in all, and, as we have seen, Ambrose did not write to him because he was an important bishop, but because he shared Ambrose's interest in the Bible. Not all letters have been written in reply to a query. Ambrose composed letters on his own initiative,[48] for his own enjoyment, because he was interested in a particular problem, or because he felt lonely. So he writes to Sabinus, first citing Cicero, *De off.* 3.1:[49]

> 'I am never less alone than when I seem to be so' … For then I summon at pleasure whom I will, and associate to myself those whom I love most, or find most congenial; no man interrupts us, or intrudes upon us. Then it is when I more intimately enjoy you, and confer with you on the Scriptures.

Moreover Ambrose sometimes – we do not know how regularly – sent copies of a letter to more than one individual.[50]

---

[39] *Ep.* 9 (M67).   [40] *Ep.* 40 (M32).   [41] *Ep.* 54 (M64).

[42] *Ep.* 15 (M69).   [43] *Ep.* 12 (M30).   [44] *Ep.* 63 (M73).

[45] *Ep.* 13 (M74).   [46] *Ep.* 68 (M26).

[47] But see Faller and Zelzer 1990: xxi, n. 6.

[48] *Ep.* 64 (M74),1; instigated by the day's reading Ambrose tackles the problem of why there are so many things in the Law of the Old Testament which are abrogated by the Gospel.

[49] *Ep.* 33 (M49).

[50] A number of letters continue an argument started in an earlier letter which in the collection is addressed to a different individual. It follows that both letters must have been sent to both addressees, e.g. *Epp.* 39 (M46) and 40 (M32), 64 (M74) and 65 (M75), 50 (M25) and 68 (M26).

This raises the question whether some – or indeed most – of these letters are perhaps not genuine letters at all,[51] but treatises in letter-form like
the moral epistles of Seneca – that they are in fact moral essays, which
Ambrose composed in the form of letters and dispatched to men[52] whom
he knew to be interested in biblical problems, and who would appreciate
his inventiveness in proposing ingenious interpretations that made difficult biblical texts confirm Christian teachings, or convey some message
relevant to problems of contemporary life. Doing this, he would have
behaved like the secular orators Libanius and Symmachus, who sent their
writings to friends and acquaintances who would appreciate them. In the
case of Ambrose, many of letters that apparently answer a question posed
by a correspondent read like genuine letters. But not all letters are written
in reply to a question. So their status, as indeed that of some of the others,
remains uncertain.

The ten books

As we have seen, Ambrose's collection is divided into ten books. With
the possible exception of the letter to Justus opening the whole collection,[53] the first and last letters of each of the ten books do not have any
obvious introductory or concluding function. Neither the books themselves, nor the letters making up the books, are arranged in chronological
order. Letters in the first eight books of the collection of Symmachus' letters are arranged by recipients,[54] and there are traces of this arrangement
in the collection of Ambrose. In Book IV, all letters, with one exception,
are addressed to Irenaeus, and in Book V all but three to Orontianus. But
some letters to Irenaeus and Orontianus, concerning topics similar to
those treated in Books IV and V, are found in other books as well. A letter to Justus introduces the whole collection, but the only other letter to
Justus is in Book VIII. Moreover the predominance of a single addressee
is not observed elsewhere. Nor are letters dealing with related themes

---

[51] The question is raised by Faller and Zelzer 1990: xxxviii–ix. Zelzer considers that most of the 'letters' are sermons or tracts in letter-form, so Faller and Zelzer 1990: xxxv.

[52] His collection does not include any letters to women, in this, as in many other respects, differing
from the letters of Chrysostom. Cf. Allen 2014a.

[53] See Faller and Zelzer 1990: xxxviii–xxxix. Justus, bishop of Lyons, who had supported Ambrose at
the Council of Aquileia in 381, soon after became a hermit in Egypt. Zelzer concluded that this is
not a genuine letter but one specially composed for this position, to honour his former friend and
colleague. She points out that in ch. 15 and so also presumably in ch. 22 Ambrose appeals no longer
to Justus, but to 'you Christians', i.e. a Christian congregation. The only other letter addressed to
Justus is not a reply to a question from Justus. It too could be a free composition of Ambrose's.

[54] Seeck 1883; Cecconi 2002.

necessary juxtaposed. When assigning letters to the later books, Ambrose was evidently more concerned with achieving variety, as regards both addressees and subject matter. The collection was not to be read as an autobiography or a history, but as an anthology.[55]

The letters of Book I are addressed to different individuals, but every one includes allegorical interpretations of biblical texts derived from Philo, the Jewish philosopher writing in Alexandria in the first century.[56] A great part of Book II has evidently been lost, but many of the argument of two of its four letters are again derived from Philo.[57] Book III is missing. Six of the seven letters in Book IV are addressed to Irenaeus. One letter (*Ep.* 14) once more makes use of Philo.[58] Some of the allegorical interpretations of *Letters* 12 and 13 are derived from works of Origen, the Christian philosophical theologian.[59] *Letter* 11 even has arguments derived from the pagan philosopher Plotinus.[60] Book V is made up of nine letters. Of these six are addressed to Orontianus, a cleric who had been ordained by Ambrose. All are concerned with the soul, its route to salvation and the stuff it is made of, and all the six make use of allegorical interpretations of the Bible derived from Origen.[61] However each of the book's last three letters has a different subject. *Letter* 24 (M82) shows Ambrose acting as an arbitrator. *Letter* 25 (M53) is addressed to the emperor Theodosius I in 392/3, and deals with the burial of Valentinian II, while the last letter (*Ep.* 26 [M54]), is addressed to a friend. So the letter to the emperor has not been given any positional prominence.

The contents of Book VI are various. Four letters are to Sabinus, bishop of Placentia, a colleague whose literary and theological judgement Ambrose respected. Of these, the letter which was certainly the last to be written as it comments on the decision of Paulinus of Nola and his wife to give away their property as late as 395, is actually the first in the book.[62] This letter turns into a defence of asceticism. The second letter, which is addressed to Chromatius, bishop of Aquileia, has also been written late in Ambrose's life. It offers justification of God's way with man and makes use of Philo.[63] Two letters to

[55] Gibson shows that this was normal in ancient letter-collections; Gibson 2012: 67–70: 'arrangement by chronology is not the default position of ancient letter collections.'

[56] Philo's *Quis rerum divinarum heres* has been used in *Ep.* 1.45–53 and repeatedly in *Ep.* 2; *De fuga et inventione* in *Epp.* 3 and 4; *quod omnis probus liber sit*, in *Epp.* 6 and 7.

[57] *Quod omnis sapiens liber*, in *Ep.*7; *De fuge et inventione*, in *Ep.*10.

[58] *Epp.* 14: Philo, *De Cain et Abel*, 1.

[59] See footnotes in Faller and Zelzer 1968: 92–100.

[60] From Plotinus 1, 6: see footnotes in Faller and Zelzer 1968: 78–92.

[61] *Epp.* 18–23 (M70–1, 77, 35–6): see Faller and Zelzer 1968: 128–70.

[62] *Ep.* 27 (M58).

[63] Philo, *Vita Moysis*; see footnotes in Faller and Zelzer 1968: 187–94.

Orontianus, and one to Sabinus, deal with problems raised by the creation narrative, and again each has arguments derived from Philo.[64] This particular discussion seems to have been instigated around 386 by the appearance of the *Hexaemeron*, Ambrose's commentary on the creation narrative of Genesis. Amid these letters dealing with religious subjects, there is a highly political letter, which at least purports to be Ambrose's official report to the emperor Valentinian II on his second embassy to the usurper Maximus.[65] If the date of that embassy, which could have taken place either in 384–5 or in 386, remains uncertain, so does the true nature of the document. In my opinion, Ambrose has rewritten what may have originally been a genuine report to show that he had always been a strong and fearless opponent of the usurper.[66]

Book VII, one of the longer books in the collection, is again made up of letters addressed to different individuals on a variety of subjects. It opens with a letter to a newly appointed bishop, Constantius, advising how he should use his sermons to teach morality.[67] The book ends with three letters related to the election of a new bishop at Thessalonica. There are two letters to Sabinus and one to Irenaeus which in respect of their subject matter are similar to the letters addressed to the two men in respectively Books VI and IV.[68] A letter to Studius, who may have been *praefectus urbi* of Constantinople, gives an affirmative answer to the question whether a magistrate who has inflicted capital punishment may receive communion.[69] Three letters are concerned with problems of exegesis of the Bible.[70] This book also has a number of notes and short letters commending the carrier of the letter, of the kind that make up the bulk of secular collections.

Book VIII starts with two letters that are largely made up of a succession of allegorical interpretations derived from Philo.[71] These are followed by an intriguing pair of letters addressed to Syagrius, bishop of Verona.[72] In the first Ambrose rebukes Syagrius for demanding a physical examination by a midwife of a consecrated virgin accused of sexual impurity. The rebuke is long and indignant. Ambrose has had the case tried at Milan and found the girl not guilty. By insisting on the physical examination Syagrius has treated chastity with contempt. But the tone of the following letter is quite different. It

---

[64] *Epp.* 29, 31 and 34: Philo, *De opificio mundi.*
[65] *Ep.*30 (M24).   [66] Liebeschuetz 2005: 349–51.
[67] *Ep.* 36 (M2), making use of Philo, *Ioseph.*   [68] *Epp.* 37 (M47), 39 (M46), 40 (32).
[69] *Ep.* 50 (M25). On Studius see *PLRE* I: 859.
[70] *Ep.* 39 (M46) to Sabinus; *Ep.* 40 (M.32) to Irenaeus, using Origen's *Commentary on Jeremiah*; *Ep.* 44 (M68) with allusions to Virgil, and *Ep.* 48 (M66), using Philo, *De vita Moysis*, to Romulus, on whom see *PLRE* I: 771 *s.v.* 'Flavius Pisidius Romulus'.
[71] *Ep.* 54 (M64) to Irenaeus, and *Ep.* 55 (M8) to Justus, both using Philo, *De fuga et inventione.*
[72] *Epp.* 56–7(M5–6). *Ep.* 57 uses Josephus, *Antiquitates Iudaicae.*

offers Syagrius an elaborate retelling of the grisly narrative of Judges 19–20, the story of how thoroughly a Levite avenged the mass-rape of his wife by the Benjaminites with the slaying of no fewer than 25,000 members of the guilty tribe. The moral of the tale is said to be that it shows the high respect the people of the Bible had for chastity and the passion they displayed in avenging its violation. The tone of the second letter is quite different from the first. The reader cannot avoid feeling that Ambrose is now inviting Syagrius to enjoy a squalid horror story, expertly told in accordance with the rules which both bishops had learnt at school. Perhaps Ambrose realised that he had gone too far, and that Syagrius had every right to resent the bishop of Milan's intervention in his jurisdiction, and wrote a second letter in order to take some of the heat out of the situation, and to reconcile his colleague. Two short letters are concerned with the reconciliation by Ambrose of the father and son of a family of high officials.[73] The final brief notes are also addressed to high officials.[74]

The opening letter of Book IX gives advice to a newly consecrated bishop of Tridentum.[75] The rest interpret situations or passages from the Old Testament. Three letters are addressed to Irenaeus,[76] one to Orontianus,[77] one to an otherwise unknown Clementianus,[78] and one to a certain Constantius.[79] *Letters* 63 and 64 to Irenaeus have allegorical interpretations taken from Origen's commentary on Paul's Epistle to the Romans, perhaps read in the translation of Rufinus. *Letters* 66 to Orontianus and 65 to Clementianus both include exegesis of the Epistle to the Galatians. Since Origen's commentary on Galatians has been lost, we cannot tell whether Ambrose has also used Origen when writing these two letters.

Ambrose's use of allegorical exegesis

The survey of the contents of the first nine books has shown that letters discussing biblical problems and composed largely of arguments based on

---

[73] *Ep.* 58 (M60), *Ep.* 59 (M84) on Cynegius and Paternus see *PLRE* I: 671–2 *s.v.* 'Aemilius Florus Paternus 6', possibly related to 'Maternus Cynegius 3', PP Or 384–88, cos 388, *PLRE* I: 235–6.

[74] *Ep.* 60 (M90), *Ep.* 61 (M89), possibly Fl. Claudius Antonius 5, cos. 382 and Faltonius Probus Alypius 13, PUR 391 cf. *PLRE* I: 77 and 49.

[75] *Ep.* 62 (M19) includes a long retelling of the story of Sampson, based on Josephus, *Antiquitates Iudaicae*.

[76] *Ep.* 63 (M73) using Origen, translated by Rufinus on Paul's Epistle to the Romans; *Ep.* 64 (M74) with use of same commentary of Origen translated by Rufinus; *Ep.* 68 (M26). *Ep.* 64 (M74) and *Ep.* 65 (M75) were sent to both Irenaeus and Clementianus, and *Ep.* 68 (M26) and 50 (M. 25) were probably sent to both Irenaeus and Studius.

[77] *Ep.* 66 (M78).

[78] *Ep.* 65 (M.75), possibly with use of Origen (named in l.4).

[79] *Ep.* 69 (M72), with use of Origen-Rufinus, *In Romanos*, PG 14: 910–13.

a succession of biblical quotations predominate. That this would be so is in fact signalled in the opening letter of Book 1, which dedicates the collection to Justus bishop of Lyons. For in this letter Ambrose describes the correspondence as fables in letter-form, and as a conversation at a distance devoted to the interpretation of the heavenly oracle, that is of scripture.[80] The letter itself is a discussion of Ex. 30:12–16. All the subsequent five letters making up Book 1 concern problems of interpretation of biblical texts; and biblical texts dominate Books iii–vi and ix. They are less prominent in Books vii and viii, but they are present there too. They are absent only from the political Book x.

Ambrose's interpretation is invariably allegorical. Augustine's account of his conversion illustrates why allegory was employed so widely in biblical commentaries, sermons and dogmatic controversy in late antiquity and subsequently. The young Augustine was strongly drawn to Christianity, not least through the influence of Monica, his mother, but he was long held back from full commitment by the fact the Bible included many passages that seemed far from edifying. When he came to Milan and heard Ambrose interpreting such awkward passages allegorically, the difficulty disappeared. 'The Catholic faith … I now concluded with myself, might well be maintained without absurdity … after I had heard one or two places of the Old Testament resolved … which when I understood literally, I was slain.'[81] The fact that Christianity is a religion of the Book was an advantage it had over the traditional cults which originated in pre-literate times. But fundamentalist interpretation raised difficulties – as it still does – which allegorical interpretation of the awkward passages could, and can, by-pass.

The difficulties which troubled Ambrose and his correspondents are generally not as fundamental as those that kept Augustine from becoming a fully committed Christian. The Arian controversy, in which Ambrose took so prominent and aggressive a part on the Nicene side, does not figure at all prominently in these discussions. Many of the questions seem to be motivated by interest in the problem raised, rather than doubts threatening the questioner's faith, though some are about important questions of doctrine or conduct. Ambrose generally replies in a relaxed style which is quite different from the intense aggressiveness of his dogmatic writings. Ambrose learnt his allegorical technique from Philo, and, as we have seen,

---

[80] *Ep.* 1 (M7), 1–2: *ut epistulares fabulas et sermonem absentium ad interpretationem conferamus oraculi caelestis.*

[81] Augustine, *Conf.* v.14, tr. Watts 1996/1: 258.

a majority of these letters offer numerous interpretations taken from recognisable passages in works of that Jewish philosopher.[82] In fact, the questions Ambrose was asked by his correspondents are very much like the questions Philo set himself to answer in his commentaries on episodes in the Old Testament. For other letters Ambrose has derived interpretations mainly from Origen, or from the Latin translations of Origen made by Jerome and Rufinus.[83] As we have seen, letters predominantly influenced by Philo are found in different books from those making use mainly of Origen. Ambrose does not name Philo, Origen or Jerome, but it may well be that Ambrose was inspired to write letters by reading particular works of one or other of these authors. It is also the case that while Ambrose appropriated many interpretations from his Greek sources, he has worked them into a composition which is essentially his own, and he certainly also enjoyed inventing striking and original interpretations himself.

While these letters consist of a succession of exegetical material, they do not provide a systematic interpretation of a single text. Ambrose uses his correspondent's request for information only as the starting-point for a chain of moral or doctrinal reflections all backed up by citations from the Bible, many to be understood allegorically, others literally. This procedure demonstrates Ambrose's formidable knowledge of the text of the Bible, as well as remarkable sensitivity to the power of biblical language. The sequence of allegories sometimes takes Ambrose a long way from his original problem. His procedure is not that of a scholar, but rather of a preacher, trying to preach a lively sermon. As one edifying admonition is followed by another and another and so on, it is often difficult to recognise any logical thread linking successive ideas. Ambrose was of course among other things a poet, and it might be said that he composed these letters as a poet composes poetry, and it was surely Ambrose the poet who was impressed by the vivid, though quite unclassical imagery of the Bible, and enjoyed adopting biblical metaphors to illustrate and give authority to his own arguments.

There is a certain ambiguity about Ambrose's use of biblical quotations in these letters. Ambrose, like all the Fathers of the church, believed that the Bible was inspired by God.[84] Following Philo and Origen,[85] he assumed that it could be read not only for the information conveyed by the literal meaning of its words, but for moral and doctrinal truths, which

---

[82] Lucchesi 1977; Savon 1977.
[83] *Epp.* 18 (M70), 21 (M34) to 23 (M36), 40 (M32), 63 (M73), 65 (M75), 69 (M72).
[84] Hanson 1959: 186–209, mainly about Origen's reconciliation of inspiration and allegory.
[85] Hanson 1959: 45–53 (Philo), 162–86 (Origen).

could be accessed by allegorical interpretation.[86] While for Ambrose all three kinds of interpretation were equally valid in theory, he certainly considered the two deeper kinds of spiritual interpretation more important. So it would seem that when he cites a sentence from scripture to support an argument, he is not only illustrating a point, but also intending to give it divine authority. Nevertheless when one reads some Ambrose's more extravagant interpretations, one wonders whether he really believed that they conferred more authority on his teaching than quotations from traditional Classics, above all from Virgil, were thought to give to the orations of secular orators.

Book x

Book x is different from the others in several respects. Its letters are exclusively concerned with historical events, and Ambrose the bishop is from the beginning to the end at the centre of the narrative. Moreover, we are introduced to a different Ambrose, not the good colleague, the caring pastor and above all the man to consult if you have a problem understanding the Bible, but the fearless upholder of the rights of the church, ready to contradict the highest authorities to prevent any concessions being made to pagans, sectarians or Jews. Book x is also much the longest book.

The first letter addressed to Theophilus, bishop of Alexandria in 392, shows Ambrose as spokesman of western bishops assembled at the Council of Capua, asking Theophilus to broker an agreement between two rival claimants to the see of Antioch, and to end a dispute that had long divided the church. In the second letter Ambrose, once again writing on behalf of the bishops assembled at Capua, calls on the bishops of Macedonia to investigate the case of Bonosus, bishop of Naisus (Nish) or perhaps of Serdica (Sofia), whom the bishops at Capua had found guilty of heresy and deposed.

There follows a dossier of documents which shows Ambrose the politician in action at the highest level of politics. In 384 Symmachus, prefect of the city of Rome and the chairman of the Roman senate, petitioned the emperor Valentinian II to restore to the senate chamber the Altar of Victory which had been removed in 357 by the pious Christian emperor Constantius II. Ambrose immediately wrote a letter opposing the request and the petition was duly rejected. The collection includes Symmachus' speech arguing for the restoration, Ambrose's letter opposing it, and finally

---

[86] Prologue to *Commentary on Luke*.

what amount to a full refutation, argument by argument, of the speech of Symmachus. The affair of the Altar of Victory has often been seen as the decisive engagement in a conflict of religions, signifying the final victory of Christianity over the traditional religion of Rome. It is, however, hardly noticed by other writers of the period. It owes its fame to its presentation in the collection of Ambrose.

There follows a letter which Ambrose purports to have written in winter 388/9 to the emperor Theodosius I warning him neither to punish the participants in the burning of a synagogue in the frontier fortress city of Callinicum, nor to compel the local bishop to rebuild it. The letter, as we read it in the collection, implies that the bishop was at the time still under orders to have the synagogue rebuilt. In fact careful reading of the letter shows that the emperor has already rescinded the order.[87] Much of what Ambrose tells the emperor in this letter, the emperor evidently knows already, and has even acted upon. It looks as if Ambrose has redacted the original letter[88] to turn it into a full statement of Ambrose's case, not only for the emperor but for the record and to guide posterity.[89]

The last episode to be documented in the collection is a conflict between Ambrose and the imperial rulers of the West, Valentinian II and his wife Justina, which was drawn out from around Easter 385 to Easter 386. It arose over imperial support for an Arian bishop at Milan, and more specifically over repeated demands that Ambrose should allow one of his churches to be used for Arian services. Ambrose refused, organised a sit-in in the threatened church, got the besieged congregation to sing hymns, and displayed not only courage, but also great demagogic skill to prevail against the imperial authorities. The last document in the dossier describes the discovery of relics of the martyrs Gervase and Protase which Ambrose evidently interpreted – or wished his readers to interpret – as a sign that God approved the stand that he had taken.

Book x is certainly not simply a collection of correspondence. The dossier on the Altar of Victory includes a speech of Symmachus and a 'letter' that is in fact a speech answering Symmachus' speech. The letter to Theodosius about the synagogue at Callinicum reads as if it had been heavily edited to make what is in effect a presentation of Ambrose's case addressed to a wider public. The letters that refer to Ambrose's conflict

[87] *Ep. ex.* 1 (M41), 27. The fact is half admitted in *Ep.* 74.9

[88] A parallel case is *Ep.* 30 (M24), Ambrose's purported report to Valentinian II on his second embassy to the usurper Maximus, which cannot possibly represent what Ambrose actually wrote to the emperor. See Liebeschuetz 2005: 349–51.

[89] Note that *Ep. ex.* 1A is a version of this letter without the final threat that Ambrose will raise this matter in church and in public if Theodosius will not hear him in the privacy of the palace.

with Justina include *Letter* 75A, which is in fact a sermon with which Ambrose successfully won the support of his congregation. They also include *Letters* 76 and 77, addressed to Marcellina, the sister of Ambrose, but clearly aimed at a much wider public. The succession of documents bearing on the conflict of 385/6 is interrupted by a long oration on the death of the emperor Theodosius I, which happened nine years later. The insertion provides variety, but it also makes the point that while Ambrose would always resist even an emperor who transgressed into the sphere of the church, he would nevertheless always remain a loyal subject of a pious Nicene emperor.

Conclusion

Book x clearly has been composed to present Ambrose as he wanted to be seen by contemporaries and posterity. Though Ambrose compiled his collection perhaps only two years before Augustine wrote his *Confessions*, Ambrose's work is not an autobiography. Ambrose always keeps his distance. The letters nevertheless tell us a great deal about Ambrose, the man. They reveal an extraordinarily gifted and versatile personality. Ambrose was obviously exceptionally strong-willed, and an extremely skilful politician. He was also outstandingly learned, and he enjoyed discussing the meaning of difficult biblical texts. He was not a literary critic in the modern sense. His motivation was of course ultimately theological, yet he had a poet's sensitivity. His must always have been an overwhelming presence, but he could be very sociable, and he sometimes wrote a letter simply because he felt lonely in his high and responsible office. Above all he was a conscientious pastor, ever anxious for the well-being of his flock. In short, posterity's image of none of the Fathers of the church owes as much to his letters as that of Ambrose.

CHAPTER 8

The letters of Basil of Caesarea and the role of letter-collections in their transmission

Anna Silvas

The last comprehensive series of critical editions of Basil's works by the Maurist Benedictines was published between 1721 and 1730, and no small advance in methodologies has been made since those days. Throughout the twentieth century, investigation of the transmission of Basil's letters made enormous strides. This chapter examines that scholarly progress and the bearing it has on the possibility of a new critical edition of Basil's works, the proposed *Basilii Caesariensis Opera*. The first volume of such a series would be dedicated to a new critical edition of Basil's letters, one of the largest corpora of letters in the Greek language from late antiquity.[1]

Awareness of the extremely complex history of transmission began with the work of Bessières and Turner, who published his work (1923), and was carried forward by Cavallin in the 1940s and Rudberg in the 1950s. A significant change of tack was taken by Fedwick (1993), who reanalysed the functioning of the primitive letter-collections and on that basis reassessed the significance of the sequence of the letters in the text families. The features of these ancient collections will be examined in terms of their addressees, content and style, to give an idea of the rationales of their collators. The early aggregation of letters by Basil's brother, Gregory of Nyssa, will then be compared. Finally I consider whether Fedwick's recommendation that a new edition of Basil's letters be based on these early sub-collections, using the so-called 'batch-style method', should be followed in a new edition.

History of editions of Basil's letters

Editions of Basil's letters began with a small collection published by the Aldine Press in 1499. More than two centuries of editions followed, in

[1] Such a project is, at writing, still a proposal, endorsed by a team of scholars and tentatively approved by Brill, but awaiting further news of funding. Silvas is the volunteer for the first volume.

which editors showed a growing awareness of attending critically to the manuscript sources. The culmination of this earlier phase came with the great edition of all Basil's works, *S.P.N. Basilii Opera Omnia*, by the Maurist Benedictines, Doms Julien Garnier, Prudent Maran and François Faverolles. Garnier had spent twenty years on the project before Maran took over and completed it. Between 1721 and 1730 three tomes appeared comprising Greek text and Latin translation. This was a pioneering exercise in text-critical method. Maran wrote a detailed *Vita* of Basil,[2] and as the fruit of that biographical investigation put the letters into a putative chronological sequence. This new 'Benedictine' numbering became the standard form of referencing Basil's letters for centuries to come. The principal manuscripts collated by the Maurists for Basil's letters were, as far as can be determined, as follows, beginning with the Maurists' own nomenclature:[3]

1   Coislinianus primus, Parisinus Coislinianus 237 (o1 in Fedwick's schema).
2   Harleanus, Parisinus 1020 S (v1).
3   Mediceus, Florence, BML Plut. iv,14 (n1)
4   Regius primus, Parisinus 506 (Regius 2293) (b1).
5   Regius secundus, Parisinus 967 (e2)
6   Coislinianus secundus, Parisinus 1021 S (Coislinianus 288) (e1).
7   Vaticanus gr. 434 (c6)
8   'Insignis ecclesiae Parisiensis codex', Paris, BN Suppl. gr. 334 (d3)
9   Claromontanus, Berolinensis, DSB Phill. 1427 (gr. 23) (w2)[4]

Of this list, however, it seems that only the first three were consistently used throughout the edition.

Investigation of Basil's letters in the early twentieth century

Before and during the period of the First World War, Abbé Marius Bessières (d. 1918) carried out the first exhaustively critical study of the transmission of Basil's letters. Bessières' results were published

---

[2] Maran 1730 = PG 29: 5–177. Originally Maran's *Vita Basilii* was published in the third and final volume (1730). However, the three volumes were rearranged by J.-P. Migne as four, PG 29–32. PG 29 and 30 cover vol. 1 of Garnier and Maran's edition, with the *Vita* reassigned to the very beginning of PG 29 as a kind of preface to the whole *Opera omnia*.

[3] See Fedwick 1993: 288.

[4] To this list, Fedwick 1993: 288 adds the comment: 'The Reg. 2502 is u2. f6 is quoted wrongly as Reg. 2896 (instead of 2986). Amand de Mendieta stands also correction with regard to Reg. 2897,2 which is no other than u2.'

posthumously: introduced at length, edited and annotated by C. H. Turner.[5] In choosing his sources, Bessières excluded anthologies of fewer than a hundred letters and mutilated manuscripts. In all, he found acceptable and collated some twenty-seven manuscripts, far more than the eight or nine that had been collated, some more thoroughly and some less, by the Benedictines. Bessières used three criteria to discern the relationship of manuscripts:

1 the age of the MS;
2 the order of the letters in each MS;
3 variant readings.

Focusing especially on the sequence of the letters of each collection, Bessières discerned two main branches according to the order in which each codex presents the letters. He called these branches A and B, under which he grouped several sub-branches or families. It seemed to Bessières (and this is a very important point) that the more systematic arrangements of the letters reflected the later intervention of copy-editors. Such, notably, are sub-collections of letters to the same addressee, which is a feature of his Ab, Ac and B text families.

Fedwick cites Turner's summary of that editorial criterion which is based on the logical or illogical arrangement of letters:

> [S]ince there would probably be in the minds of scribes and editors a desire to classify the *disiecta membra* of an extensive correspondence by grouping together letters directed to the same correspondent or letters bearing on the same or similar subjects, a group of [manuscripts] where this sort of classification is extensively adopted is likely to belong to a later stage of development of the collection than a group in which the letters are less logically arranged.[6]

It was with such reasoning that Bessières concluded that the Aa family, with its more disorderly aggregation (or collections) of letters, was the most primitive witness to the transmission of Basil's letters.

Bessières' discernment of the two main text branches and the several text families within each branch was, in the main, accepted, corroborated and amplified by subsequent research throughout much of the twentieth century. The great names of later researchers of Basil's letters begin with Anders Cavallin (1944). His *Studien zu den Briefen des hl. Basilius* confirmed and gave further precision to Bessières' twofold

---

[5] Bessières and Turner 1919–22, and 1923.
[6] Turner, 'Introduction', in Bessières 1923: 2. See Fedwick 1993: xxviii.

classification of manuscripts. Cavallin was the first to address seriously questions of authenticity, demonstrating that Basil was *not* the author of several letters, notably 'Basil's' *Letter* 38 on the distinction between *ousia* and *hypostasis*, which he reassigned to Gregory of Nyssa.[7] Nine years later, another Swedish scholar, Rudberg (1953), published his *Études sur la tradition manuscrite de saint Basile*.[8] He built on the work of both Bessières and Cavallin, and advanced the cause by identifying a further nine manuscripts not known to Bessières. He brought the tally of accredited codices to about thirty-five.[9] Bessières, Cavallin and Rudberg maintained the view that branch A represented an older transmission than branch B, and that within A, the Aa family was nearest to the primitive collection of letters.

Beginning in 1957, Yves Courtonne published his new critical edition of the letters of Basil, together with a French translation.[10] In the main he made a judicious selection from the codices recommended by the earlier scholars of the twentieth century, although he missed collating some codices that perhaps might have been used. He maintained the Benedictine chronological arrangement, and paid little attention to questions of authenticity.

Such were some seventy years of the critical study of the transmission of Basil's letters, in which the scholars of the period more or less confirmed and extended Bessières' thesis. Then came the work of Paul Jonathan Fedwick (1993), comprising one volume of his monumental *Bibliotheca Basiliana Vniversalis*.

Fedwick's textual analyses advocated a significant modification of approach, or, to speak more truly, instituted a revolution in the approach to the transmission of Basil's letters.

After noting the 'messiness' of the order of Aa, and the more orderly sequence of the other families and of the whole of Branch B, Fedwick reports Bessières' conclusion, that 'Bz, of which the distinguishing mark is the great messiness of its order, is the more primitive collection, first, of B, and then even of Aa'.[11] Even Turner pointed out the inadmissibility of this claim, if Bessières Aa is the sole ultimate source of the rest. The coherence of these two statements requires further probing.

Fedwick quotes Turner in a partial answer to Bessières' question by conjecturing that within Aa itself, certain suture lines between earlier

---

[7] Cavallin 1944: 71–7.
[8] Rudberg 1953. See also Rudberg 1981: esp. 55–6, 61–2.
[9] The information here is taken from Courtonne 2003/1: xv–xvi.
[10] Courtonne 2003.   [11] Fedwick 1993: xxvi.

sub-collections can be discerned. This hypothesis of aggregation became a certainty for Gribomont. Bessières had suggested that the first hundred letters of Aa might be the same as the letters first sent by Gregory Nazianzen to Nicoboulus. Rudberg however thought that they might be represented by the anthology in Bx.

Fedwick set out the arguments for his own arrangements and his new system of nomenclature.[12] In his considered opinion, Bessières' criteria of classification are of doubtful value. It seems that Fedwick was first put on the track of reprioritising the text families by Paul Gallay's work on the transmission of Gregory Nazianzen's letters.[13] Gallay had found it necessary to investigate also the transmission of Basil's letters, because a number of these manuscripts also contain letters of Gregory Nazianzen. Gallay agreed with the priority of Ab over Aa in the transmission of Basil's letters. Fedwick explains:

> There are, however, at least three reasons for preferring Bessières' Ab to Aa. First, the titles in Ea [= Ab] are short, whereas in Ec [= Aa] they are longer. Although neither is original, it is obvious that the compiler of corpus Ec is not as innocent of editorial intervention as claimed by Bessières.[14] It is to the author of Ea that such credit should go since he limited himself to the shortest identifications possible. Second, the keeping in one place of the letters addressed to the same person was indicative to Gallay of a more ancient origin. But not so to Bessières, who considered the messier [manuscripts] to be the more reliable ... Finally Ea provides the text of the approximately 40 untitled letters omitted by Ec. The source of these so called ἀνεπίγραφοι has been looked for in B. But is this certain or even necessary? I do not think so. A more plausible suggestion is that initially all the letters existed *in batches*, that is, Basil kept together in his files letters addressed to the same correspondents together. Undoubtedly some of his correspondents like Eusebius of Samosata and Gregory of Nazianzus also kept copies of these letters together. In my opinion, it was the author of Ec who dismembered these blocks and not that of Ea who put them back together. In other words, corpus Ea stems from the simple, almost mechanical, assembling of scattered lots, whereas Ec originates from a desire to choose some of the letters.[15]

Fedwick explains why he departs from the criterion espoused by Bessières, and how he would reprioritise the criteria for judging the manuscript

---

[12] Fedwick 1993: xxvii–xxxiii.

[13] Fedwick 1993: xxix. See Gallay 1957: 20, and 2003: xx–xiv.

[14] Fedwick 1993: xxxi adds: 'The author of Ea gives us in some instances the original titles of some letters, whereas the author of Ec makes these titles their incipits.'

[15] Fedwick 1993: xxix.

families of Basil's letters (his term is the 'corpora') according to the following criteria:[16]

1   textual variants;
2   the titles of letters;
3   the ordering of the letters;
4   omissions of the same work;
5   inclusions of a rare work (usually spurious).

For Fedwick, the most important criterion is the first; the rest are in
descending order of importance. Using these criteria he completely over-
hauled the classification of manuscripts, taking into his account many
other manuscripts, generally of a later vintage, that he located through
an exhaustive search of library catalogues. Fedwick's ordering of the letters is based on a revaluation of the role of primitive letter-collections. He
explains:

> Rather than basing itself on the unreliable chronological order, *this sys-
> tem reproduces the batch-style method* whereby letters addressed to the same
> recipients are kept together. It follows thus the system of the most authori-
> tative [manuscripts] of both families A and B except for the numbers
> themselves. In the [manuscripts] in very few instances the same numbers
> are assigned consistently to the same letters. However, one can ascertain
> in them a definite McTaggart pattern: i.e. almost always the same letters
> appear before other letters.[17] Hence, any of my numbers, e.g. in the corres-
> pondence with Eusebios of Samosata, reflect which letter is placed before
> another letter. In other words, my numbers, despite not being exactly the
> numbers of any given MS, reflect precisely which letters are placed before
> or after other letters.[18]

As a specimen of his new system of nomenclature, Fedwick gives a portion of his listing of letters according to the 'batch' method, and in
alphabetical order.[19] The Benedictine chronological numeration is also
noted, in the case of multiple letters to the same addressee, after the
back-slash.[20]

---

[16] Fedwick 1993: xxx.
[17] i.e. the succession of letters is commonly the same in the manuscripts.
[18] Fedwick 1993: 673 (emphasis mine).   [19] Fedwick 1993: xii–xiii.
[20] Mar 203: *Maritimis episkopis* ('to the bishops of the seaboard'); Mart 74: *Martiniano* ('to
Martinianus'); MaxPh 9: *Maximo philosopho* ('to Maximus the philosopher'); MaxSc 277: *Maximo
scholastic* ('to Maximus the scholasticus'); MelAnt 1/57: *Meletio Antiocheno* ('to Meletius of
Antioch') 1/57, MelAnt 2/68, MelAnt 3/120, MelAnt 4/129, MelAnt 5/216 and MelAnt 6/89;
MelArc 193: *Meletio archiatro* ('to Meletius the archphysician'); Mil 106: *Militi* ('to a soldier'); Mod
1/279: *Modesto praefecto* ('to Modestus the Prefect') 1/279, Mod 2/280, Mod 3/111, Mod 4/110, Mod
5/281 and Mod 6/104:

Fedwick, in discussing variant readings, airs the possibility that Basil himself may have made changes to his own text, but dismisses it.[21] Perhaps this was a little too precipitate. In my edition of the *Asketikon of St Basil the Great*, I particularly targeted his dismissal of this possibility in deciding which historical format of the *Great Asketikon* had most to commend it.[22] Certainly, with the *Asketikon* at least, Basil was an incessant 'copy-editor' of his own work. In my considered opinion, the Pontic recension, otherwise known as the Vulgate, may well have been Basil's last revision, during his last (lengthy) visit to Annisa in about 376, and his brother Peter may also well have had a hand in it, indeed may even have suggested it to Basil, being himself a monastic father at Annisa.[23]

The primitive collections: some conjectures

Now that the importance of the primitive collections of letters prior to the later aggregations is being highlighted, it is opportune to speculate on how these primitive collections of Basil's letters might have come about.

It seems obvious that so good an administrator as Basil, and one not entirely careless of legal realities, kept an archival copy of his letters that dealt with controversial political and doctrinal matters, or letters that were appeals to government officials. It seems likely, therefore, that some considerable body of letters is to be sourced in his chancery in Caesarea. Such a core of letters is not exactly an 'authorial' collection in the sense of an *epistolarion* deliberately put together for literary and/or autobiographical purposes, as for example, with Gregory Nazianzen. The copies kept in Basil's chancery archives were primarily motivated by pragmatic considerations: they were an insurance against the misuse and interpolation of his letters for polemical purposes by those hostile to him and the causes he represented. All the same, Basil was not oblivious of the legacy of documentation he would leave after his death.[24]

One letter, to Eustathius of Sebasteia (*Ep.* 223), is the most highly autobiographical of all Basil's letters, a kind of *apologia* of all his dealings with the once admired ascetic model of his youth, but whose covert Arianising politics Basil could no longer deny. This letter was fraught with both political and doctrinal significance, and was obviously a public letter

---

[21] Fedwick 1993: 667–8. [22] Silvas 2005: 11–13.
[23] Annisa was the family country villa, one day's journey west of Neocaesarea in Pontus, which under Macrina the Younger's guidance was gradually transformed into a classic 'Basilian' coenobitic community.
[24] To infer from his lifelong work of augmenting, editing and re-editing of the *Asketikon*.

significant on a macro-ecclesial level, so there can be no doubt that he kept a reserve copy in Caesarea. The one surviving letter to Ambrose of Milan dealt with macro-ecclesial politics, and was surely copied for his files; likewise the surviving letters to Athanasius of Alexandria, to the bishops of the West, to various named bishops of Syria, and to the church at Nicopolis. The body of letters sent to the young bishop Amphilochius of Iconium often have a warm personal note, but are on the whole truly public letters, since they report authoritatively on the church's administration of penance. These too were surely backed up in Basil's files. Yet Amphilochius himself must also have retained them for ready reference, and perhaps even had them copied and circulated. Some of these letters survived, not in early collections of Basil's letters, but by their own unique stream of transmission in the literature of church canons.

A range of letters sent to officials and persons of rank are in the nature of public letters of advocacy or of consolation or of rebuke, and copies of these too must have been kept in Caesarea. Some of these addressees are known only by their function, as in *Letters* 84 (to a governor), 85/86 (to the governor), 88 (unaddressed, for the tax-collector), 257 (to monks harassed by the Arians), 283/1196/1197 (to a widow), 286 (to a prison superintendent), 303 (to the count of the [imperial] private estates), 311 (to a superior), 333 (to a notary). It is notable that most of these letters occur towards the end of the collections. One immediately thinks of them as a cache of official letters in Basil's files, rather than a posthumous muster of letters from private sources.

The addressees of other letters are named – such addressees, for example, as Aburgius, Sophronius, Modestus the prefect, Eustathius the physician, Terentius the count, Candidianus, Leontius the sophist, Helladius the count, the noblewoman Simplicia, the noblewoman Caesaria, the canoness Theodora, Sophronius the magistrate, Magninianus, Julitta the widow and many others.

When discussing Fedwick's ideas, Benoît Gain remarked to me that recipients of Basil's letters may also have kept their own files. When one looks for a likely candidate, immediately Eusebius of Samosata comes to mind. To him we may very probably trace the collection of nineteen letters that Basil wrote to the spiritual mentor and closest friend of his later years. On the whole these were highly confidential letters between intimate friends, although issues of church politics also entered in. Even so, Basil was more reporting his own personal struggles amidst the severities of church life than writing formal notices to a fellow prelate. The tone of most of these letters does not suggest they were intended for broad publication as news bulletins. It does pose the question: how did a recipient know what 'register' along the spectrum between private and public to accord a letter received from Basil? Much must have depended on the discretion of close friends, such as the tried-and-true inner circle of neo-Nicene bishops and leaders.

Four letters that surely came from private sources and not from Basil's files were the very early letters to and from Apollinarius (*Epp.* 361–4). In the 350s the latter was an apparently orthodox upholder of the Nicene *homoousios*, but in time became the heresiarch of the Christological heresy that bears his name. When the letters between Basil and Apollinarius were later brandished by Eustathius against Basil (with interpolations?), the latter had forgotten all about them, but when reminded he did not deny having written to Apollinarius twenty years before when they were laymen. So controversial were and are these letters that they are included by the Benedictine editors and by Fedwick among the *dubia*, although for myself, I have little doubt of their genuineness. Again, who would have kept them originally? Not Basil, as his remarks in *Letter* 223 indicate. And how did Eustathius come by copies of them? Might some contemporary Apollinarians have exploited them for their own agenda?

In addition to the sub-collections of letters to Athanasius, to Eusebius of Samosata, to Amphilochius and to the church at Nicopolis as already mentioned, other 'batches' (more than two in number) of letters to the same addressee are the letters to Aburgius, Eustathius of Sebasteia, Meletius of Antioch, Gregory Nazianzen,[25] Modestus the Prefect, 'Kensitor', the Neocaesareans, Sophronius the magistrate, to the churches in the West, and to Libanius.[26]

We may also wonder about the *absence* from the general muster of what one might have expected to be among early collections. It is extraordinary that only one letter from Basil to his brother Gregory survives. Clearly it poses the question: did Basil keep a file of his letters to Gregory? We know for example that when Gregory was in exile 'over the border' (*Ep.* 231) between about 374 and 378, i.e. Basil's last years, the brothers were in clandestine communication. Was it politic that Basil *not* keep a second copy of these letters sent to an outlaw, even if his own brother? Then there is also the fact of the far smaller collection of Gregory's own letters that

---

[25] Although it is a smaller number than one might have thought. Much has been lost. Similarly, little survives of the known long correspondence between Gregory Nazianzen and Gregory of Nyssa.

[26] Fedwick 1993: xv–xvii, lists six as *dubia*, twenty as *spuria*.

have survived. No doubt Basil's enduring fame was a major factor in the large number of his letters that were preserved and copied.

There can be little doubt that Basil also corresponded with his brother Peter, and presumably with his elder sister Macrina, both of whom lived at Annisa in Pontus,[27] but nothing whatsoever of this correspondence survives. This leads to the speculation that perhaps most of the early letter-collections are to be sourced further south, in Cappadocia and neighbouring regions, especially to the east.

One whose early archival and editorial work on Basil's letters is documented, is, of course, Gregory Nazianzen. He certainly possessed his own file of Basil's letters, and in his retirement had the means to have a scribe make copies. In his *Letters* 51–5 to his grand-nephew Nicoboulus, he discusses the collection of letters he is sending as specimens of epistolary style. Nicoboulus had asked him for a treatise on the art of letter-writing, and Gregory sent his laconic 'treatise' in the form of his *Letter* 51, together with a collection of specimen letters, in which he put forward copies of Basil's letters as well as some of his own. His *Letter* 53 answers Nicoboulus' surprise at this, by saying that he, Gregory, thinks that Basil's letters are a superior kind of letter-writing to his own – with which judgement on the whole we might concur.

This preliminary speculation on the earliest sub-collections of Basil's letters suggests that after his death there were two general repositories in which to begin looking for copies:

1 Basil's archival records in Caesarea, mostly in the case of formal and/or public letters that required a reserve copy;
2 private individuals who had kept their own files of Basil's letters, which the latter himself might not have kept.

There is no doubt that the remarkable trajectory of Basil's comparatively short life, as an ascetic leader, a church Father, a theologian and a pastor, acted as a spur towards preservation of his letters, at least in some, though not all circles.

The next stage is also to be investigated: by what process were these primary collections aggregated into larger collections? The work of conserving his literary patrimony for posterity must have begun shortly after his death, if it had not already been in train well before his death. Here, study

---

[27] Basil's impassioned *Ep.* 46 to a fallen virgin very possibly concerns his own younger sister who had undertaken the virginal life at Annisa under Macrina, but who later decamped with a lover. He rhetorically asks his addressee: 'How often did you pen letters to the holy?' If the familial interpretation of this letter is right, then this is evidence of letter-writing at Annisa. See Silvas 2008: 62–73.

of the sequence of letters in the earliest manuscript *corpora* will hopefully yield results. A third stage is already known with greater clarity, how the various larger collections in the literary transmission were further aggregated into the expanding collections of the early editors.

Comparing the aggregation of Gregory of Nyssa's letters

Since the present author has had some occasion to study the letters of Gregory of Nyssa,[28] it may be useful here, for purposes of comparison, to compare how the body of Gregory's letters was gradually built over the centuries. Far fewer of Gregory of Nyssa's letters survive than those of his brother Basil – indeed about a tenth in number, amounting to thirty-six in my edition. Yet, as Teske points out,[29] one cannot deduce from this extrinsic fact that Gregory was somehow much more reticent about writing letters than he was about writing his many other works. Hints that he was in fact a frequent letter-writer occur throughout the letters of all three Cappadocians. In the very earliest record of his existence, Basil, in *Letter* 14.1, mentions that his brother has written to him expressing his desire to meet with him. Yet, although there must have been many other letters between the two brothers over the years, not one has survived from Gregory to his brother, and alas, only one from Basil to his brother, *Letter* 58, which is a somewhat embarrassing monument to their brotherly relations. It was almost certainly preserved among Basil's archives in Caesarea. The letters of Gregory Nazianzen to the younger Gregory were clearly written in the context of years of correspondence between the two men, but again not one letter of the younger Gregory to the elder has survived. In *Letter* 74, Gregory Nazianzen urges him to write and to keep him abreast of his affairs. It suggests that the older Gregory received news bulletins from the younger Gregory from time to time.

Other letters and treatises show that Gregory often wrote in response to specific enquiries, which were more often than not requests for help in doctrinal and theological matters. *Letter* 19 was written in reply to a letter of enquiry during a critical episode of his life (see *Ep.* 19.4). Of letters of intercession to civil authorities on behalf of the disadvantaged, such a prominent function of bishops in late antiquity, only one survives (*Ep.* 7), but there must have been many other such letters, especially if Gregory

---

[28] See Silvas 2007. Subsequent reference to Gregory's letters follow this edition. Much of the following material on Gregory can also be found in the introduction there, 2007: 59–61.

[29] Teske 1997: 1.

had any influence with Emperor Theodosius' court in the 380s, which we
know he did. A great deal then has been lost.

In fact Gregory was so much of a letter-writer that the epistolary style
tended to inform much of his writing that might be assigned to other
genres. He notes the possible confusion of genres himself in the opening
sentence of the *Vita sanctae Macrinae* (*Life of Macrina*), for though it is
indeed a *Life* of his sister, it was also used as a circular letter and sent out
to a range of correspondents, as is proved by the variety of addressees in
the different textual transmissions. In fact it was even suggested to me that
the *Vita sanctae Macrinae* be included among Gregory's letters. Indeed,
what distinct borderline is there between some of the smaller dogmatic
treatises written in the form of letters to named persons, e.g. *To Ablabius,
that there are not three gods*, or *To Simplicius, on the holy Faith* on the one
hand, and letters devoted to doctrinal topics on the other hand, e.g. *Letter
3 to Eustathia and Ambrosia*, *Letter 5 to those who discredit his orthodoxy*,
Letter 24 to Heracleianus or *Letter 32 to the monk Philip*? Two letters at any
rate are included here, *Letters 33* and *35*, which fully inhabit both genres.
They are certainly small dogmatic treatises, but unmistakably letters too,
and since they were published for so long among Basil's letters, we include
them in that genre now under their rightful author's name.

From our survey of Basil's letters above, it is clear that if (a ponderable
if) Gregory had kept a file of Basil's letters, it has not survived. This was
very possibly due to the disturbed political circumstances of his life. He
had had to flee hurriedly from his see of Nyssa in about 374, and was in
exile during Basil's last years, before he returned to his see in the late summer of 378, in the last months of the emperor Valens' life and scarcely in
time to wait upon Basil's deathbed. Similar provisos apply to any archival collection he may have kept of his own letters as bishop of Nyssa.
Not much seems to have survived from this source, or certainly not in
the same proportions as letters from Basil's archival records. Sometimes
a letter survived in the transmission under Gregory Nazianzen's name
or under Basil's name. Gregory's long and immensely impressive *Letter
1* is the most outstanding example of the former case,[30] and *Letter 35* in
my collection an outstanding example of the latter case.[31] If so much of

---

[30] A remarkable specimen of literature by anyone's standard, it gives an almost Kafkaesque account of
his visit to a local synod in a mountain village. It was presided over by Helladius, Basil's successor as
metropolitan at Caesarea. The breakdown of relations between the two men was total.

[31] The *Letter to Peter his own brother on the divine* 'ousia' *and* 'hypostasis' is *Letter 38* in Basil's letters.
Beginning with Cavallin 1944: 71–81, most scholars have reassigned it to Gregory's authorship. It
has lately been the object of comprehensive stylometric analysis. See Maspero *et al.* 2010, 2012,
2013.

Gregory's correspondence has been lost, one may wonder how any of Gregory's letters come to survive at all?

In the Pasquali collection,[32] it may be observed that the manuscripts fall into two broad groups: *Letters* 1–3, each of which have come down in separate manuscript traditions, and *Letters* 4–30, which have come down for the most part in three manuscripts with a common source. It seems reasonable to suppose that *Letters* 4–30 more or less represent an early compilation of letters.

Within this slender collection it is possible to discern two sub-collections. One is a bundle of letters emanating from the crisis at Sebasteia in early to mid-380, following upon the death of Eustathius. Increasingly scholars have come to situate several letters in the specific circumstances of Gregory's strange and abortive election as metropolitan of Sebasteia and its aftermath.[33] The relevant letters are 5, 10, 12, 18, 19 and 22. It seems that there must have been a copy-book of letters from this disturbing episode in Gregory's life.[34] Since Gregory was in such a politically delicate situation where any word or utterance of his was liable to wholesale exploitation, he may well have made copies himself in his months of incarceration.

One also notices a good number of letters which have a very literary, one might even say *secular*, tone. Gregory in *Letter* 11.1 refers to his 'custom' of beginning letters with a text or passage from scripture. The fact that within the second collection (*Epp.* 4–30) only *Letters* 7 and 17 bear this out suggests that a disproportionate number of the surviving letters was selected on a criterion of secular 'literary' qualities, in which scriptural citations were less pertinent. As in the case of Gregory Nazianzen's packet of exemplary letters sent to Nicoboulus, so Gregory of Nyssa may also have put together a collection of his own letters to illustrate the epistolary style,[35] perhaps for the benefit of his son Cynegius, or for some other forum of student interest. The Hellenist manner and only the merest hint of Christian themes, if any, are characteristic of these letters.[36] The disproportionate representation of this type of letter due to unknown circumstances of choice or the hazards of survival may, however, give a somewhat skewed impression of Gregory's character as a letter-writer.

---

[32] See the thirty letters published in Pasquali 1959: 3–91.

[33] In Müller's opinion (1939: 83, n. 1), no letters survived before 380 or after 381. Maraval 1990: 18 n. 1 thinks that is too narrow a period, but agrees that the time for dating Gregory's extant letters is relatively short, perhaps a dozen years or so.

[34] Pasquali's suggestion (1923: 93), supported also by Müller 1939: 83.

[35] See also Maraval 1990: 43.

[36] *Epp.* 8, 9, 11, 13, 14, 16, 20, 21, 23, 26, 27 and 28.

It seems that the compiler of the early collection of Gregory's letters had simply to combine these two modest sub-collections, and add but very few others that could be recovered from individual recipients. Significantly, among these new letters was the fervently religious and hortatory *Letter* 17, coming from very late in Gregory's life. Since this was a formal and ecclesiastical letter – very much a public letter – a copy was surely kept in Nyssa, and if so, perhaps it was here that the primitive collection may have been compiled. These additional letters, together with the first three letters incorporated into his edition by Pasquali, and the theological and other letters recovered by scholars from false attributions[37] or from obscure trails of manuscripts and presented in the 'Supplementary Collection',[38] redress a potential imbalance of subject matter and enable us to gain a rounder view of Gregory's interests as a letter-writer.

One very interesting letter, the *Letter to Letoius*,[39] survived only because it was ecclesiastically approved as a patristic *locus classicus* for its topic: the episcopal administration of church penance. Three of Basil's letters also survived this way, in the collections of church canons. Alas, the introduction of Gregory's letter was lopped off, which is a loss, since he was something of a specialist in writing captivating introductions. Still the personal ending survives, from which we can glean some of the personal context in which the letter was written.

Selecting the manuscripts for collation

In choosing which manuscripts to collate for a new edition of Basil's letters, Fedwick's advice is noteworthy:

> It is quite clear that all in all the text of Basil's letters did not suffer much at the hands of scribes and readers. The variant readings closest to the original unified text are those preserved in some of the [manuscripts] of families Ea–Ed and Eo–Eq Eu (first part).[40]
>
> [N]o edition can ignore either family [i.e. branch], and also that it is necessary to collate not just the [manuscripts] of some of the corpora, but at least one from each.[41]

Study of the scholarship on the transmission of Basil's letters guides a provisional choice of some eighteen codices to be collated for a new edition

---

[37] *Letter to Eustathius the Physician*, which appears as *Letter* 33 in my collection – first reassigned to Gregory by Giovanni Mercati; *Letter* 38 in Basil's letters as mentioned above; *Letter 124 to Theodore* in Basil's letters, which appears as *Letter* 36 in my collection, reassigned to Gregory by Pouchet 1988: 28–46. A pericope of Gregory's *Letter* 28, *On the Rose and its Thorns*, appears as *Letter* 42 in the Benedictine numeration of Basil's letters.

[38] Silvas 2007: 211–70.   [39] *Letter* 31, Silvas 2007: 211–25.

[40] Fedwick 1993: 166.   [41] Fedwick 1993: xxxi.

of Basil's letters, as follows. To the title of each of Fedwick's 'corpora' the equivalent nomenclature in Bessières' list is added. The *sigla* of manuscripts in Courtonne's edition are also indicated.

Branch A

Corpus Ea = Ab
 a1 Venice, BNM gr. 79s. XI
 a2 Modena, BE α.O.4.15 (gr. 229)...........................s. XI/XII
Corpus Eb = Ab
 b1 Paris, BN gr. 506...s. X
 b2 Paris, BN suppl. gr. 763......................................s. XI
Corpus Ec = Aa
 c1 Athos, MB 72 (= Courtonne V)................................s. X
 c2 Athos, MI 355...s. X
 c3 Patmos, MAITh 57 (Courtonne P)............................s. X
 c4 Oxford, BL Barocci 121 (= Courtonne B).................s. XI/XII
Corpus Ed
 d1 Venice, BNM gr. 61 (coll. 500) (= Courtonne M)..........s. X
 d2 Florence, BML Plut. lvii,7 (= Gallay F)...................s. XI

Branch B

Corpus En = Bo
 n1 Florence, BML Plut. iv,14....................................s. X/XI
Corpus Eo = Bo
 o1 Paris, BN, Coislin. 237(= Courtonne L)...................s. XI
Corpus Ep = Bo
 p1 Munich, BSB cod. gr. 497....................................s. XI
Corpus Eq = Bo
 q1 Vatican City, BAV Vat. gr. 713.............................s. XIII
Corpus Eu = Bu
 u1 Vatican City, BAV Vat. 2209.................................s. X/XI
Corpus Ev = Bx
 v1 Paris, BN Suppl. gr. 1020....................................s. X/XI

The selection is restricted to the families noted by Fedwick, tending to the oldest in each corpus. In addition there are Ee1 and 2, and Ev1, which, while comparatively late, may be needed for specific letters. Several manuscripts, mostly from the corpora of Branch B, have not been collated for an edition of Basil's letters. Due to the importance of Bessières' Aa and Ab, two manuscripts will be used in each of Fedwick's equivalent 'corpora' for Ab. An important point here is that no one manuscript contains all the letters. A letter-by-letter approach is going to be an important principle. Fortunately in Fedwick's massive tome all the detailed information necessary for tracking down which letter occurs in what families of manuscripts is supplied.

Conclusion

A matter for careful discernment is whether a proposed new edition of Basil's letters should continue with the chronological numeration, current for some three centuries, or whether one should take a cue from Fedwick's radically different arrangement, which more nearly reflects the 'batches' of letters discernible in the earliest strata of the textual transmission. There are advantages and disadvantages to either option. The Benedictine chronological sequence has much to commend it: the arrangement showcases the large collection of letters as a *de facto* autobiography of Basil and as a history of his times, and moreover, Maran's well-considered chronology has, by and large, stood the test of time. At present, however, it seems more advisable not to lose the opportunity for a thorough reshaping of the presentation of the letters to reflect the genesis of the primitive collections. Furthermore, if the letters are arranged *alphabetically* under the name of recipients, it leaves a certain amount of flexibility for future amendments to the scheme.

Another issue is how to deal with the three classes of authentic, doubtful and spurious letters of Basil. Since questions of authenticity will be indefinitely subject to review in the future, it is probably advisable to include even in a new edition all three classes of letters that occur in the historical transmission, and to leave to scholarly discussion the issue of authenticity.

A new series of critical editions, beginning with this first projected volume of Basil's letters, will collate a wider range of select manuscripts than has been used before, and attend more closely to the pattern of early collections and aggregation in the shaping of the entire corpus of letters. Should this project come it pass, it promises to become the underpinnings of a renewed analysis of the political, religious, social and cultural history of the eastern later Roman empire that the life and literary legacy of the great Basil uniquely afford.

CHAPTER 9

The ins and outs of the Chrysostom letter-collection
New ways of looking at a limited corpus

Wendy Mayer

Within the vast secondary literature concerning the Chrysostomic literary corpus, very little attention has been paid to the *c.* 240 letters that have been passed down to us. With the exception of the editing by Anne-Marie Malingrey of the seventeen letters to Olympias and of the first letter to Innocent (*Ep. 1 ad Innocentem*),[1] the analysis and edition of a small number of falsely attributed letters by Panagiotis Nikolopoulos,[2] the magisterial work by Roland Delmaire on the dating and prosopography of the remaining authentic letters,[3] and the recent translation of and historical annotation to thirty of the letters *ad diversos*,[4] only a handful of studies shed any useful light on the collection from an epistolary perspective. Because of interest by historians in the letters to Olympias, on the one hand, and the letters to Innocent, bishop of Rome, on the other, only a single study, that of Delmaire,[5] focuses on the collection as a whole. Building on Delmaire's analysis of the order in which the letters have been transmitted in the manuscripts,[6] in this study I will push our knowledge of the rationale for this one-sided and severely limited collection further by considering the few extraneous letters that survive, and examining the two ps-Chrysostom letters (*Ep. 1 ad Cyriacum*, *Ep. 233 ad episc. Antioch.*) that the collection preserves. The questions that I pose are:

Do the ps-Chrysostom letters provide a clue as to who preserved the letters in the form that they were preserved and why?
What clues do the rare letters addressed to John Chrysostom that survive in other letter-collections or sources provide?

---

[1] Malingrey 1968; Malingrey and Leclercq 1988/II: 68–94. Malingrey extracted *Ep. 1 ad Innoc.* from Palladius' *Dialogue*, where it also appears as ch. 2, and published it separately in vol. II of her edition of the latter (SC 342). Regarding the double manuscript tradition of this letter see n. 8 below.
[2] Nikolopoulos 1973b. For a summary of his conclusions regarding the dating and authorship of the letters see Nikolopoulos 1973a.
[3] Delmaire 1991, 1997.   [4] Barnes and Bevan 2013: 121–52.   [5] Delmaire 1991.
[6] Barnes and Bevan 2013: 124–6 argue for a slightly different dating for *Ep.* 147 to Anthemius.

Does the collection accurately represent the volume of letters that John wrote from exile, as Delmaire and the modern biographers assume?

A better understanding of what was left out of the corpus, as much as what it contains, will not just shed new light on the circumstances in which this collection was formed, but also elicit the kinds of information that, within the limits of the collection, can be retrieved.

The shape of the letter-collection

The collection with which we work in the present day owes its shape to two distinct editorial phases: the selection and transmission of the letters in the manuscripts, and the production of modern editions of the letters from the time of Henry Savile to the most recent, that of the sub-corpus of letters to Olympias by Malingrey (1968).[7] On the basis of the manuscripts, a number of sub-groups within the collection should be distinguished. These are sometimes grouped together in various combinations, sometimes transmitted among other non-epistolary texts on their own. Generally, these are: the cluster 'Letter to the priests and deacons imprisoned for their faith', *Letters* 1–2 to Innocent, *Letter* 1 to Cyriacus[8] and *Letters* 1–17 to Olympias; *Letters* 18–173 to various people and *Letters* 174–242.[9] The last of these clusters includes five letters (*Epp.* 237–41) written not by John, but by the Antiochene presbyter Constantius.[10] The latter are generally incorporated within the Chrysostom letter-collection rather than transmitted as a separate group in the manuscripts. Whether their inclusion provides any clue as to who originally assembled the letter-collection will be discussed in the final section of this chapter.

What is noteworthy about what the manuscripts tell us about the rationale for the collection is, firstly, the lack of consistency in the grouping of the letters. Some manuscripts contain most of the collection, but

---

[7] A new edition of the remainder of the letters (excluding *Ep. 1 ad Innoc.* and *Epp. 1–17 ad Olymp.*) is in preparation for the SC series by Guillaume Bady and Marie-Gabrielle Guérard on the basis of a collation and preliminary text prepared by Anne-Marie Malingrey (†). This will include an introduction and notes prepared by Roland Delmaire. See Bady 2012.

[8] See Malingrey 1981: 383. In the same article she points out that *Ep.* 1 to Innocent is additionally found in some manuscripts combined with all or part of the letters to Olympias, on its own, and in combination with selections from among the other letters (*Epp.* 18–241). It is further found inserted (in a slightly different form) into ch. 2 of Palladius' *Dialogue*.

[9] Regarding the last two clusters see Delmaire 1991: 72.

[10] Constantius, who was intended to replace Flavian as bishop of Antioch on the latter's death, travelled between Antioch and Cucusus after John was sent into exile, before being driven by the anti-Johannites into exile in a separate location. See Mayer 2001: 67–9. On his identity see Delmaire 1991: 120–1 *s.v.* 'Constantius 2'.

none contains all of the letters passed down to us. Secondly, within the sub-corpus of letters to Olympias and the groups that comprise *Letters* 18–242 the arrangement in the manuscripts is not chronological and the rationale for the order in which they do appear is not patent. The order in which the seventeen letters to Olympias are preserved, however, while not chronological, is consistent across the bulk of the manuscripts.[11] Within the manuscripts the arrangement of the other letters (*Epp.* 18–242) has some consistency, but the order in which they have been published since the time of Fronton du Duc (1614) does not reflect this.[12] On the basis of a study of the transmission of these letters, Delmaire is able to show that there are a number of small clusters that consistently appear together in the manuscripts, most likely indicating packets of letters that were delivered by the same courier.[13] The smallest and most typical consist of only two letters; the largest – one of three groups of letters sent to the West in spring 406 in response to news of an ecumenical synod scheduled to be held at Thessalonica[14] – comprises twenty-nine.

The grouping of the letters in the early editions faithfully reflects the common manuscript tradition only in regard to the seventeen letters to Olympias, and then only in the case of the earliest edition, that of Savile.[15] Fronton du Duc,[16] and Montfaucon after him,[17] placed priority on a manuscript that located as *Letter* 4, the letter located as *Letter* 16 in the bulk of the manuscripts and thus, in Savile's edition, displacing by one all of the subsequent letters, with the exception of *Letter* 17.[18] This is the order duplicated by Migne, based on the second edition of Montfaucon.[19] To confuse matters further, Malingrey, recognising that, regardless of how one collates them, the way in which these letters are grouped in the manuscripts does not reflect the order in which they were written (and, presumably, delivered), in her edition chose to arrange the letters chronologically, resulting in an entirely new sequence and numbering.[20] This has proven to be of considerable benefit to historians, although it results in an awkward double numbering system and dismantles the shape this sub-corpus was consistently given by tradition.[21]

---

[11] See Table 9.1, columns 1–2, based on Malingrey 1965 and 1968: 70–98.

[12] See Delmaire 1991: 72, who labels it 'arbitraire'.

[13] Delmaire 1991: 99–103.   [14] Delmaire 1991: 86–91.

[15] Savile 1612: vol. VII.   [16] Fronton du Duc 1614: vol. IV.

[17] Montfaucon 1834–40: vol. III.   [18] See Table 9.1, column 3.

[19] See PG 52: 549–623. As Bady 2012 points out, Migne reproduced the second edition of Montfaucon, rather than the first, with some significant consequences.

[20] See Table 9.1, column 4.

[21] On the latter point see Bady 2010, whose editorial process gives priority to the manuscript tradition.

In regard to the modern editions of the remainder of the letters there are several important points to be noted. Firstly, as already observed, the arrangement of the letters in editions from Savile onwards does not reflect the common order of the letters in the manuscripts. Savile arranged the letters alphabetically by addressee,[22] whereas Fronton du Duc, for the first 173 letters, followed the sequence published before him by Jacob Cujas, except that the latter and his translator had forgotten *Letter* 236, which was in his chief manuscript intercalated between the present *Letters* 84 and 85.[23] To *Letters* 1–173 (which include the seventeen to Olympias) Fronton du Duc appended on the basis of a more complete manuscript *Letters* 174–236, the five letters authored by Constantius (*Epp.* 237–41) and another letter (*Ep.* 242) from a different manuscript in which it followed *Letter* 178.[24] The same order and numbering as that of Fronton du Duc was adopted by Montfaucon and, in turn, by Migne.[25] In these editions the letters to Olympias comprise *Letters* 1–17 and are prefaced by *Epp. 1–2 ad Innoc.* and *Ep. ad episcopos … in carcere inclusos.*[26] As Delmaire points out, Fronton du Duc's decision simply to append to those Cujas had published from a partial manuscript the remainder from the more complete manuscripts he examined, rather than retaining the order in those manuscripts, where they were intercalated among the 137 that Cujas published, simply added to the incoherence.[27] For the scholars within the Institut Sources Chrétiennes currently preparing a new edition of *Letter* 18 onwards,[28] the decision whether to follow the order preserved in the main manuscripts or to arrange the letters according to Delmaire's chronology is a difficult one.[29] A chronological arrangement, of greatest benefit to historians, would bring the process by which Chrysostom authored and dispatched his letters into clearer view. An arrangement that follows the main manuscripts would make clear for the first time the shape in which these letters were handed down by tradition. Both approaches have merit and offer a resolution to the current misshaping of the collection. Whatever

[22] See Delmaire 1991: 71. For a list of the manuscripts collated see Malingrey 1968: 86–7.

[23] Delmaire 1991: 72.

[24] Delmaire 1991: 72. For the manuscripts collated see also Malingrey 1968: 87–8.

[25] See PG 52: 623–748. Again, the implications of Migne's choice in publishing the letters from the second edition of Montfaucon (Bady 2012), not the first, should be noted.

[26] See PG 52: 529–36 and 541–2*. These letters in turn bracket two letters in Greek from Innocent to John and the church of Constantinople, preserved by the church historian Sozomen (*HE* 8.26), and another in Latin addressed by the emperor Honorius to his brother Arcadius, preserved by Palladius (*Dial.* 3). See PG 52: 537–42.

[27] Delmaire 1991: 72–3.   [28] See n. 7 above.

[29] For the order that would more or less result from following the chronology of Delmaire 1991: 176–80, see Table 9.2.

decision is made, however, will inevitably result in a second new (double) numbering system.[30]

To confuse matters further, the authentic letters published as *Letters* 18–242, not only include a small cluster of letters (*Epp.* 237–41) authored by the Johannite, Constantius, but the manuscripts (and subsequent editors) include as genuine two letters that are inauthentic (*Ep.* 125 [=1] *ad Cyriacum* and *Ep.* 233 *ad episcopum Antiochenum*).[31] These have been studied and edited in the company of three other letters falsely attributed to John but by other strands of tradition,[32] further complicating our understanding of the shape of the original collection.

The contents of the collection

When we turn to the contents of the collection, the first point of note is that all of the authentic letters, with the possible exception of *Ep. 1 ad Innoc.*, were composed by John in exile (late June 404–mid September 407). *Ep. 1 ad Innoc.* was clearly considered part of the exile correspondence in thematic terms, since it was written after the events of Easter (17 April) 404 and, depending on precisely when it was sent, John may still have been waiting for a reply when, in late June 404, he was expelled for the second and final time from Constantinople.[33] Chronologically, then, this letter can be located at the very beginning of the preserved record of John's actions and experiences throughout this three-year period. The inclusion of the five letters composed by Constantius is consistent with this rationale, since Constantius authored them during this period,[34] received the earliest letter sent from exile by John in the collection,[35] and spent time with him after John reached his assigned place of exile, Cucusus.[36] The two inauthentic letters included in the collection are

[30] This is anticipated in Delmaire 1991.

[31] Published by Migne at PG 52: 681*–85 and 739.

[32] See Nikolopoulos 1973a and 1973b. Of the other three (*ad Eudoxiam, ad Caesarium* and *ad monachos*), Nikolopoulos locates the first within the Jezebel tradition of the eighth to tenth centuries, expressed in the *Vita* by George of Alexandria, argues in regard to the second for an indirect tradition that goes back to the sixth century, and identifies in the third the conflation of an authentic letter by Basil and a hesychast text from the eleventh century, probably only accidentally assigned to Chrysostom in the manuscript tradition.

[33] Regarding the date of this letter see Delmaire 1991: 80, who calculates that it was written in April or May and not received at Rome until a month later (sometime in June). For a more recent opinion see Dunn 2005.

[34] Delmaire 1991: 180 dates all five to Oct./Nov. 404.

[35] *Ep.* 221 (4 July 404), PG 52: 732–3.

[36] See Mayer 2001: 67–9, Delmaire 2009: 288. Constantius spent at least October and November 404 in Cucusus, which supplies the date for the letters preserved in the collection.

likewise consistent with this rationale. Of the three recensions of *Ep. 1 ad Cyriacum*, the first (α) is in reality *Ep. 7 ad Olymp.* with some variants;[37] the second (β) comprises five units of which three contain complete passages from *Epp. 7* and *10 ad Olymp.* and the other two attack the empress Eudoxia and John's immediate successor, Arsacius;[38] the third (γ), found only in three manuscripts, represents a later development in which an intact second recension is augmented by a lengthy passage from *Ep. 7 ad Olymp.*[39] Thus in all its forms *Ep. 1 ad Cyriacum* constitutes part of the exile narrative. *Ep. 233 ad episc. Antioch.* similarly can be situated within the exilic discourse. It is ostensibly addressed to the anti-Johannite bishop, Porphyrius, who was hastily consecrated bishop of Antioch in place of Constantius in late July or early August 404 on the death of John's mentor, close colleague and supporter, Flavian.[40] In it the author explicitly refers to his expulsion from the city and his tenure in the wilderness, and uses the sort of allusive language that John employs when in authentic letters he describes the troubles experienced by the Johannites.[41]

The second point of note is that the letters preserved in the collection present a very particular picture of John's exile. This is one in which the inclusion of a large number of letters from the first months of exile demonstrate a bishop who, based on his previous experience of exile and rapid recall in September 403, sets out with a certain degree of optimism that his supporters will be able to influence events and ameliorate his circumstances.[42] Suggesting that in combination with local factors in Armenia the effects of the edict of 18 November 404 were devastating,[43] the letters dating from winter 404/5 to late spring 405 that are included represent a substantial reduction in volume and portray a bishop who is isolated, sick and

---

[37] See Nikolopoulos 1973a: 125, where he notes that *Ep. 1 ad Cyr.* is always found together in the manuscript tradition with *Ep. 2 ad Cyriacum*, which is in reality *Ep. 10 ad Olymp.* The numbering used to reference the letters to Olympias here and throughout the remainder of this chapter follows that of Malingrey 1968.

[38] Nikolopoulos 1973a: 126.   [39] Nikolopoulos 1973a: 126.

[40] On these events see Delmaire 1991: 76–9.

[41] Cf. Nikolopoulos 1973b: 497, and John's second letter to Innocent (PG 52: 535–6, esp. 536.12 ff.). Ubaldi 1901 attempted to explain its inclusion as a sixth letter authored by Constantius (reading it as referring to Constantius' own expulsion from Antioch where he should have been bishop). Nikolopoulos 1973a: 127 observes simply that the manuscripts in which it is preserved are late and the attribution to Chrysostom vague and uncertain.

[42] See Delmaire 1997: 309, who points out that John writes 142 letters before the end of winter 404/5, all of which assume support by clergy and members of the Constantinopolitan elite and demand visits from supporters in Syria. These represent more than half of the surviving collection.

[43] *Codex Theodosianus* 16.4.6; ed. Mommsen 2005: 224. This edict required communion with key bishops hostile to John (Theophilus of Alexandria, Arsacius of Constantinople and Porphyrius of Antioch), in consequence of which many Johannites were persecuted further and exiled.

disillusioned, and who now restricts his correspondence to certain faithful supporters.[44] The collection includes a large cluster of letters (thirty-four in total) from spring 406 sent to a variety of correspondents old and new in response to news of the western delegation to Constantinople and the proposed synod, which give the impression of reawakened hope. The number of letters included then dramatically tapers off, with only two from 407 (spring) included, implying that by this point John had been deserted by his supporters, with only the two most faithful, Olympias and Helpidius, bishop of Laodicea, remaining.[45] The contents of the collection and, as we shall see, what is missing, have thus served to shape – whether intentionally or accidentally – the picture of John's exile that has been handed down.[46]

The third point is that the rationale for the letter-collection (John's exile and response) shapes our picture of his correspondence in another way. The genre of the letters included is severely limited. The bulk of the 238 letters authored by John are brief networking (patron–client) letters, sent to shore up patronage networks or, more rarely, to initiate them.[47] Some could be described equally as letters of friendship.[48] Two letters of congratulation on the achievement of high office are included,[49] one to a previous supporter, Gemellus,[50] the other to the new *Praefectus praetorio per Orientem*, Anthemius.[51] A sole letter of consolation is incorporated, addressed to the urban prefect of Constantinople, Studius, on the death of his brother.[52] Three letters of recommendation are found within the collection: two commending the bishop Seleucus, who has been visiting John, to the care, respectively, of a fellow bishop, Tranquillinus, and a senior physician at Caesarea, Hymnetius;[53] the other, commending

[44] See Delmaire 1997: 309, who points out that by late 405 only a dozen or so of his faithful supporters remained in touch.

[45] For the chronological distribution of the letters see Tables 9.1 and 9.2.

[46] For the most part the picture described here is the one adopted in the chief biographies of John (Baur 1930, Kelly 1995, Brändle 1999, Tiersch 2002) and is the view that prevails in Delmaire's latest study of the letters (Delmaire 2009).

[47] On this point see Delmaire 2009 and Mayer 2010.   [48] See Mayer 2012: 134 n. 25.

[49] *Ep.* 116 (Sept. 404), addressed to Valentinus at Constantinople on his appointment as *Magister militum per Orientem*, could be considered a third letter of congratulation by virtue of its subject matter, but adopts a distinctly different tone. See PG 52: 671–2.

[50] *Ep.* 124 (summer 405), PG 52: 678.

[51] *Ep.* 147 (Aug./Sept. 405), PG 52: 699. Delmaire 2009: 289 points out John's error in attempting to curry favour with Anthemius, who was of Egyptian origin and thus probably allied with Theophilus. He had been in charge of the soldiers who expelled John's supporters from the church during the Easter Vigil 404 in Constantinople.

[52] *Ep.* 197 (before Dec. 404), PG 52: 721–2.

[53] See *Epp.* 37–8, PG 52: 630–1, both sent during winter 404/5. Presumably John had made Hymnetius' acquaintance at Caesarea when he himself was in need of medical care en route to

to Bishop Cyriacus, the governor of Armenia, Sopater, who has aided John.[54]

Of those letters that are not primarily part of an epistolary strategy for maintaining networks and securing favours (a mere fifteen) the bulk are best described as administrative rather than pastoral (excluding the letters John sends to Olympias concerning despair, to be discussed shortly). In these, John deals with personnel, supplies and funding for the mission in Phoenicia;[55] the mission to the Goths across the Danube and to the Persians;[56] and the spiritual and physical welfare of supporters who remain in Constantinople.[57] Letters (some thirteen in total) addressed to supporters who are being persecuted, including those in prison, do not fall strictly into the category of pastoral letters, nor do they follow the formulae of letters of consolation, although they do counsel endurance and in some cases evoke the language of martyrdom.[58] The rare pastoral letters in the collection are reserved for female supporters – in the main, Olympias. Of the seventeen addressed to her, ten are predominantly letters of counsel concerning her declining mental and spiritual state as a consequence of her own exile and persecution and the continuing lack of resolution of John's situation.[59] One letter to a female supporter at Antioch may possibly indicate that, despite the sketchy pastoral counsel in the letter itself, John communicated this verbally via the letter-carrier,[60] while in a letter to an elite female supporter at Constantinople John firmly counsels her concerning her dismissal of an individual from her household.[61]

The five letters authored by Constantius incorporated into the collection do little to broaden the limited range of categories. Two, addressed to his mother and sister, praise their courage, virtue and piety in a manner

---

Cucusus, in which case the letter also performs the function of maintaining the connection. It was in fact delivered along with a cluster of letters (*Epp.* 236, 80–4, 171–3) John sent on arrival in Cucusus to acquaintances made at Caesarea for precisely this purpose. See Table 9.2 and discussion in Mayer 2006 and 2010: 164–5.

[54] *Ep.* 64 (Sept. 404), PG 52: 644.
[55] For a list of the letters and discussion see Mayer 2010: 169–71.
[56] *Ep.* 9 *ad Olymp.*, ed. Malingrey 1964b: 218–40.
[57] For letters and discussion see Mayer 2010: 168.
[58] For letters and discussion see Mayer 2010: 166–7, where it is pointed out that, in a small number where the addressees are also ascetics, John instead requests of them a ministry of prayer for the embattled church.
[59] *Epp.* 7–8, 10–17 *ad Olymp.*, ed. Malingrey 1964b: 132–216, 242–388.
[60] *Ep.* 133 to Adolia, PG 52: 691–2. On the nature of the relationship between Adolia and the presbyter Libanius who acts as a Johannite courier between Antioch and Cucusus, see Mayer 2014. On verbal communication to the letter-bearer see Allen 2013a: 487–8.
[61] *Ep.* 117 to Theodora, PG 52: 672–3.

not dissimilar to John's praise of Olympias.[62] The other three, addressed to various fellow presbyters at Antioch, are in essence letters of friendship.[63]

The first letter to Innocent, which, as I will discuss shortly, was in fact also sent to two other Italian bishops, stands alone as a piece of diplomatic correspondence.[64] With the exception of the lengthier pastoral letters addressed to Olympias, it is also one of the longest letters included in the collection.

Finally, of the two ps-Chrysostom letters inserted in the collection, the second recension of the letter to Cyriacus (*Ep. 1 ad Cyriacum* β)[65] and *Ep. 233 ad episc. Antioch.* are both polemical. Depending on the date of the second, they most likely constitute part of a larger set of documents manufactured between 403 and *c.* 420 and circulated under John's name as authentic, as both Johannites and anti-Johannites attempted to sway opinion at various levels concerning the legality of how John was treated.[66]

As a fourth point of note, just as the genre of the letters is constrained by the overall rationale for the collection, so too is the identity of the addressees. The latter are analysed in detail by Delmaire in his lengthy prosopographical study.[67] His much briefer summary of the 'Johannite' correspondents is more useful, however, for our immediate purpose.[68] The first point to be made is that they are all overt supporters or people whom John and his supporters thought might prove to be sympathetic to his cause. Whether or not an addressee turned out to be a supporter or sympathetic in reality – Delmaire argues convincingly that John made a number of mistakes[69] – this is a letter-collection constructed exclusively from a Johannite perspective. These 'Johannite' addressees can be divided into six categories: bishops,[70] clergy in Constantinople and Syria,[71] and laity in Asia Minor,[72] Constantinople and Syria.[73] This provides a general

---

[62] *Epp.* 237–8, PG 52: 741–5.

[63] *Epp.* 239–41, PG 52: 745–6, addressed to Valerius and Diophantes, Castus and Cyriacus, respectively. Six letters (*Epp.* 222, 22, 62, 66, 107, 130) authored by John to these same four are included in the collection, extending from late 404 into spring 406. See Table 9.2.

[64] Mayer 2012: 131–6. The letter provides useful insight into the protocols involved and the role of bishops (from the petitioning bishop's domestic synod?) as legates between episcopal peers.

[65] For the text of this recension see Nikolopoulos 1973b: 395–411.

[66] See Wallraff 2008 and Mayer 2013. This campaign included constructing John's arch-enemy Theophilus as heretical and John as orthodox, on which point see also Barry 2013.

[67] Delmaire 1991: 103–75.

[68] Delmaire 1997, esp. the concluding table at 311–13.

[69] This is particularly the case with elite males at Constantinople who held imperial administrative office. See Delmaire 1997: 307–8 regarding, among others, Anthemius, Gemellus, Paeanius and Valentinus.

[70] Delmaire 1997: 303.   [71] Delmaire 1997: 303–6.

[72] Delmaire 1997: 306.   [73] Delmaire 1997: 306–9.

sense of the exiled bishop's support networks and communicative radius. That is, the two chief nodes are Constantinople and Antioch, with radii into other parts of Syria, and some initial networking with potentially influential provincial elite in Asia Minor situated along the path John travelled between Constantinople and Cucusus.[74] To put this in perspective, at a rough count the proportion of addressees who reside in Antioch and the Syrian provinces is 37 per cent; those who continue to reside in Constantinople or who originate in that city, 31 per cent. The western bishops and small number of lay elite to whom the three packets of letters were sent in spring 406 (a further 12 per cent) expand the geographic focus temporarily,[75] although it is to be noted that the initial letter sent to Innocent in Rome indicates at its conclusion that identical letters were also dispatched at that time to two other Italian bishops, Chromatius of Aquileia and Venerius of Milan,[76] who, like Innocent, are among the recipients of the renewed western correspondence in spring 406.

Notable among the numerous letters, specific and generic, to western addressees in 406 are three addressed to elite Roman women.[77] This raises the issue of the gender differential among the addressees represented in the collection. Of female addressees, the remainder constitute both clergy and laity in Antioch and Constantinople, the majority of elite or noble status. Twenty-seven letters are addressed to seven different women who originate in Constantinople;[78] a further twenty-four to seven different women who reside in Antioch.[79] The two letters addressed by the presbyter Constantius to women in his family at Antioch expand the overall number. The letters addressed to women preserved in the collection constitute roughly a quarter of the total and are divided more or less evenly between the two chief nodes of correspondents.

A final, perhaps obvious point is that all of the letters are written, or at least preserved, in Greek. This is of interest from two angles. First, in a letter to one woman of elite status, John says that the lack of a scribe is no excuse, since she is capable of writing in her own language and hand.[80] Delmaire speculates that her native language is Latin.[81] Second, whereas

---

[74] Delmaire 1997: 306 points out that the chief focus was Caesarea, which was in sufficient proximity to Cucusus for people to visit, and that, among others, John targets the governor of Cappadocia, the chief physician of the city, and a resident sophist.

[75] See Table 9.2 and Delmaire 1991: 86–90 and 2009: 289–90.

[76] Malingrey 1981: 386–7.   [77] Epp. 168–70, PG 52: 709–10.

[78] Including Olympias. For the identification of the bulk of these as ascetic deacons see Broc 1993.

[79] See Mayer 2014. On letters to women in Christian antiquity see Allen 2014a.

[80] Ep. 103 to Amprucla, PG 52: 663.

[81] Delmaire 1991: 107. That John was literate in Latin is confirmed by ps-Martyrius (Or. funeb. 50, Wallraff and Ricci 2007: 102).

the initial letter sent to Innocent and all of the letters sent to western bishops and Italian women in spring 406 are preserved in Greek, Sozomen, as we shall see shortly, indicates that any letters sent by Innocent were translated into Greek from their original Latin.[82]

What is missing?

If we consider how many letters John must have generated as bishop of Constantinople (February 398–June 404), the number of letters missing from the collection is substantial and, as already noted, distorts the range of genres represented.[83] With the exception of *Ep. 1 ad Innoc.*, dictated at the very end of his tenure of the Constantinopolitan see when John was under house arrest and his duties severely restricted, there are no letters authored by John during the ordinary course of his episcopate. This point will be of interest when I consider the question of who instigated the collection. Two letters sent to John, one during his exile, one from the early years of his episcopate, survive outside the collection, and two other letters by him dealing with administrative matters are referenced in an external source. There is also a reference to a number of letters sent back and forth to Rome in the months following the Synod of the Oak and into the early period of his exile. All of these will be discussed shortly. Of particular pertinence to the collection is the number of letters sent by John in exile that are not included in the collection but the existence of which can be surmised from evidence internal to the letters that are included. Noticeably absent is any letter from the anti-Johannite perspective. Finally, what is not included, either from the period of John's episcopate or from the period of exile, is a single letter addressed to him.[84]

Letters outside the collection

As already mentioned, a small number of letters addressed to and by John survive outside the Chrysostom letter-collection. A rare letter sent to him at Constantinople that dates from early in his episcopate survives

---

[82] On the date and translation of John's own writings into Latin see Bady 2008.

[83] Of the nine categories of episcopal letters listed by Neil in the introduction, in John's letters we have no pieces of a dogmatic or disciplinary nature, and none on decree and judgement. In other cases categories blur. The letters sent to the delinquent presbyters at Constantinople that I have labelled administrative (*Epp.* 203, 212), could also be considered letters of admonition. Similarly John's pastoral letters could also be considered letters of advice.

[84] The two letters by Innocent preserved in Sozomen's ecclesiastical history are inserted into the modern editions for completeness. See n. 26.

in Latin. The letter is sent by an Italian bishop, Vigilius of Tridentum
(Trent), in company with relics extracted from recently martyred clergy
from Anaunia.[85] This appears to be another example of a networking letter
in which the Italian bishop, with a gift, seeks to attach John as a patron,
since it is clear that John knows nothing about these martyrs and Vigilius
makes the same approach to the bishop of Milan.[86] It could also be viewed
as a diplomatic letter, intended to establish or strengthen communion,
since the sees of Milan and Constantinople were both considered strategic
at this time.

Two letters sent during the period of John's exile by Innocent of Rome,
one to John, one to the clergy and laity of Constantinople, are recorded
by Sozomen.[87] The first follows the conventions of a letter of consolation;
the second is a hybrid of *consolatio*, letter of advice and letter of decree.
What is significant is that Sozomen notes that he found both translated into Greek from Latin[88] which suggests that they survived in the
Constantinopolitan archives at the time that Sozomen wrote his history
(*c.* 439–50).[89] Recent argument identifies the first letter as one couriered
back to the East from Rome in July/August 404.[90] The second letter was
sent after October 404.[91]

Two letters written by John during his exile exist outside the collection.[92] These are lengthy pastoral letters, better described as treatises in
letter form,[93] written and sent in the last year of his exile (407). The first
(*Quod nemo laeditur nisi a se ipso*) is addressed to Olympias and her community, and is explicitly mentioned by John in the last letter to her that
appears in the collection.[94] The second (*Ad eos qui scandalizati sunt*) is

---

[85] PL 13: 552–8 (= Vigilius, *Ep.* 2). On the state of the Latin, which may be corrupt, see Menestò 1985.
     On the manuscript tradition of this letter see Cagni and Sironi 1984. The three martyrs were killed
     in 397 CE.

[86] Vigilius, *Ep.* 1, PL 13: 549–52. That the letter to John is significantly longer than the letter to
     Simplicianus reinforces the suspicion that not just the martyrs but Vigilius himself are largely
     unknown to John.

[87] Soz., *HE* 8.26, GCS NF 4: 384–7.   [88] *HE* 8.26.1, GCS NF 4: 384.13–14.

[89] On the date see Van Nuffelen 2004: 59–61.

[90] Dunn 2005: 169. In July 404 Theotecnus had brought news to Rome of the burning of the Great
     Church at Constantinople and the exile of John (Pall., *Dial.* 3).

[91] Dunn 2005: 157.

[92] There exist a further four treatises in letter form dating from John's early career in Antioch (*Ad
     Theodorum lapsum, Ad Stagirium a daemone vexatum, Ad Stelechium,* and *Ad Demetrium de com-
     punctione*), but their length is much greater, some being divided into books, and their genre thus
     more questionable. Regarding their publication during John's lifetime see Bady 2010: 161.

[93] See Malingrey 1961: 11–15 on the genre of the second, which she describes as neither homily, nor
     letter, nor treatise, but more than all three.

[94] *Ep. 17 ad Olymp.* 4.c (spring 406), ed. Malingrey 1964b: 384.32–5. John says he sent it recently. For
     the text see Malingrey 1964b.

identified by Malingrey as the treatise he says he is sending to Olympias with *Letter* 17.[95] In four out of thirty manuscripts the first (*Quod nemo laed.*) is located together with a small number of letters from exile; in two others it is located together with the second letter/treatise.[96] Given the paucity of letters in the collection from the third and final year of John's exile, the date of these two letters is of particular interest.

Evidence of letters from external sources

Evidence of a number of letters authored by John or that constitute part of the exile correspondence exists in three Johannite sources. Firstly, Theodoret in his ecclesiastical history refers to two administrative letters that he personally witnessed and that most likely date from John's episcopate.[97] The first, addressed to Leontius, bishop of Ancyra, contained a description of the conversion of the Goths along the Danube and asked that Leontius supply personnel to continue their (Nicene) instruction.[98] The second, addressed to a predecessor to Theodoret as bishop of Cyrrhus, concerned Marcionite heretics in that region. In it, John instructed him to 'drive out the plague' and offered imperial edicts to assist him. The question to be asked here is whether Theodoret viewed both letters in the Constantinopolitan archives or had access to the second via the episcopal archives at Cyrrhus.

Secondly, Palladius, in the early chapters of his *Dialogue*, documents a number of letters that in the middle of 404 passed back and forth between Alexandria and Rome, on the one hand, and Constantinople and Rome, on the other.[99] Many of these do not survive beyond Palladius' reference, although he does cite in full or part a letter from Innocent to Theophilus and one from the emperor Honorius to his brother, Arcadius.[100] To this cluster belong *Ep. 1 ad Innoc.* and the first of the two letters sent by Innocent mentioned earlier. Among those missing, according to Palladius, are two letters to Innocent from Theophilus of Alexandria, a letter of communion

---

[95] Malingrey 1961: 7.

[96] Malingrey 1964b: 418–19 and 1962, who points out that the second is preserved in a much larger number of manuscripts due to its being identified in the tenth to twelfth centuries as one of the homilies *De incomprehensibili Dei*. For the text of both see Malingrey 1961, 1964b. Like *Quod nemo laed.*, *Ad eos qui scand.* is grouped with documents pertaining to John's exile in only a small number of manuscripts.

[97] Theod., *HE* 5.31, GCS NF 5: 331.

[98] In *Ep. 9 ad Olymp.* 5.b, ed. Malingrey 1964b: 236–8 John discusses with Olympias a request conveyed in a letter from the king of the Goths for a new bishop.

[99] See the discussion in Delmaire 1991: 80–6 and Dunn 2005.

[100] Pall., *Dial.* 3, Malingrey and Leclercq 1988/I: 66–8, 82–4.

to Theophilus from Innocent, letters to Innocent from bishops allied to John and from Anysius of Thessalonica, and letters from bishops of Caria and presbyters of Antioch (brought by Demetrius, bishop of Pisinum, who had toured the diocese of Oriens gathering support). In addition Palladius notes that he himself arrived with a copy of an eastern edict of confiscation of property directed at those who received bishops and clergy in communion with John; that two presbyters of Constantinople arrived with an inventory of the Constantinopolitan church treasury and news of violence directed toward the clergy; and that another presbyter of that city arrived with further news of the torture, trial and imprisonment of fellow clergy, elite women and consular families. This indicates that between June and September 404 a large number of letters and ecclesiastical embassies were going back and forth between Constantinople, Alexandria and Rome, of which only a tiny fraction is included in the collection. Palladius also witnesses to what must have been only a small fraction of the letters generated by the anti-Johannite side of the conflict.

Thirdly and finally, there is a single clear echo in the earliest Johannite source, the funeral oration of ps-Martyrius, of the language John repeatedly uses throughout the letters within the collection to describe his isolation in exile.[101] This could be attributed to a number of sources: that the author of the funeral oration was one of John's correspondents in exile, that he was one of the clergy from either Constantinople or Antioch who acted as couriers for many of the letters,[102] or that he was closely linked to the network of one of the recipients of John's letters and heard them read aloud in that individual's company.[103]

Letters cited by John that are not included in the collection

Of perhaps greatest interest concerning the rationale for the collection is a comparison of the letters John sent (as reported by him) that are included in the collection, and those that are not. The bulk of the missing letters date from the first six to eight months of exile. As examples, in November 404 John tells Adolia that he has sent five previous letters to her,[104] but only three are included.[105] Theodora is told that he has sent three or four letters

---

[101] Ps-Marty., *Or. funeb.* 117.4–8, Wallraff and Ricci 2007: 170. For a discussion of this language and how John exploits it see Mayer 2006.

[102] Regarding their identity see Delmaire 1991: 97–103, Dunn 2005, Mayer 2006.

[103] Wallraff argues that the author was a member of the inner circle of Johannites (i.e. clergy who worked closely with John), possibly Philip of Side. Wallraff and Ricci 2007: 17 and 37 n. 51.

[104] *Ep.* 179.   [105] *Epp.* 133, 57, 231.

beforehand,[106] but no earlier letter appears in the collection. In a number of cases he says that he has written often, but no earlier letter is found.[107] Similarly, in writing to Theophilus, a presbyter at Constantinople, John tells him that he has written to many people on his behalf,[108] but there is no record of this correspondence. By contrast, in three instances all of the letters that John claims he sent form part of the collection,[109] suggesting that in these other instances his claim concerning the number of letters sent is not an exaggeration. Rather their absence is a consequence of how the collection has been formed.

Who compiled the collection?

What we have, thus, is a collection limited to letters written (or purported to be written) by John in exile, and by the Antiochene presbyter Constantius during a two-month visit to him. The collection is further restricted in that it does not include every known letter sent to or from Armenia during that three-year period. The chief question that remains is whether inclusion or not in the collection is deliberate or accidental.

Delmaire's conclusion that John continued in exile to maintain an archive of copies of letters sent and of original letters received, as was common among men of letters in late antiquity, and that the bulk of the letters in the collection (*Epp.* 1–17 to Olympias and *Epp.* 18–242) derive from it, is inescapable.[110] Given the geographic spread and number of the recipients and the number of couriers involved,[111] it is difficult to imagine how the letters could have been assembled, unless collected at the point of origin. Delmaire finds support in the precision with which John refers to the number of letters previously written to a particular correspondent.[112] The

---

[106] *Ep.* 120.

[107] *Ep.* 101 to Severus; *Ep.* 206 to Theodoulos; *Ep.* 219 to Severina and Romula. All three addressees reside at Constantinople. Cf. *Ep.* 202 to Cyriacus, also at Constantinople; one earlier letter to him, *Ep.* 64, does appear in the collection.

[108] *Ep.* 115.

[109] See *Ep.* 67 (summer 406) to Theodotus, deacon of Antioch, which refers to two letters sent previously (*Epp.* 59, 135); *Ep.* 22 to Castus *et al.* (winter 404/5) presbyters of Antioch, in which John says he is also sending a letter to another Antiochene presbyter, Romanus (*Ep.* 91), for them to pass on; and *Ep.* 180 to Hypatius, presbyter of Constantinople, in which John indicates that he sent one previous letter (*Ep.* 90).

[110] Delmaire 1991: 97–8.

[111] Thirteen couriers are mentioned by name, ranging from clergy to personal servants to praetorian guards. A number of presbyters are explicitly mentioned, but go unnamed. John generally assumes that anyone arriving or departing will bring or take letters. See Stander 2010: 55–6; Allen 2013a.

[112] Delmaire 1991: 98, who also argues that the assemblage within the manuscripts of letters delivered together as a packet is evidence of their having been filed together in an archive.

most likely scenario, thus, is that the collection was compiled by one of the clergy who, when not delivering letters back and forth to Italy, Syria and Constantinople, remained at John's side in exile.[113] The inclusion of five letters authored by Constantius, the presbyter intended as the successor to the Antiochene episcopate but replaced by an anti-Johannite candidate, may tip the scales in favour of locating the compiler within the Johannite network at Antioch. That might also explain the inclusion of the letters concerning the Antiochene mission in Phoenicia. It is equally possible, however, that Constantius' letters are included simply because they were present in the archive by virtue of their point of origin and because the possession of the Antiochene see by an enemy was viewed by Johannites as a major blow. That is, Constantius' situation was viewed as comparable to that of John, and the collection thus contains a narrative of two Johannites in exile. The inclusion of two ps-Chrysostom letters is less easy to explain in this scenario, since, if they were indeed deliberately generated by one or the other side in response to the conflict, those archiving the letters (John or one or more of his aides) would have known that they were inauthentic.

This leads to the question of intentionality in compiling the collection. If we accept the archive thesis, then the failure to include all of its contents is already a sign that the shape of the collection is intentional. A simple examination of the chronological termini of the collection reinforces this conclusion. No letters from after spring 407 are included, which, given that in late summer that year John was forcibly removed from Cucusus (?) and sent under guard towards a more remote location,[114] is perhaps not surprising. That only two letters from 407 make it into the collection,[115] however, is significant in light of that decision. The latter indicates concern that, three years on, John's place of exile was proving to be insufficiently isolated. If the impression the collection conveys (that support from Constantinople had by this time been largely cut off) is accurate,[116] the visitors and letters he was continuing to receive in 407 most likely came predominantly from Armenia and

---

[113] In spring 406, for instance, despite withdrawing to a more remote location (Arabissus) because of Isaurian raids, John has two deacons and three presbyters at his disposal. See Mayer 2006.

[114] See Kelly 1995: 283–4. Whether at that time he was back in Cucusus or still in Arabissus is uncertain.

[115] Delmaire 2009: 290 counts three, including the letter-treatise *Quod nemo laeditur*. If we add *Ad eos qui scand.*, the number is four. However, the manuscripts do not consider either part of the collection.

[116] The reading of Delmaire 1991 and 2009.

Syria.[117] The failure to preserve evidence of this suggests that it did not suit the purposes of the compiler. At the other end of the spectrum, aside from John's initial letter to Innocent and his peers, the collection ignores the flurry of diplomatic letters that were sent back and forth between Constantinople and the West from late June to the promulgation of the edict of November 404 requiring communion with John's enemies. Palladius records this activity because of his own apologetic interests;[118] their absence here suggests that the compiler's interest lay elsewhere.

That interest may well have been in creating the narrative that we have inevitably extracted from the collection: that of a bishop focused on regaining his rightful see, who starts out in hope, moves to despair and has his hopes reawakened, only to be deserted in the end by all but his most faithful supporters.[119] The contents of the archives (in Constantinople?) that preserved the letters viewed by both Sozomen and Theodoret are likely to have been deemed irrelevant to this agenda. Likewise, if by 407 John had become convinced that rehabilitation was unlikely and he was becoming increasingly engaged in local Armenian affairs, this may well have been viewed by Johannites as a betrayal. We must also admit, however, that what is both in and out of the collection may be the result of a mixture of design and accident. On at least five occasions John was obliged to move from his current location in exile, twice hastily or unexpectedly.[120] It is easy to imagine that some copies may have been lost in the process. In the end, beyond recognising that this is a Johannite collection that in some way serves Johannite interests, we can only speculate.

Conclusions

That speculation, however, leads in some interesting directions. To review what we have learnt thus far, firstly, the shape of the original letter collection is not faithfully presented in any of the modern editions. Either, due to the greater weight placed on them by historians, the sub-corpus of letters to Olympias has been published separately or, for a variety of reasons,

---

[117] In support of this point see ps-Mart., *Or. funeb.* 134.15–16, Wallraff and Ricci 2007: 190 ('all [of his activities in Armenia] virtually transplanted the entire city of Antioch to him'); and Mayer 2006.

[118] See Katos 2011 and Van Nuffelen 2013.

[119] Delmaire 2009.

[120] From Caesarea en route to Cucusus (mid Aug. 404), from Cucusus to Arabissus (early 406), from Arabissus to a remote fort (autumn 406), back to Cucusus (?), from Cucusus (?) to Pityus (late Aug. 407). See Delmaire 1991: 75, 174, Kelly 1995: 256, 260, 283–4.

the sequence of the letters *ad diversos* has been altered. Additionally, the manuscripts themselves do not consistently group all of the letters together. They are, however, for the most part coherent in the way they present the letters to Olympias, which are usually found grouped together, and in the way they configure small clusters among the other letters. The latter appear to constitute groups of letters that were delivered on the same occasion by the same letter-carrier. Secondly, the contents of the collection are selective. With the exception of *Letter* 1 to Innocent I, dictated in Constantinople while he was under house arrest, only letters sent by John in exile or by the presbyter Constantius during a two-month visit to Cucusus are included. All letters are in Greek, although John indicates that he could read Latin and for some 12 per cent of his correspondents that was their primary language. Not a single letter received by John is incorporated in the collection. Even within these constraints, there is evidence that letters that John sent from exile are missing from the collection. That is, the collection does not transmit the full contents of an archive. The archive itself, however, may have been incomplete, some copies of letters having been left behind or destroyed in the upheaval of translocation. Thirdly, regardless of the latter possibility there is evidence of intentionality regarding the shape of the collection. This diminishes the likelihood that the collection simply represents an archive maintained by an exiled bishop with gaps due to the accident of survival, preserved because of the status of the bishop in question. Rather, the collective evidence, particularly the inclusion of two polemical ps-Chrysostom letters, suggests that this is a Johannite collection that has been shaped to present a Johannite point of view, most likely for the benefit of the Johannite community that survived him.

In fact, if we shift our focus from the question of who compiled the collection to that of where it was assembled, it may be that we can further refine our understanding of the rationale behind the collection. As already mentioned, the inclusion of five letters by another author (Constantius) is intriguing. They cannot have been incorporated simply by accident, since we can identify other clergy from both Antioch and Constantinople who came to visit John for periods long enough for them to have initiated and included among the outgoing letters personal correspondence with their own networks.[121] If Constantius' letters had

---

[121] For the networks to which the deacon Theodotus and presbyter Libanius were attached in Antioch, for example, see Mayer 2014: Table 1.

simply been filed together with John's as a matter of course, then the letters of other inner-circle clergy ought to have comprised part of the archive also. We already raised the possibility that it was Constantius' letters that were selected precisely because of his status as the Johannite candidate destined to assume the neo-Nicene Antiochene episcopate on Flavian's death. When we add this choice to the incorporation of such a large number of letters addressed by John to supporters in Antioch and to the inclusion of letters that relate to the Antiochene-based mission in Phoenicia, the impression of an Antiochene bias to the collection becomes inescapable. It may also explain the inclusion of the ps-Chrysostom letter *Ep. 233 ad episc. Antioch.*, offering some support for Ubaldi's thesis.[122] If we speculate that the most likely source of the impetus to cut off John's support-base in mid-407 came from Porphyrius, the anti-Johannite bishop of Antioch consecrated in Constantius' place, and that his concern was sparked off by the fact that communication between John and his supporters in Antioch was continuing unabated, persecution of the Johannites there being either less aggressive or less effective, an alternative possibility arises. That is, the putative archive on which the collection is based was not attached to the person of John and thus assembled in Armenia, but was assembled, on the contrary, in Antioch.

Could it be that the Antiochene interest that the collection demonstrates is due to the activity of one or more of the Antiochene deacons and presbyters who shuttled back and forth, acting at times as John's scribe, at others as his letter-carriers? A number of inner-circle Johannites engaged in these roles may well have brought back copies systematically for safe-keeping. Given the instability of the region in which John was exiled and the numerous translocations he experienced, it may make more sense to posit that the collection was assembled in secret in Antioch in the household of one of his key lay supporters. Ultimately, this is pure speculation, the available evidence being insufficient to confirm or deny it. It does suggest, however, that in future the Chrysostom letter-collection should be read alongside the *Dialogue* of Palladius and the funeral oration by ps-Martyrius as an integral part of the Johannite defence of John and their particular shaping of his memory.

---

[122] i.e., that this is a sixth letter written by Constantius. See n. 41 above. The other possibility is that the letter is a ps-Constantius construct, crafted to accord him the same status as John (that of a 'bishop' wrongfully cast out of his church and city). The important point in either case is that it directly addresses and accuses the current bishop of Antioch, Porphyrius.

Table 9.1 Sequence of *Epp.* 1–17 to Olympias

Order in bulk of manuscripts (edited by Savile)	Date (Delmaire)	Fronton du Duc, Montfaucon (= Migne, PG 52: 549–623)	Chronological sequence (edited by Malingrey 1968)
1 [S]	end Sept./Oct. 404	1 [S] = 1 [M]	10 [S] 11 [M] = 1 [SC]
2 [S]	Oct. 404	2 [S] = 2 [M]	9 [S] 10 [M] = 2 [SC]
3 [S]	end 404	3 [S] = 3 [M]	8 [S] 9 [M] = 3 [SC]
		16 [S] = 4 [M]	11 [S] 12 [M] = 4 [SC]
4 [S]	beg. 405	4 [S] = 5 [M]	7 [S] 8 [M] = 5 [SC]
5 [S]	spring 405	5 [S] = 6 [M]	12 [S] 13 [M] = 6 [SC]
6 [S]	summer 405	6 [S] = 7 [M]	1 [SM] = 7 [SC]
7 [S]	mid Aug. 404	7 [S] = 8 [M]	2 [SM] = 8 [SC]
8 [S]	beg. Aug. 404	8 [S] = 9 [M]	13 [S] 14 [M] = 9 [SC]
9 [S]	3 July 404	9 [S] = 10 [M]	3 [SM] = 10 [SC]
10 [S]	end June 404	10 [S] = 11 [M]	4 [S] 5 [M] = 11 [SC]
11 [S]	mid Aug. 404	11 [S] = 12 [M]	5 [S] 6 [M] = 12 [SC]
12 [S]	mid Sept. 404	12 [S] = 13 [M]	6 [S] 7 [M] = 13 [SC]
13 [S]	end Nov. 404	13 [S] = 14 [M]	15 [S] 16 [M] = 14 [SC]
14 [S]	spring 406	14 [S] = 15 [M]	14 [S] 15 [M] = 15 [SC]
15 [S]	405	15 [S] = 16 [M]	17 [SM] = 16 [SC]
16 [S]	spring 407		16 [S] 4 [M] = 17 [SC]
17 [S]	end 406	17 [S] = 17 [M]	

Note: [S] = Savile; [M] = Montfaucon; [SC] = *Sources chrétiennes*.

Table 9.2 Chronological order of authentic letters written by John Chrysostom (*Epp.* 18–124, 125–232, 234–6)*

No. (PG = Montfaucon)	Date (Delmaire)	Addressee	Location of addressee
221	4 July 404	Constantius 2	Antioch
118	summer 404	bishops and priests in prison	Constantinople?
174	summer 404	bishops and priests	Chalcedon
119	Aug. 404	Theophilus	Constantinople
120	Aug. 404	Theodora	Constantinople
121	Aug. 404	Arabius	Constantinople
123	end Aug./beg. Sept. 404	priests and monks	Phoenicia

* The table excludes *Epp.* 23, 31, 42, 45, 63, 71, 78, 145, 175, 177, 192 and 195, which Delmaire was unable to date with any precision.

Table 9.2 (*cont.*)

No. (PG = Montfaucon)	Date (Delmaire)	Addressee	Location of addressee
193	beg. Sept. 404	Paeanius	Constantinople
194	beg. Sept. 404	Gemellus	Constantinople
223	beg. Sept. 404	Hesychius 2	Constantinople
234	beg. Sept. 404	Brison	Constantinople
235	beg. Sept. 404	Porphyrius	Rhosos
236	beg. Sept. 404	Carterius	Caesarea
80	beg. Sept. 404	Firminus	Caesarea
81	beg. Sept. 404	Hymnetius	Caesarea
82	beg. Sept. 404	Cytherius	Caesarea
83	beg. Sept. 404	Leontius	Caesarea
84	beg. Sept. 404	Faustinus	Caesarea
171	beg. Sept. 404	Montius	Caesarea
172	beg. Sept. 404	Helladius	Caesarea
173	beg. Sept. 404	Evethius	Caesarea
85	beg. Sept. 404	Lucius	Palestine
86	beg. Sept. 404	Mares 1	Palestine
87	beg. Sept. 404	Eulogius	Caesarea in Palestine
88	beg. Sept. 404	John 1	Jerusalem
89	beg. Sept. 404	Theodosius 2	Scythopolis
90	beg. Sept. 404	Moises 1	Antarados?
108	beg. Sept. 404	Urbicius	Cilicia
109	beg. Sept. 404	Rufinus 4	Cilicia
110	beg. Sept. 404	Bassus	Cilicia
111	beg. Sept. 404	Anatolius 2	Adana
112	beg. Sept. 404	Theodorus 4	Mopsuestia
222	beg. Sept. 404	Castus and company	Antioch
53	mid Sept. 404	Nicolaos	Zeugma
54	mid Sept. 404	Geontius 2	Zeugma
72	Sept. 404	Alphius	Antioch
74	Sept. 404	Hesychius 3	Antioch
75	Sept. 404	Armatus	Antioch
133	Sept. 404	Adolia	Antioch
48	Sept. 404	Arabius	Constantinople
64	Sept. 404	Cyriacus 2	Constantinople
115	Sept. 404	Theophilus	Constantinople
116	Sept 404	Valentinus	Constantinople
188	Sept. 404	Macellinus	Constantinople
189	Sept. 404	Antiochus 2	Constantinople
134	Sept. 404	Diogenes	Syria?
196	Sept. 404	Aetius	?
228	end Sept. 404	Theodorus 2	Caesarea
95	end Sept./beg. Oct. 404	Paeanius	Constantinople
96	end Sept./beg. Oct. 404	Amprucla	Constantinople

Table 9.2 (*cont.*)

No. (PG = Montfaucon)	Date (Delmaire)	Addressee	Location of addressee
97	end Sept./beg. Oct. 404	Hypatius	Constantinople
103	end Sept./beg. Oct. 404	Amprucla	Constantinople
202	Sept./beg. Oct. 404	Cyriacus 2	Constantinople
186	beg. autumn 404	Alypius	Constantinople
94	Oct. 404	Pentadia	Constantinople
220	Oct. 404	Paeanius	Constantinople
26	Oct. 404	Magnus	Syria?
57	Oct. 404	Adolia	Antioch
231	Oct. 404	Adolia	Antioch
114	Oct. 404	Helpidius 1	Laodicea
230	Oct. 404	Helpidius 1	Laodicea
224	Oct. 404	Marcian and Marcellinus	Antioch
226	Oct. 404	Marcian and Marcellinus	Antioch
225	Oct. 404	Constantius 1	Antioch
227	Oct. 404	Carteria	Antioch
232	Oct. 404	Carteria	Antioch
229	Oct. 404	Severa	Antioch
101	Oct./Nov. 404	Severus	Constantinople
191	autumn 404	Amprucla	Constantinople
190	autumn 404	Brison	Constantinople
28	autumn 404	Basil	Syria/Phoenicia
73	autumn 404	Agapetus	Antioch
18	end Oct./Nov. 404	Carteria	Antioch
242	end Oct./beg. Nov. 404	Chalcidia and Asyncritia	Antioch
76	Nov. 404	Chalcidia	Antioch
77	Nov. 404	Asyncritia	Antioch
179	Nov. 404	Adolia	Antioch
24	end autumn 404	Hesychius 3	Antioch
25	end autumn 404	Helpidius 1	Laodicea
27	end autumn 404	Domnus	Syria?
187	end autumn 404	Procopius	Constantinople
198	end autumn 404	Hesychius 2	Constantinople?
203	end Nov. 404	Sallustius	Constantinople
204	end Nov. 404	Paeanius	Constantinople
205	end Nov. 404	Anatolius 3	Constantinople
206	end Nov. 404	Theodoulos	Constantinople
207	end Nov. 404	Gothic monks	Constantinople

Table 9.2 (*cont.*)

No. (PG = Montfaucon)	Date (Delmaire)	Addressee	Location of addressee
208	end Nov. 404	Acacius	Constantinople
209	end Nov. 404	Salvio	Constantinople
210	end Nov. 404	Theodore 3	Constantinople
211	end Nov. 404	Timothy	Constantinople
212	end Nov. 404	Theophilus	Constantinople
213	end Nov. 404	Philip	Constantinople
214	end Nov. 404	Sebastian	Constantinople
215	end Nov. 404	Pelagius 2	Constantinople
216	end Nov. 404	Musonius	Constantinople
217	end Nov. 404	Valentinus	Constantinople
218	end Nov. 404	Euthymius	Constantinople
197	before Dec. 404	Studius	Constantinople
52	beg. Dec. 404	Adolia	Antioch
144	beg. winter 404	Diogenes	Syria?
199	beg. winter 404	Daniel	Constantinople
200	beg. winter 404	Callistratus	Isauria
20	Dec. 404	Agapetus	Antioch
39	Dec. 404	Chalcidia	Antioch
40	Dec. 404	Asyncritia	Antioch
201	end 404?	Herculius	Constantinople
122	end 404	Marcianus 2	Constantinople
219	end 404	Severina and Romula	Constantinople
176	end 404	Hesychius 3	Antioch
19	end 404	Marcian and Marcellinus	Antioch
47	end 404	Namaea	Antioch
92	end 404?	Moises 2	Syria?
30	end 404	Heortius	?
113	end 404	Palladius	?
32	end 404/beg. 405	Euthalia	Constantinople?
178	end 404/beg. 405	Euthalia	Constantinople?
117	winter 404/5 at earliest	Theodora	Constantinople
60	end 404/beg. 405	Chalcidia and Asyncritia	Antioch
65	winter 404/5	Marcian and Marcellinus	Antioch
98	winter 404/5	Chalcidia	Antioch
99	winter 404/5	Asyncritia	Antioch
43	winter 404/5	Bassiana	Antioch
21	winter 404/5	Alphius	Antioch
49	winter 404/5	Alphius	Antioch
22	winter 404/5	Castus and company	Antioch
62	winter 404/5	Castus and company	Antioch

Table 9.2 (*cont.*)

No. (PG = Montfaucon)	Date (Delmaire)	Addressee	Location of addressee
66	beg. 405	Castus and compnay	Antioch
137	beg. 405	Theodotus 3	Antioch
91	winter 404/5	Romanus	Antioch
33	winter 404/5	Adolia	Antioch
34	winter 404/5	Carteria	Antioch
35	winter 404/5	Alphius	Antioch
36	winter 404/5	Maron	Syria?
37	winter 404/5	Tranquillinus	?
38	winter 404/5	Hymnetius	Caesarea
41	winter 404/5	Valentinus	?
46	winter 404/5	Rufinus 2	?
55	winter 404/5	Symeon and Mares	Apamea
56	winter 404/5	Romulus and Byzos	Apamea?
93	winter 404/5	Aphtonius	Zeugma
104	winter 404/5	Pentadia	Constantinople
180	winter 404/5	Hypatius	Constantinople
140	spring 405	Theodotus 3	Antioch
129	spring 405	Marcian and Marcellinus	Antioch
29	spring 405	Chalcidia and Asyncritia	Antioch
138	spring 405	Helpidius 1	Laodicea
105	summer 405	Chalcidia	Antioch
106	summer 405	Asyncritia	Antioch
130	summer 405	Castus and company	Antioch
139	summer 405	Theodore 3	Antioch
50	summer 405	Diogenes	Syria?
51	summer 405	Diogenes	Syria?
146	summer 405	Theodotus and company	Zeugma
124	summer 405	Gemellus	Constantinople
195	summer 405	Pentadia	?
147	Aug./Sept. 405	Anthemius	Constantinople
100	summer/autumn 405	Marcian and Marcellinus	Antioch
126	summer/autumn 405	Rufinus 3	?
59	beg. 406	Theodotus 3	Antioch
61	beg. 406	Theodotus 2	?
79	spring 406	Gemellus	Constantinople
135	spring 406	Theodotus 3	Antioch
107	spring 406	Castus and company	Antioch
69	spring 406	Nicolaos	Zeugma
70	spring 406	Aphtonius	Zeugma
127	spring 406	Polybius	?

Table 9.2 (*cont.*)

No. (PG = Montfaucon)	Date (Delmaire)	Addressee	Location of addressee
128	spring 406	Marinianus	?
151	spring 406	Asellus	?
149	spring 406	Aurelius	Carthage
150	spring 406	Maximius	Turin?
155	spring 406	Chromatius	Aquileia
148	spring 406	Cyriacus and company	Rome
168	spring 406	Proba	Rome
169	spring 406	Juliana	Rome
170	spring 406	Italica	Rome
182	spring 406	Venerius	Milan
183	spring 406	Hesychius 1	Salona
184	spring 406	Gaudentius	Brescia
164	spring 406	Alexander	Corinth
152	spring 406	bishops	Thessalonica
153	spring 406	bishops	Thessalonica
154	spring 406	bishops	Thessalonica
156	spring 406	bishops	Thessalonica
157	spring 406	bishops	Thessalonica
158	spring 406	bishops	Thessalonica
159	spring 406	bishops	Thessalonica
160	spring 406	bishops	Thessalonica
161	spring 406	priests	Thessalonica
162	spring 406	Anysius	Thessalonica
163	spring 406	bishops of Macedonia	Thessalonica
165	spring 406	bishops	Thessalonica
166	spring 406	bishops	Thessalonica
167	spring 406	bishops	Thessalonica
181	spring 406	bishops	Thessalonica
131	spring/summer 406	Helpidius 1	Laodicea
136	spring/summer 406	Theodotus 4	?
143	spring/summer 406	Polybius	?
68	beg. summer 406	Theodotus 3	Antioch
67	summer 406	Theodotus 3	Antioch
102	summer 406	Theodotus 4	?
141	summer 406	Theodotus 2	?
132	summer 406	Gemellus	Constantinople
142	spring 407	Helpidius 1	Laodicea

CHAPTER 10

The letters of Theodoret of Cyrrhus
Personal collections, multi-author archives and historical interpretation

Adam M. Schor

In 434, Theodoret, bishop of Cyrrhus in Syria, sent two letters dealing with apparently divergent issues.[1] One concerned doctrinal disputes. Since 430, bishops had split over how to describe the human and divine in Christ. Initially, most bishops in Syria joined in supporting 'two natures' in opposition to Cyril of Alexandria. By 434, Syrian clerics had turned on each other. Notably Alexander of Hierapolis refused communion with John of Antioch, because John had negotiated peace with Cyril and accepted him as orthodox. After trying and failing to mediate, Theodoret sided with Alexander in schism, even as the emperor demanded that everyone join communion with Cyril and John.

In this letter, Theodoret wrote to Alexander with new information. General Titus had asserted that 'he would toss us out ... if we did not acquiesce to become peaceful'. These threats Theodoret could laugh off: if deposed, he would return to his monastery; but then came more troubling news. Titus had requested help from three famous ascetics, Baradatus, Jacob of Cyrrhestica and Symeon Stylites, whom Theodoret counted as friends. 'The holy monks afflicted me badly, asking of us many things for the sake of peace, as if they held us guilty.' Theodoret could not ignore the monks' wish to assemble the feuding parties, so he asked Alexander how to restart negotiations.[2]

The other letter concerned a non-clerical judicial matter. Theodoret had a friend named Palladius, a non-Christian 'philosopher' who paid a soldier to protect him. When the soldier was denounced in military court, Palladius asked Theodoret to plead with the presiding general. 'Justice has many enemies', he wrote, 'but injustice yields to it when the lovers of justice truly join the fray.' Luckily, this general was a 'most brilliant

---

[1] Citations of Theodoret's letters employ this shorthand: P = *Collectio Patmensis*, Azéma 1964–98, vol. 1; S = *Collectio Sirmondiana*, Azéma 1964–98, vols. 11–111. Conciliar letters are cited by titles and numbers in *CPG*, and by location in document collections.

[2] Theodoret, *Ep. ad Alexandrum Hierapoltianum* (*CPG* 6249), ACO 1/4: 170–1.

contender'. Theodoret insisted that the soldier be permitted to work for Palladius; he asked for an 'unbribed judgment' for the sake of this 'philosopher' and the accused soldier.[3] This case would seem unrelated to clerical feuding, except that Theodoret was writing to Titus, the very general threatening to depose him. Nor was this their only social contact, for Titus and Theodoret shared several acquaintances[4] and the bishop even tried to offer the general spiritual advice.[5]

Theodoret's correspondence, to which these letters belong, illuminates late-antique society in striking ways. Many entries display the workings of key social and political institutions; others showcase the development of the Christological controversy which fractured the church. Above all, the letters depict the career of Theodoret, a supremely educated monk, elected bishop in 423, who gained prominence during the Nestorian controversy (429–36), sustained influence by his writings and elite connections, endured condemnation by the Second Council of Ephesus in 449 and went into exile, only to be freed in 450 and vindicated by the Council of Chalcedon the next year.[6] Historians have plumbed Theodoret's letters for social 'facts' and doctrinal positions.[7] Yet scholars often stress the rhetorical nature of these texts and wonder how much they reflect reality.[8]

This chapter surveys Theodoret's letters from the perspective of a historian seeking evidence. This correspondence presents interpretative problems. The 233 extant notes[9] are not only rhetorical; they were never one text. Two single-author collections, which barely overlap, are augmented by scattered entries in multi-author records from church councils. Each of Theodoret's letter-sets had its own editors with aims that differ from his.

Nevertheless, Theodoret's letters remain powerful sources for social history, if we take a careful approach. Different letter types and textual

---

[3] Theodoret, *Ep.* P11, Azéma 1964–98/1: 83.

[4] E.g. Eurycianus the tribune, who conveyed Titus' threats (Theodoret, *Ep. ad Alexandrum Hierapolitanum* [*CPG* 6249], ACO 1/4: 170–1), also carried personal tidings between Theodoret and the sophist Isocasius (*Ep.* P38, Azéma 1964–98/1: 102–3), and received Theodoret's condolence (*Ep.* P47, Azéma 1964–98/1: 111–17, see below).

[5] Theodoret, *Ep.* P6, Azéma 1964–98/1: 78–9.

[6] On Theodoret's life, see Urbainczyk 2002: 10–28; Pásztori-Kupán 2006: 3–27; Vuolanto 2012. See also Young 1983: 322–7.

[7] On social facts, see Jones 1986/1: 355, 385, 542, 633; 11: 854; Tompkins 1993. On doctrinal positions, see Devreesse 1948, 1931; Richard 1977d, 1941–2, 1936; Diepen 1953; Liébaert 1970; Mandac 1971; Evieux 1974; van Esbroeck 1987; Clayton 2007; Fairbairn 2007a, 2007b.

[8] On Theodoret's epistolary rhetoric, see Wagner 1948; Azéma 1981; Spadavecchia 1985; Calvet-Sebasti 1998; Rousseau 2005; Millar 2007.

[9] This count is augmented by twenty-two conciliar letters that Theodoret probably co-authored. See below.

traditions support different forms of analysis, for example where personal collections are helpful for exploring the author's rhetoric and social strategies, multi-author conciliar records allow for mapping certain clerical relations amid conflict. Viewed together, segments of Theodoret's collection gain value, affording multiple perspectives on a bishop navigating his social world.

Theodoret's personal collections: *Patmensis*

Most studies of Theodoret's letters examine his 'personal' collections, fifty-two letters of the *Patmensis* manuscript and 142 unique entries in the *Sirmondiana* edition. These are notable for their rich portrayal of the author and memorable social scenes.

But what can historians conclude from Theodoret's personal correspondence? As source material, it has limitations. No replies are included, and some entries may be excerpts. Late-antique clerical letters drew on classical educational traditions, rhetorical handbooks, and specifically Christian customs, all of which channelled what Theodoret said.[10] Many of Theodoret's letters lack key contextual information; many mention couriers conveying messages only hinted at in writing.[11]

Perhaps the deepest limitation is our lack of knowledge about editors. We know neither who first gathered the personal letters,[12] nor who shaped the two extant collections. The fourteenth-century Byzantine scholar Nikephoros Kallistos knew of about 500 letters by Theodoret.[13] *Patmensis* and *Sirmondiana* are probably drawn from part or all of this pool.[14] Somehow the shorter manuscript ended up in a monastery on Patmos, to be published by Johannes Sakkelion in 1885. The longer manuscript was brought to Italy, replicated and published by the Jesuit Jacques Sirmond in 1642.[15] What guided the editors' arrangements and selections is unclear.

---

[10] On sophistic epistolography and handbooks, see Kim 1972; Constable 1976; Stowers 1986; Malherbe 1988; Trapp 2003; Van Dam 2003: 131–8; Hodkinson 2007; Rees 2007. On Christan epistolary customs, see Porter and Adams 2010; Mullett 1981; Stirewalt 1993.
[11] On oral supplementation see Liebeschuetz 1972: 18–22; Stirewalt 1993: 4–5; Mullett 1997: 36–37; Schor 2011: 35–8; Allen 2013a: 487–8.
[12] Theodoret never hints that he self-published.
[13] Nikephoros Kallistos, *Historiae* 14.54, PG 146: 1257.
[14] The single source pool is suggested by consistency in letter titles, and the five repeated entries, four of which appear in the same order.
[15] On *Patmensis*'s and *Sirmondiana*'s textual history, see Azéma 1964–98/I: 66–72, II: 9–18.

Yet, Theodoret's personal collection remains ripe for historical study through a socio-rhetorical approach. By this I mean to treat correspondence as a partial record of past communications. Scholars have noted the personal letters' linguistic consistency, which suggests one author.[16] The addressees' role is less clear, but some entries clearly belong to ongoing exchanges. We can fairly assume that Theodoret really sent these messages, to convey certain signals of affinity to particular audiences. Extant entries may not be representative of Theodoret's (thousands of) original letters, but the letters still show us people with whom Theodoret sought to interact and the means he employed to court them. Thus we gain a subjective glimpse at his social world.[17]

We start with the *Patmensis* collection, which features fifty-two letters (or excerpts), all but one less than thirty-six Greek lines. All but two entries name addressees – thirty-seven people in total (the main text names twenty-five more).[18] Such prosopography matters because it supplies our only grounds for dating *Patmensis* letters. All of Theodoret's extant letters post-date his election in 423; all but one make most sense before the Council of Chalcedon in 451.[19] Some notes in other collections can be precisely dated, but most *Patmensis* entries are only time-limited by the name and title of addressees.[20]

The *Patmensis* letters fall into categories of purpose. Three offer condolence; twenty ask favours for Theodoret's clients; two give thanks for past help; one answers a request for Theodoret's patronage; thirteen profess friendship; three offer officials or ex-officials advice; two ask elite men to embrace baptism; two ask existing Christians to enrich their faith; six rebuke addressees for improper actions or associations; and one invites someone to a feast honouring 'Prophets and Apostles'.[21]

The *Patmensis* letters furnish samples of Theodoret's socio-rhetorical tactics – how he tailored words to fit different situations and addressees. Consider Theodoret's friendly letters, which include one to Aerius, a Christian sophist. The letter began with a mock accusation: 'O best of men, you do wrong, in not giving us a taste of your education, as the

---

[16] See Rousseau 2005.

[17] On this approach, see Schor 2011; for slightly different approaches, see Mullett 1997 and McLean 2007.

[18] Even for Theodoret, *Ep.* P31, P33, Azéma 1964–98/1: 97–9, scholars can deduce addressees' social position.

[19] Except Theodoret, *Ep. ad Iohannem Aegeatem* (*CPG* 6278), Nau 1919: 190–1. See Gray 1984.

[20] E.g., Titus led troops in Syria in late 433 and 434. Theodoret, *Ep. ad Alexandrum Hierapolitanum* (*CPG* 6249), ACO 1.4: 170–1; and *Ep.* P11, Azéma 1964–98/1: 83, must date then.

[21] Theodoret, *Ep.* P35, Azéma 1964–98/1: 100.

saying goes, "on the tips of your fingers", (Zenobius 1.61), rather over-
looking the thirsty and hiding the springs of words.' The letter extended
this words-as-water metaphor: 'They say that the unreachable reservoirs
exhaust those who would drink from them, but the reachable ones provide streams sweeter and purer.' Sophists were not usually known for the
'silence of Pythagoras', so the bishop asked for more writing. 'If you are
silent only to us, tell us why, so that we may convince you that you are
silent unjustly.'[22] Many letters lament infrequent communication, but,
with a close associate, Theodoret made this trope a game. Playful rhetoric
and allusions signalled the classical learning and emotions they shared,
but not all Theodoret's friendly letters played this game. Some were more
coldly formal, while others alluded mainly to scripture and avoided classical learning, or called it a 'cheap casing', the 'writings of sinners'.[23] Much
depended on the socio-cultural positioning of addressees.

Theodoret's condolence notes also reveal variation. Consider his words
to Axia the deaconess after her daughter's death. 'You know that human
nature is mortal, and you have been taught the hopes of resurrection', he
began. 'Both reasons together are sufficient to blunt sadness' but when
a person 'has exited life gloriously, it is proper to extinguish our pain
entirely'. Theodoret urged Axia to let the 'blessings of all ... console your
Piety; for everyone sings of [your daughter's] praiseworthy life'. Theodoret
urged the deaconess to 'Consider this separation from your daughter to
be an exercise in philosophy, and persuade yourself that she has left for a
greater land ... to claim the rewards of virtue'.[24] By the mid-fifth century,
a long tradition informed Christian condolence, but Theodoret chose
themes suited to an ascetic woman: her 'philosophy' and faith in heavenly
rewards. Change the audience, however, and the discourse shifts, as in
Theodoret's letter to the tribune Eurycianus, who also lost a daughter. 'I
know the gloominess of winter storms and the violence of the waves', he
began. 'The present life holds nothing ... lasting, except the beauty of virtue.' And yet, 'it is the right time to remind you of divine dogmas, to lead
you from suffering to great hope'. He followed with one hundred lines of
biblical interpretation concerning Christian immortality, repeatedly praising the 'virtue' of Eurycianus and his child.[25] With this imperial official,

---

[22] Theodoret, *Ep.* P10, Azéma 1964–98/1: 82.
[23] Playful letter: Theodoret, *Ep.* P49, Azéma 1964–98/1: 119; formal friendly letter: *Ep.* P15, Azéma 1964–98/1: 86–7. Both quote scripture. Dismissal of classical learning: *Ep.* P12, Azéma 1964–98/1: 83–8, to Palladius!
[24] Theodoret, *Ep.* P48 Azéma 1964–98/1: 118.
[25] Theodoret, *Ep.* P47, Azéma 1964–98/1: 111–17.

Theodoret did not share ascetic values, but he could offer Christian basics, as he simulated a family panegyric for his elite friend.

Another sort of variation characterises *Patmensis* letters that counsel changes in behaviour or policy. For instance, Theodoret wrote three decurions of nearby Zeugma a blunt message: 'We have heard that people from your town betroth daughters to their nephews and that maternal uncles make wives of their own nieces.' Such acts, he said, 'are dared among Persians, not Romans reared in piety'. Such unions might accord with Roman law, but the emperor 'cannot dissolve sins'.[26] Provincial governors were (temporarily) more powerful than such *curiales*, so Theodoret advised them more obliquely. Thus he wrote to Governor Neon on taxation enforcement by praising his gentleness. 'Having used kind words', he wrote, 'you have made collection of taxmen better… for, since they are ashamed at the sight of your gentleness, those compelled to pay forget their poverty and strip themselves of their miserable rags.' Theodoret urged patient calm, even amid coin shortage, 'for thus shall you serve the God of the universe and protect the cities that the emperor entrusted to you'.[27] Here Theodoret criticised past policy and intruded into the governor's basic business, but always via panegyrical tones.

Rhetorical variations in *Patmensis* letters portray Theodoret and the social landscape. In these letters Theodoret plays roles proper to a bishop, his words casting him as a steadfast moral corrector, a skilful comforter and a loyal friend. Theodoret's words also characterise the social and cultural standing of his audience. They reveal his assumptions about the significance of imperial rank, gender, and cultural affiliation, and how he might navigate this social world.

Theodoret's personal collections: *Sirmondiana*

The *Sirmondiana* manuscripts also contain personal correspondence, but their contents call for separate analysis. Initially *Sirmondiana* looks like *Patmensis* writ larger. It features 147 letters, five of which are repeated.[28] As in *Patmensis*, most entries in *Sirmondiana* name addressees,[29] including

---

[26] Theodoret, *Ep.* P8, Azéma 1964–98/i: 79–81. *Ep.* P9, Azéma 1964–98/i: 81–2, suggests that the *curiales* heeded Theodoret.

[27] Theodoret, *Ep.* P37 Azéma 1964–98/i: 101–2. Perhaps the message worked; *Epp.* P39–40, Azéma 1964–98/i: 103–4, praised Neon's job performance.

[28] Repetitions include thank-you notes for recommendations (S19–20, Azéma 1964–98/ii: 66–8), calls for officials to embrace baptism (S22, S58, Azéma 1964–98/ii: 78, 134–6), and an appeal for poor tenant-farmers (S23, Azéma 1964–98/ii: 80).

[29] Fifteen have a generic headline.

eighty-five additional souls (the main text adds thirty-eight more). Early in *Sirmondiana*, we see mostly short disconnected letters, datable only by prosopography, but we soon encounter clusters of interrelated letters. The result is more contextual information; hence, a majority of *Sirmondiana* entries are dateable by year (or even by season).

Fifty-six *Sirmondiana* letters follow patterns similar to *Patmensis*. They are mostly short (all but six last fewer than forty-one lines) with only vague chronological markings. Many fall into familiar categories: ten requests for friendship, eight notes of condolence, two singular appeals for clients, two thank-you notes, two notes praising courtiers, three invitations to the 'Feast of the Prophets and Apostles', five notes of advice (three of which urge baptism), and one rebuke. Intermixed we find slight letter-form variations. We encounter sixteen festal letters, that is, feast day greeting cards.[30] We read two long letters of encouragement to bishops facing persecution in Persian Armenia.[31] We find biblically rooted musings on a related question – if compelled to sacrifice to demons on a boat, should one jump overboard or wait to be killed?[32] In these letters (the first portion of the *Sirmondiana* collection), Theodoret's rhetorical tropes fall within the same general range as they do in the *Patmensis* letters: the same sorts of quotations, allusions, comparisons, metaphors, formal figures and most importantly the same sort of tailoring of these cues to fit with Theodoret's perceptions of the social location of his addressees. These letters alone (if the *Sirmondiana* included only them) would thus not lead us to many new conclusions about Theodoret or his social perceptions and strategies, beyond what the *Patmensis* letters support.

Ninety-one *Sirmondiana* letters, however, break new ground, with interrelated entries[33] confronting specific historical situations. Seventeen of these letters concerned larger-scale patronage. Eleven recommended refugees from North Africa, fleeing the Vandals. By 443, several refugees reached Syria, and Theodoret wrote to bishops, officials and others to win them hospitality or protection. Six letters defended Cyrrhus' taxpayers, as the city faced reassessment during the census of 446. Cyrrhus had complained about its past tax burdens, and won minor revisions, but now someone (a deposed Syrian bishop) was alleging that Cyrrhus was defrauding the fisc. So Theodoret wrote to many officials, coordinating with

---

[30] Syrian festal letters differ from the Alexandrian festals, which announced the date of Easter and guided preaching. See Brok 1951; Evieux *et al.* 1991; bibliography in Allen 2010: 196 n. 5.

[31] Theodoret, *Epp.* S77–8, Azéma 1964–98/II: 166–82.

[32] Theodoret, *Ep.* S3, Azéma 1964–98/II: 22–30, to Irenaeus of Tyre (see below).

[33] Cribiore 2007: 233 terms such clusters in Libanius' correspondence 'dossiers'.

civic leaders, bishops and a holy man. Individually these pleas scarcely stand out. Four *Patmensis* entries advocated for taxpayers or refugees,[34] but the context from multiple letters reveals more of the author's guiding strategies.

Theodoret's pleas for refugees are notable for how they combined to address this problem. Consider the seven notes he wrote for the decurion Celestiacus and his family. When Theodoret wrote to a civil official, he portrayed Celestiacus as a tragic figure now finding piety. 'The sufferings of the Carthaginians', he began, 'would require the tragic poetry of Aeschylus or Sophocles.' Theodoret recalled the glorious history of Carthage and its elite. Seeing these refugees, he said he was 'struck with fear, for *I do not know*, as scripture says, *what tomorrow may bring* (Prov. 27:1)'. Theodoret said he admired Celestiacus, who 'makes his change of circumstance an occasion for philosophy,' and asked the official to 'deem him worthy of the kindliness ... of Abraham' (cf. Gen. 18).[35] Thus he mixed classical and historical allusions with biblical examples, to inspire sympathy. When Theodoret wrote about Celestiacus to the sophist Aerius, he struck a different tone. 'Now is the time', he began, 'for your Academy to demonstrate the usefulness of fancy words.' Theodoret noted Celestiacus' rank and past generosity, so he told Aerius: 'Become his tongue ... persuade those of your assembly who are capable to show the hospitality of Alcinous' (cf. Homer, *Odyssey* 7–8).[36] Variations continued in other refugee appeals: to civic leaders, the coming of Celestiacus signified the fickleness of fortune,[37] while to clerics, it warned of punishments all sinners could expect from God.[38] We see how requests were customised to attract elites of various cultural preferences, but Theodoret did not court random wealthy men. He chose people in specific leadership roles, and he motivated them to echo his requests within specific demographics. Together these letters reveal a strategy to maximise the scope of generosity, geographically and socially.[39]

Theodoret's appeals for taxpayers offer their own rhetorical flourishes. Consider his fullest account of the situation, to Constantine the prefect. 'If I sent a letter to Your Greatness with no imposing necessity', he began, 'I would have likely been found guilty of presumption',

---

[34] Taxpayers: Theodoret, *Epp*. P17, P20, Azéma 1964–98/i: 88–9, 92; see Allen and Neil 2013: 61–6. Refugees: *Epp*. P22–3, Azéma 1964–98/i: 92–4; see Allen and Neil 2013: 94–6.

[35] Theodoret, *Ep*. S29, Azéma 1964–98/ii: 86–8.

[36] Theodoret, *Ep*. S30, Azéma 1964–98/ii: 88–90.

[37] Theodoret, *Ep*. S33 Azéma 1964–98/ii: 94–6, to Stasimus the *principalis*.

[38] Theodoret, *Ep*. S32, Azéma 1964–98/ii: 92–4, to Theoctistus of Beroea.

[39] On Theodoret's refugee strategy, see Schor 2011: 166–7; Allen and Neil 2013: 61–66.

but the lies of an excommunicated cleric compelled him to write (or write again – Theodoret assumes Constantine knew the basic circumstances). To counter these lies, Theodoret offered technical detail, which we modern scholars struggle to reconstruct. In the last census Cyrrhus was assessed, he claims, at 62,500 *iuga* (47,500 *iuga* on private holdings, 15,000 *iuga* on imperial estates). However, collectors reportedly could not meet requirements with so many abandoned lands. Reassessments, he said, had transferred 2,500 *iuga* from imperial to freehold lands, without reducing Cyrrhus' liability.[40] Theodoret noted support from the 'holy man Jacob', and he urged the prefect to 'put aside false accusations' and 'leave to the generations an eternal memory of glory'.[41] Including these details in his letter to Constantine made sense, since the prefect officially commanded the land tax bureaux. For other figures of influence, he changed his approach; to Empress Pulcheria, Theodoret offered tales of suffering and praise of piety. 'Since you adorn the purple by your faith', he began, 'we are so bold as to write you.' He begged her to 'deem our miserable territory worthy of mercy', to ignore the 'false accusations' of a man 'making war on the countless poor'. Rather than quote liability figures, he dramatised the problem of abandoned lands with images of people left begging. 'The shape of the city is reduced to one man, and he will not hold out, unless a remedy is applied.'[42] The empress lacked a bureaucratic portfolio but had broad influence and a record of charitable support; Theodoret simply called her to extend her pious patronage.

The strategy guiding Theodoret's tax appeals, while more intricate, can be reconstructed.[43] Initial efforts to minimise Cyrrhus' taxes (in 445) relied on Philip the decurion to work with the tax bureaucrats and their superiors, aided by Constantinople's bishop,[44] but countering an active accuser demanded broader efforts. So Theodoret's later letters (in 446) first courted the prefect and the empress, then the same prefect again, a former official and a friendly general. Throughout they drew help from a lawyer,

---

[40] The *iugum* was an assessment unit of land area modified to account for different crops, labour regimes and fertility. A total *iugatio* was fixed for each city territory, and served as the basis for assigning actual tax burdens. Also significant was assessment in gold vs. in kind. On tax terms and the *agri deserti*, see Grey 2007; Gascou 1977; on gold taxation, see Banaji 2007; on Theodoret's figures, see Tompkins 1993: 96–123.

[41] Theodoret, *Ep*. S42, Azéma 1964–98/II: 106–12.

[42] Theodoret, *Ep*. S43 Azéma 1964–98/II: 112–14. See Tompkins 1993: 112–13.

[43] Tompkins 1995 reconstructed the chronology. For slight modifications, see Schor 2011: 167–9, 263 n. 83.

[44] Theodoret recollected this journey in *Ep*. S47, Azéma 1964–98/II: 122–4. He must have also then written P17, Azéma 1964–98/I: 88–9. The bureaucrats involved would have been the *praefectiani* (for freeholdings) and the *palatini* (for imperial land).

a bishop and Jacob the hermit.[45] These letters and in-person pleas followed a clear plan: to ostracise the accuser, and to surround key decision-makers with favourable arguments.

The third *Sirmondiana* cluster overshadows the collection: seventy-four letters lengthily defend Theodoret's and his allies' orthodoxy during the 'Eutychean' controversy (448–51). Most of these letters are arranged at the end of the collection in rough chronological order[46] and supply key information about the controversy. We hear about accusations of clerical misconduct targeting Theodoret and his allies in early 448. We see Theodoret respond by recounting his career: 'In my twenty-five years as bishop, I was neither sued by anyone, nor did I accuse another ... I never received an obol or a garment ... I gladly led eight villages of Marcionites ... one of Arians, and one of Eunomians, to the truth.'[47] We find Theodoret instructing allies on how to assist; later one ally helped to condemn the monk Eutyches.[48] We read Theodoret's complaints as supporters abandoned him, before his condemnation and exile.[49] We read his plea to Pope Leo, who may have helped convince the new emperor to release him,[50] and we observe his quest for support before the Council of Chalcedon.[51] Here Theodoret cast himself as persecuted defender of orthodoxy. Other sources supply alternate perspectives, yet even those that cast Theodoret as villain echo impressions left by *Sirmondiana*, portraying him as doctrinal party leader with important but limited support.[52]

Whatever their accuracy, the 'Eutychean' letters remain ripe for socio-rhetorical analysis. It is striking to whom Theodoret wrote *apologiai*. Most elite figures he courted as friends or patrons, consoled or advised elsewhere in *Sirmondiana* reappear here as (hoped-for) supporters. A few

---

[45] Earlier contact with Constantine is implied by Theodoret, *Ep.* S42, Azéma 1964–98/II: 106–12. Empress: *Ep.* S43, Azéma 1964–98/II: 112–14. Ex-official: *Ep.* S44, Azéma 1964–98/II: 116–18. General: *Ep.* S45, Azéma 1964–98/II: 118–20. Lawyer: *Ep.* S46, Azéma 1964–98/II: 122. Bishop: *Ep.* P20, Azéma 1964–98/I: 92. Jacob is mentioned in *Epp.* P20, Azéma 1964–98/I: 92; S42, S44, Azéma 1964–98/II: 112, 116–18.

[46] Five 'Eutychean' letters (Theodoret, *Epp.* S 9, 11–12, 16, 21) appear earlier in *Sirmondiana*; others break sequence.

[47] Theodoret, *Ep.* S81, Azéma 1964–98/II: 196.

[48] See Theodoret, *Epp.* S79, S85, S92, S110–12, Azéma 1964–98/II: 182–8, 222–4, 242–4, III: 38–56. Basil of Seleucia helped to condemn Eutyches in November 448 (*Acta concilii Chalcedonensis*, session I, ACO II.I.I: 123–47).

[49] On lack of replies, see Theodoret, *Epp.* S80–1, S90–1, S93–4, Azéma 1964–98/II: 188–98, 238–46.

[50] Theodoret, *Ep.* S113, Azéma 1964–98/II: 56–66. Leo's reply (*Ep.* 120, PL 54: 1046–55), if genuine, must post-date the Council of Chalcedon (see Silva-Tarouca 1934–5). Yet Leo appealed generally to the empresses Galla Placidia and Pulcheria for mistreated bishops.

[51] Theodoret, *Epp.* S138–47, Azéma 1964–98/III: 138–232.

[52] See *Acts of the Second Council of Ephesus*, Flemming 1917: 84–128; tr. Perry 1881: 270–363.

allies now become turncoats.[53] It is also striking how Theodoret organised his defence. With some clerics and (a few) courtiers he shared details of theology.[54] Once condemnation seemed unavoidable, he played confessor, decrying injustice while standing firm for orthodoxy,[55] but Theodoret's foes only attacked his 'heresy' after assaulting his conduct as bishop. So his main approach was to defend his sociability and benefaction. 'When did we ever act offensively about anything to his Serenity [Theodosius II]; when were we ever obnoxious to … illustrious landowners here?' Rather, he had spent church revenues, 'building stoas and baths, repairing bridges, and caring for the common needs'.[56] Through these letters we see how Theodoret strategised, employing dozens of helpers to avoid condemnation (unsuccessfully), then to regain his see. Throughout, his prime means of claiming orthodoxy was to sustain his elite contacts and reputation as a patron.[57]

Because of the patronage and 'Eutychean' clusters, *Sirmondiana* letters enrich our picture of Theodoret and his social scene. We still see Theodoret's words casting him in suitable episcopal roles: advocate, adviser and friend, and we still see his assumptions about the segmented social landscape, but *Sirmondiana* also exhibits the scale of Theodoret's patronage operations, and it demonstrates, through autobiographical letters, the wrenching experience of being targeted in a theological conflict. The result is a sympathetic, fragmentary narrative, and a darker portrait of the clergy and wider elite.

Multi-author collection: Theodoret's conciliar letters

Theodoret's remaining letters lead down another path of interpretation. In thirty-nine more letters (or fragments) Theodoret is named as author. Another twenty-two probably involve his pen. All of them are linked to fifth- and sixth-century church councils, with one that may be inauthentic.[58] A majority of these conciliar notes are only preserved in translation.

[53] One 'turncoat' was Basil of Seleucia; see Theodoret, *Ep.* S102, Azéma 1964–98/III: 20–2. For others, see Theodoret, *Epp.* S84, S135–6, Azéma 1964–98/II: 220–2, III: 128–36.
[54] Detailed theology: Theodoret, *Epp.* S83–5, S104–5, S112–13, S116, Azéma 1964–98/II: 204–24, III: 24–30, 46–72.
[55] Theodoret, *Epp.* S112, S119, S124–5, S131, S133–4, Azéma 1964–98/III: 46–56, 76–82, 90–8, 110–28.
[56] Theodoret, *Ep.* S79, Azéma 1964–98/II: 182–8.
[57] On self-defence strategies, see Schor 2011: 174–9.
[58] Theodoret, *Ep. ad Iohannem Antiochenum, cum mortuus esset Cyrillus* (*CPG* 6287), ACO IV.1: 135, was condemned by the Second Council of Constantinople in 553. The letter muses on Cyril's death to John of Antioch, even though John died three years before Cyril. For more, see Richard 1941–2: 420–1.

Translated texts raise problems in evaluating rhetoric, beyond the mere loss of context, and these letters starkly illustrate the power of the collectors: one (Latin) letter also survives in a Greek excerpt that nearly reverses its message![59]

These conciliar letters focus on doctrinal conflicts among clerics and officials. As we have noted, church leaders of the 430s and 440s were divided over how to describe Christ. Divergent doctrinal language came to light in 428, thanks to Nestorius. Then the argument became regionalised. Theodosius II called the First Council of Ephesus in 431 to judge heresy and clarify orthodoxy, but the meeting split into two camps, each claiming to be the holy council. For two years, the court urged bishops to negotiate doctrinal language and restore communion. In April 433, John of Antioch and Cyril agreed to condemn Nestorius, publishing a vague 'Formula of Reunion',[60] but Alexander of Hierapolis, Theodoret and almost half of Syria's bishops refused this deal. Then came government threats, and the monks' plea for peace, which prompted Theodoret's new attempts to mediate.[61] By spring of 435, only eight bishops held out and were soon exiled, but the imposed agreement scarcely ended the conflict. New arguments arose in 437 over whether bishops had to condemn two supposed teachers of Nestorius.[62] Yet the Syrian bishops resisted new pressures by clinging to the compromise of 433. Only in 447–8 did Theodoret and his new main foe, Dioscorus of Alexandria, reignite conflict. These twists of church politics could not be precisely followed without conciliar letters, including Theodoret's.[63]

And yet the conciliar letters enable deeper socio-historical analysis, for two reasons. First, Theodoret's conciliar notes never stand alone. Most respond to other people's extant writings (or statements); most occasioned further responses. Some documents neither by nor to Theodoret still furnish key context,[64] and some words Theodoret shared with his allies in

---

[59] Theodoret, *Ep. ad Iohannem Antiochenum*, C21a–b (*CPG* 6266). Casiniensis 183 preserves whole letter in Latin, which accepts Cyril's orthodoxy but refuses his communion unless he accepts Nestorius. MS Atheniensis 128 preserves in Greek only the acceptance of Cyril's orthodoxy.

[60] See Cyril of Alexandria, *Ep. ad Iohannem Antiochenum de pace* (also known as *Laetentur coeli*) (*CPG* 5339), ACO 1.1.4: 15–20.

[61] For more, see Schor 2011: 81–113.

[62] I.e. Diodore of Tarsus and Theodore of Mopsuestia. On this conflict, see Schwartz 1914; Devreesse 1931 and 1948; Abramowski 1956; Richard 1977b: sec. 50; Winkler 1985; Garsoïan 1995, 1999; Constas 2003.

[63] Studies employing these letters include Devreesse 1931, 1948; Richard 1936, 1941–2, 1977: sec. 50; Bacht 1951; Pericoli-Ridolfini 1954; Abramowski 1956; Evieux 1974; McGuckin 1988, 1996, 2004; Leppin 1996; Sillett 1999.

[64] Notably, letters (now in Greek and Armenian) exchanged between Constantinople and Armenia. See Winkler 1985; Garsoian 1995, 1999; Constas 2003.

petitions and reports. Furthermore, nearly all the conciliar letters can be roughly sequenced and dated, at least by season. As a result, the whole conciliar collection forms a contextualised set of overlapping conversations.[65]

Secondly, the conciliar letters were generally transmitted by known parties with clearer motives. As we noted, after the First Council of Ephesus ended in schism, each party saved records that supported its claim to represent the church. At the Second Council of Ephesus, in 449, Dioscorus of Alexandria preserved the only transcript, part of which survives in Syriac translation. At the Council of Chalcedon in 451, imperial courtiers collected all records, preserving (mostly Cyril's) *acta* from the First Council of Ephesus, and excerpted transcripts from the Second.[66] These records were augmented by later disputes. In the 540s and 550s Emperor Justinian tried to settle doctrinal feuds by condemning the 'Three Chapters', three sets of past writings, including some by Theodoret.[67] All told, these (mostly) Greek collections contain three of Theodoret's letters, plus twenty more, officially by John of Antioch but possibly drafted by Theodoret.[68]

Then there are alternate records, saved by those who lost in these councils. Several small alternative archives are preserved,[69] but the most important is *Collectio Casiniensis*, a Latin collection that began with a disgruntled ally of Theodoret. Irenaeus had been an imperial count, charged with security at the First Council of Ephesus. When the imperial court abandoned Nestorius, Irenaeus was exiled, but then escaped notice.[70] In 443 he became bishop of Tyre, with Theodoret's support, but was exiled again in 448 amid renewed controversy.[71] While Theodoret returned to office, Irenaeus remained in exile, where he gathered records and added commentary to compose his '*Tragedy*'. A copy of Irenaeus' records wound up in the Monastery of the Sleepless, near Constantinople, and was found

---

[65] For a list of every relevant conciliar letter, see Schor 2011, bibiliography.

[66] On transcripts from Ephesus in 431, see Devreesse 1929; Galtier 1931; Sillett 1999: 12–40. On the *Acts of the Second Council of Ephesus*, see Flemming 1917; ACO ii.i.i; Price and Gaddis 2005: introduction. See also Lim 1995.

[67] On the Three Chapters, see Gray 1979; Chazelle and Cubitt 2007.

[68] Theodoret, *Epp.* (*CPG* 6242, 6264, 6276); John of Antioch, *Epp.* (*CPG* 6318–19, 6323–31, 6337–8, 6341–3, 6349–51) and the easterners' pronouncement in Ephesus in 431.

[69] Alternate archives include Rabbula of Edessa's correspondence, mostly in Overbeck 1865; and three collections by defenders of the 'Three Chapters': Facundus (Clement and Vander Plaetse 2003–6); Pope Pelagius I (Devreesse 1932); and Codex Vaticanus Graecus 1431 (Schwartz 1927). On the letters of Pelagius I, see Neil's Chapter 12 in this volume.

[70] Theodoret, *Ep.* P14, Azéma 1964–98/i: 86, describes the difficulties of Irenaeus' (secret?) travel and correspondence.

[71] On Irenaeus' second exile, see Theodoret, *Ep.* S110, Azéma 1964–98/iii: 38–42; *Codex Iustinianus* I.1.3, Krueger 1877: 5–6.

there by Rusticus, a deacon working for the pope in the 540s; he made a partial Latin translation and commentary, to inform allies in the 'Three Chapters' fight.[72] The resulting text included thirty-three of Theodoret's notes, plus two he likely co-wrote,[73] amid hundreds of other dateable letters.

Dateable conversations enable different kinds of socio-historical interpretation. The archive features interactive signals from Theodoret, his allies and his foes, and amid these letters, we can discern key social cues sent within clerical alliances – the call and response that indicated shared orthodoxy. For Theodoret and his confidants, the exchange of cues included explicit doctrinal terms (such as 'two natures and a difference between them').[74] But often the bishops preferred to trade catchphrases (such as praising doctrinal 'exactness'),[75] salutes to favourite past teachers (such as Theodore of Mopsuestia)[76] and lists of heretical *bête noires* (such as 'Arius, Eunomius and Apollinarius'),[77] alongside displays of intimacy and emotion. Surveying the whole conciliar collection, we see the same signals repeated within a group by multiple members.[78] Thus we have evidence for personal relationships and collective bonds reciprocated for some length of time.

Meanwhile, the letters' textual transmission inspires some trust in their social information. Extant letters may be incomplete or distorted by translation.[79] Irenaeus had his own editorial agenda, which included criticising Theodoret and portraying him as disloyal,[80] but Irenaeus' agenda differs from that of Rusticus,[81] and their goals differed from those of other editors. In any case, no one agenda governs the entire conciliar collection. The result, when we analyse the whole collection, is an 'averaging effect',

---

[72] On the textual history of *Casiniensis*, see ACO 1.4 introduction.

[73] John of Antioch, *Epp.* (*CPG* 6339, 6344).

[74] Theodoret, *Ep. ad Iohannem Antiochenum*, C21a (*CPG* 6266), ACO 1.1.7: 164.

[75] E.g., ibid.; *Epp. ad Alexandrum Hierapolitanum* (*CPG* 6250–51), ACO 1.4: 170, 172; John of Antioch *et al.*, *Acta et Sententia synodi Orientalium* (*CPG* 6351), ACO 1.1.5: 121.

[76] See John of Antioch, *Ep. ad Cyrillum episc. Alexandriae* (*CPG* 6312), ACO 1.5: 310, which reports on Theodore's reputation to Cyril; Ibas of Edessa, *Ep. ad Marim Persam* (*CPG* 6500), ACO ii.1.3: 32–4.

[77] Theodoret, *Ep. ad Iohannem Antiochenum* (*CPG* 6264), ACO 1.1.6: 107–8; Andreas of Samosata, *Ep. ad Alexandrum Hierapolitanum* (*CPG* 6375), ACO 1.4: 100–1; Alexander of Hierapolis, *Ep. ad Theodoretum episc. Cyri* (*CPG* 6416), ACO 1.4: 187; and John of Antioch *et al.*, *Acta et Sententia synodi Orientalium* (*CPG* 6352), ACO 1.1.5: 122.

[78] On this approach, see Schor 2011: 19–39.

[79] On translation, see esp. Brock 1977, 1979, 1983 and 1994; Millar 2006.

[80] In one letter preserved by Irenaeus, Theodoret swore never to abandon Nestorius (e.g. *Ep. ad Alexandrum Hierapolitanum* [*CPG* 6248], ACO 1.4: 135). Irenaeus' commentary, Rusticus reported, highlighted Theodoret's about-face.

[81] Rusticus distanced himself from Irenaeus' critical comments. See note 80.

revealing patterns of social interaction beyond any one person's or party's control.

Clusters of conciliar letters illuminate the shifting of alliances during the Nestorian controversy. For example, one cluster reveals the tense interactions affecting Syrian bishops' positions during the negotiations for restoring communion in early 433. Some details discussed by John of Antioch and Cyril of Alexandria had leaked to Alexander of Hierapolis, Andreas of Samosata and Theodoret. These three men knew they agreed on Christology, but on reading Cyril's words, they came to different judgements. Alexander claimed to see through Cyril's subterfuge, 'since he neither casts out heretical dogma nor openly confesses that Christ was both God and man'.[82] Andreas agreed, at first. Thus he wrote to Alexander about a nightmare he had had: 'I was with your piety ... when you said to me that the heretic Apollinarius was still alive.' Later in the dream, Andreas said, he saw this heretic blessing John of Antioch and his peace deal, joining everyone in forced communion. Haunted by heretics, Andreas worried that he was being compelled to embrace them.[83] Theodoret took another view, namely, that Cyril might have shifted toward orthodoxy, so he wrote to Andreas, promising to keep defending Nestorius while supporting negotiations.[84] Andreas then asked Alexander to suspend judgement, until full agreements were known.[85] Here we catch a rare glimpse of how some doctrinal judgements were made through personal interactions.

Another cluster of letters affords insight into how Theodoret, a suffragan bishop, rose in influence. In late 434, the imperial court was losing patience with the nearly forty Syrian bishops still avoiding communion with Egypt. Theodoret had found a way to rejoin communion with a clear conscience.[86] Now he wrote to John of Antioch, and imperial officials (including Titus), asking that Alexander and other recalcitrants be given more time.[87] Meanwhile, he wrote numerous letters, and planned visits, to convince reluctant colleagues, claiming that 'excessive exactness' might displease God, 'because we tend to what is ours and do not consider what is useful for the laity'.[88] He even wrote to Nestorius, urging him to convince Alexander to rejoin communion – to cease defending Nestorius' own cause.[89] Alexander rebuffed Theodoret, and was dragged

---

[82] Alexander of Hierapolis, *Ep. ad Andream Samosatenum* (*CPG* 6394), ACO 1.4: 99–100.
[83] Andreas of Samosata, *Ep. ad Alexandrum Hierapolis* (*CPG* 6375), ACO 1.4: 100.
[84] Theodoret, *Ep. ad Andream Samosatenum* (*CPG* 6256), ACO 1.4: 102.
[85] Andreas of Samosata, *Ep. ad Alexandrum Hierapolis* (*CPG* 6376), ACO 1.4: 102–3.
[86] Theodoret, *Ep. ad Cyrillum Adanae* (*CPG* 6258), ACO 1.4: 181.
[87] Theodoret, *Ep. ad Iohannem Antiochenum* (*CPG* 6267), ACO 1.4: 191–2.
[88] Theodoret, *Ep. ad Alexandrum Hieropolitanum* (*CPG* 6251), ACO 1.4: 174.
[89] Theodoret, *Ep. ad Nestorium* (*CPG* 6271), ACO 1.4: 189.

to the mines by soldiers several months later,[90] but most other reluctant bishops rejoined communion. As Helladius of Tarsus did so, he wrote to Nestorius to explain: 'May your Divine Love find your share on the day of judgment ... With those who congregate around Theodoret, one may count us.'[91] These letters reveal the social arrangements that effectively ended the schism. They also indicate how Theodoret, already a failed mediator, finally won a position of informal leadership.[92]

Yet the greatest benefit of these letters comes from surveying the entire conciliar collection. Whenever letters can be sequenced and dated, they support diachronic narration, tracing shifts in rhetoric and social tactics. In this case, we can also follow shifts of intersubjective social position, and we can analyse synchronically. We can scan all letters sent within some period (such as 429–40), for the exchange of certain social cues (signalling doctrinal agreement and friendship, or the opposite), and we can map these social interactions to reconstruct some (temporary) clerical social relations.[93] Conciliar collections are hardly a flawless archive because the social maps that they support are incomplete and may mislead, but the conciliar letters of the 430s offer the most detailed view we have of a (mostly clerical) doctrinal network, as it transformed amid conflict.

Conclusion: combining methods and collections

Theodoret's letters present historians with interpretative problems, which vary with the letters' form, content and textual circumstances, but far from being a drawback, the complexities of Theodoret's correspondence enhance its historical value. The approaches that I have recommended for different letter-sets can be profitably combined. Frequently, they lead to compatible conclusions. When perspectives do clash, we gain insight into how textual representations diverge from intersubjective social relations.

One benefit of combining the personal and conciliar letters is a broadened sample of social rhetoric. *Patmensis* and *Sirmondiana* showcase Theodoret playing multiple roles tied to his elite status and clerical office. Together, they convey how Theodoret sought connections across

---

[90] Alexander of Hierapolis, *Ep. ad Theodoretum episc. Cyri* (*CPG* 6416), ACO 1.4: 186–7. On Alexander's ouster, see Libianus, governor of Euphratensis, *Relationes ad vicarium Titum* (*CPG* 6429–30), ACO 1.4: 200–2; Irenaeus, *Quanti a sanctis eclesiis exierunt nolentes suam conscientiam vulnerare* (*CPG* 6431), ACO 1.4: 203–4.

[91] Helladius of Tarsus, *Ep. ad Nestorium* (*CPG* 6441), ACO 1.4: 205.

[92] Theodoret's rise to prominence involved other steps. See Schor 2011: 81–130.

[93] Hence the limited network analysis of Schor 2011: 19–56. On network analysis, see Boissevain 1974; Wasserman and Faust 1994; Scott 2000; Watts 2003; Barabási 2003.

elite Roman society, from the leading monks and the clergy to pagan (and Christian) educators, from decurions and bureaucrats to civil and military leaders. They also reveal the range of ways Theodoret sought connections, from signalling shared doctrinal preferences to touting classical learning, from begging favours for clients to urging people to repent for sins. The broader Theodoret's social signalling, the more we see, within the limits of extant text, his sense of his social surroundings. From Theodoret's authorial perspective, late-antique society appears both hierarchical (even within the elites) and culturally segmented, and he presented himself as the learned bishop who bridged social and cultural divides.

Another benefit of combining the letter-sets is the sharper picture of Theodoret's intersubjective relational webs. Conciliar records allow us to map some reciprocated social connections, especially among bishops and officials doctrinally allied to Theodoret. Personal letters extend this mapping in limited ways. A few doctrinal allies reappear as such in the Eutychean letters, joined by new recruits. When these alliances are also noted in (hostile) records of the Second Council of Ephesus, we have clear evidence for a theological party, centred on Theodoret and his confidants, lasting (in some form) until 449.[94] But Theodoret's social world was broader than battles over doctrine. His personal letters reveal probable links to doctrinal foes, and many uninvolved in the conflict. Yet even his relations with doctrinal allies are shown to involve cultural affinity, friendship, shared pastoral work and patronage cooperation, intermixed with shared orthodoxy. The personal letters suggest that Theodoret joined many layers of social networks, even if they cannot be precisely mapped. At the same time, those letters showcase an inner core of Theodoret's allies (clerics, monastic leaders, and officials), recasting them as multiform friends.[95]

Perhaps the greatest benefit of combining methods is what they reveal about the dynamic link between textual rhetoric and intersubjective social relations. Like his other writings, Theodoret's letter-collections represent aspects of his social world idiosyncratically, and represent the author in self-serving ways.[96] Yet Theodoret did not write in a vacuum. His subjects were known to his audience, or part of his audience, and his audience could reply. Reading all the letters in context, one can see that Theodoret neither just reported his prominent social position nor invented it. Rather,

---

[94] The extent of this partisan network is unclear. See Schor 2011: 40–56, 81–94, 104–9, 128–30.
[95] See Schor 2011: 20–39, 113–30, 153–5, 159–79.
[96] See esp. Urbainczyk 2002; Krueger 2004; Rousseau 2005; Vuolanto 2012.

by letters and other texts, he tried to push existing relationships in his preferred directions. His diverse elite contacts were what enabled him to play doctrinal expert, diligent pastor, committed ascetic and cultured friend. They allowed him to advocate for a troubled soldier and a philosopher, and to mediate clerical disputes. Those same connections also pushed Theodoret to work with other influential figures and embrace compromise, or face losing his claim to orthodoxy and his position within his social world.

PART IV

Collecting early papal letters

Collectio Corbeiensis, Collectio Pithouensis, and the earliest collections of papal letters

Geoffrey D. Dunn

Among the more than two hundred manuscripts that have come down to us containing canons from various church synods and councils together with letters or decretals from Roman bishops, those from Merovingian Gaul are particularly significant. From the sixth century onward, particularly in the south, a large number of manuscripts of such material started to be produced, although most do not survive. It has been argued that these were generally regional and unofficial.[1] Identifying which canons from which synods and which letters from which Roman bishops and the order in which they are all arranged (as well as other peculiarities) has enabled scholars both to group individual manuscripts together as belonging to the same tradition or family and to distinguish manuscripts as belonging to different traditions or families. Two of these families, the *Collectio Corbeiensis* and the *Collectio Pithouensis*, each known from a single surviving manuscript, are of particular importance in tracing the history of the transmission of mediaeval canon law, and papal letters in particular. It has long been known that there are close connections between the two and that there is evidence that they both utilised an earlier, common source.

In fact, most of the surviving letters of Roman bishops prior to the time of Gregory I are to be found in these canon law manuscripts. It tells us more about the interests and concerns of the early mediaeval communities that preserved them than it does of the interests and concerns of the Roman bishops themselves, since these bishops are known to have written about much more than just the regulation of Christian, particularly clerical, life, even though not many examples of that broader interest were deemed worthy of transmission.

Yet, some of this process of gathering letters of Roman bishops together might go back to the Roman bishops themselves. A fresh examination of the common source material in the two manuscripts and of some of the

---

[1] Halfond 2010: 161.

other component pieces will challenge some long-held conclusions and address the concerns raised recently by Rosamond McKitterick that scholars treat collections as though they were integral texts. She mentions these two collections in particular to refute the notion that they should be seen as established texts.[2] While it is true that the copying of an earlier manuscript tells us something of the needs of the times and ought to receive more consideration than hitherto, nonetheless it remains legitimate and profitable for us to ask about the stages of the composition of the components of these two manuscripts and what the needs of those times were. This chapter seeks to cast new light on that process of letter-collecting. It concludes that Leo I, in the middle of the fifth century, might have been responsible for distributing a small corpus of letters from some of his recent predecessors to the churches in Gaul on questions relating to clerical qualification. That this material was reused to fashion larger collections of canonical material over successive centuries contributed in no small way to the growing authority of the Roman bishop in the western church.

Collectio Corbeiensis in previous scholarship

Paris, BnF lat. 12097 is the oldest extant manuscript containing letters of Roman bishops, as parts of it were definitely written in the sixth century. Once identified as Corbeiensis 26, this half-uncial, single-column document had belonged at some point to the Abbey of Corbie, a Merovingian foundation established in Picardy on the Somme at its confluence with the Ancre in about 660 by Balthild, widow of Clovis II, but after Cardinal Richelieu ordered the removal of much of the abbey's library to the Abbey of Saint-Germain-des-Prés in Paris in 1638, it was renumbered as Sangermanensis 936. After the dispersal of that abbey's library during the French Revolution, the manuscript came into the possession of the Bibliothèque Nationale de France (BnF).[3]

Pierre Coustant consulted this manuscript to prepare his still-standard 1721 edition.[4] Pietro and Girolamo Ballerini, whose three-volume correction to the edition produced by Pasquier Quesnel of Leo I's writings appeared between 1753 and 1757,[5] began the critical process of identifying

---

[2] McKitterick 2004: 254.   [3] See Kéry 1999: 47–8.
[4] See e.g. Coustant 1721: cols. 739–40, 745–8, 750–4, 757–9.
[5] Quesnel's (1675) edition relied upon the *Collectio Grimanica* found in Paris, Bibliothèque Mazarine 1645, a ninth-century manuscript from Friuli, and the *Collectio Quesnelliana*.

differing collections of canonical and decretal material. They drew attention to the list of popes at the beginning of this manuscript, which ended with the death of Vigilius in 555.[6] They noted that a block of letters from several fifth-century Roman bishops – Innocent I (402–17), Zosimus (417–18), Celestine I (422–32) and Leo I (440–61) – appears between canons from the 340 Synod of Gangra (modern Çankırı), thereby splitting the material from that synod into two.[7] Finally, they concluded that this collection was put together in Gaul because of the heavy emphasis on Gallic synodal material.[8]

In the nineteenth century Friedrich Maassen dubbed this manuscript the sole example of the *Collectio Corbeiensis*, observing that the popes' length in office was measured by year, month and day, down to Hormisdas (514–23), but from John I (523–6) only by year. He noted that after this list (and a list of provinces) come two tables of contents,[9] and that by comparing them with each other and with the following contents, as well as the manuscript with the *Collectio Albigensis* and *Collectio Pithouensis*, one could determine the original shape of the *Collectio Corbeiensis* and the various stages of addition to the original material, the latest of which are the canons from the fourth Synod of Paris in 573.[10] The original canonical synodal material (nos. I–III, XV–XVIII) was all in the Isidorian version.[11] Although the canons from Nicaea are no longer present in that part of the manuscripts (only the preface and episcopal subscriptions remain; the canons reappear later in the manuscript), it is obvious that they would have been in the form combined with the canons from the Synod of Serdica (modern Sofia), which is commonly found in the earliest Italian and Gallic manuscripts.[12] In the first half of the manuscript – up to fol. 139v was written in the one hand – he argued that there was evidence, since the tables of contents conclude with material found in fol. 91r, that the second part (91v–139v) of that half, mainly concerned with Leo I, was an addition to the original (1r–91r).[13]

With regard to the Roman episcopal letters that the Ballerini brothers had identified as having been inserted into the middle of that earlier

---

[6] Ballerini 1865 = PL 56: 131.   [7] Ballerini 1865.

[8] Ballerini 1865 = PL 56: 132. See discussion of the Gallic *libri canonum* in Mathisen 2014.

[9] Lowe 1950: 29 (no. 619). The first is more detailed than the second, the latter of which contains forty-three items. See Table 11.1 where they are listed as 3a and 3b, since the prefixed material at the front of the manuscript contains two other tables of contents of the whole manuscript in seventeenth- and eighteenth-century hands.

[10] Maassen 1870: 556.

[11] These numbers are taken from the first table of contents (3a).

[12] Maassen 1870: 560–1.   [13] Maassen 1870: 568–9.

material (as nos. IV–XII), Maassen simply noted that the two tables of contents listed number VIII differently: the first (3a) identifying it as Innocent's letter *Magna me gratulatio* (JK 303) (although not mentioning the recipients), and the second (3b) as Celestine's letter *Cuperemus quidem* (JK 369). Both letters are present in the manuscript but do not both appear in both tables of contents.[14] Maassen thought that the failure to list JK 303 in the second table proved ('bewiesen') some connection with the *Collectio Albigensis*.[15] The *Collectio Pithouensis*, on the other hand, is claimed to be following the first table of contents in the *Collectio Corbeiensis* in not mentioning JK 369.[16] He did not speculate at all about why this material interrupted the material from the Synod of Gangra, other than to note the close relationship between these various collections.[17]

In a 1913 article Morin mentioned the collection and a possible relationship with Arles but did not add to our knowledge of it.[18] The Jesuit Karl Silva-Tarouca saw some of the later material in the second half of the Paris manuscript (that after fol. 139v) coming from the area of Paris, and perhaps the earlier material being assembled in Vienne, on the basis of the inclusion of Leo's letter *Diuinae cultum* (JK 407) (unnumbered in the first table of contents) to the bishops of that province.[19] He was interested in the similarities with the *Collectio Albigensis* and the *Collectio Pithouensis*, arguing against dependence by the latter two on our manuscript and instead for a common source for all three.[20] Some years later he expressed the opinion that the earliest material had been sent from Rome to Arles, but his interest lay in some of the rubrics to Leo's letters and the

---

[14] However, Maassen is wrong in this assertion. While it is true that the second table of contents does not list JK 303, it is not true that the first table of contents omits JK 369, which he claims was 'nur durch Versehen ausgelassen' (Maassen 1870: 558). In fact both of Celestine's letters are mentioned in the first table of contents, although inaccurately, something Maassen overlooked. See Table 11.1.

[15] Since Toulouse, Bm, 364, is missing its first three gatherings, we are left to rely upon the table of contents preserved in Albi, Bm, 2. On fol. 2 it lists at item XXVII: *Canones urbicani*; as item XXVIII: *epistola Innocenti papae ad episcopos*; and as item XXIX: *epistola Zosimi papae ad Esitium episcopum Salonitanum*. Item XXIV is listed as: *epistola ex canonibus urbicanis*. In the text itself item XXVI is given the rubric: *incipiunt auctoritates uel canones urbicani*; and is JK 293, while the next item (unnumbered) is the opening of JK 303 (fol. 50v), and item XXVIII is JK 339. JK 303 is repeated (unnumbered), this time in full, starting on fol. 59r, after an extract (also unnumbered) headed: *ex canonibus urbicanis* on fol. 58v. Contrary to Maassen, the manuscript in Albi does mention JK 303 (although ambiguously) as item XXVIII in the table of contents. On the *Collectio Albigensis* see Turner 1901: 266–73.

[16] Maassen 1870: 558. No table of contents survives from the *Collectio Pithouensis*, so it is hard to make an argument from that, but the manuscript certainly includes JK 369. The *Collectio Albigensis* neither mentions JK 369 nor includes it.

[17] Maassen 1870: 574.

[18] Morin 1913. See Turner 1915–16: 241; and Mathisen 1997.

[19] Silva-Tarouca 1919: 668–9.   [20] Silva-Tarouca 1919: 669.

way they parallel what is found later with letters in the papal chancery from the ninth century and the fact that the compiler of the collection did not seem to have had original copies of all the letters, given some of the subscriptions reproduced.[21]

C. H. Turner's 1928–9 article on this manuscript was one in a series dedicated to the Latin manuscripts of early canonical material.[22] He had expressed his opinion previously that the collection was Gallic, and although he doubted the manuscript was from Arles, he accepted that the nucleus of the material (up to fol. 91r, where the tables of contents can be followed) might have been put together in Arles about 525.[23] He noted that there were six leaves attached to the front of the manuscript containing Rufinus' translation of Gregory of Nazianzus' *Apologeticum*, in a hand not earlier than the ninth century.[24] The compiler of the first part of the manuscript seems to have been the person who added the material from 91r to 139v (concerned on the whole with a western interest in the Council of Chalcedon and Leo I) sometime just before 560 during the pontificate of Pelagius I (555–61), Vigilius' successor.[25] Some of the material at the end of the tables of contents from the fourth Synod of Arles and the Synod of Epaon is not in the manuscript, probably because it had fallen out or faded in our manuscript's exemplar.[26] In 1929, Turner's principal interest was to look at the appendices – that material found in fols. 139v–43v and 144r–232v. While the first few of those folios contain material written into the blank leaves of the final gathering of the original manuscript, the latter group comprises six appendices, each starting with a new gathering added to the manuscript. The appendices contain sixth-century material and are not our concern here, although this is an important topic.[27] Turner's conclusion was that the archetype was written about 523 to 526, the original manuscript (until fol. 139v) about 560, with the appendices added until 625.[28] His view about the nature and purpose of the original core of the manuscript is worth repeating at length:

> C [the *Collectio Corbeiensis*] and K [the *Collectio Coloniensis*, represented by the MS Köln, EBDDB, 212] are handbooks of all the Canon Law that had validity in the Gallican Church, native and foreign alike. The presence of

---

[21] Silva-Tarouca 1932: 58–60.   [22] Turner 1928–9.   [23] Turner 1915–16: 237.

[24] Turner 1928–9: 226. He made no comment about the six other leaves at the very front of the manuscript containing the first two tables of contents.

[25] Turner 1928–9: 233–4.   [26] Turner 1928–9: 234.

[27] Turner 1928–9: 227–32. Except, one may note, that Leo I, *Quanta fraternitati* (JK 411), *Subditis responsionibus* (JK 544) and Siricius, *Directa* (chapters 5–15) (JK 255) occupy fols. 184r–92r.

[28] Turner 1928–9: 234.

Greek and African material enforces the idea that Canon Law is an inheritance common to the whole Church, though it develops in each region on its own lines. The presence of papal decretals implies that the Roman Church has its separate contribution to make, and that it is made not by councils and canons but by the personal initiative of Popes. And the additional presence of the papal list, and especially as the preface to the collection, marks the time when the Church of Gaul took on a new orientation toward Rome as the centre of the Church, and towards the Pope as the unifying element of what might otherwise have seemed a vast congeries of ecclesiastical legislation, always growing, always developing in each district in some sort of independence of the rest. That centripetal movement acquired force and momentum in Arles, the capital of south-eastern Gaul, at the end of the fifth and beginning of the sixth century. The original Corbie MS was written at some place near enough, and at some date late enough, to experience something of the effect of the new movement.[29]

However, on the small group of letters inserted in the middle of the material on the Synod of Gangra, Turner only wrote that they represent a very primitive collection of important decretals, 'but by what accident the insertion was made at so arbitrary a point we can no longer decide'.[30] He noted parallels with the *Collectio Albigensis* on this matter.

In his foundational study of the *Collectio Dionysiana*, Hubert Wurm made comparison between that collection and earlier ones, including the *Collectio Corbeiensis*, which he labelled as one of the Gallic collections. He accepted the sixth-century date of composition and early sixth-century date of the first part of the collection. While noting that this collection was extremely valuable and takes us back nearly to original sources, and had striking parallels in the arrangement of some material with the *Collectio Albigensis*, the *Collectio Coloniensis* and the *Collectio Pithouensis*, Wurm also noted the fact that canons and decretals seem hardly separable in this collection.[31] In considering the relationship between the *Collectio Corbeiensis* and the *Collectio Pithouensis*, Wurm drew attention to the fact that in both there is that small collection of similarly arranged material, although he did not mention the fact that in the *Collectio Corbeiensis* it divides material from the Synod of Gangra into two. He argued that the small nucleus consisted originally of only five letters: Innocent's JK 286, 293 and 303,[32] and Celestine's

---

[29] Turner 1928–9: 233.   [30] Turner 1928–9: 235.   [31] Wurm 1939b: 93–4.

[32] Wurm 1939b: 135: the differences between the *Collectio Corbeiensis* and the *Collectio Pithouensis* in the addresses for JK 303 would also indicate that they both took their list of names of recipients from the same tabluar presentation, which the former copied incorrectly (reading down each column instead of across to create a running list), while the latter copied correctly preserving the tabular style.

JK 369 and 371. His claim was that only the first letter (Innocent's *Etsi tibi*) has a rubric or 'Protokoll'.[33] In both collections those five letters are preceded by Zosimus' *Exigit dilectio* (JK 339), which, because it preserves its own rubric and is like this in both collections, must have been added to the original collection but early enough to have been in the source document for both collections to have drawn from that expanded version. Wurm then notes that the inclusion of Innocent's *Si instituta* (JK 311) prior to Zosimus' letter in the *Collectio Corbeiensis* but its omission from the *Collectio Pithouensis* would indicate that it was not to be found in the source document.[34] Elsewhere he noted the similarity of readings in the two collections for both Innocent's *Consulenti tibi* (JK 293) and Leo's *Vt nobis gratulationem* (JK 402).[35]

Schwartz's brief comment on the collection adds nothing to our knowledge.[36] Lowe stated that the first 139 folios were copied about 523 (he made no reference to the division at fol. 91r, although stating that popes listed after Hormisdas were in a second hand, disagreeing with Turner that the list was in one hand only)[37] in somewhere like Arles or Lyons, and the rest of the manuscript was added in stages until the seventh century, and that by the eighth century the manuscript was at Corbie.[38]

Hubert Mordek looked for parallels between the *Vetus Gallica* and other early collections. With regard to the *Collectio Corbeiensis* he noted the similarities in presentation between Celestine's JK 369 in both.[39] While in the first half of the manuscript it would appear that it and the *Collectio Pithouensis* used a common source, it is evident, Mordek argues, that in the appendices of the Corbie manuscript, at least with regard to Siricius' *Directa* to Himerius of Tarragona (ancient Tarraco) (JK 255), that this manuscript has borrowed here from the *Collectio Pithouensis* in adding an extra chapter to that letter.[40] Of course, his concern was with the extent to which the *Vetus Gallica* borrowed from either.

In his brief comments on the *Collectio Corbeiensis* Jean Gaudemet ignored the work of Wurm and simply noted the near parallel with another primitive collection, known as the *canones urbicani* and found in the *Collectio Laureshamensis*, in which six out of seven items appear

---

[33] Wurm 1939b: 119: 'In der ältesten Form der Quelle stand nur J¹ [JK 286] – C² [JK 371], die Dekretalen J² [JK 293] – C² folgen in beiden Sammlungen ohne besondere Überschriften auf die J¹.' As we shall see, this needs correcting.

[34] Wurm 1939b: 119–20.　[35] Wurm 1939a: 52 and 81.

[36] Schwartz 1936: 85.　[37] I would agree with Turner here.

[38] Lowe 1950: 29–30 (nos. 619 and 620).　[39] Mordek 1975: 58.

[40] Mordek 1975: 90–1.

in both.[41] However, although he acknowledges that other material is also included in the Corbie manuscript, what Gaudemet has not drawn attention to is the fact that these six items in the manuscript are not together as a group. Perhaps Gaudemet was simply noting similarities but he seems to suggest some dependence.

In his chapter on the development of canonical material until the time of Gregory the Great, Detlev Jasper summarises this research in the context of the two other primitive collections, the *canones urbicani* and the *epistolae decretales*.[42] Wolfgang Kaiser has provided the most recent summary of all this evidence, although he has nothing to say about the small primitive collection.[43] He accepts that there are two hands in the papal list,[44] that the core material runs to fol. 92r,[45] and that the material from the Synod of Gangra is in the Isidorian version before the papal letters and in the Priscan version after the papal letters.[46]

We may now turn our attention to the *Collectio Pithouensis* and its sole manuscript and see what scholarship has noted about it, before making a fresh comparison between the two collections.

Collectio Pithouensis in previous scholarship

The sixteenth-century French lawyer, Pierre Pithou, who barely escaped with his life during the St Bartholomew Day massacre in August 1572, died in 1596 owning a large collection of mediaeval manuscripts, most of which eventually came into the possession of the BnF. One of these manuscripts, lat. 1564, which also had been in the possession of Louis XIV's finance minister, Jean-Baptiste Colbert (where it was numbered 1863) in the seventeenth century, contains the same kind of material as lat. 12097, but in a way unique enough for it to be called the single example of the *Collectio Pithouensis* by Maassen.[47] The single-columned manuscript, written by several hands in Carolingian minuscule, is to be dated to the late eighth or early ninth century (785–810) and was produced in northern France, possibly Chelles.[48] The gatherings are numbered from VIIII to XXV,

---

[41] Gaudemet 1985: 90. The seven items in the *Collectio Laureschamensis* are JK 293, JK 339, JK 371, JK 255, JK 286, Damasus' *Per filium* (JK 235) to Paulinus of Antioch and Symmachus' *Hortatur nos* (JK 764) to Caesarius of Arles. Siricius' letter is the one identified as missing in the *Collectio Corbeiensis*. It ought to be noted that Siricius' letter does appear in the collection but only in one of the later appendices.
[42] Jasper 2001: 26.   [43] Kaiser 2006.
[44] Kaiser 2006: 66 and 84–6.   [45] Kaiser 2006: 67.
[46] Kaiser 2006: 68 and 71.   [47] Maassen 1870: 604–11.
[48] Silva-Tarouca 1919: 672; Lowe 1950: no. 529; and Kéry 1999: 48–9.

meaning that the first eight (128 folios) are missing. The original exemplar is dated to the late sixth or early seventh century since there is no material later than that present in our manuscript.[49] Halfond prefers Sens or Auxerre for its composition.[50] It has not attracted nearly as much investigation as the Corbie manuscript.

Coustant also used this manuscript in his edition.[51] Maassen pointed to the fact that a significant portion of the manuscript parallels what is found early in the *Collectio Corbeiensis*, like XLVIII–LI, then JK 339 (unnumbered in the *Collectio Pithouensis* following LIII) to LXI, LXIV–LXIX[52] and LXXIV–LXXXVI, which for him meant that this manuscript borrowed from the *Collectio Corbeiensis*.[53] Wurm noted that it was a manuscript of 'außerordentlich vielen Schreibfehler', makings its use in text editing problematic,[54] but that it was important in tracing the history of the collections.[55] This is because he found embedded within this collection a smaller collection of material, as mentioned in the previous section. A look at the superscript (or salutation) of JK 303 makes it clear that Pithou's manuscript did not copy from the Corbie manuscript.[56] Mordek has demonstrated that the compiler of the *Vetus Gallica* made substantial use of the *Collectio Pithouensis* in preparing that collection.[57] Jasper, who accepts Wurm, dates this group of letters to the 430s.[58] He repeats the opinion of Wurm, which is the most recent consideration of the matter, that there is a small, primitive collection of letters consisting of JK 286, 293, 303, 369 and 371 found in both manuscripts.[59]

Fresh consideration of the primitive letter-collection

The antiquity of the Corbie manuscript and the obvious physical fact that the product we have today was assembled in stages makes it particularly

---

[49] Stürner 1969: 153–4.   [50] Halfond 2010: 161.

[51] Coustant 1721: cols. 792 and 794.

[52] Misnumbered by Maassen 1870: 611 as LXIII to LXXII.

[53] Maassen 1870: 610–11.

[54] One may note, for example, in the rubric for JK 286 that the compiler has *ad Victricio*, suggesting a scribe not very competent with Latin. The material in Table 11.2 reproduces what is found in the manuscript, with some footnotes to suggest what the Latin ought to read.

[55] Wurm 1939b: 283.

[56] Wurm 1939b: 135, n. 65, points out that the compiler of the manuscript has produced a running list of recipients of this letter by reading down a series of columns rather than across, for Rufus, the bishop of Thessalonica, was the principal recipient. This was not a mistake one would expect the compiler of Pithou's manuscript could have corrected just from the Corbie manuscript itself; he must have been copying from the exemplar and read the columns correctly.

[57] Mordek 1975: 56–7.   [58] Jasper 2001: 26.   [59] Jasper 2001: 26.

significant. Pithou's manuscript is essentially different, especially since so much of it, including the opening folios, is missing. While Wurm's opinion about a small, primitive collection being discernible within these manuscripts has stood now for more than eighty years, it is time for a fresh consideration, for Wurm's position is not completely accurate. What interests me here is not so much individual letters themselves as products of their authors but these letters as the preserved material of mediaeval collectors.

Let us consider the material in the *Collectio Corbeiensis* that interrupts the flow of material on the Synod of Gangra. Wurm's point was that because in the *Collectio Corbeiensis* JK 311, 339 and 286 all have rubrics of their own, while the letters following 286 (293, 303, 369 and 371) did not, and because JK 311 is in a different position in the *Collectio Pithouensis*, that the last five formed a primitive collection to which the first two were attached later (as well as the material following JK 371).[60] The problem is with the fact that in the Corbie manuscript there is a rubric for JK 303 (*item*) and in Pithou's manuscript both JK 369 (with *incipit Caelestini*) and 371 (with *epistola Celestini ad episcopis per Apuliam et Calabriam*) have rubrics. Further, Wurm's claim that JK 402 in both manuscripts has a rubric does not appear to be the case with the Corbie manuscript. Either Wurm failed to notice some of these points or there must be some methodological assumption at work here to enable him to discount the evidence, which would seem to be that where there are now rubrics (like *item* in JK 303 in the Corbie manuscript) originally there were not, and that this inclusion must be the work of the later compiler. Could we not, however, ask for better proof that the opposite (that it is the work of later compilers in deleting rubrics in JK 369 and 371 where they are missing in the Corbie manuscript or *item* missing in Pithou's manuscript) is not the case? Indeed, we may note also that where a letter like JK 286 does have a rubric appear in both manuscripts the wording may differ: the Corbie manuscript refers to *capitola* while Pithou's refers to *epistola decretalis* and calls him *papa* (cf. the previous letter in the latter manuscript – JK 339 – where Innocent's successor, Zosimus, is referred to simply as *episcopus*),[61] so the parallels between these five letters in the two manuscripts are not quite as close as Wurm stated. I would contend that since JK 293

---

[60] See n. 33 above.
[61] The rubrics for JK 402 in Pithou's manuscript and JK 405 in both manuscripts refer to Leo I as *papa*.

is the only one of the five letters not to have any trace of a rubric in either manuscript that Wurm's identification of them being an original group is not as firm as he claimed.

However, this does not mean that his hypothesis must be abandoned entirely. If the compiler of Pithou's manuscript (or the compiler of its exemplar) was responsible for altering[62] or inserting the rubrics for JK 286, 369, 371 and 402, then Wurm's position remains intact, with two qualifications: the presence of *item* as a rubric in JK 303 in the Corbie manuscript is still unexplained as is the addition of the first letter from Leo (JK 402) to that group of five, since it lacks a rubric in the Corbie manuscript. This would make a primitive collection from sometime after 443. Given Leo's interest in Gaul, evidenced by his visit there prior to becoming bishop, it could even be suggested that he was responsible for putting together this small collection of letters from his recent predecessors for distribution in Gaul to address issues of clerical qualification that were likely to be raised among the various churches to show them how the church in Rome had dealt with them.

Still, this must remain rather speculative. Perhaps a more realistic avenue of investigation concerns the larger group of documents (including these items) in the Corbie manuscript that interrupts the Synod of Gangra. This amounts to fourteen items (4–17 in my list). All of them appear in Pithou's manuscript (as items 19–22 and 25–34 in my list for that manuscript).[63] While items 15–17 from the Corbie manuscript (*Breuiarium Hipponense*, Synod of Thélepte, and *Regula formatarum*) no longer follow item 14 from the manuscript in Pithou's manuscript but precede it (separated by canons from the 517 Synod of Epaon and the 524 Synod of Arles), all the others, from JK 339 to the letter of Faustinus and Marcellinus are in order (fols. 18v–55r in the Corbie manuscript and 30r–55v in Pithou's manuscript).

What binds much of this material together is its wide-ranging focus on clerical qualification, although why Leo's *In consortium uos* (JK 405) from 444 about Manichees in Italy[64] or *Quam laudabiliter* (JK 412) from 447 on the Trinity[65] should be thought appropriate to follow one about qualifications for clerical office is not immediately

---

[62] If JK 286 was the only letter of the small group originally to have a rubric, then it is easier to imagine the compiler of the exemplar of Pithou's manuscript inserting *papa* than the compiler of the exemplar of the Corbie manuscript deleting it from the source they both used.

[63] The material from *Breuiarium Hipponense* is divided into 19 and 20 in Pithou's manuscript.

[64] Leo I, *Ep.* 7; PL 54: 620–2.   [65] Leo I, *Ep.* 15; PL 54: 677–92.

apparent.[66] The presence of *De confessione uerae fidei* of Faustinus and Marcellinus, clerical supporters of Ursinus against Damasus and followers of the staunchly anti-Arian Lucifer of Cagliari (ancient Calaris) and the letter supposedly of Atticus of Constantinople to Boniface I of Rome (*Regula formatarum*), is also surprising.[67] Yet the rest of the material does have thematic coherence, with each letter generally canvassing a variety of related topics. JK 402 states that slaves and others of low rank are not to be admitted to the priesthood, by which we should understand the episcopate, and any from such a background are to be removed; that those bishops who had married twice or whose wives had been widows at the time of marriage to them also ought to be removed from office; and that clerics ought not be engaged in usury.[68] The five letters before that, from Innocent and Celestine, also treat the same topic of clerical qualifications. A section of Celestine's letter to the bishops of Vienne and Narbonne dealt with irregular ordinations[69] and in his letter to the southern Italian bishops he stressed the need for following the clerical *cursus honorum*.[70] Innocent's letter to Victricius is replete with discussion about the rights of metropolitans, clerical qualification, especially with regards to marriage, and clerical life, including celibacy.[71] In the letter to Exsuperius there is discussion about how to treat clerics who fail in celibacy and again on the question of marriage and clerical qualification.[72] The eligibility for clerical office for those married was also discussed at length in Innocent's letter to the Macedonian bishops, as was the question of the readmission to communion and the holding of clerical office of those ordained in schism.[73] Zosimus' letter also dealt with the clerical *cursus honorum*[74] and Siricius' JK 258, surviving in the *Acts* of the Synod of Thélepte, also deals with clerical qualification for office as does the African *Breuiarum Hipponense* of 397.

---

[66] These letters from Leo are to be distinguished from the group of them later in the manuscripts, on which see Jasper 2001: 45.

[67] See Canellis 2006 and the earlier edition in Guenther 1895/1: 5–44.

[68] Leo I, *Ep.* 4; PL 54: 610–14. See Wessel 2008: 127.

[69] Celestine I, *Ep.* 4; PL 50: 429–36.   [70] Celestine I, *Ep.* 5; PL 50: 436–8.

[71] Innocent I, *Ep.* 2; PL 20: 468–85. See Dunn 2011.

[72] Innocent I, *Ep.* 6; PL 20: 495–502.

[73] Innocent I, *Ep.* 17; PL 20: 526–7. See Dunn 2008.

[74] See Dunn 2013. Of course, since Zosimus' letter is out of chronological sequence, it does support Wurm's hypothesis about the small primitive collection to which this and the other material were attached.

It could be suggested that the occasion in 443 of Leo writing about the topic of eligibility for clerical office and clerical behaviour was an opportunity to bundle together a few letters and canons from the last few decades that had also dealt with these issues, making the group of six letters, perhaps in an effort to point to the consistency of Roman teaching, which was then expanded to a total of fourteen items, but this would not explain the presence of Leo's two letters from 444 and 447, nor would it provide a rationale for including the non-Roman material or even the document from Faustinus and Marcellinus. A satisfactory theory that incorporates every one of the fourteen items together into a unity remains elusive.

Conclusions

McKitterick's point about not viewing a canonical and decretal collection as a discrete entity is well made; we need to pay attention to manuscripts just as much as to collections and to the various phases of compilation within a manuscript. Two manuscripts in Paris, each of which has been identified as the sole example of a collection (BnF lat. 12097 – the *Collectio Corbeiensis* and BnF lat. 1564 – the *Collectio Pithouensis*) exemplify this. Wurm's reconstruction of the small primitive collection of five papal letters from Innocent I and Celestine I was based upon the presence and absence of rubrics. Here I have suggested that the evidence upon which he reached that conclusion is not as firm as he indicated, but perhaps one could detect, provided that inconsistencies in the assertions about rubrics could be resolved, that the group was actually six not five (if one includes Leo's JK 402). Then, I would argue, there was a second stage in the process of compilation: the addition of the other material before and after that group to make the total of fourteen items. It was this second-stage primitive collection that served as the source for both the exemplars of the Corbie manuscript and Pithou's manuscript. For the Corbie manuscript a third stage was the incorporation of that bundle into a document exemplified by the tables of contents that now cover up to fol. 91r. The fourth stage was the writing of the Corbie manuscript as far as fol. 139v. Subsequent stages were the addition of further gatherings (fols. 144r–232r) and the completion of the final gathering of the original manuscript (fols. 139v–143v). Pithou's manuscript does not show such clear evidence of stages of composition. It could be suggested that in the third stage of the compilation of the *Collectio Pithouensis*, when the exemplar for our manuscript was written, the compiler split up the source document of fourteen items, placing the canonical material (fols. 23r–26v) in the appropriate chronological position among the canonical material already gathered (the missing gatherings and fols. 1r–30r), before adding the decretal material (fols. 30r–48v).[75] If we believe that the compiler was more interventionist than the one for the Corbie manuscript, it makes sense that he, incompetent though he was in Latin, added a number of rubrics, perhaps inspired by other manuscripts in his library, calling Innocent *papa* for example, thereby weakening our ability to detect more primitive stages in the composition of the source material within the manuscript. So perhaps the version in the Corbie manuscript remains more faithful to the style of the small primitive collection, which still reveals that it contains an even earlier nucleus of six (instead of Wurm's five) letters.

How did this, a small collection of fourteen items, come together? Who bundled this material together? How did the even smaller nucleus of six letters of that primitive collection come together? There is a very clear thematic unity here, since all the letters deal with broadly relevant issues of clerical life and discipline, but whether Leo was responsible for gathering this group together as a kind of handbook of Roman rules for clerical eligibility and behaviour and sending it to south-eastern Gaul, or whether someone there combined them out of some archive remains elusive. There are still inconsistencies and tensions within this theory put forward here with items that do seem entirely appropriate, but perhaps future research will shed more light on this.

There is no immediately apparent reason why Leo would have sent his letter to southern Gaul, although we know that he engaged at some length with Hilary of Arles about the extent of the latter's authority over the Gallic churches. So perhaps we can posit a probable reason from that situation. Indeed, Leo's letter of 445 (JK 407) to the bishops of the province of Viennensis, mentioned earlier, although not in the small first or second stage of the *Collectio Corbeiensis* (it is also in the *Collectio Pithouensis*)

---

[75] Since the material from Faustinus and Marcellinus (fols. 48v–55r) is a letter it makes sense that it remained with the decretals rather than with the synodal canons. The only weakness in this theory is why synodal canons from Orléans in the sixth century (fols. 55v–63r) follow the decretals and were not incorporated into the synodal. As a speculative suggestion, which is why it remains a footnote, perhaps the original manuscript, with a compiler prepared to shuffle material around, ended at fol. 63r in the current manuscript, and that a later compiler merely added fresh material at the end (the Orléans canons and then more decretals and other material [fols. 63r–136v]).

reveals the extent of antagonism between Leo and Hilary.[76] So there is every reason to suspect that Leo would have been interested in sending to Arles documents illustrating the history of the evolution of metropolitan and super-metropolitan rights of Gallic bishops and of Rome's relationship with the Gallic churches. Since Arles was the problem in Leo's opinion, the inclusion of JK 303 would serve the purpose of showing that Rome retained an authority over Illyricum even though the bishop of Thessalonica acted as head of the local churches (much as the bishops of Arles had been attempting in Gaul for the past generation), given that letter shows the bishop of Thessalonica consulting Rome rather than ignoring it, as Hilary is charged with doing.

One could argue that Leo was concerned that Hilary was writing Rome out of the equation and that by sending a bundle of documents from Rome, which illustrated Roman teaching on clerical eligibility and discipline and procedures for enforcing that teaching, he hoped to check Hilary's ambition.

Of course this is hypothetical, but it would support the notion that the *Collectio Corbeiensis* could have been compiled in Arles around a nucleus of earlier material sent from Rome, to which other letters were added over time, including JK 407 itself, until the end of the first quarter of the sixth century when the first version of the Corbie manuscript was produced. For whatever reason, the compiler of Pithou's manuscript also found this source material useful but was much happier to try to rearrange it for his own purposes, whatever they might have been. Mediaeval manuscripts give us evidence that over various generations early papal letters were found useful and relevant in fresh contexts and situations and were copied and distributed with increasing frequency.

---

[76] Leo I, *Ep.* 10; PL 54: 628–36; Honoratus of Marseille, *Life of Hilary*, ed., tr. Jacob 1995. See Wessel 2008: 57–88.

Table 11.1 Contents of Paris, BnF, lat. 12097 (fol. 1 to fol. 139v) with emphasis on papal letters

Folio	My item no.	Item no. in MS (according to 3a)	Item no. in MS (according to 3b)	Description	No. of canons	JK
I				Table of Contents 1a		
II–V				Table of Contents 1b		
A				Table of Contents 2		
b–g				Gregory of Nazianzus Incipit: *Proficiscenti mihi*		
1r–1v				List of popes		
2r–2v				List of provinces		
2v–8r				Table of Contents 3a		
8v–9r				Table of Contents 3b		
9r–12r	I	I	I	Synod of Ancyra in 314	25	
12r–13v	II	II	II	Synod of Neocaesarea in c. 314	14	
13v–15v	[III]	[III]	III	Synod of Gangra in 340	19	
15v–18v	[IV]	[IV]	IV	**Innocent I** Contents 3a: *Incipiunt capitula decretalia Innocenti* Contents 3b: *Decretalia Innocenti* Rubric: *Incipiunt capitula decretalia Innocenti* Superscript: *Innocentius Dicenio episcopo Egubino* Incipit: *Si instituta*	7	311
18v–19v	V	V	V	**Zosimus** Contents 3a: *Incipiunt capitula de epistula Iosemi ad Esy*ᵃ *episcopo* Contents 3b: *Decretalia Iosumi ad Isychio*ᵇ Rubric: *Incipit Iosimi* Superscript: *Iosimus Esychio*ᶜ *episcopo Salonitano* Incipit: *Exigit dilectio*	5	339

20r–23r	6	VI	**Innocent I** Contents 3a: *Incipiunt capitula Innocenti Victricio episcopo* Contents 3b: *Item Innocenti ad Victricio*[d] Rubric: *Incipiunt capitola Innocenti Victricio episcopo Rotomagensi* Superscript: none Incipit: *Etsi tibi*	15[e]	286
23v[f]–26r	7	VII	**Innocent I** Contents 3a: *Item Innocenti Exsuperio episcopo Tolosano* Contents 3b: *Item Innocenti ad Exsuperio*[g] Rubric: none Superscript: none Incipit: *Consolent*[h] *tibi*	7	293
26r–30v	8	VIII	**Innocent I** Contents 3a: *Innocenti* Contents 3b: not listed Rubric: *Item* Superscript: *Innocentius Eustasio, Eugenio, Policronio, Helario, Zosimo, Hermogeni, Therentiano, Rufo, Claudio, Gerontio, Suffronio, Macedonio, Profuturo, Vincentio, Herodiano, Eusebio, Maximiano, Iohanni, Flauiano, Calecrati, Nicitae, Asiologo, Martiano, episcopis Macedonibus et diaconibus in deo*[i] *salutem* Incipit: *Magna me*	12	303
30v–33r	9[j]	VIII	**Celestine I** Contents 3a: *Incipit Caelestini ad uniuersos episcopos* Contents 3b: *Caelestini ad uniuersos episcopos* Rubric: none Superscript: *Caelestinus uniuersis episcopis per Viennensim et Narbonensim*[k] *prouincias constitutis* Incipit: *Cuperemus quidem*	11	369

Table 11.1 (*cont.*)

Folio	My item no.	Item no. in MS (according to 3a)	Item no. in MS (according to 3b)	Description	No. of canons	JK
33r–33v	10	[IX][1]	IX	**Celestine I** Contents 3a: *Caelestinus uniuersis episcopis* Contents 3b: *Item alia* Rubric: none Superscript: *Caelestinus episcopus uniuersis episcopis per Apuliam et Calabriam constitutis* Incipit: *Nulli sacerdotum*	4	371
34r–35r	11	X	X	**Leo I** Contents 3a: *De epistula pape Leonis* Contents 3b: *Epistola papae Leonis* Rubric: none[m] Superscript: *Leo uniuersis episcopis per Campaniam, Ticinum, Tuscia[n] et per uniuersis prouincias constitutis in domino salutem* Incipit: *Vt nobis gratulationem*	3	402
35v–36r	12	XI	XI	**Leo I** Contents 3a: *Item Leo de uniuersis episcopis* Contents 3b: *Item alia papae Leonis* Rubric: *Incipit eiusdem papae Leonis de Manichaeis* Superscript: *Leo uniuersis episcopis per diuersas prouincias constitutis in domino salutem* Incipit: *In consortium uos*	1	405
36r°–44v	13	XII	XII	**Leo I** Contents 3a: *Item Leo Corebio Astosacensium* Contents 3b: *Item alia* Rubric: none Superscript: *Leo Chorebio[p] Asathoracensi reg[q]* Incipit: *Quam laudabiliter*	16[r]	412

Folio	No.			Content	
44v–55r	14	XIIIs		Faustinus and Marcellinus, *De confessione uerae fidei* Incipit: *Deprecamur mansuetudinem*	
55v–59v	15t	[XIIIA]u	XIII	*Breuiarium Hipponense*	27
59v–61v	16	XIV	XIV	Synod of Thélepte/**Siricius** Contents 3a: *Incipiunt xiv capitula concilii Telense* Contents 3b: *Concilium Telensim* Rubric: *Incipit concilium Telinsim super tractatu' sancti Syrici episcopi papae urbis Romae per Africam* Superscript: none Incipit: *Post consulatum/Cum in unum*	8
61r–62r	17	[XIVA]w		*Regula formatarum*	
62r–62v	18x	XV	XV	Synod of Gangra in 340 – continued	
62v–64v	19	XVI	XVI	Council of Nicaea in 325 – preface and episcopal subscriptions	
64v–69v	20	[XVA]y	XVII	Synod of Antioch in 341	24
69v–73v	21	XVI	XVIII	Synod of Laodicea in 363	37
73v–74v	22	XVII	XIX	Synod of Constantinople in 448	2
74v–77r	23	XVIII		Synod of Carthage in 397 – letter of Aurelius and Mizonius and *Breuiarum Hipponense*, can. 2–16	
77r–78r	24	XVIII	XX	Council of Nicaea in 325 – creed and bishop list	
				Capitola canonum de ordinationibus clericorum	
			XXI	*Capitola canonum CCCXVIII de exemplaribus papae Innocenti*	
			XXII	Synod of Arles	
			XXIII	Synod of Carthage	
			XXIV	*Item de conuersatione episcopi*	
78r	25	XIX	XXV	Synod of Valence – rubric only	
		XX		*Exemplaria de litteris episcoporum ad ecclesiam Focumiuli*	
		XXI	XXVI	Synod of Turin	6

Table 11.1 (*cont.*)

Folio	My item no.	Item no. in MS (according to 3a)	Item no. in MS (according to 3b)	Description	No. of canons	JK
78r–81v	26	XXII	XXVII	**Innocent I** Contents 3a: *Epistula Innocenti papae ad uniuersos episcopos ecclesiae Tolosanae* Contents 3b: *Epistola Innocenti ad uniuersos episcopos ecclesiae Tolosane* Rubric: *Innocentius uniuersis episcopis in Tholosana synbodo constitutis* Superscript: *Dilectissimis fratribus in domino salutem* Incipit: *Saepe me*		292
			XXVIII	Synod of Riez in 439		
			XXIX	Synod of Orange in 441		
			XXX	Synod of Vaison in 442		
			XXXI	Synod of Arles in 443 or 452		
			XXXII	Synod of Agde in 506		
			XXXIII	Synod of Orleans in 511		
82r–86v	27	XXIV^z	XXXIV	**Leo I** Contents 3a: *Epistula papae Leonis ad Viennensem prouinciam de fuga Hilari episcopi* Contents 3b: *Capitola papae Leonis ad Viennensi* Rubric: none Superscript: *Dilectissimis fratribus uniuersis episcopis per Viennensim*[aa] *prouinciam constitutis Leo* Incipit: *Diuinae cultum*		407

Folio	No.			Contents	JK
86v–87v	28	XXXV	XXXV–XXXVI	**Hilary I** Contents 3a: *Epistola sancti Hilari papae ad Leontium, Veranum, Victurum episcopi ad petitionem Ingenui episcopi datum* Contents 3b: *Capitola papae Helari de primatibus ecclesiae Ebridunensis* Rubric: none Superscript: *Dilectissimis fratribus Leontio, Verano, Victuro episcopis Hilarius papa* Incipit: *Mouimur ratione*	562
87v–88r	29	XXXVI	XXXVII	Synod of Arles in 314	
88r	30	XXXVII	XXXVIII	**Innocent I** Contents 3a: *Epistula Innocenti papae Rufo et Eusebio de his, qui duas accipiunt uxores* Contents 3b: *Epistola papae Innocenti de bigamis* Rubric: none Superscript: *Innocentius Rufo et Eusebio* Incipit: (ch. 2 only)	303
88v–89r	31	XXXVIII	XXXIX	**Symmachus** Contents 3a: *Epistula sancti Simmaci papae ad Caesarium episcopum datam* Contents 3b: *Epistola papae Simmachi ad Caesarium episcopum* Rubric: none Superscript: *Dilectissimo fratri Caesario Symmachus* Incipit: *Hortatur nos*	764
89r–90v	32	XXXIX	XL	**Damasus** Contents 3a: *Epistula Damasi ad Paulinum data de anatematezandis heresibus* Contents 3b: *Epistola Damasi de anathemathezandis heresibus* Rubric: none Superscript: *Dilectissimo fratri Paulo Damasus* Incipit: *Per ipsum filium*	235

Table 11.1 (cont.)

Folio	My item no.	Item no. in MS (according to 3a)	Item no. in MS (according to 3b)	Description	No. of canons	JK
90v–91r	33	XLI	XL	Augustine, *Sermo* 392.2		
91r–92r		XLII	XLI	Synod of Arles in 314 – bishop list	4	
		XLIII	XLII	Fourth Synod of Arles		
		[XLIV]	XLIII	Synod of Epaon	39	
92r–93r	34			Paulinus Incipit: *Scribere uobis*		
93r–97r	35			Synod of Constantinople in 448, *actio* 7		
97r–98v	36			**Leo I** Rubric: *Incipit epistula Flauiani episcopi Constantinopolitae ad Leonum urbis Romae episcopum* Superscript: *Domino beatissimo et Deo amabili patri Leoni Flauianus in domino salutem* Incipit: *Nulla res*		
98v–103v	37			**Leo I** Rubric: none Superscript: *Dilectissimo fratri Flauiano episcopo Leo episcopus* Incipit: *Lectis dilectionis*		423
103v–104v	38			**Leo I** Rubric: none Superscript: *Dilectissimis fratribus Rustico, Rauennio, Venerio et ceteris episcopis per Gallias constitutis Leo* Incipit: *Impletis per misericordiam*		480
104v–107r	39			**Leo I** Rubric: *Incipit epistula papae Leonis ad Pulcheriam Augustam* Superscript: none Incipit: *Quantum praesidii*		425

107r–109r | 40

Leo I
Rubric: *Incipit ad Iulianum episcopum*
Superscript: none
Incipit: *Licet per nostros*

429

109r–110v | 41

Leo I
Rubric: *Incipit ad Iouenalem episcopum*
Superscript: none
Incipit: *Acceptis dilectionis tuae*

514

110v–113v | 42

Leo I
Rubric: *Incipit eiusdem papae Leonis ad Constantinopolitanos ciues*
Superscript: none
Incipit: *Licet de his*

447

113v–118v | 43

Leo I
Rubric: *Incipit epistula papae Leonis ad Leonem imperatorem contra Eutychen*
Superscript: *Leo Leoni Augusto*
Incipit: *Promisisse me*

542

118v–119r | 44

Leo I
Rubric: *Incipit epistula papae Leonis ad Gallias et Hisanias de paschae sollemnitate*
Superscript: *Dilectissimis fratribus uniuersis episcopis catholicis per Gallias et Hispanias constitutis Leo*
Incipit: *Cum in omnibus*

512

119r–120v | 45

Leo I
Rubric: none
Superscript: *Dilectissimo fratri Theudoro episcopo Leo episcopus*
Incipit: *Sollicitudinis quidem*

485

Table 11.1 (cont.)

Folio	My item no.	Item no. in MS (according to 3a)	Item no. in MS (according to 3b)	Description	No. of canons	JK
120v–124r	46			**Leo I** Rubric: none Superscript: *Dilectissimo fratri Torebio Leo* Incipit: *Quam laudabiliter*[b] *Breuiarium aduersus hereticos*	8	412
124r–139v	47			Incipit: *Errare hereticos*		

[a] Presumably this should ready *ad Esychium episcopum* or *Esychio episcopo*.
[b] One may note the use of *ad* with the ablative instead of the accusative.
[c] Kaiser 2006: 68 mistakenly reads *Etychio* here.
[d] One may note the use of *ad* with the ablative.
[e] Wurm 1939b: 273 states there are fifteen chapters. The first table of contents lists fourteen, but the text itself has fifteen.
[f] Kaiser 2006: 68 mistakenly has the letter begin on fol. 23r.   [h] Presumably this should read *consulenti*.
[g] One may note the use of *ad* with the ablative.
[i] Wurm 1939b: 273 reads *domino* here.
[j] Wurm 1939b: 273 lists this as 8a. Consequently, all his numbers hence are one lower than mine.
[k] Presumably this should read *Viennensem et Narbonensem*.
[l] According to Maassen 1870: 558, there is nothing listed in this table for the preceding letter (hence he assigns no number to it and ix to the following letter), but he is mistaken.
[m] Wurm 1939b: 273 reads *Incipiunt decreta papae Leonis* but Kaiser 2006: 69 does not see any rubric. None appears in the microfilm. This will require a further inspection of the actual manuscript itself.
[n] One would expect this to read *Tusciam*.
[o] Wurm 1939b: 273 states that the letter begins on fol. 36v.
[p] Kaiser 2006: 69 reads *thorebio*.
[q] Wurm 1939b: 273 notes that this last word is inserted later. Kaiser 2006: 69 notes it is in another hand. Both read it as *req(uire)*.
[r] Wurm 1939b: 273 states there are sixteen chapters. The first table of contents lists fifteen, but the text itself has sixteen.

s Maassen 1870: 559, has the heading *Incipit epistula episcoporum ad imperatorem* although the manuscript actually reads *Incipit epistula episcoporum ad imperatores breuis staturo* (for *statutorum*), as does the heading for this item in table 3b, which he noted. This merging of two headings means that the next item, *Breuis Hipponensis*, is listed without number simply by its first chapter *delictoribus*.

t Wurm 1939b: 274, lists this as 13b. Consequently, all his numbers hence are two lower than mine.

u Maassen 1870: 559 assigns no number to this entry.

v Kaiser 2006: 70 reads *per tractatus*.

w Maassen 1870: 559, assigns no number or listing for this entry in 3a, but it is clearly listed as a later insertion, in the same hand, but without number, alongside the last chapter heading for the letter of Siricius contained in the Synod of Thélepte: *Explicit XV incipit regola formatorum*.

x Wurm 1939b: 274, lists this as 15b. Consequently, all his numbering hence is three lower than mine.

y Maassen 1870: 561 assigns no number to this entry.

z Maassen 1870: 566 has no further numbers for items from 3a, but a number are visible on the right-hand side of the manuscript.

aa Presumably this should read *Viennensem*.

ab The manuscript reads *Pro catholicae fidei ueritate quam laudabiliter*, although PL 54: 678 reads *Quam laudabiliter pro catholicae fidei ueritate* and Jaffé and Kaltenbrunner 188; 61 (JK 412) give the incipit as *Quam laudabiliter*.

Table 11.2 Contents of Paris, BnF, lat. 1564 with emphasis on papal letters

Folio	My item no.	Item no. in MS	Description	No. of canons	JK
1r–2r	1	[xxx]	Synod of Orange in 441	37	
2r–3r	2	xxxi	Synod of Vaison in 442	7	
3r–4v	3	xxxii	Synod of Arles in 443 or 452 – can. 26–56	25	
4v–5v	4a	xxxiii	Synod of Agde in 506 – can. 48–70	9	
5v–6r	5	xxxiii	**Innocent I** – can. 1 Rubric: *Epistolae sancti Innocenti episcopi* Superscript: *Dilectissimê fratri Exuperio Innocentius.* Incipit: *Consulenti tibi*		293
6r–9v	4b		Synod of Agde in 506 – continued	39 (to 48)	
9v–11r	6	xxxv	Synod of Clermont in 535	15	
11r–14r	7	xxxvi	Isaak Christinus, *Liber fidei de sancta trinitate*		
14r–14v	8	xxxvii	*Tituli ex canones excepti* (Synods of Orléans in 533, Clermont in 535, and Orléans in 538)		
14v–16r	9	xxxviii	*Regula beatissimi Macharii abbati*		
16r–18r	10	xxxix	Caesarius of Arles: *Regula sancto Teridio*		
18v–19r	11	xl.	Lupus and Euphronius: *Epistula*		
19r–20v	12	xli	Synod of Vannes in 465		
20v–21r	13	xlii	Leo, Victurus and Eustochius: *Epistula*		
21r	14	xliii	Troianus: *Epistula*		
21r	15	[xliv]	Honorius, *Inter publicas necessitates*		
21v–22r	16	xlv	Synod of Rome in 378		
22r–23r	17	xlvi	*Fides Romanorum*		
23r	18	xlvii	Gennadius		
23r–23v	19	xlviii	*Breuis statutorum* (*Breuiarum Hipponense*) – can. 1–6		
23v–24v	20	xlix	Synod of Carthage (*Breuiarum Hipponense*) – can. 16, 19–22, 35–37		

Folio	No.	Roman	Content		Page
24v–26r	21	L	Synod of Thélepte/**Siricius**. Rubric: *Incipit concilium Telinse per tractatus sancti Syrici papae urbis Romae per Africam.* Superscript: *Dilectissimis fratribus et coepiscopis per Africa Syricius diuersa quamuis.* Incipit: *Post consulatum/Cum in unum*	8	258
26r–26v	22	LI[b]	*Regula formatorum*	2	
26v–29v	23	LII	Synod of Epaon in 517	40	
29v–30r	24	LIII	Synod of Arles in 524	4	
30r–31r	25		**Zosimus**. Rubric: *Episcopus Zosimi ad Esicio episcopo Salunitano*[c] decretalis. Superscript: *Zosimus Eycio episcopo Saunitano*[d] . Incipit: *Exegit dilectio*	3	339
31r–34r	26	LIV	**Innocent I**. Rubric: *Epistola decretalis Innocenti papae ad Victricio episcopo*[e] *Rotomagensi.* Superscript: *Innocencius Victricio episcopo Rotomagense*[f]. Incipit: *Exsit ibi*[g]	15	286
34r–35v	27	LV	**Innocent I**. Rubric: none. Superscript: *Innocentius Exsuperio episcopus*[h] *Tholosano.* Incipit: *Consolenti*[i] *tibi*	7	293
35v–39r	28		**Innocent I**. Rubric: none. Superscript: *Innocentius, Rufos, Eusebius, Eustasius, Claudius, Maximianus, Eugenius, Reroncius, Iohannis, Polecronius, Sofronius, Flauianus, Helarius, Machedonius, Calecratius, Zosimos, Profuturus, Nicetius, Hermogenius, Vincencius, Asiologus, Terentianus, Herudianus et Marcianus*[j] *episcopis Machedonibus et diaconibus in Deoldomino salutem.* Incipit: *Magna me*	12	303
39r–40v	29	LVI	**Celestine I**. Rubric: *Incipit Caelestini.* Superscript: *Caelestinus uniuersis episcopus per Viennensim et Namnensium*[k] *prouincias constitutis.* Incipit: *Copiremus*[l] *quidem*	11[m]	369
40v–41r	30	LVIII[n]	**Celestine**. Rubric: *Epistola Celestini ad episcopis per Apuliam et Calabriam.* Superscript: *Caelestinus episcopus uniuersis episcopis per Apuliam et Calabriam constitutis.* Incipit: *Nulli sacerdotis*	4	371
41r–42v	31	LVIII	**Leo I**. Rubric: *Incipiunt decreta papae Leonis.* Superscript: *Leo uniuersis episcopis per Campaniam, Ticinam, Tusciam et per uniuersas prouincias constitutis in domino salutem.* Incipit: *Vt nobis gratulationem*	3	402

Table II.2 (cont.)

Folio	My item no.	Item no. in MS	Description	No. of canons	JK
42v–43r	32	LIX	**Leo I.** Rubric: *Incipit eiusdem papae Leonis de Manicheis.* Superscript: *Leo uniuersis episcopis per diuersas prouincias constitutis in Domino salutem.* Incipit: *In consortium uos*		405
43r–48v	33	LX	**Leo I.** Rubric: none. Superscript: *Leo Chorebio episcopo Astoracensi.* Incipit: *Quam laudabiliter*	15	412
48v–55v	34	LXI	Faustinus and Marcellinus, *De confessione uerae fidei.* Incipit: *Deprecamur mansuetudinem*		
55v–58r	35	LXII	Synod of Orleans in 511	27	
58r–63r	36	LXIII	Synod of Orleans in 538	33	
63r–65v	37	LXIV	**Innocent I.** Rubric: *Innocentius diuersis episcopis in Tolosana synodo constitutis.* Superscript: *Dilectissimis fratribus in domino salutem.* Incipit: *Sepe me*		292
65v–68v	38	LXV	**Leo I.** Rubric: none. Superscript: *Dilectissimis fratribus uniuersis episcopis per Viennensem prouinciam constitutis Leo.* Incipit: *Diuine cultum°*		407
68v–69v	39	LXVI	**Hilary I.** Rubric: none. Superscript: *Dilectissimis fratribus Leoncio, Verano, Victuro episcopo Hilarius papa.* Incipit: *Monemur racione*		562
69v–70r	40	LXVII	**Symmachus.** Rubric: none. Superscript: *Dilectissimo fratri Caesario Symmachus.* Incipit: *Hortatur nos*		764
70r–71r	41	LXVII	**Damasus.** Rubric: none. Superscript: *Dilectissimo fratri Paulino Damasius°.* Incipit: *Per ipsum filium*		235
71r–71v	42	LXIX	Augustine, *Sermo 392.2*		
71v–72r	43	LXX	Faustus of Riez, *Ep. 4.* Incipit: *Scribere uobis*		
72v–75v	44	LXXI	Faustus of Riez, *Ep. 5.* Incipit: *Admiranda mihi*		
75v–77r	45	LXXII	Faustus of Riez, *Ep. 6.* Incipit: *Magnum pietatis*		
77r–79v	46	LXXIII	Faustus of Riez, *Ep. 7.* Incipit: *Honoratus officio*		
79v–83r	47	LXXIV	Synod of Constantinople in 448, ch. 7		

Folio	No.		Description	Date
83r–84r	48	LXXV	**Leo I** (*Ep.* 22). Rubric: *Incipit epistola Flauiani episcopi Constantinopolitani de*^A *Leonem orbis Romanae episcopum.* Superscript: *Domino beatissimo et deo amabile patri Leone Flauianus in domino salutem.* Incipit: *Nulla res*	
84r–87v	49	LXXVI	**Leo I**. Rubric: none. Superscript: *Dilectissimo fratre Flauiano episcopo Leo episcopus.* Incipit: *Lectis dilectionis*	423
87v–88r	50	LXXVII	**Leo I**. Rubric: none. Superscript: *Dilectissimis fratribus Rustico, Rabennio, Venerio et ceteris episcopis per Gallias constituti Leo.* Incipit: *Impletis per misericordiam*	480
88r–88v	51	LXXVIII^r	**Leo I**. Rubric: *Incipit exemplar epistolae Pascasinus episcopis Lillibitanus et Lugensis episcopis Ascolanus et Bonifacius prebiter*^s *ecclesiae maximae orbis Romae uecarii sanctissimi ac beatissimi papae Leonis apostolicae sedis antestites*^t *pronunciauerunt.* Superscript: none. Incipit: *Manifesta sunt*	
88v–90v		LXXIX	**Leo I**. Rubric: *Incipit ad Pulciriam Augustam.* Superscript: none. Incipit: *Quantum praesidii*	425
90v–92r	52	LXXX	**Leo I**. Rubric: *Incipit ad Iulianum episcopum.* Superscript: none. Incipit: *Licet per nostros*	429
92r–93r	53	LXXXI	**Leo I**. Rubric: *Incipit ad Iuuenalem episcopum.* Superscript: none. Incipit: *Acceptis dilectionis tuae*	514
93r–95r	54	LXXXII	**Leo I**. Rubric: *Incipit eiusdem papae Leonis ad Constantinopolitanum ciuis.* Superscript: none. Incipit: *Licet de his*	447
95r–99r	55	LXXXIII	**Leo I**. Rubric: *Incipit epistola papae Leonis ad Leonem imperatorem contra Eutycin.* Superscript: *Leoni Augusto.* Incipit: *Promisisse me*	542
99r	56	LXXXIV	**Leo I**. Rubric: *Incipit epistola papae Leonis ad Gallias et Hispanias.* Superscript: *Dilectissimis fratribus uniuersis episcopis catholicis per Gallias et Hispanias constitutis Leo.* Incipit: *Cum in omnibus*	512
99r–100v	57	LXXXV	**Leo I**. Rubric: *Teudero episcopo Leo episcopus.* Superscript: *Dilectissimo fratri Teudero episcopo Leo episcopus.* Incipit: *Sollicitudinis quidem*	485
100v–111v	58	LXXXVI	*Breuiarium aduersus hereticos.* Incipit: *Errare hereticos*	
111v–114r	59	LXXXVII	Council of Chalcedon in 451	

Table 11.2 (cont.)

Folio	My item no.	Item no. in MS	Description	No. of canons	JK
114r–118v	60	LXXXIX	**Siricius.** Rubric: *Incipit exitus epistolae Syrici ad Ierio episcopo Tarraconinsi.* Superscript: *Siricius Hierio episcopo Tarraconensi.* Incipit: *Directa*	12	255
118v–121v	61	LXXXVIII	Synod of Rome in 499		
121v–122r	62	XC	John the deacon, *Epistula ad Symmachum.* Incipit: *Quia me*		
122r–125v	63		Synod of Rome in 502		
125v–126r	64[a]		**Zosimus.** Rubric: *Zosimus commoneturium*[b] *presbyterorum et diaconorum qui Rauenna sunt.* Superscript: none. Incipit: *Ex relatione*		345
126r–126v	65	XCI	*Theodoric, Epistula ad Laurentium, Marcellinum et Petrum.* Incipit: *Vos quidem*		
126v–127v	66	XCII	*Theodoric, Epistula ad synodum Romae.* Incipit: *Romanae ecclesiae*		
127v–128r	67	XCIII	Synod of Rome in 501. Incipit: *Agemus Deo*		
128r–128v	68	XCIV	*Theodoric, Epistula ad synodum Romae.* Incipit: *Decuerat quidem*		
128v–129r	69	XCV	*Theodoric, Epistula ad synodum Romae.* Incipit: *Si mihi*		
129r–132v	70	XCVI	Synod of Rome in 501		
132v–133r	71	XCVII	**Symmachus.** Rubric: none. Superscript: *Dilectissimo fratri Caesario Symmachus.* Incipit: *Ortatur nos*		764
133r–134r	72	XCVIII	**Pelagius II.** Rubric: none. Superscript: *Dilectissimo fratri Aunario Pelagius urbis Romae.* Incipit: *Laudanda tuae*		1048
134r–136v	73	XCIX	Augustine, *De diuersis heresibus*	69	

a Presumably this should read *dilectissimo.*
b Maassen 1870: 606 reads LII, but one of the IS, written above LI, refers to the canon.
c One may note the use of *ad* with the ablative.
d Presumably this should read *Salunitano.*
e One may note the use of *ad* with the ablative.

f   Presumably this should read *Rotomagensi*.

g   Presumably this should read *Etsi tibi*.

h   Presumably this should read *episcopo*.

i   Presumably this should read *consulenti*.

j   One may note that most of the recipients' names are in the nominative.

k   Presumably this should read *Viennensem et Narbonensem*.

l   Presumably this should read *Cuperemus*.

m   Wurm 1939b: 284 states there are seven chapters, but the manuscript lists eleven.

n   This is a mistake in the manuscript for LVII, which does not appear in the manuscript. Wurm 1939b: 284 simply numbers it as 57.

o   Wurm 1939b: 285 mistakenly reads this as *cultu*.

p   Presumably this should read *Damasus*.

q   Presumably this should read *ad*.

r   Maassen 1870: 608 omits this letter.

s   Incorrectly for *presbiter*.

t   Incorrectly for *antistitis*.

u   Maassen 1870: 609 does not mention this letter.

v   Presumably this should read *commonitorium*.

CHAPTER 12

De profundis

The letters and archives of Pelagius I of Rome (556–561)

Bronwen Neil

Almost all letters by bishops of Rome from beginning of the fifth century (Innocent I) up to 590 (Gregory I) are preserved only in mediaeval letter-collections. Due to the nature of the canon law-collections and the rationale behind their compilation, that of providing authorities on questions of clerical discipline and doctrinal error, the content of papal letters that survive is remarkably homogeneous. This, together with a preference for letters addressed to important figures such as members of the imperial family, and other well-known bishops, has meant that questions of the collator's intention are thus generally removed from the contemporary sphere to mediaeval concerns with providing epistolary precedents for canon law.

The letters of Pelagius I are an exception to the rule. The production and preservation of ninety-six letters from his pontificate merit scholarly attention. The content of these letters covers much the same ground as the *Registrum* of Gregory the Great (590–604): defence of doctrine, management of papal property and revenues, care for the poor and needy, especially clergy, involvement in disputed episcopal elections and clerical discipline. In this broad focus, we can see a distinct change from previous papal collections, and an often-overlooked precursor to Pope Gregory I. First let us consider the Pelagian collection in the context of papal archive production in the fifth and sixth century, before turning to the mediaeval transmission of the collection, and its highly varied contents.

Papal archives from the fifth and sixth centuries

Two of the largest Latin corpora of episcopal letters before Gregory's were produced by Leo the Great (440–61) and Gelasius (492–96). The third largest was that of Pelagius I (556–61).[1] The survival of so many

---

[1] Pelagius' pontificate was long dated from 555 to 560 (see e.g. Ewald 1880; Löwenfeld 2010; Jaffé and Kaltenbrunner 1885). That the correct dates were one year later was established by Gassó and Batlle 1956.

letters from Pelagius I casts doubt on Noble's assertion that the papal archives before Gregory I do not survive 'in even fragmentary form'.[2] Pelagius' father, John, was a *vicarianus*, either a deputy to the praetorian prefect of a civil diocese, or a civil servant on the staff of a *vicarius*.[3] His son would probably have been well aware of the importance of imperial practices of archiving, and he employed a notary, Valentine, to help him produce and distribute letters, as was customary in the papal administration by this time.[4]

The *primicerius notariorum* is first mentioned in the *LP* entry for Pope Julius (337–52), as the official responsible for church documents including bonds, deeds, donations, exchanges, transfers, wills, declarations and manumissions.[5] Other early mentions of the papal archives occur in Innocent I's *Letter* 13[6] and in the *LP* entry for Celestine (422–32).[7] *LP* also records that the archive of the church library preserved five books authored by Gelasius against Eutyches and Nestorius and two against Arius.[8] At the end of Gelasius' *Ep.* 30, the copyist identifies himself as a secretary (*notarius*) from the archive.[9] There is also an interpolation in the *LP* Gelasius to the effect that his five books against Nestorius and Eutyches 'are preserved today in the archive of the church library'.[10] The notaries of the papal archive were among the pope's closest advisors and were often used as envoys, due to the knowledge they had gained in the course of producing papal documents, particularly letters on sensitive subjects.

Every pope from Innocent I to Gregory I produced at least one surviving letter, with the exception of six, including Pelagius' immediate successors, Popes John III and Benedict I.[11] We note that there was a ten-month

---

[2] Noble 1993: 397.

[3] *LP* I, Duchesne 1955–7/I: 303. See Davis 2000: 141, *s.v. vicarianus*. On Pelagius generally, see also Sotinel 2000a, and the bibliography cited therein.

[4] *LP* I, Duchesne 1955: 303.   [5] *LP* I, Duchesne 1955: 205.

[6] Innocent, *Ep.* 13 to Rufus, bishop of Thessalonica, PL 20: 516B–517A: *Omnem sane instructionem chartarum in causa archivorum cum presbytero Senecione, viro admodum maturo, fieri jussimus. Itaque et ex priore nostra epistola, et ex his chartulis, bene recensens quid agere debeas, recognosce.* 17 June 412.

[7] *LP* I, Duchesne 1955: 230: *Hic fecit constitutum de omnem ecclesiam, maxime et de religione, quae hodie archivo ecclesiae detenentur recondite.* '[Celestine] issued a decree about the whole church and especially (one) about religious life, which are kept safe today in the church archive.' Tr. Davis 2000: 35, modified.

[8] *LP* I, Duchesne 1955: 255.

[9] *Ep.* 30, Thiel 1867 [2004]: 447: *Sixtus notarius sanctae Romanae ecclesiae jussu domini mei beatissimi papae Gelasii ex scrinio edidi.*

[10] *LP*, Mommsen 1898: 117: *qui hodie bibliotheca ecclesiae archivo reconditi tenentur.* This is an interpolation to the text of *LP*.

[11] Popes John I (523–6), Silverius (536), John III (561–74) and Benedict I (575–9).

interregnum between the pontificates of John III and Benedict I. The difficulty of maintaining proper records in times of great upheaval clearly impacted on the survival rates of letters produced in this latter period. Four of these collections were substantial. Pope Leo I produced 143 letters; another thirty addressed to him were preserved with these; Pope Gelasius I was the author of some 102 letters and fragments, including one addressed to him.[12] From Pope Hormisdas, we have a 'collection' of ninety-three letters, as well as thirty-one addressed to him.[13] These three significant collections, together with the large Pelagian corpus, are proof that the archiving techniques of the papal archive (*scrinium*) were well practised before the episcopate of Gregory the Great. Other works attributed to Pelagius are the six books *In defensione trium capitulorum*, to be discussed below, and a translation of the Greek *Sayings of the Desert Fathers* (*Apophthegmata Patrum*). The Latin translation, known as *Vitae patrum*, by the deacon Pelagius and subdeacon John, has been attributed to Pelagius I and the later pope John III,[14] but the question of authorship remains open.

Transmission of the collection

The ninety-six letters of Pelagius, now conveniently collected in a critical edition,[15] enjoyed mixed popularity over the five centuries after their composition. Eleven letters of Pelagius were preserved in the mid-sixth-century Gallic collection, *Liber auctoritatum Arelatensis ecclesiae*, along with five letters of Pope Symmachus and nine of Vigilius.[16] These are *Letters* 1–11, written between 556 and 558, and collated in Arles in those years.[17] Nine of these eleven letters of Pelagius are addressed to either Sapaudus of Arles or King Childebert, and concern the rights and privileges of Bishop Sapaudus as the pope's vicar in Gaul.[18] (Two of the letters are found in

---

[12] Thiel 1867 [2004]: 287–510.

[13] Thiel 1867 [2004]: 741–990. Another twenty-six in the collection are neither written by Hormisdas nor addressed to him.

[14] PL 73: 855–1022 (*CPG* 5570.) Kelly 1986: 63–64, and Straw 1988: 14. The new edition by Gassó signalled in *CPG* has not appeared.

[15] Gassó and Batlle 1956. Their numbering reflects their approximate chronological order, from 556 to 561, and not the order in which the letters appeared in their manuscripts.

[16] Jasper 2001: 67. The *Collectio Arelatensis*, Gundlach 1892, survives in three manuscripts in the BnF, two from the ninth century and one from the tenth to twelfth: Gassó and Batlle 1956: xxvii–xxviii. The ongoing disputes between the bishops of Arles, Vienne and other Gallic centres have been treated by Geoffrey Dunn in Chapter 11.

[17] JK 938–48.

[18] The remaining two, *Epp.* 10 and 11, Gassó and Batlle 1956: 31–4 and 35–40, were confessions of faith written in the context of the Three Chapters controversy.

an appendix to Gregory I's *Registrum*.[19] Gregory I's *Letter to Leo, bishop of Catena* is the oldest witness to Pelagius I's letter-writing activity, where he tells Leo that 'My predecessor Pelagius of blessed memory gave an instruction to Helpidius, your predecessor'.)[20] This mini-collection on the bishop of Arles's privileges was used by various Gallic bishops in the ninth century, and one of Pelagius' letters was cited almost completely in the letter of Pope Nicholas I (858–67) to Emperor Michael III,[21] surely one of the most sophisticated put-downs ever received by a Byzantine emperor.[22] This is the letter in which Pelagius reprimanded Childebert for allowing Sapaudus to be brought before a secular court at the request of another bishop for an unspecified crime. It also contained a thinly veiled threat that God would not uphold the king's rule if he did not respect ecclesiastical laws and protect the integrity of clerical orders.[23] Its value to Nicholas I in his struggles for primacy over the bishop (and emperor) of Constantinople in the mid-ninth century is obvious. Nicholas' inclusion of this letter suggests a well-organised papal archive (*scrinium*) was in place with records that reached back well before the *Registrum* of Gregory.[24]

The *scrinium* at the end of the seventh century included a chief secretary (*primicerius notariorum* or *scriniarius*), who supervised the notaries, the papal library and the archive, and his deputy (*secundicarius*). Both are mentioned in the retinue of the Syrian Pope Constantine (708–15), but the *primicerius notariorum* was first mentioned in the sixth-century *Liber Pontificalis* as appearing in the pontificate of Julius (337–52).[25] It seems safe to assume that such an officer was also in charge of papal correspondence and records during Pelagius' pontificate. Gregory I refers to his private secretary (*chartularius*), who was sent to manage the Sicilian papal estates in 603.[26] The papal notaries were among the pope's closest advisors, and were often used as envoys, especially on sensitive matters, due to their intimate knowledge of papal business.

---

[19] *Ep.* 5 to Sapaudus of Arles, and *Ep.* 6 to Valerian the Patrician, Gundlach 1892: 442–6.

[20] Gregory I, *Ep.* 14.16, Hartmann 1899: 436, lines 6–7.

[21] *Ep.* 8 (JK 948). See Jasper 2001: 67 n. 287. Pope Nicolas, *Ep.* 88, Perels 1978: 465 (28 September 865). See Gassó and Batlle 1956: xxxi, on the two Vatican codices that preserve this letter-within-a-letter, plus one codex from Monte Cassino and one from Valencia.

[22] See discussion of *Ep.* 88 in Neil 2006: 16–17.

[23] Gassó and Batlle 1956: 27, lines 20–5: *Et huiusmodi causis sollicitam uos in reliquo decet exhibere cautelam, ne quid contra ecclesiasticas regulas menti uestrae, non aliter Deo nostro recte potest regalis deuotio famulari, nisi prouidentia eius ecclesiasticorum ordinum seruetur integritas.*

[24] On the contents of the *Registrum*, see Neil 2013b: 17–26; on the role of the papal *scrinium* in the production and preservation of Gregory's letters, see Pollard 2013.

[25] Constantine: *LP* 1, Duchesne 1955: 389; Julius: *LP* 1, Duchesne 1955: 205. See Neil 2013b: 9–10.

[26] *Ep.* 13.20, Norberg 1982: 1020–1.

Unfortunately, the papal archives from the fifth and sixth centuries survive only in fragmentary form, and most have to be pieced together from recipients' copies or from special collections like the *Collectio Avellana*,[27] a sixth-century collection that consists mostly of papal correspondence, and includes almost all of the letters of Hormisdas (514–23).

In modern times, the letters of Pelagius the British Collection (*Collectio Britannica*), a mediaeval Italian collection of papal letters from the sixth, ninth and eleventh centuries but now held in London, was first edited by Ewald in 1880.[28] The eighty-four letters by Pelagius included in this collection date from 1 September 658 until March 561, the year of Pelagius' death. Many of Pope Gelasius' letters from 492 to 496 were also preserved in the British Collection, with some reassigned to Pelagius. For example, Ewald reassigned *Fragment 3 To Dulcius the defensor* (attributed to Gelasius by Thiel),[29] to Pelagius on the basis of manuscript evidence that was not available to Thiel, which showed that the names Pelagius and Gelasius were often confused by scribes.[30] *Ep.* 73 in Ewald's edition (*To the count Hostilius*) was correctly reascribed there to Gelasius.[31]

The British Collection is so-called after the manuscript in which it is found, London BM Add. MS 8873, an eleventh- or twelfth-century codex copied in Italy. This preserves seventy-two letters and letter fragments of Pelagius (fols. 21–38), the only witness to the majority of letters that are missing from the older *Collectio Arelatensis*, the eighty-four that are numbered *Letters* 12 to 96 in Gassó and Batlle's edition.[32] It represents an early private effort to collect various letters relevant to canon law. Letters from later popes include selections from Pelagius II (578–90),[33] Leo IV (847–55),[34] John VIII (872–82),[35] Stephan VI (885–91), Alexander II (1061–73) and Urban II (1088–99).[36] The final section of the manuscript includes letters from various popes before Pelagius I, from Clement I to Hormisdas,[37] as well as many later popes and bishops of other sees than Rome, such as Ambrose of Milan. Also included are letters from Boniface of Mainz (747–55). This collection, or one just like it, was the basis of Bishop Ivo

---

[27] Noble 1993: 397.

[28] Ewald 1880: 277 (Pelagian letters are listed in Ewald 1880: 533–62); see also Jasper 2001: 67–8.

[29] Thiel 1867 [2004]: 484–5.

[30] *Ep.* 16, Ewald 1880: 542 n. 6 (JK 949). Amory 1997: 356 accepted Pelagian authorship, but I think this one too is better assigned to Gelasius.

[31] Ewald 1880: 592–3.　　[32] Gassó and Batlle 1956: xxxiii.

[33] Two letters (fols. 38–38v.).　　[34] Forty-five letters (fols. 159v–171).

[35] Fifty-five letters (fols.120–136v).　　[36] Ewald 1880: 279.

[37] Ewald 1880: 239 calls this 'Varia Pars 2'. The contents of these seventy-seven items are listed in Ewald 1880: 572–6. They are not always full letters, but sometimes a series of excerpts.

of Chartres' collection of papal decretals in 1094–5.[38] A similar collection, which is the sole witness to several fragments of Pelagius' letters,[39] was made by the Italian Cardinal Deusdedit of the Church of the Apostles in Eudoxia in 1083–7. Several decades later, in 1119–23, a collection of papal decretals arranged in chronological order from the pseudo-Isidorean decretals appeared, the work of Anselm of Lucca.[40] Several of Pelagius' letters were excerpted in the *Decretum* of Gratian, perhaps the most influential collection of canon-law documents.[41] Each collator 'cherry-picked' the papal letters to illustrate particular points of canon law that were relevant to his own age.

The famous theorist of papal primacy, Walter Ullmann, posited that the British Collection was forged, on the basis that it included accommodating letters from Gelasius to the Arian king Theodoric that did not accord with Ullmann's sense of the pope's ideological stance towards secular rulers in his region. The supposition of forgery has since been definitively quashed.[42]

Seventy-two Pelagian letters from the British Collection were listed by Ewald, and those not previously edited by Thiel were edited by him.[43] Seventeen letters or fragments from the British Collection were included in Löwenfeld's 'previously unedited' papal letters.[44]

Contents of the Pelagian collection

The content of Pelagius' correspondence shows a bishop under stress, trying to juggle the competing demands of preserving doctrinal purity and ecclesial unity from the attacks of heretics and schismatics; managing papal properties and dispensing pastoral care; and maintaining clerical discipline.[45] Five areas of activity dominate the surviving correspondence of Pelagius I. What distinguishes this from previous papal letter-collections is the collator's willingness to show the problems that the bishop of Rome was undergoing, and how he attempted to deal with them. This is a sharp contrast to the other, heavily doctored, collections of previous papal correspondence from the fifth and sixth centuries, such

---

[38] Fronteau *et al.* 1647, vol. II. See further Gassó and Batlle 1956: xxxii and xliii–xliv.
[39] Gassó and Batlle 1956: xxxix.   [40] Gassó and Batlle 1956: xl.
[41] Mansi 1960–1/IX: 749–50 lists those decretals taken from the Third Council of Paris in 557, selected by Gratian and other decretalists.
[42] See Amory 1997: 198 and 200 n. 22.
[43] Ewald 1880: 533–62.   [44] Löwenfeld 2010: 12–21.
[45] On Pelagius' pontificate, see Sotinel 2000a, with literature.

as the letters of Innocent I,[46] Leo I,[47] Gelasius I[48] and Hormisdas,[49] whose focus is on papal primacy and disciplinary and doctrinal matters. The earlier collections depict 'business as usual' for the bishop of Rome, in spite of invasions, sieges, diplomatic defeats, and starvation and plague in the city of Rome and surrounding countryside. While papal primacy and clerical discipline and doctrinal orthodoxy also appeared to be priorities in the Pelagian correspondence, so too do household matters and the protection of papal property.

Defence of doctrine and papal authority

One of the first issues that Pelagius was forced to address was the ongoing Three Chapters controversy, which threatened to undermine his authority as a newly elected bishop.[50] Justinian's condemnation of the Three Chapters was strenuously opposed in the West because it was seen as a betrayal of the ecumenical Council of Chalcedon. Pelagius I's predecessor, the hapless Pope Vigilius (537–55), initially opposed Justinian's initiative.[51] Vigilius was forced to capitulate in person in 548 while being detained in Constantinople. He made an initial qualified condemnation of the Three Chapters in his first *Constitutum*,[52] before capitulating to imperial pressure fully in 553 with a second *Constitutum*.[53] The Council of Constantinople, held in the same year, confirmed Justinian's position against Theodoret, Theodore and Ibas. Vigilius, after being held in Constantinople under house arrest for several years, died on the journey back to Rome in 555.[54] The archdeacon Pelagius was the candidate of the Byzantine general Narses, chosen to replace the recalcitrant Vigilius.

---

[46] See Dunn's Chapter 11.   [47] See Neil 2009.   [48] See Neil and Allen 2014.

[49] Neil and Allen are preparing a translation with commentary of Hormisdas' letters.

[50] After the Council of Chalcedon (451) had condemned the works of three bishops perceived as anti-Cyrillian – Theodoret of Cyrrhus, Theodore of Mopsuestia and Ibas of Edessa – their works were condemned again by the opponents of Chalcedon in 532, as 'Nestorian'. The contested works of these three authors, known as the Three Chapters, were to cause ecclesial division for a century after Chalcedon. Justinian first tried to achieve compromise over the Three Chapters, but in 543 or the following year the emperor promulgated an edict condemning them. For background on the controversy, see the collected essays in Chazelle and Cubitt 2007, with literature; and Grillmeier and Hainthaler 1995: 411–62.

[51] On the episode of Vigilius in Constantinople, see Sotinel 1992 and 2000b.

[52] *Collectio Avellana* 82, Guenther 1895: 230–320 (JK 936). Also called the *Scandala*. See Price 2009/ II: 141–4.

[53] Also known as *Aetius*; ACO IV.2: 138–68 (JK 937). See Price 2009/II: 219–20.

[54] On Vigilius' death in Syracuse on the way home from his unfortunate sojourn in Constantinople see Allen and Neil 2013: 58–61.

The circumstances of Pelagius' election made him an unpopular choice with the nobility and clergy of Rome, where he was seen as a traitor to the Three Chapters cause. The people of Rome suspected that he was implicated in Vigilius' death, and refused to enter into communion with him, according to the *LP*.[55] As a consequence, it was difficult to find a bishop who would ordain him. On Narses' advice, Pelagius had to avow his innocence in public, before 'the entire populace and the plebs' would enter into communion with him. Many clergy in northern Italy also refused to enter into communion with him and demanded that he ratify their schism.[56] He also faced opposition from the Gallic bishops, prompting him to send a confession of faith to Childebert (*Ep.* 7), and asking the king to obstruct those who were causing divisions in the Gallic church.

In an unprecedented step the new pope Pelagius wrote an open letter to 'all the people of God', seeking to remove all suspicion about the orthodoxy of the see of Rome by sending his profession of faith to all the faithful in the world.[57] Although he declares that he accepts the decrees of the four councils, and whatever was laid down by his predecessors, particularly Pope Leo I, Pelagius in this early letter accepts Theodoret and Ibas as orthodox.[58] This was quite a departure from the second *Constitutum* of Vigilius. It seems that Pelagius was endeavouring to distance himself from the failures of his predecessor, in order to garner support from bishops in Gaul and northern Italy.

When he was still a deacon and legate (*apocrisiarius*) in Constantinople, Pelagius had written six books defending the Three Chapters, a work known as *In defensione trium capitulorum*.[59] The many stylistic similarities between this work and Vigilius' first *Constitutum* suggest that Pelagius composed the latter for Vigilius while he was still deacon.[60] Confirming this theory is the fact that, soon after his ordination as bishop, the bishops of Aemilia accused him of writing a letter *against* the Three Chapters. Writing to Simeon the *illustris*, Pelagius rejects the accusation that he was the author of the letter that the bishops of Aemilia want to attribute to him, insisting that he sent no other letters while he was in Constantinople, apart from a refutation of the Three Chapters condemnation and the work *In defensione trium capitulorum*.[61]

---

[55] *LP* 1, Duchesne 1955: 303. Cf. Sotinel 2000a: 529–36.
[56] *Ep.* 10 to the bishops of Tuscia Annonaria (JK 939), 16 April 557; Gassó and Batlle 1956: 31–4.
[57] *Ep.* 11 (JK 938), Gassó and Batlle 1956: 35–40.
[58] *Ep.* 11 (JK 938), Gassó and Batlle 1956: 35–40.
[59] Devreesse 1932 (*CPL* 1703).   [60] Ertl 1937: 68–70.
[61] *Ep.* 80 to Simeon the *illustris* (JK 972), Gassó and Batlle 1956: 196–7.

Persecuting schismatics

A distinctive development in the sixth century was the Roman bishop's willingness to use secular force in disciplinary matters. These misdemeanours often went hand-in-hand with schism. This collection contains two groups of letters that show Pelagius bringing imperial force to bear on schismatics. These are not identified but the context suggests that they were Three Chapters supporters.

The first group (*Epp.* 65, 66, 67) concerns the case of the fraudulent papal administrator Maximilian, a member of a schismatic community. On account of the aberrations of Maximilian and the schismatic bishops, Pelagius sends the presbyter Peter and the *notarius* Proiectus to tell the *magister militum* Carellus to use force if necessary.[62] Pelagius signals his desire to remove business affairs from Maximilian and put them into presbyter Peter's hands.[63] In addition, he asks the count Anilanus to protect Peter and Proiectus so that they can perform their duties.[64]

The second group (*Epp.* 60, 69, 70, 71) concerns a dishonest bishop, Paulinus of Fossombrone, one of a group of schismatics. Pelagius enquires about the delay in the arrival of Paulinus, whom Narses had promised to deliver on another occasion, and urges the general to punish the crimes that Paulinus and other schismatics have committed through Narses' negligence.[65] Pelagius informs Narses that, as a patrician, he should use his authority to exert force on the dishonest, who are tearing the church apart, because the laws advise that those who have civil powers should contain rebels. Pelagius requests the Byzantine *magister militum* John, for the sake of the peace of the church, to put the pseudo-bishop Paulinus in chains and send him to the pontiff.[66] The *defensores* also have a crucial role to play. Pelagius asks the *defensores* Basil and Oclatinus to help John in the struggle with Paulinus, in order to bring not only military but also ecclesiastical clout to bear.[67] Pelagius has to repeat his request to the *magister militum* to arrest Paulinus and send him to Rome. John is to put into chains all the other clergy designated by the letter-bearer, and either hand them over to the bishop or send them to Rome.[68] It is interesting that the list of names

---

[62] *Ep.* 65 to Carellus *magister militum* (JK 1024), Gassó and Batlle 1956: 171–2.
[63] *Ep.* 66 to Peter the presbyter (JK 1025), Gassó and Batlle 1956: 174.
[64] *Ep.* 67 to Anilanus *comes* (JK 1026), Gassó and Batlle 1956: 175–6.
[65] *Ep.* 60 to Narses the patrician (JK 1019), Gassó and Batlle 1956: 159–61.
[66] *Ep.* 69 to John *magister militum* (JK 952), Gassó and Batlle 1956: 178–9.
[67] *Ep.* 70 to Basil and Oclatinus *defensores* (JK 1028), Gassó and Batlle 1956: 180–1.
[68] *Ep.* 71 to John *magister militum* (JK 1029), Gassó and Batlle 1956: 182.

of the guilty was not entrusted to writing but only to the memory of the letter-bearer. Pelagius adds confidently that the *defensores* Basil and Oclatinus will assist the church, having just been asked to do so.[69]

Exercising clerical discipline

Two legal avenues that were open to bishops to pursue such infringements of clerical discipline as that with which Paulinus was charged were secular law and the bishop's court (*audientia episcopalis*). Both were overloaded in the fifth and sixth centuries, as episcopal correspondence of Augustine of Hippo, Gelasius of Rome and Theodoret of Cyrrhus shows.[70] While the bishops of Rome were concerned to represent themselves as 'exceptional judges', to quote Uhalde,[71] it seems that this ideal was compromised by the workings of pontifical agents and other bishops, as the Pelagian correspondence demonstrates. Pelagius shared with Leo I and Gelasius I the expectation that misdemeanours of clergy would be dealt with by ecclesiastical rather than secular courts. Pelagius thus reproved King Childebert for permitting Bishop Sapaudus to be called to appear in court at the behest of another bishop, requesting that in future the laws of the church not be repealed.[72] Sapaudus had recently been appointed vicar of the apostolic see, at the request of Childebert,[73] and so could reasonably expect papal protection from a secular lawsuit. In the case of a deacon who had attracted public notoriety by committing incest, Pelagius instructs that the culprit is to be punished because of the bad publicity.[74] He is pleased to tell other bishops how to resolve law cases which are unworthy of Christians.[75] He also tells Benegestus the *defensor* how to conduct himself in judicial cases pertaining to clerics.[76] A cleric of any rank must address his complaint against a layperson to the judge of the province, but a layperson who wants to get a cleric of any rank deposed must direct his complaints to the bishops in the same city or territory.[77] Obviously

---

[69] See *Ep.* 70 cited above, n. 67.
[70] See the case-studies in Allen and Neil 2013: 158–70, 180–91.
[71] Uhalde 2007: 10–12, 47–76.
[72] *Ep.* 8 to King Childebert (JK 948), Gassó and Batlle 1956: 26–7 (cf. *Ep.* 5).
[73] *Ep.* 5 to Sapaudus (JK 944), Gassó and Batlle 1956: 14–17; *Ep.* 6 to King Childebert (JK 945), Gassó and Batlle 1956: 18–19. Pelagius indicates that he has agreed to his request: Sapaudus has become vicar of the see of Rome and has the use of the *pallium*.
[74] *Ep.* 95 to Bishop Peter of Potentia (?) (JK 945), Gassó and Batlle 1956: 225–7.
[75] *Ep.* 96 to Bishop Eleutherius (no JK no.), Gassó and Batlle 1956: 227–8. *Igitur, auctoritate potiore ducta ad medium, benignior et humanior intellectus qui reperiri poterit ibi, doceat terminare litem, instruat sententiam proferre, prout tempus et res uel qualitas personarum expostulat.*
[76] *Ep.* 91 to Benegestus the *defensor* (JK 964), Gassó and Batlle 1956: 217–18.
[77] *Ep.* 81 to Sergius the *cancellarius* (JK 965), Gassó and Batlle 1956: 198–9.

the segregation of ecclesiastical and secular business was calculated to favour the cleric under suspicion, not the lay plaintiff.

Managing the papal 'household'

The recent work of Kristina Sessa has highlighted the ways in which the bishop of Rome saw himself, and presented himself, as *paterfamilias*, or head of the household. This entailed careful stewardship of 'the most material aspects of estate management, that is, those involving property, agriculture, labour and production'.[78] An important aspect of this role was pastoral care for the people of Rome, both in the provision of basic needs in times of want, and in protection from social abuses. One of the most important avenues of assistance for late-antique bishops in stemming social abuses, either with regard to civil or church office-holders, was their epistolary networks. These considerations about late-antique bishops' axes of influence, horizons and culture demonstrate the validity of the arguments adduced by several scholars recently,[79] namely that these bishops were often impotent in the face of ecclesiastical or civil crisis, and that what today we call human rights were not issues for them.[80] However, we can also see them trying to intervene in cases involving laypersons, those seeking asylum in churches, victims of usury or of extortionate taxation, orphans or virgins who have been defrauded of their property. While this was typically not the main focus of concern of papal letter-collections, some examples may be found in the canon law-collections of Leo I's letters[81] and those of Gelasius.[82] An even greater portion of Pelagius I's correspondence concerns such 'household' issues.

In the sixth century socio-economic conditions had worsened in Italy, as first the Gothic wars and later the Lombard invasions from the 570s left many dioceses unable to provide for the basic needs of their clergy or other needy in their district. Out of dire necessity Pelagius I was forced to

---

[78] Sessa 2012: 124.   [79] See Lepelley 2007: 16–17; Uhalde 2007: 38–43.

[80] See, for example, Holman 2000.

[81] Leo, *Ep.* 4.3; see Allen *et al.* 2009: 199–200. Note that Leo's ruling on usury by laypersons is in the context of a prohibition of clerical usury. Clerical discipline is the focus of letters chosen for inclusion in the early canon law-collections of the late fifth and sixth centuries: *Collectio Avellana, Collectio Dionysiana, Collectio Corbeiensis, Collectio Coloniensis, Collectio Pithouensis, Collectio Thessalonicensis, Collectio Quesnelliana* and *Collectio Grimanica*. See Jasper 2001: 41–53; Dunn, Chapter 11 in this volume. On the *Dionysiana* and the inclusion within it of twenty-eight decretals from Gelasius, *Ep.* 14 *ad episcopos Lucaniae, Brutii et Siciliae* (PL 67: 301–12), see Neil 2013a.

[82] E.g. Gelasius, *frag.* 1 *ad Iohannem*, Thiel 1867 [2004]: 483–4 (JK 671), recommending the widow Antonina to the bishop's care; *frag.* 6 *ad Hereleuvam*, Thiel 1867 [2004]: 502 (JK 683), a letter to the mother of the Gothic king Theodoric, in which Gelasius asks the queen to help the poor; see more examples in Neil forthcoming b.

take an interest in the poor and to watch closely the management of his own estates and of private foundations. It has been plausibly suggested that the tightening of episcopal control over such appointments was a response to the breakdown of the old system of senatorial management of rural estates, as a result of the Gothic wars.[83] In a rather pathetic letter written at the end of 556, Pelagius asked Sapaudus to send him the revenue from the papal estates in Gaul, because 'the estates in Italy have been rendered desolate and there is no one to recover their value'.[84] This is one of a very few references in the Roman epistolary record to the waves of plague and famine that wracked Italy from the 540s, during and as a consequence of the Gothic wars. In particular Pelagius requests items of clothing for the poor, even 'white tunics' which were only worn by the wealthy. He reports that subdeacon Homobonus has been dispatched to deliver relics to the monks of Lérins at the request of King Childebert. It seems that the bishop of Rome has been reduced to exchanging holy relics for material sustenance.[85] *Letter* 20 records another gift of relics – filings from St Peter's chains – to Eutychius, bishop of Constantinople, between December 558 and 2 February 559. Pelagius repeated his request for aid in 557, when he again commended to Sapaudus' care the Romans who had taken refuge in Arles, and asked him to help the poor of Rome.[86]

His instructions to Count Gurdimer to prune his trees within five or six days before they drop their seeds might incline one to suspect that Pelagius had not enough to do.[87] However, his main concern is that the fields be maintained in an arable state, with food production for the city at a premium in the countryside around Rome. In a letter to the bishop of Heracleia, Pelagius professes himself overcome by grief because of the lack of scruples of those people who demand tribute from the church for fields that are uncultivated. Poverty is everywhere; Pelagius has nothing to live on and as a result cannot help the poor.[88] Toward the end of his pontificate – between 560 and 8 March 561 – Pelagius wrote in desperation to the praetorian prefect of Africa, seeking help. He admits to Boethius that after

---

[83] Pietri 2002: 262.

[84] *Ep.* 4 (14 December 556) to Sapaudus (JK 943), Gassó and Batlle 1956: 11–13. In his appointment of Sapaudus, Pelagius seems to have continued his predecessor's practice of making clerical appointments that would protect both Rome's doctrinal and domestic interests. On Vigilius' appointment of the deacon Sebastian as the chief agent in charge of papal estates in Dalmatia, and simultaneous guardian of orthodoxy on the Three Chapters question there, see Sessa 2012: 122–3. Cf. Vigilius, *Ep.* 14 (JK 923).

[85] *Ep.* 20 (JK 979), Gassó and Batlle 1956: 62–3.

[86] *Ep.* 9 (JK 947), Gassó and Batlle 1956: 28–30.

[87] *Ep.* 76 to Gurdimer *comes* (JK 1034), Gassó and Batlle 1956: 191.

[88] *Ep.* 94 to Bishop Benignus of Heracleia (556–61) (no JK no.), Gassó and Batlle 1956: 223–4.

twenty-five years of war and devastation in Italy, he needs subsidies to be
sent from islands and remote locations to the church of Rome for clerics
and the poor.[89] In a letter that probably reflects a breakdown of good relations with his patron, he tells the patrician Narses in no uncertain terms
not to give the property of the poor to those who suffer no want.[90] Some
decades later, Pelagius II (579–90) is said to have converted his own house
into an almshouse for the aged poor.[91]

Protecting papal property

The number of letters concerned with management of papal property
and its revenues may seem disproportionate against the three or four
letters this pope wrote on behalf of the poor. His concern to defend
the property and the revenues of his own church reflects the extreme
regionalism of Roman bishops' strategies to manage crises, even within
Italy. He rebuked John, bishop of Nola, for requesting permission to
sell the sacred vessels of the parish of Suessula.[92] If this parish cannot
possibly survive because of its abject poverty, Pelagius writes, John
should incorporate it into the church of Nola and its cult. He added
that it would be necessary for Bishop John to look after cultivation of
the fields so that at least the church of Nola will be up to paying its
revenues.

A letter to a couple, John and Hilaria, contains the remark that bishops
of Rome were forbidden to bequeath goods acquired during their term
as pope.[93] Following a decree issued by Basil, praetorian prefect under
Odovacer, to an assembly of Roman clergy in St Peter's, after the death
of Pope Simplicius in 483, no pope was allowed to alienate the goods and
ornaments of the churches, under penalty of anathema to the vendor.[94]
This was apparently to avoid prospective popes from bribing their way into
election. That this had become a common practice in general throughout the empire has been demonstrated by Sabine Huebner.[95] According to
the *LP*, Pelagius also used the occasion of his speech to the populace to
declare his opposition to the practice of simony in attaining preferment to

[89] *Ep.* 85 to Boethius, praetorian prefect of Africa (JK 963), Gassó and Batlle 1956: 207–8.
[90] *Ep.* 90 to Narses the patrician (JK 962), Gassó and Batlle 1956: 216.
[91] *LP* i, Duchesne 1955: 309.
[92] *Ep.* 17 to John, bishop of Nola (JK 976), Gassó and Batlle 1956: 51–2.
[93] *Ep.* 26 to Hilaria and John (JK 985), Gassó and Batlle 1956: 81.
[94] The decree was reversed at the Roman Synod of 502, *Acta synodhodorum Romae*, Mommsen
1894: 445.
[95] Huebner 2009: 167–80.

any clerical order, from doorkeeper to bishop.[96] Not only were the popes forbidden to sell their church's goods, but apparently they could not even leave them as bequests.

Two letters of 558 show the careful auditing of the administration of papal estates. In the first, Pelagius reproves Dulcitius, *defensor* of Apulia, for falsifying the date in collecting payments and accumulating funds, thereby causing financial and administrative headaches for Pelagius.[97] In the second letter, Pelagius orders the *defensor* Vitus to supervise the administration of the papal estates because he will have to collect revenue from the seventh indiction, and requests him to send a report to be lodged in the papal archive, 'as is customary'.[98] The importance of the papal notaries in administrating the patrimonies is obvious in *Letter* 88 to Melleus the subdeacon. Papal notaries have told Pelagius that since Melleus was put in charge of the *patrimonium*, no accounts have been forthcoming from him. Melleus is warned to rectify this omission for his own sake and that of the church.[99]

Pelagius was just as involved in the pressing problems of feeding and clothing the Roman population, and supervising litigation of laypersons and clergy, as he was in the Three Chapters controversy. It is impossible to say if this breadth of activity indicates a change in management style, from a primary focus on heresy and doctrinal matters to the *minutiae* of papal administration, or just the increasingly scrupulous preservation practices of recipients of papal correspondence. Again it is difficult to determine whether Pelagius' involvement in so many levels of papal administration was the product of necessity *in extremis*, or his personal style. In any case, the range of functions that Pelagius adopted as well as the meticulous recording of papal correspondence was carried on by Gregory I, and it seems that Pelagius I set the beginning of a trend.

Conclusion

The Pelagian correspondence offers a rare glimpse of the range of issues that claimed a bishop's attention in mid sixth-century Rome, and suggests

[96] *LP* 1, Duchesne 1955: 303.
[97] *Ep.* 12 to Dulcitius, *defensor* (JK 949), Gassó and Batlle 1956: 41–2. Gassó and Batlle 1956: 41, suggest that this is the same person as the recipient of *Ep.* 29 (JK 988), Dulcius *defensor* of Apulia, who is informed that a deacon and a bishop have been ordained for the town of Luceria in February 559.
[98] *Ep.* 13 to Vitus, *defensor* (JK 950), Gassó and Batlle 1956: 43.
[99] *Ep.* 88 to Melleus the subdeacon (JK 957), Gassó and Batlle 1956: 214; cf. *Ep.* 28 to Melleus, on what kind of person is to be ordained abbot of a monastery.

that the shift to 'micro-management' had taken place well before Gregory I. It is rich in the material pertaining to the day-to-day running of the Roman see that is so conspicuously absent in the letters of fifth-century Roman bishops, with the exception of Gelasius I. The spheres of activity reflected in Pelagius' letters include the management of papal property, clerical discipline and practical support for the people of Rome in a time of war, as well as the traditional episcopal roles of defending doctrine and persecuting schismatics. In this respect the Pelagian corpus supports Noble's contention that 'The routine business of papal government, and the duties of the pope as an Italian metropolitan always took precedence over everything else, even if the narrative sources are crisis oriented and seem to focus on the great events of late-antique history'.[100] Letters like these are an important corrective to contemporary narrative sources such as Count Marcellinus' *Chronicle*, Prosper's *Epitome chronicon* and Jordanes' *Gaetica*.

The preservation of the majority of Pelagius' letters in the *Collectio Britannica* is a fortunate accident of history. These letters were preserved because they were relevant to questions of canon law that emerged from the ninth century onward. Such questions included the running of the papal household and the protection of papal property, uncanonical elections of bishops in other Italian sees, and the primacy of the bishop of Arles over other sees in Gaul.

---

[100] Noble 1993: 398, a statement made in connection with Gelasius' correspondence over the Acacian schism.

Bibliography

Abramowski, L. (1956) 'Der Streit um Diodor und Theodor zwischen den beiden ephesinischen Konzilien', *Zeitschrift für Kirchengeschichte* 67: 252–87.

Alexander, L. C. A. (1989) 'Hellenistic letter-forms and the structure of Philippians', *Journal for the Study of the New Testament* 37: 87–101.

Alishan, L. (ed.) (1868) *Lettre d'Abgar ou histoire de la conversion des Edesséens par Laboubnia, écrivain contemporain des apôtres traduite sur la version arménienne du Ve siècle.* Venice.

Allen, P. (1999) 'Severus of Antioch and pastoral care', in *Prayer and Spirituality in the Early Church*, vol. II, eds. P. Allen, W. Mayer and L. Cross. Brisbane: 387–400.

(2006a) 'The horizons of a bishop's world: The letters of Augustine of Hippo', in *The Spiritual Life, Prayer and Spirituality in the Early Church*, vol. IV, eds. W. Mayer, P. Allen and L. Cross. Strathfield, NSW: 327–37.

(2006b) 'It's in the post: Techniques and difficulties of letter-writing in antiquity with regard to Augustine of Hippo', A.D. Trendall Memorial Lecture 2005, *The Australian Academy of the Humanities, Proceedings 2005.* Canberra: 111–29.

(2006c) 'The Syrian church through bishops' eyes: The letters of Theodoret of Cyrrhus and Severus of Antioch', *SP* vol. XLII. Leuven: 3–21.

(2009) *Sophronius of Jerusalem and Seventh-Century Heresy: The Synodical Letter and Other Documents.* Oxford Early Christian Texts. Oxford.

(2010) 'Cyril of Alexandria's Festal Letters: The politics of religion', in *Studies of Religion and Politics in the Early Christian Centuries*, eds. D. Luckensmeyer and P. Allen. Early Christian Studies 13. Strathfield, NSW: 195–230.

(2011) 'Episcopal succession in Antioch in the sixth century', in *Episcopal Elections in Late Antiquity*, eds. J. Leemans, P. Van Nuffelen, S. W. J. Keough and C. Nicolaye. Arbeiten zur Kirchengeschichte 119. Berlin and Boston: 23–38.

(2013a) 'Prolegomena to a study of the letter-bearer in Christian antiquity', *SP* vol. LXII. Leuven: 481–91.

(2013b) 'Religious conflict between Antioch and Alexandria *c.* 565–630 CE', in *Religious Conflict from Early Christianity to the Rise of Islam*, eds. W. Mayer and B. Neil. Arbeiten zur Kirchengeschichte 121. Berlin and Boston: 187–99.

(2014a) 'Bishops and ladies: How, if at all, to write to a woman in Christian late antiquity', in *Reading Men and Women in Early Christianity*. eds. W. Mayer and I. Elmer. Early Christian Studies 18. Strathfield, NSW: 185–98.

(2014b) 'The festal letters of the patriarchs of Alexandria: Evidence for social history in the fourth and fifth centuries', *Phronema* 29/1: 1–20.

(forthcoming) 'Christian correspondences: The secrets of letter-bearers', in *The Art of Veiled Speech. Self-Censorship from Aristophanes to Hobbes*, eds. H. Baltussen and P. Davis. Philadelphia, Pa.

Allen, P. and Hayward, C. T. R. (2004) *Severus of Antioch*. The Early Church Fathers. London and New York.

Allen, P. and Neil, B. (2013) *Crisis Management in Late Antiquity: A Survey of the Evidence from Episcopal Letters (410–590 CE)*. VCS 121. Leiden.

Allen, P., Neil, B. and Mayer, W. (2009) *Preaching Poverty in Late Antiquity: Perceptions and Realities*. Arbeiten zum Kirchen- und Theologiegeschichte 28. Leipzig.

Alpi, F. (2009a) *La route royale: Sévère d'Antioche et les églises d'Orient (512–518)*, vol. I *Texte*, vol. II *Sources et documents*. Bibliothèque archéologique et historique 188. Beirut.

(2009b) 'La correspondance du patriarche Sévère d'Antioche (512–518): Un témoignage sur les institutions et la discipline ecclésiastique en Orient protobyzantin', in *Correspondances: Documents pour l'histoire de l'antiquité tardive*, eds. R. Delmaire, J. Desmulliez and P.-L. Gatier. Lyon: 333–48.

Amidon, P. R. and O'Keefe, J. J. (trs.) (2009) *St. Cyril of Alexandria. Festal Letters 1–12*. The Fathers of the Church 118. Washington, DC.

Amory, P. (1997) *People and Identity in Ostrogothic Italy, 489–554*. Cambridge Studies in Medieval Life and Thought. Cambridge.

Anderson, W. B. (1936) *Sidonius. Poems. Letters I–II*. LCL 296. Cambridge, Mass. and London.

Arras, V. (ed.) (1963) *Collectio Monastica*. CSCO 238–9. Louvain.

Arzt-Grabner, P. (2014) *2. Korinther: Papyrologische Kommentare zum Neuen Testament 4*. Göttingen.

Aune, D. E. (1987) *The New Testament in Its Literary Environment*. Library of Early Christianity 8. Philadelphia, Pa.

Azéma, Y. (1954) 'Sur la chronologie de trois lettres de Théodoret de Cyr', *Revue d'études grecques* 67: 82–94.

(1981) 'Citations d'auteurs et allusions profanes dans la correspondance de Théodoret', in *Überlieferungsgeschichtliche Untersuchungen*, ed. F. Paschke. Berlin: 5–13.

(ed., tr.) (1964–98) *Théodoret de Cyr. Correspondance*, vol. I, 2nd edn. SC 40 bis (1982), vol. II. SC 98 (1964), vol. III. SC 111 (1965), vol. IV. SC 429 (1998). Paris.

Bacht, H. (1951) 'Die Rolle des orientalischen Mönchtums in die kirchen-politischen Auseinandersetzungen um Chalkedon (431–519)', in *Das Konzil von Chalkedon: Geschichte und Gegenwart*, vol. II, eds. A. Grillmeier and H. Bacht. Würzburg: 193–314.

Bady, G. (2008) 'Les traductions latines anciennes de Jean Chrysostome: motifs et paradoxes', in *Formation et transmission des collections textuelles de l'Antiquité tardive au Moyen Âge central (IVe–début XIIIe siècle)*, eds. S. Gioanni and B. Grévin. Collection de l'École française de Rome. Rome: 303–16.

(2010) 'La tradition des oeuvres de Jean Chrysostome, entre transmission et transformation', *Revue des Etudes Byzantines* 68: 149–64.

(2012) '*L'editio Parisina altera* des œuvres de Jean Chrysostome et la *Patrologie grecque* de Migne', *Eruditio antiqua* 4: 1–17.

Bagnall, R. S. (2002) 'Public administration and the documentation of Roman Panopolis', in *Perspectives on Panopolis: An Egyptian Town from Alexander the Great to the Arab Conquest*, eds. A. Egberts, B. P. Muhs and J. van der Vliet. Leiden: 1–12.

(2006) *Hellenistic and Roman Egypt: Sources and Approaches*. Aldershot.

Bagnall, R. S. and Cribiore, R. (2006) *Women's Letters from Ancient Egypt, 300 BC–AD 800*. Ann Arbor, Mich.

Ballerini, P. and G. (1865) *De antiquis collectionibus et collectoribus canonum*, Paris.

Banaji, J. (2007) *Agrarian Change in Late Antiquity: Gold, Labour, and Aristocratic Dominance*. Oxford.

Barabási, A. L. (2003) *Linked: How Everything is Connected to Everything Else and What it Means for Business, Science and Everyday Life*. New York.

Barnes, T. D. and Bevan, G. (trs.) (2013) *The Funerary Speech for John Chrysostom*, TTH 60. Liverpool.

Barnett, A. E. (1941) *Paul Becomes a Literary Influence*. Chicago.

Barrett, C. K. (1961) *Luke the Historian in Recent Study*. London.

Barry, J. (2013) 'Dis/placement in Late Antiquity: The Formation of Orthodox Identities through Exilic Discourse', PhD diss. Drew University, Madison, NJ.

Baur, C. (1929–30) *Johannes Chrysostomus und seine Zeit* (2 vols.). Munich; Eng. tr. (1959–60) *John Chrysostom and His Time* (2 vols.). Westminster, Md.

Beard, M. (2002) 'Ciceronian correspondences: Making a book out of letters', in *Classics in Progress: Essays on Ancient Greece and Rome*, ed. T. P. Wiseman. Oxford: 103–44.

Bell, H. I. (1924) *Jews and Christians in Egypt: The Jewish Troubles in Alexandria and the Athanasian Controversy*. London.

Bessières, M. and Turner, C. H. (1919–22) 'La tradition manuscrite de la correspondance de saint Basile', *JTS* 21: 1–9, *JTS* 22 (1922): 113–33, *JTS* 23 (1922): 225–49, 337–58.

(1923) *La tradition manuscrite de la correspondance de Saint Basile*. Oxford.

Betz, H. D. (1985) *2 Corinthians 8 and 9: A Commentary on Two Administrative Letters of the Apostle Paul*. Philadelphia, Pa.

(1992) 'Corinthians, Second Epistle to the', in *Anchor Bible Dictionary*, ed. D. N. Freedman. New York, vol. 1: 1148–54.

Bevan, G. A. and Gray, P. T. R. (2009) 'The trial of Eutyches: A new interpretation', *Byzantinische Zeitschrift* 101/2: 617–57.

Beyenka, M. M. (tr.) (1967) *Letters of Saint Ambrose*. Fathers of the Church 26, rev. edn. Washington, DC, 1954.

Bidez, J. and Hansen, G. C. (eds.) (1995) *Sozomenus. Kirchengeschichte*. GCS NF 4. Berlin.

Bieringer, R. and Lambrecht, J. (1994) *Studies on 2 Corinthians*. Bibliotheca ephemeridum theologicarum Lovaniensium 112. Leuven.

Blaudeau, P. (2007) 'Motifs et structures des divisions ecclésiales: Le schisme acacien (484–519)', *Annuarium Historiae Conciliorum* 39: 65–98.

Blum, G. G. (1969) *Rabbula von Edessa: Der Christ, der Bischof, der Theologe*. Louvain.

Boissevain, J. (1974) *Friends of Friends: Networks, Manipulators and Coalitions*. Oxford.

Boon, A. (ed.) (1932) *Pachomiana Latina: Règle et épîtres de s. Pachome, épitre de s. Théodore et 'liber' de s. Orsiesius*. Louvain.

Borg, M. (forthcoming) 'Pliny and the senatorial opposition to Domitian', PhD diss., University of Sydney.

Boud'hors, A. and Heurtel, C. (2010) *Les ostraca coptes de la TT 29. Autour du moine Frangé* (2 vols.). Brussels.

Brändle, R. (1999) *Johannes Chrysostomus. Bischof-Reformer-Märtyrer*. Stuttgart, Berlin and Cologne.

Bratož, R. (2000) 'Gelasio', in *Enciclopedia dei Papi*, vol. i. Rome: 458–62.

Broc, C. (1993) 'Le rôle des femmes dans l'Eglise de Constantinople d'après la correspondance de Jean Chrysostome', *SP* vol. xxvii. Berlin: 150–4.

Brock, S. P. (1977) 'Greek into Syriac and Syriac into Greek', *Journal of the Syriac Academy* 3: 1–17 (422–406, reverse pagination).

(1979) 'Aspects of translation technique in antiquity', *Greek, Roman and Byzantine Studies* 20: 69–87.

(1983) 'Towards a history of Syriac translation technique', *Orientalia Christiana Analecta* 221: 1–14.

(1994) 'Greek and Syriac in late antique Syria', in *Literacy and Power in the Ancient World*, eds. A. K. Bowman and G. Wolf. Cambridge: 149–60.

Brok, M. F. A. (1951) A propos des lettres festales', *VC* 5/2: 101–10.

Brooks, E. W. (ed., tr.) (1902–3) *The Sixth Book of the Select Letters of Severus Patriarch of Antioch in the Syriac Version of Athanasius of Nisibis* (2 vols.). Oxford and London (repr. Westmead, Hants., 1969).

(1930) 'The Patriarch Paul of Antioch and the Alexandrine schism of 575', *Byzantinische Zeitschrift* 30: 468–76.

(ed., tr.) (1915) 'A collection of letters of Severus of Antioch, from numerous Syriac manuscripts. Letters i to lxi'. *Patrologia Orientalis* 12/ii 165–342.

(ed., tr.) (1920) 'A collection of letters of Severus of Antioch, from numerous Syriac manuscripts. Letters lxii to cxviii', *Patrologia Orientalis* 14/i: 1–310.

(ed.) (1935) *Iohannis Ephesini Historiae Ecclesiasticae Pars Tertia*. CSCO 105 (text), Scr. Syr. 54. Louvain.

(tr.) (1936) *Iohannis Ephesini Historiae Ecclesiasticae Pars Tertia*. CSCO 106 (text), Scr. Syr. 55. Louvain (repr. Louvain 1964).

Bruce, F. F. (1988) *The Canon of Scripture*. Downers Grove, Ill.

Bumazhnov, D. (2009) *Visio Mystica im Spannungsfeld frühchristlicher Überlieferungen*. Tübingen.

Bunge, G. (2006) *Briefe aus der Wüste*. Trier.

Byrne, B. (1996) *Romans*. Collegeville, Minn.

Cagni, G. and Sironi, E. (1984) 'Contributo alla tradizione del testo delle lettere di san Vigilio di Trento a S. Sempliciano e a S. Giovanni Crisostomo', *Barnabiti Studi* I: 209–26.

Cain, A. (2009) *The Letters of Jerome: Asceticism, Biblical Exegesis, and the Construction of Christian Authority in Late Antiquity*. Oxford Early Christian Studies. Oxford.

Calvet-Sebasti, M.-A. (1998) 'Comment écrire à un païen: l'exemple de Grégoire de Nazianze et de Théodoret de Cyr', in *Les apologistes chrétiens et la culture grecque*, eds. B. Pouderon and J. Doré. Paris: 369–81.

Calvet-Sebasti, M.-A. and Gatier, P.-L. (1989) (eds., trs.) *Firmus de Césarée: Lettres*. SC 350. Paris.

Cancik, H. (1967) *Untersuchungen zu Senecas Epistulae morales*. Spudasmata 18. Hildesheim.

Canellis, A. (ed., tr.) (2006) *Fausinus: Supplique aux empereurs (Libellus precum et Lex augusta) précédé de Confession de foi*. SC 504. Paris.

Caner, D. (2002) *Wandering, Begging Monks. Spiritual Authority and the Promotion of Monasticism in Late Antiquity*. Berkeley, Calif.

Cavallin, A. (1944) *Studien zu den Briefen des hl. Basilius*. Lund.

Cecconi, G. A. (2002) *Commento storico al libro II dell' epistolario di Q. Aurelio Simmaco*, Pisa.

Chabot, J.-B. (ed., tr.) (1899–1901) *Chronique de Michel le Syrien Patriarche Jacobite d'Antioche (1166–1199)* (4 vols.). Paris and Brussels (repr. Brussels 1963).

  (ed.) (1908) *Documenta ad origines monophysitarum illustrandas*. CSCO 17. Scr. Syr. 37. Louvain.

  (tr.) (1933) *Documenta ad origines monophysitarum illustrandas*. CSCO 103. Scr. Syr. 52. Louvain.

Champerius, S. (ed.) (1516) *Epistolae sanctissimorum*. Paris.

Champlin, E. (1974) 'The chronology of Fronto', *Journal of Roman Studies* 64: 136–59.

Chapa, J. (1994) 'Is First Thessalonians a letter of consolation?', *New Testament Studies* 40: 150–60.

Chazelle, C. and Cubitt, C. (eds.) (2007) *The Crisis of the* Oikoumene: *The Three Chapters and the Failed Quest for Unity in the Sixth-Century Mediterranean*. Studies in the Early Middle Ages 14. Turnhout.

Chesnut, R. C. (1976) *Three Monophysite Christologies: Severus of Antioch, Philoxenus of Mabbug and Jacob of Sarug*. Oxford.

Chitty, D. (tr.), revised with an introduction by S. Brock (1979) *The Letters of Ammonas. Successor of Saint Antony*. Oxford.

Choat, M. (2010) 'Early Coptic epistolography', in *The Multilingual Experience in Egypt from the Ptolemies to the Abassids*, ed. A. Papaconstantinou. Aldershot: 153–78.

(2013a) 'The epistolary culture of monasticism between literature and papyri', *Cistercian Studies Quarterly* 48: 227–37.

(2013b) 'Monastic letter collections in late antique Egypt: structure, purpose, and transmission', in *Cultures in Contact: Transfer of Knowledge in the Mediterranean Context. Selected Papers*, eds. S. Torallas Tovar and J. P. Monferrer-Sala. Cordoba: 73–90.

(2013c) 'The *Life of Antony* in Egypt', in *Ascetic Culture: Essays in Honor of Philip Rousseau*, eds. B. Leyerle and R. Darling Young. Notre Dame, Ind.: 50–74.

Chryssavgis, J. (ed.) (2006–7) *Barsanuphius and John: Letters*, vols. I–II. Fathers of the Church 113–14. Washington, DC.

Claassen, J.-M. (1999) *Displaced Persons: The Literature of Exile from Cicero to Boethius*. Madison, Wis.

Clabeaux, J. J. (1989) *A Lost Edition of the Letters of Paul: A Reassessment of the Text of the Pauline Corpus Attested by Marcion*. Washington, DC.

Clarysse, W. (2003) 'Tomoi Synkollēsimoi', in *Ancient Archives and Archival Traditions: Concepts of Record-Keeping in the Ancient World*, ed. M. Brosius. Oxford: 344–59.

Clayton, P. B. (2007) *The Christology of Theodoret of Cyrus: Antiochene Christology from the Council of Ephesus (431) to the Council of Chalcedon (451)*. Oxford.

Clement, J. and Vander Plaetse, R. (eds., trs.), Fraisse-Betoulières, A. (tr.) (2003–6) *Facundus d'Hermiane: Défense des trois chapitres (à Justinien)* (5 vols.). SC 471, 478, 479, 484, 499. Paris.

Constable, G. (1976) *Letters and Letter-Collections*. Typologie des Sources du Moyen Âge occidental, fasc. 17. Turnhout.

Constas, N. (2003) *Proclus of Constantinople and the Cult of the Virgin in Late Antiquity*. Leiden.

Cooper, K. (2007) 'Poverty, obligation and inheritance: Roman heiresses and the varieties of senatorial Christianity in fifth-century Rome', in *Religion, Dynasty and Patronage in Early Christian Rome, 300–900*, eds. K. Cooper and J. Hillner. Cambridge: 165–89.

Courtonne, Y. (ed., tr.) (2003) *Sainte Basile: Correspondance*, vol. I: *Lettres I–C*, vol. II: *Lettres CI–CCXVIII*, vol. III: *Lettres CCXIX–CCCLXVI*. 2nd edn. Paris.

Coustant, P. (ed.) (1721) *Epistolae Romanorum Pontificum et quae ad eos scriptae sunt a S. Clement I usque ad Innocentum III*, vol. I. Paris.

Cracco Ruggini, L. (1998) '"Vir sanctus": il vescovo e il suo "pubblico ufficio sacro" nella città', in *L'évêque dans la cité du IVe au Ve siècle: image et autorité*, eds. E. Rebillard and C. Sotinel. Collection de l'École française de Rome 248. Rome: 3–15.

Cribiore, R. (2007) *The School of Libanius in Late Antique Antioch*. Princeton, NJ.

Crum, W. E. (1902) *Coptic Ostraca from the Collections of the Egypt Exploration Fund, the Cairo Museum and Others*. London.

(1909) *Catalogue of the Coptic Manuscripts in the Collection of the John Rylands Library*. Manchester.

Dahlman, B. (2013) 'The *Collectio Scorialensis parva*: An alphabetical collection of old apophthegmatic and hagiographic material', *SP* vol. LV. Leuven: 23–34.

Dam, R. Van, (2003) *Families and Friends in Late Roman Cappadocia.* Philadelphia, Pa.

Davies, M. (forthcoming) *A Commentary on Seneca's Letters Book 4.*

Davis, R. (tr.) (2000) *The Book of Pontiffs (Liber Pontificalis). The Ancient Biographies of the First Ninety Roman Bishops to AD 715.* TTH 6, 2nd edn. Liverpool.

Davis, S. J. (2004) *The Early Coptic Papacy: The Egyptian Church and Its Leadership in Late Antiquity.* Cairo.

Deissmann, A. (1910) *Light from the Ancient East: The New Testament Illustrated by Recently Discovered Texts of the Graeco-Roman World,* tr. L. R. M. Strachan. London.

Dekker, R. (forthcoming) 'A relative chronology of the *Topos* of Epiphanius: the identification of its leaders', in *Proceedings of the Tenth Congress of the International Association for Coptic Studies, Rome 2012.* Leuven.

Delmaire, R. (1991) 'Les "Lettres d'exil" de Jean Chrysostome: Etudes de chronologie et de prosopographie', *Recherches Augustiniennes* 25: 71–180.

(1997) 'Jean Chrysostome et ses "amis" d'après le nouveau classement de sa correspondance', *SP* vol. xxxiii. Leuven: 302–13.

(2009) 'Les lettres de Jean Chrysostome: Espérances et désillusions d'un évêque en exil', in *Correspondances. Documents pour l'histoire de l'antiquité tardive,* eds. R. Delmaire, J. Desmulliez and P.-L. Gatier. Collection de la Maison de l'Orient et de la Méditerranée 40, Série littéraire et philosophique 13. Lyon: 283–91.

Delmaire, R., Desmulliez, J. and Gatier, P.-L. (eds.) (2009) *Correspondances. Documents pour l'histoire de l'antiquité tardive.* Actes du colloque international Université Charles-de-Gaulle-Lille 3, 20–22 novembre 2003. Collection de la Maison de l'Orient et de la Méditerranée 40, série littéraire et philosophique 13. Lyon.

Devreesse, R. (1929) 'Les actes du concile d'Ephèse', *Revue des sciences philosophiques et théologiques* 18: 223–42.

(1931) 'Après le concile d'Ephèse: Le rétour des Orientaux à l'unité', *Echoes d'Orient* 30: 271–92.

(1948) *Essai sur Théodore de Mopsueste.* Vatican City.

(ed.) (1932) *Pelagii Diaconi in defensione trium capitulorum.* Studi e Testi 57. Vatican City.

Diepen, H. M. (1953) 'La christologie des amis de Nestorius', in *Les Trois Chapitres au Concile de Chalcédoine.* Oosterhout: 30–45.

Dijkstra, J. H. F. and Greatrex, G. (2009) 'Patriarchs and politics in Constantinople in the reign of Anastasius (with a reedition of "O.Mon. Epiph." 59)', *Millennium* 6: 233–64.

Divjak, J. (1983) 'Zur Struktur Augustinischer Briefcorpora', in *Les Lettres de saint Augustin découvertes par Johannes Divjak: Communications présentées au colloque des 20 et 21 septembre 1982.* Etudes augustiniennes. Paris: 13–27.

(1996–2002) 'Epistulae', in *Augustinus-Lexikon* 2, eds. C. Mayer *et al.* Basel: 893–1057.

Donfried, K. P. (1993) 'The theology of 1 Thessalonians', in *The Theology of the Shorter Pauline Letters,* eds. K. P. Donfried and I. H. Marshall. Cambridge: 3–27.

Duc, F. du (ed.) (1636) *Sancti Patris Nostri Ioannis Chrysostomi archiepiscopi Constantinopolitani opera omnia* (4 vols.). Paris.

Duchesne, L. (1955–7) *Le Liber Pontificalis,* ed. C. Vogel, 2nd edn. (3 vols.). Paris.

Ducloux, A. (1994) *Ad ecclesiam confugere: Naissance du droit d'asile dans les églises (IVe–milieu du Ve s.).* De l'archéologie à histoire. Paris.

Dunn, G. D. (2005) 'The date of Innocent I's *epistula* 12 and the second exile of John Chrysostom', *Greek, Roman, and Byzantine Studies* 45: 155–70.

(2008) 'Innocent I and the Illyrian churches on the question of heretical ordination', *Journal of the Australian Early Medieval Association* 4: 65–81.

(2011) 'Canonical legislation on the ordination of bishops: Innocent I's letter to Victricius of Rouen', in *Episcopal Elections in Late Antiquity,* eds. J. Leemans, P. Van Nuffelen, S. W. J. Keough and C. Nicolae. Arbeiten zur Kirchengeschichte 119. Berlin: 145–66.

(2013) 'The clerical *cursus honorum* in the late antique Roman church', *Scrinium* 9: 132–45.

Dunn, J. D. G. (1996) *The Epistles to the Colossians and to Philemon: A Commentary on the Greek Text.* New International Greek Testament Commentary. Grand Rapids, Mich.

(1988) *Romans 9–16.* Word Biblical Commentary 38B. Dallas, Tex.

Dunn, M. (2000) *The Emergence of Monasticism.* Oxford.

Ebied, R. Y., Wickham, L. R. and Van Roey, A. (1981) *Peter of Callinicum: Anti-Tritheist Dossier.* Orientalia Lovaniensia Analecta 10. Leuven.

Ehrman, B. D. (2004) *The New Testament: A Historical Introduction to the Early Christian Writings.* 3rd edn. Oxford.

(2013) *Forgery and Counterforgery: The Use of Literary Deceit in Early Christian Polemics.* Oxford.

Ellis, E. E. (1971) 'Paul and his co-workers', *New Testament Studies* 17: 435–52.

Elmer, I. J. (2008) 'I, Tertius: Secretary or co-author of Romans', *Australian Biblical Review* 56: 45–60.

(2009) *Paul, Jerusalem, and the Judaisers: The Galatian Crisis in Its Broadest Historical Context.* Wissenschaftliche Untersuchungen zum Neuen Testament 2. Reihe, 258. Tübingen.

Emmel, S. (2004) *Shenoute's Literary Corpus* (2 vols.). Leuven.

Ertl, N. (1937) 'Diktatoren frühmittelalterlicher Papstbriefe', *Archiv für Urkundenforschung* NF 1/1: 6–132.

Esbroeck, M. van (1987) 'Who is Mari, the addressee of Ibas' letter?' *JTS* ns 38/1: 129–35.

1987. 'Who is Mari, the Addressee of Ibas' Letter?', *JTS* 38/1: 129–35.

Evieux, P. (1974) 'André de Samosate: un adversaire de Cyrille d'Alexandrie durant la crise nestorienne', *Revue d'études byzantines* 32: 255–300.

(1995) *Isidore de Péluse.* Théologie historique 99. Paris.

(ed.) (1997, 2000) *Isidore de Péluse. Lettres*. SC 422, 454. Paris.

Evieux, P., Burns, W.H., Arragon, L., Boulnoios M.-O., Forrat, M. and Meunier, B. (eds., trs.) (1991, 1993, 1998, 2009) *Cyrille d'Alexandrie. Lettres festales I–VI.* SC 372 bis, 392, 434. Paris.

Ewald, P. (1880) 'Die Papstbriefe der Brittischen Sammlung, I. und II.', *Neues Archiv* 5: 275–414, 503–96.

Fairbairn, D. (2007a) 'Allies or merely friends: John of Antioch and Nestorius in the Christological controversy', *Journal of Ecclesiastical History* 58/3: 383–99.

(2007b) 'The puzzle of Theodoret's Christology: A modest suggestion', *JTS* ns 58/1: 100–33.

Faller, O. and Zelzer, M. (eds.) (1968–1996) *Sancti Ambrosii Opera, Pars X, Epistulae et Acta*. CSEL 82/I (1968), 82/II (1990), 82/III (1982), 82/IV (1996) (4 vols.). Vienna.

Farag, G. (2012) 'Les lettres attribuées à Antoine dans la deuxième collection arabe (Lettres 8–20)' PhD diss. University of Strasbourg.

Faraggiana di Sarzana, C. (1997) '*Apophthegmata Patrum*: Some Crucial Points of their Textual Transmission and the Problem of a Critical Edition', *SP* vol. XXIX: 455–67.

Fedwick, P. J. (1993) *Bibliotheca Basiliana Vniversalis I. The Letters*. Turnhout.

Ferrari, R. J. (tr.) (1952) *Early Christian Biographies*. Fathers of the Church 15. Washington, DC.

Festugière, A.-J. (ed., tr.) (1971) *Historia monachorum in Aegypto: Edition critique du text grec et traduction annotée*. Brussels.

Flemming, J. P. G. (ed.) (1917) *Akten der Ephesinischen Synode vom Jahre 449: Syrisch*. Abhandlungen der Königlichen Gesellschaft der Wissenschaften zu Göttingen, Philologisch-Historische Klasse, NF 15.1. Berlin.

Foerster, R. (ed.) (1927) *Libanii Opera*, vol. IX. Leipzig.

Fortescue, A. (1955) *The Reunion Formula of Hormisdas*. Garrison, NY.

Fraipont, J. (ed.) (1968) *Sancti Fulgentii espiscopi Ruspensis Opera*. CCSL 91. Turnhout.

Frend, W. H. C. (1972) *The Rise of the Monophysite Movement: Chapters in the History of the Church in the Fifth and Sixth Centuries*. Cambridge.

Fronteau, J., Souchet, J.-B. and Cottereau, L. (1647) *D. Ivonis Carnotensis Episcopi Opera omnia: in duas partes distributa, prior continet eximium illud decretorum opus quod decretum Ivonis vulgo nuncupatur, ad exemplar manuscriptum insignis Bibliothecæ S. Victoris Parisiensis revisum, & ab infinitis quibus scatebat mendis repurgatum* (2 vols.). Paris.

Furnish, V. P. (1994) 'On putting Paul in his place', *JBL* 113/1: 3–17.

Gallay, P. (1957) *Les manuscrits des lettres de saint Grégoire de Nazianze*. Paris.

(2003) *Saint Grégoire de Nazianze: Correspondance*, vol. I: *Lettres I–C*. 2nd edn. Paris.

Galtier, P. (1931) 'Le centenaire d'Ephèse: Les actes du concile – Rome et le Concile', *Recherches de sciences religieuses* 21: 169–99.

(1953) 'Nestorius mal compris, mal traduit', *Gregorianum* 34: 427–33.

Gamble, H. Y. (1985) *The New Testament Canon: Its Making and Meaning*. Guides to Biblical Scholarship, New Testament Studies. Philadelphia, Pa.

  (1990) 'The Pauline corpus and the early Christian book', in *Paul and the Legacies of Paul*, ed. W. S. Babcock. Dallas, Tex.: 265–80.

Garitte, G. (1939) 'A propos des lettres de Saint Antoine l'erémite', *Le Muséon* 52: 11–31.

  (1955a) 'Une "Lettre de S. Arsène" en géorgien', *Le Muséon* 68: 259–78.

  (1955b) *Lettres de Saint Antoine: Version géorgienne et fragments coptes*. CSCO 148–9. Louvain.

  (1956) *Catalogue des manuscrits géorgiens littéraires du mont Sinaï*. CSCO 165. Louvain.

  (1976) 'De unius ex Ammonae epistulis versione iberica', *Le Muséon* 89: 123–31.

Garnier, J., Maran, P. and Faverolles, F. (eds.) (1721–30) *Basilii Caesareae Cappadocii Archiepiscopi Opera Omnia* (3 vols.). Paris.

Garsoïan, N. (1995) 'Acace de Mélitène et la présence de dyophysites en Arménie au début du Ve siècle', *Res Orientales* 7: 74–5.

  (1999) *L'église arménienne et le grand schisme d'Orient*. CSCO 574, Subsidia 100. Leuven.

Gascou, J. (1977) 'KLEROI APOROI: (Julien, Misopogôn, 370d–371b)', *Bulletin de l'Institut français d'archéologie orientale* 77: 235–55.

Gassó, P. M. and Batlle, C. M. (eds.) (1956) *Pelagii I Papae epistulae quae supersunt (556–561)*. Scripta et Documenta 8. Montserrat.

Gatier, P.-L. (2009) 'Hiérarchie et politesse dans les correspondances grecques de l'antiquité tardive: Les exemples de Firmus de Césarée et de Denys d'Antioche', in *Correspondances: Documents pour l'histoire de l'antiquité tardive*, eds. R. Delmaire, J. Desmulliez and P.-L. Gatier. Collection de la Maison de l'Orient et de la Méditerranée 40, série littéraire et philosophique 13. Lyon: 115–23.

Gaudemet, J. (1985) *Les sources du droit de l'Eglise en Occident, du IIe au VIIe siècle*. Initiations au christianisme ancien. Paris.

Géhin, P. (1999) 'Le dossier macarien de l'*Atheniensis gr.* 2492', *Recherches Augustiniennes* 31: 89–147.

Gibson, B. J. and Rees, R. D. (eds.) (2013) *Pliny the Younger in Late Antiquity*, Special Edition of *Arethusa* 46.2.

Gibson, R. K. (2012) 'On the nature of ancient letter collections', *Journal of Roman Studies* 102: 56–78.

  (2013a) 'Letters into autobiography: The generic mobility of the ancient letter collection', in *Generic Interfaces in Latin Literature: Encounters, Interactions and Transformations*, eds. T. D. Papanghelis, S. J. Harrison and S. Frangoulidis. Trends in Classics. Berlin: 386–416.

  (2013b) 'Pliny and the letters of Sidonius: From Constantius and Clarus to Firminus and Fuscus', in *Pliny the Younger in Late Antiquity*, eds. B. J. Gibson and R. D. Rees. Special Edition of *Arethusa* 46.2: 333–56.

Gibson, R. K. and Morello, R. (2012) *Reading the Letters of Pliny the Younger: An Introduction*. Cambridge.

Gibson, R. K. and Morrison, A. D. (2007) 'What is a letter?', in *Ancient Letters*, eds. R. Morello and A.D. Morrison. Oxford: 1–16.

Gillett, A. (2003) *Envoys and Political Communication in the Late Antique West, 411–533*. Cambridge.

Gioanni, S. (ed., tr.) (2006, 2010) *Ennode de Pavie. Lettres. Tome I, livres I et II*. Collection des Universités de France. Paris.

(2013a) 'Les lettres de chancellerie et la genèse d'un langage diplomatique commun dans la péninsule italienne', in *La corrispondenza epistolaria in Italia 2. Forme, stili e funzioni della scrittura epistolare nelle cancellerie italiane (secoli V–XV)*, eds. S. Gioanni and P. Cammarosano. Convegno di studio, Roma, 20–21 giugno 2011. Trieste and Rome: 9–19.

Gioanni, S. and Cammarosano, P. (eds.) (2013) *La corrispondenza epistolaria in Italia 2. Forme, stili e funzioni della scrittura epistolare nelle cancellerie italiane (secoli V–XV)*, Convegno di studio, Roma, 20–21 giugno 2011. Trieste and Rome.

Glimm, F. (tr.) (1947a) 'The letter of St Clement of Rome to the Corinthians', in *Apostolic Fathers*, eds. F. Glimm, J. M. F. Marique and G. G. Walsh. Baltimore, Md.: 9–58.

(tr.) (1947b) 'The letter of Polycarp to the Philippians', in *Apostolic Fathers*, eds. F. Glimm, J. M. F. Marique and G. G. Walsh. Baltimore, Md.: 135–43.

Godlewski, W. (1986) *Deir el-Bahri V: Le monastère de St Phoibammon*. Warsaw.

Goehring, J. E. (1990) *The Crosby-Schøyen Codex MS 193 in the Schøyen Collection*. CSCO 521, Subsidia 85. Leuven.

(1993) 'Melitian monastic organization: A challenge to Pachomian originality', *SP* vol. xxv. Berlin: 388–95 (repr. in Goehring 1999: 187–95).

(1999) *Ascetics, Society, and the Desert: Studies in Early Egyptian Monasticism*. Harrisburg, Pa.

(2008) 'Pachomius and the White Monastery', in *Christianity and Monasticism in Upper Egypt*, vol. I, *Akhmim and Sohag*, eds. G. Gabra and H. N. Takla. Cairo: 47–57.

Goodspeed, E. J. (1927) *New Solutions of New Testament Problems*. Chicago.

(1937) *An Introduction to the New Testament*. Chicago.

Grant, R. M. (1971) *A Historical Introduction to the New Testament*. London.

Gray, P. T. R. (1979) *The Defense of Chalcedon in the East (451–533)*. Leiden.

(1984) 'Theodoret on the "One Hypostasis": An Antiochene reading of Chalcedon', *SP* vol. xv/I. Berlin: 301–5.

Greatrex, G. (ed.), Phenix, R. R. and Horn, C.B. (trs.) (2011) *The Chronicle of Pseudo-Zachariah Rhetor: Church and War in Late Antiquity*. TTH 55. Liverpool.

Gregg, R. C. (1975) *Consolation Philosophy. Greek and Christian Paideia in Basil and the Two Gregories*. Patristic Monograph Series 3. Cambridge, Mass.

Grey, C. (2007) 'Revisiting the problem of *agri deserti* in the late Roman Empire', *Journal of Roman Archaeology* 20: 362–82.

Grillmeier, A. with Hainthaler, T. (1995) *Jesus der Christus im Glauben der Kirche 2, part 2, Die Kirche von Konstantinopel im 6. Jahrhundert*. Freiburg, 1989;

trs. J. Cawte and P. Allen, *Christ in Christian Tradition* 2, part 2. *The Church of Constantinople in the Sixth Century*. London and Louisville, Ky.

(2002) *Jesus der Christus im Glauben der Kirche. Die Kirche von Jerusalem und Antiochien nach 451 bis 600*, Bd 2/3. Freiburg.

Grünbart, M. (2006) 'Byzantine letter collections: Aspects of their function and order', in *Proceedings of the 21st International Congress of Byzantine Studies London, 21–26 August 2006. Theme II. Abstracts of Panel Papers*, ed. E. Jeffreys, with the assistance of J. Galliland. Ashgate: 144–5.

Guenther, O. (ed.) (1895) *Epistulae imperatorum pontificum aliorum inde ab a. CCCLXVII ad a. DLIII datae* (2 vols.). CSEL 35. Vienna.

Guillemin, A.-M. (ed.) (1961) *Cornélius Népos: Oeuvres*. Paris.

Gundlach, W. (ed.) (1892) *Pelagii I: Epistulae*. MGH Epp. 3. Berlin: 442–6, 448–50.

Guthrie, D. (1990) *New Testament Introduction*, 4th rev. edn. The Master Reference Collection. Downers Grove, Ill.

Guy, J.-C. (1962) *Recherches sur la tradition grecque des Apophthegmata Patrum*. Subsidia Hagiographica 36. Brussels.

(1993) *Les Apophthegmes des Pères. Collection systématique*, vol. 1. SC 387. Paris.

Haacke, W. (1939) *Die Glaubensformel des Papstes Hormisdas im Acacianischen Schisma*. Rome.

Haenchen, E. (1966) 'The Book of Acts as source material for the history of early Christianity', in *Studies in Luke-Acts: Essays Presented in Honour of Paul Schubert*, eds. L. E. Keck and J. L. Martin. Nashville, Tenn.: 258–78.

Halfond, G. I. (2010) *Archaeology of Frankish Church Councils, AD 511–768*. Medieval Law and Its Practice 6. Leiden.

Halkin, F. (ed.) (1932) *S. Pachomii vitae Graecae*. Brussels.

Halm, K. F. von (ed.) (1863) *Rhetores Latini Minores: Ex codicibus maximam partem primum adhibitis*. Leipzig.

Hanson, R. P. C. (1959) *Allegory and Event*. London.

Harmless, W. (2004) *Desert Christians: An Introduction to the Literature of Early Monasticism*. Oxford.

Harnack, A. von (1926) *Die Briefsammlung des Apostels Paulus und die anderen vorkonstantinischen christlichen Briefsammlungen: Sechs Vorlesungen aus der altkirchlichen Literaturgeschichte*. Leipzig.

Harries, J. (1994) *Sidonius Apollinaris and the Fall of Rome AD 407–485*. Oxford.

Hartmann, L. (ed.) (1899) *Pelagii II. Epistulae*. MGH Epp. 2. Berlin: 440–67.

Hauben, H. (2012) *Studies on the Melitian Schism in Egypt (AD 306–335)*, ed. P. Van Nuffelen. Farnham.

Hefele, J. (1972) *A History of the Councils of the Church*. Edinburgh.

Hengel, M. (1979) *Acts and the History of Earliest Christianity*, tr. J. Bowden. London.

Hermann, T. (1928) 'Patriarch Paul von Antiochia und das Alexandrinische Schisma von Jahre 575', *Zeitschrift für die Neutestamentliche Wissenschaft* 27: 263–304.

Hillner, J. (2007) 'Families, patronage and the titular churches of Rome, *c.* 300–*c.* 600', in *Religion, Dynasty, and Patronage in Early Christian Rome, 300–900,* eds. K. Cooper and J. Hillner. Cambridge: 225–61.

Hodkinson, O. (2007) 'Better than speech: Some advantages of the letter in Second Sophistic', in *Ancient Letters: Classical and Late Antique Epistolography,* eds. R. Morello and A. D. Morrison. Oxford: 283–300.

Holman, S. R. (2000) 'The entitled poor: Human rights language in the Cappadocians', *Doctores Ecclesiae, Pro Ecclesia* 9/4: 476–88.

Honigmann, E. (1951) *Evêques et évêchés monophysites d'Asie antérieure au IVe siècle.* CSCO Subsidia 127, vol. II. Louvain: 195–205.

Hout, M. P. J. van den (ed.) (1988) *M. Cornelii Frontonis Epistulae Schedis tam editis quam ineditis Edmundi Hauleri usus iterum editum.* Bibliotheca Scriptorum Graecorum et Romanorum Teubneriana. Berlin.

(1999) *A Commentary on the Letters of M. Cornelius Fronto.* Mnemosyne Supplementum 190. Leiden.

Huebner, S. R. (2009) 'Currencies of power: The venality of offices in the later Roman Empire', in *The Power of Religion in Late Antiquity,* eds. A. Cain and N. Lenski. Aldershot: 167–80.

Iordanites, A. (ed.) (1911) *Tou hosiou patros hemon abba Esaiaou logoi 29.* Jerusalem.

Jacob, P.-A. (ed., tr.) (1995) *Honorat de Marseille: La Vie d'Hilaire d'Arles.* SC 404. Paris.

Jaffé, P. (1885–8) *Regesta pontificum Romanorum ab condita ecclesia ad annum post Christum natum MCXCVIII,* eds. F. Kaltenbrunner (to a. 590), P. Ewald (to a. 882), S. Löwenfeld (to a. 1198). 2nd edn. (2 vols.). Leipzig.

Jasper, D. (2001) 'The beginning of the decretal tradition: Papal letters from the origin of the genre through the pontificate of Stephen V', in *Papal Letters in the Early Middle Ages,* eds. D. Jasper and H. Fuhrmann. History of Medieval Canon Law. Washington, DC: 1–133.

Jasper, D. and Fuhrmann, H. (eds.) (2001) *Papal Letters in the Early Middle Ages.* History of Medieval Canon Law. Washington, DC.

Jewett, R. (1970) 'The epistolary thanksgiving and the integrity of Philippians', *Novum Testamentum* 12: 40–53.

Joest, C. (1994) 'Ein Versuch zur Chronologie Pachoms und Theodoros', *Zeitschrift für die Neutestamentliche Wissenschaft* 85: 132–44.

(1996) 'Die Geheimschrift Pachoms: Versuch einer Entschlüsselung, mit Übersetzung und Deutung der Pachom-Briefe 9a und 9b', *Ostkirchliche Studien* 45: 268–89.

(2002) 'Die Pachom-Briefe 1 und 2: Auflösung der Geheimbuchstaben und Entdeckungen zu dem Briefüberschriften', *Journal of Coptic Studies* 4: 25–98.

(2009) 'Die *Praecepta* Pachoms: Untersuchung zu dem größten Abschnitt der Pachom-Regeln', *Zeitschrift für Antikes Christentum* 13: 430–51.

(2010) 'Die *Instituta* des pachomianischen Regelcorpus', *Journal of Coptic Studies* 12: 33–65.

(2012) 'Die *Leges* Pachoms und die Mönchsregeln der Pachomianer', *VC* 66: 160–89.

Johnson, L. T. (tr.) (2008) *The First and Second Letters to Timothy: A New Translation with Introduction and Commentary.* London.

Johnson, W. A. and Parker, H. (eds.) (2009) *Ancient Literacies: The Culture of Reading in Greece and Rome.* Oxford.

Jones, A. H. M. (1986) *The Later Roman Empire, 284–602: A Social, Economic and Administrative Survey* (2 vols.). Baltimore, Md.

Jouguet, P. (1928) *Papyrus grecs.* Paris.

Kahle, P. E. (1954) *Bala'izah: Coptic Texts from Deir el-Bala'izah in Upper Egypt* (2 vols.). London.

Kaiser, W. (2006) 'Beobachtungen zur Collectio Corbeiensis und Collectio Bigotiana (Hs. Paris BN lat. 12097 und Hs. Paris BN lat. 2796)', *Zeitschrift der Savigny-Stiftung für Rechtsgeschichte* 123, Kanonistische Abteilung 92: 63–110.

Kalvesmaki, J. (2013) 'Pachomius and the mystery of the letters', in *Ascetic Culture. Essays in Honor of Philip Rousseau*, eds. B. Leyerle and R. Darling Young. Notre Dame, Ind.: 11–28.

Karmer, B. and Shelton, J. C. (1987) *Das Archiv des Nephoros und verwandte Texte.* Aegyptiaca Treverensia 4. Mainz: 11–20.

Katos, D. (2011) *Palladius of Helenopolis: The Origenist Advocate.* Oxford Early Christian Studies. Oxford.

Kelly, J. N. D. (1986) *Oxford Dictionary of Popes.* Oxford (repr. 1996).

(1995) *Golden Mouth: The Story of John Chrysostom – Ascetic, Preacher, Bishop.* London.

Kennedy, G. A. (tr.) (2003) *Progymnasmata: Greek Textbooks of Prose Composition and Rhetoric.* Writings from the Greco-Roman World 10. Atlanta, Ga.

Kéry, L. (1999) *Canonical Collections of the Early Middle Ages (ca. 400–1140): A Bibliographical Guide to the Manuscripts and Literature.* History of Medieval Canon Law. Washington, DC.

Kim, C. H. (1972) *Form and Structure of the Familiar Greek Letter of Recommendation.* Missoula, Mont.

Klauck, H.-J. (2003a) 'Compilation of letters in Cicero's correspondence', in *Early Christianity and Classical Culture: Comparative Studies in Honor of Abraham J. Malherbe*, eds. J. T. Fitzgerald, T. H. Olbricht and L. M. White. Leiden: 131–55.

(2003b) *Religion und Gesellschaft im frühen Christentum: Neutestamentliche Studien.* Tübingen.

(2006) *Ancient Letters and the New Testament: A Guide to Context and Exegesis.* Waco, Tex.

Kmosko, M. (ed.) (1915) *Ammonii Eremitae Epistolae.* Patrologia Orientalis 10. Paris: 555–639.

Knox, J. (1959) *Philemon among the Letters of Paul: A New View of Its Place and Importance*, rev. edn. New York.

Kramer, B., Römer, C. and Hagedorn, D. (1982) *Kölner Papyri*, vol. IV. Opladen.

Krawiec, R. (2002) *Shenoute and the Women of the White Monastery.* New York.

Kropp, A., Hermann, A. and Weber, M. (1968) *Demotische und Koptische Texte*, part 2. Opladen.

Krueger, D. (2004) *Writing and Holiness: The Practice of Authorship in the Early Christian East*. Philadelphia, Pa.

Krueger, P. (ed.) (1877) *Corpus Iuris Civilis*, vol. II: *Codex Iustinianus*. Berlin.

Krusch, B. (ed.) (1887) *Fausti aliorumque epistulae ad Ruricium aliosque*. MGH AA 8. Berlin.

Krusch, B. and Levison, W. (eds.) (1951) *Gregorii Episcopi Turonensis decem libri historiarum*. MGH Scriptores rerum merovingicarum I.I. Hanover.

Kuhn, K. H. (1956) *The Letters and Sermons of Besa*. CSCO 158. Louvain.

Kurth, D., Thissen, H.-J. and Weber, M. (1980) *Kölner ägyptische Papyri*. Opladen.

Kurz, W. S. (1996) '2 Corinthians: Implied readers and canonical implications', *Journal for the Study of the New Testament* 62: 43–63.

Laourdas, B. (1951) 'The codex Ambrosianus Graecus and Photius', *Byzantinische Zeitschrift* 44: 370–2.

Layton, B. (2007) 'Rules, patterns, and the exercise of power in Shenoute's monastery: The problem of world replacement and identity maintenance', *JECS* 15: 45–73.

(2009) 'Some observations on Shenoute's sources: Who are our fathers?', *Journal of Coptic Studies* 11: 45–59.

Lebon, J. (1909) *Le monophysisme sévérien: Etude historique, littéraire et théologique sur la résistance monophysite au Concile de Chalcédoine jusqu'à la constitution de l'Eglise Jacobite*. Louvain.

(1951) 'La christologie du monophysisme syrien', in *Das Konzil von Chalkedon. Geschichte und Gegenwart*, vol. II, eds. A. Grillmeier and H. Bacht. Würzburg: 425–580.

Leipoldt, J. (1903) *Shenute von Atripe und die Entstehung des national ägyptischen Christentums*. Leipzig.

(ed.) (1908) *Sinuthii Archimandritae vita et opera Omnia*, vol. III. Paris.

Lepelley, C. (1998) 'Le patronat épiscopale aux IVe et Ve siècles', in *L'évêque dans la cité du IVe au Ve siècle: Image et authorité*, eds. E. Rebillard et C. Sotinel. Collection de l'École française de Rome 248. Rome: 17–33.

(2007) 'Facing wealth and poverty: Defining Augustine's social doctrine', The Saint Augustine Lecture 2006, *Augustinian Studies* 38: 1–17.

Leppin, H. (1996) 'Zum kirchenpolitischen Kontext von Theodorets Mönchsgeschichte', *Klio* 78: 212–30.

Leroy-Molinghen, A. (1980) 'Naissance et enfance de Théodoret', in *L'enfant dans les civilisations orientales*, ed. A. Theodorides. Louvain: 153–58.

Liébaert, J. (1970) 'L'évolution de la christologie de saint Cyrille d'Alexandrie à partir de la controverse nestorienne', *Mélanges de Science Religieuse* 27: 27–48.

Liebeschuetz, J. H. W. G. (1972) *Antioch: City and Imperial Administration in the Later Roman Empire*. Oxford.

(tr.) (2005) *Ambrose of Milan: Political Letters and Speeches*. TTH 43. Liverpool.

Lightfoot, J. B. (ed.) (1885–90) *The Apostolic Fathers* (5 vols.) 2nd edn. London.

Lim, R. (1995) *Public Disputation, Power and Social Order in Late Antiquity.* Transformations of the Classical Heritage 23. Berkeley, Calif.

Lizzi, R. (1987) *Il potere episcopale nell'oriente romano: Rappresentazione ideologica e realtà politica (IV–V sec. d. C.).* Filologia e Critica 53. Rome.

Longenecker, R. N. (1974) 'Ancient amanuenses and the Pauline epistles', in *New Dimensions in New Testament Study*, eds. N. Longenecker and M. C. Tenny. Grand Rapids, Mich.: 281–97.

Lovering, E. H. (1988) 'The collection, redaction, and early circulation of the *corpus Paulinum*', PhD diss., Southern Methodist University.

Lowe, E. A. (1950) *Codices Latini Antiquiores*, vol. v, *France: Paris.* Oxford.

Löwenfeld, S. (ed.) (2010 [1895]) *Epistolae pontificum Romanorum ineditae.* Leipzig (repr. Charleston, SC, 2010).

Lucchesi, E. (1977) *L'usage de Philon dans l'oeuvre de saint Ambroise.* Leiden.

Luckensmeyer, D. (2009) *The Eschatology of First Thessalonians.* Novum Testamentum et Orbis Antiquus/Studien zur Umwelt des Neuen Testaments 71. Göttingen.

Luckensmeyer, D. and Neil, B. (forthcoming) 'Consoling Christians and pagans: *Consolatio* in First Thessalonians and Seneca'.

Luetjohann, C. (ed.) (1897) *Gai Solii Apollinaris Sidonii epistulae et carmina: Accedunt Fausti aliorumque epistulae ad Ruricium aliosque Ruricii epistulae.* MGH AA 8. Berlin.

Luttenberger, J. (2012) *Prophetenmantel oder Bucherfutteral? Die Personlichen Notizen in den Pastoralbriefen im Licht antiker Epistolographie und literarischer Pseudepigraphie.* Arbeiten zur Bibel und ihrer Geschichte 40. Leipzig.

Maassen, F. (1870) *Geschichte der Quellen und der Literatur des canonischen Rechts im Abendlande bis zum Ausgange des Mittlealters*, vol. i. Graz.

Macé, C. (2006) 'Letters as a distorting mirror of reality: Gregory of Nazianzos' and Basil of Caesarea's practices of letter writing', in *Proceedings of the 21st International Congress of Byzantine Studies London, 21–26 August 2006. Theme II. Abstracts of Panel Papers* (ed.) E. Jeffreys with the assistance of J. Galliland. London: 144.

McGing, B.C. (1990) 'Melitian Monks at Labla', *Tyche* 5: 67–73.

McGuckin, J. A. (1988) 'The Christology of Nestorius of Constantinople', *Patristic and Byzantine Review* 7/1: 2–3.

(1996) 'Nestorius and the political factions of fifth-century Byzantium: Factors in his personal downfall', *Bulletin of the John Rylands University Library of Manchester* 78: 7–21.

(2003) 'Cyril of Alexandria: Bishop and pastor', in *The Theology of St Cyril of Alexandria. A Critical Appreciation*, eds. T. G. Weinandy and D. A. Keating. London and New York: 205–36.

(2004) *St Cyril of Alexandria: The Christological Controversy, Its History, Theology and Texts.* Crestwood, NY.

McKitterick, R. (2004) *History and Memory in the Carolingian World*, Cambridge.

McLean, P. D. (2007) *The Art of the Network: Strategic Interaction and Patronage in Renaissance Florence.* Durham, NC.

McLynn, N. B. (2001) 'Gregory Nazianzen's Basil: The literary construction of a Christian friendship'. *SP* vol. xxxvii. Leuven: 178–93.

McNary-Zak, B. (2000) *Letters and Asceticism in Fourth-century Egypt.* Washington, DC.

(2011) *Useful Servanthood. A Study of Spiritual Formation in the Writings of Abba Ammonas. With the Greek Corpus of Ammonas in English Translation by N. Conic, L. Morey and R. U. Smith.* Cistercian Studies Series 224. Collegeville, Minn.

Mai, A. (ed.) (1815) *M. Cornelii Frontonis et M. Aurelii imperatoris epistulae.* Rome.

(ed.) (1823) *M. Cornelii Frontonis et M. Aurelii imperatoris epistulae.* 2nd edn. Rome.

Malherbe, A. J. (1988) *Ancient Epistolary Theorists.* Society of Biblical Literature, Sources for Biblical Study 19. Atlanta, Ga.

(tr.) (2000) *The Letter to the Thessalonians: A New Translation with Introduction and Commentary.* Anchor Bible 32b. New York.

Malingrey, A.-M. (1961) *Jean Chrysostome: Sur la Providence de Dieu.* SC 79. Paris.

(1964a) 'Etude sur les manuscrits d'un texte de Jean Chrysostome: Lettre d'exil à Olympias et à tous les fidèles', *Traditio* 20: 418–27.

(1965) 'Etude sur les manuscrits des lettres de Jean Chrysostome à Olympias', *Traditio* 21: 425–44.

(1981) 'La double tradition manuscrite de la lettre de Jean Chrysostome à Innocent', *Traditio* 37: 381–8.

with Leclercq, P. (ed., tr.) (1988) *Palladios: Dialogue sur la vie de Jean Chrysostome.* SC 341–2. Paris.

(ed., tr.) (1962) 'Etude sur les manuscrits d'un texte de Jean Chrysostome, De providentia Dei, incipit: *Iatron men paides*', *Traditio* 18: 25–68.

(ed., tr.) (1964b) *Jean Chrysostome: Lettre d'exil. A Olympias et à tous les fidèles (Quod nemo laeditur).* SC 103. Paris.

(ed., tr.) (1968) *Lettres à Olympias.* SC 13 bis. Paris.

Mandac, M. (1971) 'L'union christologique dans les oeuvres de Théodoret antérieures au concile d'Ephèse', *Ephemerides Theologicae Lovanienses* 1: 64–96.

Mansi, G. D. (ed.) (1960–1 [1759–98]) *Sacrorum conciliorum nova et amplissima collectio* (53 vols.). Florence (repr. Graz, 1960–1).

Maran, P. (ed.) (1730) *Vita sancti Basilii magni archiepiscopi Caesariensis*, in *Basilii Caesareae Cappadocii Archiepiscopi Opera Omnia*, vol. iii, eds. J. Garnier, P. Maran and F. Faverolles Paris (repr. in PG 29: 5–177).

Maraval, P. (ed., tr.) (1990) *Grégoire de Nysse: Lettres, introduction, texte critique, traduction, notes et index.* SC 363. Paris.

Marriott, G. L. (1918) '*Macarii anecdota*: Seven unpublished homilies of Macarius', *Harvard Theological Studies* 5: 47–8.

Marshall, I. H. (1980) *The Acts of the Apostles.* The Tyndale New Testament Commentaries. Grand Rapids, Mich.

Marshall, P. K. (ed.) (1977) *Cornelii Nepotis vitae cum fragmentis.* Leipzig.

Martin, A. (1994) 'Archives privées et cachettes documentaires', in *Proceedings of the 20th International Congress of Papyrologists, Copenhagen 23–29 August 1992*, ed. A. Bülow-Jacobsen. Copenhagen: 569–77.

Martin, H. (1960) 'La controverse trithéite dans l'empire byzantine au VIe siècle', diss. Catholic University of Louvain.

Martin, R. P. (1986) *New Testament Foundations: A Guide for Christian Students*, vol. II, rev. edn. Grand Rapids, Mich.

(1994) *The Epistle of Paul to the Philippians: An Introduction and Commentary*, rev. edn. The Tyndale New Testament Commentaries. Grand Rapids, Mich.

Martini, A. and Bassi, D. (1906) *Catalogus Codicum Graecorum Bibliothecae Ambrosianae*. Milan.

Maspero, G., with Degli Esposti, M. and Benedetto, D. (2010) 'Who wrote Basil's *Epistula* 38? A possible answer through quantitative analysis', in *Gregory of Nyssa's* Contra Eunomium *III: Proceedings of the Twelfth International Gregory of Nyssa Colloquium (Leuven, 14–17 September 2010)*, eds. J. Leemans and M. Cassin. Leuven: 579–94.

(2012) 'Authorship attribution and small scales analysis applied to a real philological problem in Greek patristics', in *Methods and Applications of Quantitative Linguistics*, eds. I. Obradović, E. Kelih and R. Köhler. Belgrade: 11–20.

(2013) 'The puzzle of Basil's *Epistula* 38? A mathematical approach to a philological problem', *Journal of Quantitative Linguistics* 20: 267–87.

Mathisen, R. (1997) 'The "Second Council of Arles" and the spirit of compilation and codification in Late Roman Gaul', *JECS* 5: 511–54.

(2014) 'Church councils and local authority: the development of Gallic *libri canonum* during late antiquity', in *Being Christian in Late Antiquity: A Festschrift for Gillian Clark*, eds. C. Harrison, C. Humfress and I. Sandwell. Oxford: 175–93.

(ed., tr.) (1999) *Ruricius of Limoges and Friends: A Collection of Letters from Visigothic Gaul.* TTH 30. Liverpool.

Maurach, G. (1970) *Der Bau von Senecas Epistulae Morales*. Bibliothek der klassischen Altertumswissenschaften. NF 30. Heidelberg.

Maurist Congregation (eds.) (1690) *Sancti Ambrosii Mediolanensis episcopi opera … emendata studio et labore monachorum Ordinis S. Benedicti, e congregatione S. Mauri*, 2nd edn. Rome.

(eds.) (1965) *Lettere. Opere di Sant'Agostino*. Nuova biblioteca Agostiniana, vols. XXI–XXIIIa. Rome.

Mayer, W. (2001) 'Patronage, pastoral care and the role of the bishop at Antioch', *VC* 55: 58–70.

(2006) 'John Chrysostom: Deconstructing the construction of an exile', *Theologische Zeitschrift* 62/2: 248–58.

(2010) 'The bishop as crisis manager: An exploration of early fifth-century episcopal strategy', in *Studies of Religion and Politics in the Early Christian Centuries*, eds. D. Luckensmeyer and P. Allen. Early Christian Studies 13. Strathfield, NSW: 159–71.

(2012) 'John Chrysostom as crisis manager: The years in Constantinople', in *Ancient Jewish and Christian Texts as Crisis Management Literature: Thematic Studies from the Centre for Early Christian Studies*, eds. D. Sim and P. Allen. Library of New Testament Studies 445. London and New York: 129–43.

(2013) 'Media manipulation as a tool in religious conflict: Controlling the narrative surrounding the deposition of John Chrysostom', in *Religious Conflict from Early Christianity to the Rise of Islam*, eds. W. Mayer and B. Neil. Arbeiten zur Kirchengeschichte 121. Berlin: 151–68.

(2014) 'John Chrysostom and women revisited', in *Reading Men and Women in Early Christianity*, eds. W. Mayer and I. Elmer. Early Christian Studies 18. Strathfield, NSW: 215–30

Menestò, E. (1985) 'Le lettere di S. Vigilio', *Atti della Accademia Roveretana degli Agiati. Classe di Scienze umane, Lettere ed Arti* 25: 383–8.

Menze, V. L. (2008) *Justinian and the Making of the Syrian Orthodox Church*. Oxford Early Christian Studies. Oxford.

Messeri G. (2001) 'Official and private archives in the papyri', in *First International Symposium of Archivists. Archival Prospectives in the New Millennium, Cyprus, 4–6 May 2000*. Athens: 61–9.

Metzger, B. M. (1987) *The Canon of the New Testament: Its Origin, Development and Significance*. Oxford.

Mews, C. and Chiavaroli, N. (2009) 'The Latin West', in *Friendship: A History*, ed. B. Caine. London: 73–110.

Millar, F. (2006) *A Greek Roman Empire: Power and Belief under Theodosius II*. Berkeley, Calif.

(2007) 'Theodoret of Cyrrhus: A Syrian in Greek dress?', in *From Rome to Constantinople: Studies in Honour of Averil Cameron*, eds. H. Amirav and B. ter Haar Romeny. Leuven: 105–25.

Mitchell, M. M. (2005) 'Paul's letters to Corinth: The interpretive intertwining of literary and historical reconstruction', in *Urban Religion in Roman Corinth: Interdisciplinary Approaches*, eds. D. N. Schowalter and S. J. Friesen. Cambridge, Mass.: 307–38.

Mitton, C. L. (1951) *The Epistle to the Ephesians: Its Authorship, Origin and Purpose*. Oxford.

Mommsen, T. (ed.) (1894) *Acta synodhodorum habitae Romae a. CCCCXCVIIII. DI. DII*. MGH AA 12. Berlin.

(ed.) (1898) *Liber pontificalis*. Gestorum Pontificum Romanorum. Berlin.

(ed.), Rougé, J. (tr.) (2005) *Code Théodosien, livre XVI*. SC 497. Paris.

Montfaucon, B. de (ed.) (1834–40) *Sancti Patris Nostri Ioannis Chrysostomi archiepiscopi Constantinopolitani opera omnia quæ exstant, uel quæ eius nomine circumferentur*. 2nd edn. Paris.

Mordek, H. (1975) *Kirchenrecht und Reform im Frankenreich*. Beiträge zur Geschichte und Quellenkunde des Mittelalters, Bd. 1. Berlin and New York.

Moreau, D. (2010) '*Non impar conciliorum extat auctoritas*. L'origine de l'introduction des lettres pontificales dans le droit canonique', in *L'étude des correspondances dans le monde romain de l'Antiquité classique à l'Antiquité tardive: Permanences et mutations*, eds. J. Desmulliez, C. Hoët-van Cauwenberghe, J.-C. Jolivet. Actes du XXXe Colloque international de Lille, 20–22 novembre 2008. Villeneuve-d'Ascq: 487–506.

Morello, R. and Morrison, A. D. (eds.) (2007) *Ancient Letters: Classical and Late Antique Epistolography*. Oxford.

Morgenstern, F. (1993) *Die Briefpartner des Augustinus von Hippo: Prosopographische, sozial- und ideologiegeschichtliche Untersuchungen.* Bochumer historische Studien. Bochum.

Morin, G. (1913) 'Les *Statuta ecclesiae antiqua* sont-ils de S. Césaire d'Arles?', *Revue Bénédictine* 30: 334–42.

Morris, L. (1988) *The Epistle to the Romans.* Grand Rapids, Mich.

Mowry, L. (1944) 'The early circulation of Paul's letters', *JBL* 63: 73–86.

Mratschek, S. (2002) *Der Briefwechsel des Paulinus von Nola. Kommunikation und soziale Kontakte zwischen christlichen Intellektuellen.* Hypomnemata 134. Göttingen.

Müller, F. (1939) 'Der zwanzigste Brief des Gregors von Nyssa', *Hermes* 74: 66–91.

Mullett, M. (1981) 'The classical tradition in the Byzantine letter', in *Byzantium and the Classical Tradition,* eds. M. Mullet and R. Scott. Birmingham: 75–93.

(1997) *Theophylact of Ochrid: Reading the Letters of a Byzantine Bishop.* Birmingham Byzantine and Ottoman Monographs 2. Aldershot and Brookfield, Vt.

Mundó, A. (1957) 'L'authenticité de la Regula S. Benedicti', *Studia Anselmiana* 42: 105–98.

Murphy-O'Connor, J. (1995) *Paul the Letter Writer: His World, His Options, His Skills.* Good News Studies 41. Collegeville, Minn.

Musurillo, H. (ed., tr.) (1972) *The Acts of the Christian Martyrs: Introduction, Texts and Translations.* Oxford.

Naber, S. A. (ed.) (1867) *M. Cornelii Frontonis et M. Aurelii imperatoris epistulae post Angelum Maium cum codicibus Ambrosiano et Vaticano iterum contulit G. N. du Rieu.* Leipzig.

Nadjo, L., Gavoille, E., Laurence, P. and Guillaumont, F. (2002–06) *Epistulae antiquae,* i–v (5 vols.). Leuven.

Nau, F. (1906) 'La version syriaque de la première lettre de Saint Antoine', *Revue d'Orient Chrétien* 14: 282–97.

(1916) *Ammonas, successeur de saint Antoine. Textes grecs et syriaques.* Patrologia Orientalis 11. Paris.

(ed.) (1919) *Documents pour servir à l'histoire de l'Eglise nestorienne.* Patrologia Orientalis 13. Paris.

Neil, B. (2003) 'Rufinus' translation of the *Epistola Clementis ad Jacobum*', *Augustinianum* 43: 25–39.

(2006) *Seventh-century Popes and Martyrs: The Political Hagiography of Anastasius Bibliothecarius.* Studia Antiqua Australiensia 2. Turnhout and Sydney.

(2009) *Leo the Great.* The Early Church Fathers. London and New York.

(2013a) 'The decretals of Gelasius I: Making canon law in late antiquity', in *Lex et religio in età tardoantica, XL Incontro de Studiosi dell'Antichità Cristiana (Roma, 10–12 maggio 2012)*. Studia Ephemeridis Augustinianum 135. Rome: 657–68.

(2013b) 'The papacy in the age of Gregory the Great', in *A Companion to Gregory the Great*, eds. B. Neil and M. dal Santo. Brill's Companions to the Christian Tradition. Leiden and Boston: 3–27.

(forthcoming a) 'Papal letter collections', in *A Critical Introduction and Reference Guide to Letter Collections in Late Antiquity*, eds. E. Watts, B. Storin and C. Sogno. Berkeley and Los Angeles.

(forthcoming b) 'The letters of Gelasius (492–496): A new model of crisis management?' in *The Bishop of Rome in Late Antiquity*, ed. G. D. Dunn. Aldershot.

Neil, B. and Allen, P. (trs.) (2014) *Letters of Gelasius I, Micro-manager and Pastor of the Church of Rome*. Adnotationes 1. Turnhout.

Neri, M. (ed., tr.) (2009) *Ruricio di Limoges: Lettere*. Pubblicazioni della Facoltà di Lettere e Filosofia della Università di Pavia 122. Pisa.

Neunhaus, D. R. (2007) *Not by Paul Alone: The Formation of the Catholic Epistle Collection and the Christian Canon*. Waco, Tex.

Nikolopoulos, P. (1973a) 'Les lettres inauthentiques de saint Jean Chrysostome', in *SYMPOSION. Studies on St. John Chrysostom*. Analekta Blatadon. Thessalonica: 125–8.

(1973b) Αἱ εἰς τὸν Ἰωάννην τὸν Χρυσόστομον ἐσφαλμένως ἀποδιδόμεναι ἐπιστολαί. Athens.

Noble, T. F. X. (1993) 'Theodoric and the papacy', in *Teodorico il Grande e i goti d'Italia. Atti dei congressi 13*. Spoleto: 395–425.

Norberg, D. (ed.) (1982) *S. Gregorii Magni Registrum Epistularum libri I–XIV* (2 vols.). CCSL 140, 140a. Turnhout.

Norman, A. F. (ed., tr.) (1992) *Libanius: Autobiography and Selected Letters* (2 vols.). LCL 478, 479. London and Cambridge, Mass.

Nuffelen, P. Van (2004) *Un héritage de paix et de piété: Etude sur les histoires ecclésiastiques de Socrate et de Sozomène*. Orientalia Lovaniensia Analecta 142. Leuven.

(2013) 'Palladius and the Johannite schism', *Journal of Ecclesiastical History* 64: 1–19.

Oates, J. F., Willis, W. H., Sosin, J. D., Bagnall, R. S., Cowey, J., Depauw, M., Wilfong, T. G. and Worp, K. A. *Checklist of Greek, Latin, Demotic and Coptic Papyri, Ostraca and Tablets*. http://scriptorium.lib.duke.edu/papyrus/texts/clist.html (accessed 28 September 2014).

Outtier, B. (1971) 'Un patéricon arménien', *Le Muséon* 84: 299–351.

(1985) *Lettres des Pères du Désert: Ammonas, Macaire, Arsène, Serapion de Thmuis*. Spiritualité Orientale 42. Bégrolle-en-Mauges.

Overbeck, J. (ed.) (1865) *S. Ephraemi Syri, Rabulae episcopi Edesseni Balaei aliorumque opera selecta*. Oxford.

Palanque, J. R. (1931) *Saint Ambroise et l'empire romain: Contribution à l'histoire des rapports de l'Église et de l'État à la fin du quatrième siècle*. Paris: 480–556.

Paoli-Lafaye, E. (2002) 'Messagers et messages: La diffusion des nouvelles de l'Afrique d'Augustin vers les régions d'au-delà des mers', in *L'information et la mer dans le monde antique*, eds. J. Andreau and C. Virlouvet. Rome: 233–59.

Parmentier, L. and Hansen, G. C. (eds.) (1998) *Theodoret. Kirchengeschichte*. GCS NF 5. Berlin.

Parmentier, M. (1990) 'A letter from Theodoret of Cyrus to the exiled Nestorius (*CPG* 6270) in a Syriac version: [facsim.]', *Bijdragen* 51: 234–45.

Parys, M. van (1971) 'L'évolution de la doctrine christologique de Basile de Séleucie', *Irénikon* 44: 493–514.

Pasquali, G. (1923) 'Le lettere di Gregorio di Nissa', *Studi Italiani de Filologia Classica* ns 3: 75–136.

    (ed.) (1959) *Gregorii Nysseni Epistulae, editio altera*. Gregorii Nysseni Opera vol. VIII/2. Leiden.

Pásztori-Kupán, I. (2006) *Theodoret of Cyrus*. The Early Church Fathers. London and New York.

Peiper, R. (ed.) (1961) *Alcimi Ecdicii Aviti Viennensis episcopi opera quae supersunt*. MGH AA 6/II. 2nd edn. Berlin.

Perels, E. (ed.) (1978) *Nicholae I. epistulae*. MGH Epp. 6, *Epistolae Karolini aevi* 4. Berlin: 454–87.

Pericoli-Ridolfini, F. (1954) 'La controversia tra Cirillo d'Alessandria e Giovanni d'Antiochia nell'epistolario di Andrea di Samosata', *Rivista degli Studi Orientali* 29: 187–217.

Perry, S. G. F. (tr.) (1881) *The Second Synod of Ephesus, English Version*. Dartford.

Pervo, R. I. (2010) *The Making of Paul: Constructions of the Apostle in Early Christianity*. Minneapolis, Minn.

Peterson, W. (ed.) (1916) *M. Tulli Ciceronis Orationes: Divinatio in Q. Caecilium. In C. Verrem*. Oxford (repr. 1967).

Petrie, W. M. F. (1907) *Gizeh and Rifeh*. London.

Pietersma, A. and Comstock, S. (2011) 'Two more pages of Crosby-Schøyen codex MS 193: A Pachomian Easter lectionary?', *Bulletin of the American Society of Papyrologists* 48: 27–46.

Pietri, L. (2002) 'Evergétisme chrétien et fondations privées dans l'Italie de l'antiquité tardive', in *Humana Sapit: Études d'antiquité tardive offertes à Lellia Cracco Ruggini*, eds. R. Lizzi Testa and J.-M. Carrié. Turnhout: 253–63.

Pietrini, S. (2002) *Religio e ius romanum nell'epistolario di Leone Magno*. Materiali per una palingenesi delle costituzioni tardo-imperiali 6. Milan.

Pollard, R. (2013) 'A cooperative correspondence: the letters of Gregory the Great', in *A Companion to Gregory the Great*, eds. B. Neil and M. dal Santo. Brill's Companions to the Christian Tradition. Leiden and Boston: 291–312.

Porter, S. E. (ed.) (1999) *The Paul of Acts: Essays in Literary Criticism, Rhetoric, and Theology*. Wissenschaftliche Untersuchungen zum Neuen Testament 115. Tübingen.

(2009) *The Pauline Canon*. Pauline Studies. Atlanta, Ga.

(2011) 'Paul and the Pauline letter collection', in *Paul and the Second Century*, eds. M. F. Bird and J. R. Dodson. London: 19–36.

Porter, S. E. and Adams, S. (eds.) (2010) *Paul and the Ancient Letter Form*. Leiden.

Pouchet, J. B. (1988) 'Une lettre spirituelle de Gregoire de Nysse identifiée', *VC* 42: 28–46.

Price, R. (2009) *The Acts of the Council of Constantinople 553 with Related Texts on the Three Chapters Controversy*, with tr. and comm. (2 vols.). TTH 51. Liverpool.

Price, R. and Gaddis, M. (2005) *The Acts of the Council of Chalcedon*, with tr. and comm. (3 vols.). TTH 45. Liverpool.

Quecke, H. (1974) 'Ein neues Fragment der Pachombriefe in koptischer Sprache', *Orientalia* 43: 66–82.

(ed.) (1975) *Die Briefe Pachoms: griechischer Text der Handschrift W. 145 der Chester Beatty Library. Anhang: Die koptischen Fragmente und Zitate der Pachombriefe*. Regensburg.

Quesnel, P. (ed.) (1675) *Sancti Leonis Magni papae primi Opera omnia*. Paris.

Rapp, C. (2005) *Holy Bishops in Late Antiquity: The Nature of Christian Leadership in an Age of Transition*. Berkeley, Los Angeles and London.

Rees, R. (2007) 'Letters of recommendation and the rhetoric of praise', in *Ancient Letters: Classical and Late Antique Epistolography*, eds. R. Morello and A. D. Morrison. Oxford: 149–68.

Reicke, B. (1951) *Diakonie, Festfreude und Zelos in Verbindung mit der altchristlichen Agapenfeier*. Uppsala.

(1969) *The New Testament Era: The World of the Bible from 500 BC to AD 100*, tr. D. E. Green. London.

(2001) *Re-Examining Paul's Letters: The History of the Pauline Correspondence*. Harrisburg, Pa.

Reynolds, L. D. (ed.) (1983) *Texts and Transmission: A Survey of the Latin Classics*. Oxford.

Richard, M. (1936) 'Notes sur l'évolution doctrinale de Théodoret', *Revue des sciences philosophiques et théologiques* 24: 83–106.

(1941–2) 'La lettre de Théodoret à Jean d'Egées', *Les sciences philosophiques et théologiques* 2: 415–23; repr. in *Opera Minora* ii, sec. 48.

(1977a) *Opera Minora* ii. Turnhout and Leuven.

(1977b) 'Acace de Mélitène, Proclus de Constantinople et la Grande Arménie', in *Opera Minora* ii: sec. 50. Turnhout and Leuven.

(1977c) 'Proclus de Constantinople et le Théopaschisme', in *Opera Minora* ii: sec. 52. Turnhout and Leuven.

(1977d) 'Théodoret, Jean d'Antioche et les moines de l'orient', in *Opera Minora* ii: sec. 47. Turnhout and Leuven.

Richards, E. R. (1991) *The Secretary in Paul's Letters*. Wissenschaftliche Untersuchungen zum Neuen Testament 2. Reihe, 42. Tübingen.

(2004) *Paul and First-Century Letter Writing: Secretaries, Composition, and Collection*. Downers Grove, Ill.

Richter, T. S. (2008) 'Coptic Letters', in *Documentary Letters from the Middle East: The Evidence in Greek, Coptic, South Arabian, Pehlevi, and Arabic (1st–15th c. CE)*, eds. E. M. Grob and A. Kaplony. Bern: 739–70.

Roberts, W. R. (ed., tr.) (1932) *Demetrius: On Style*. LCL, rev. edn. London and Cambridge, Mass.

Robinson, J. (2011) *The Story of the Bodmer Papyri: From the First Monastery's Library in Upper Egypt to Geneva and Dublin*. Eugene, Ore.

Roey, A. Van (1981) 'La controverse trithéite depuis la condemnation de Conon et Eugène jusqu'à la conversion de l'évêque Elie', in *Von Kanaan bis Kerala. Festschrift für Prof. Mag. Dr. Dr. J.P.M. van der Ploeg O.P. zur Vollendung des siebzigsten Lebensjahres am 4. Juli 1979*, eds. W.C. Delsman, J. T. Nelis, J. R. T. M. Peters, W. H. P. Römer and A. S. van der Woude. Veröffentlichungen zur Kultur und Geschichte des Alten Orients und des Alten Testaments 211. Neukirchen.

(1985) 'La controverse trithéite jusqu'à l'excommunication de Conon et d'Eugène (557–569)', *Orientalia Lovaniensia Periodica* 16: 141–65.

Roey, A. Van and Allen, P. (eds., tr.) (1994) *Monophysite Texts of the Sixth Century*. Orientalia Lovaniensia Analecta 56. Leuven.

Rolfe, J. C. (ed.) (1929) *Lucius Annaeus Florus: Epitome of Roman History. Cornelius Nepos*. London (repr. London1966).

Roques, D. (1989) *Etudes sur la correspondance de Synésios de Cyrène*. Collection Latomus 205. Brussels.

Ross, G. M. (1974) 'Seneca's philosophical influence', in *Seneca*, ed. C. D. N. Costa, Greek and Latin Studies. Classical Literature and Its Influence. London and Boston: 116–65.

Rousseau, P. (1999) *Pachomius: The Making of a Community in Fourth-Century Egypt*. 2nd edn. Berkeley, Calif.

(2005) 'Knowing Theodoret: Text and self', in *The Cultural Turn in Late Ancient Studies*, eds. D. Martin and P. Cox Miller. Durham, NC: 278–97.

Rubenson, S. (1995) *The Letters of St Antony: Monasticism and the Making of a Saint*, 2nd rev. edn. Studies in Antiquity and Christianity. Minneapolis.

(2004) 'Wisdom, *paraenesis* and the roots of monasticism', in *Early Christian Paraenesis in Context*, eds. J. Starr and T. Engberg Pedersen. Beihefte zur Zeitschrift für die neutestamentliche Wissenschaft und die Kunde der älteren Kirche, Band 125. Berlin and New York: 521–34.

(2009) '"As already translated to the kingdom while still in the body". The transformation of the ascetic in early Egyptian monasticism', in *Metamorphoses: Resurrection, Body and Transformative Practices in Early Christianity*, eds. T. K. Seim and J. Økland. Berlin: 271–90.

(2011a) 'Antony and Ammonas: Conflicting or common tradition in early Egyptian monasticism', in *Bibel, Byzanz und Christlicher Orient. Festschrift für Stephan Gerö*, ed. D. Bumazhnov. Orientalia Christiana Analecta 187. Leuven: 185–201.

(2011b) 'Athanasius und Antonius', in *Athanasius Handbuch*, ed. P. Gemeinhardt. Tübingen: 141–45.

(2013) 'The formation and reformations of the *Sayings of the Desert Fathers*', *SP* vol. LV, ed. M. Vinzent. Leuven: 5–22.

Rudberg, S. Y. (1953) *Études sur la tradition manuscrite de saint Basile*. Lund.

(1959) Review of *Saint Basile, Lettres, Tome 1*, ed. Y. Courtonne, *Gnomon* 31: 123–8.

(1963) Review of *Saint Basile, Lettres, Tome 2*, ed. Y. Courtonne, *Gnomon* 35: 262–4.

(1968) Review of *Saint Basile, Lettres, Tome 3*, ed. Y. Courtonne, *Gnomon* 40: 776–8.

(1981) 'Manuscripts and editions of the works of Basil of Caesarea', in *Basil of Caesarea: Christian, Humanist, Ascetic. A Sixteen-hundredth Anniversary Symposium*, ed. P. J. Fedwick (2 parts). Toronto: 49–65.

Russell, D. A. (1974) 'Letters to Lucilius', in *Seneca*, ed. C. D. N. Costa. Greek and Latin Studies. Classical Literature and Its Influence. London and Boston: 70–95.

Russell, D. A. and Wilson, N. G. (eds.) (1981) *Menander Rhetor*. Oxford.

Russell, N. (2000) *Cyril of Alexandria*. The Early Church Fathers. London and New York.

(tr.) (1981) *The Lives of the Desert Fathers*. Kalamazoo, Mich.

Sakissian, P. (1885) *Vark' srboc' haranc'* (*Lives of the Holy Fathers*), vol. II. Venice.

Sardella, T. (2000) 'Ormisda, santo', in *Enciclopedia dei Papi*, vol. I. Rome: 476–82.

Savile, H. (ed.) (1612–13) *Tou en hagiois patros hemon Ioannou archiepiskopou Konstantinoupoleos tou Chrysostomou ton heuriskomenon tomos (a-h)*. [= *S. Johannis Chrysostomi opera omnia*]. (8 vols.). Eton.

Savon, H. (1977) *Saint Ambroise devant l'exégèse de Philon le Juif*. Paris.

Schanzer, D. and Wood, I. (trs.) (2002) *Avitus of Vienne: Letters and Selected Prose*. TTH 38. Liverpool.

Schiller, A. A. (1971) 'Introduction', in *Koptische Rechtsurkunden des achten Jahrhunderts aus Djême (Theben)*, eds. W. E. Crum and G. Steindorff. 2nd edn. Leipzig.

Schmeller, T. (2004) 'Die Cicerobriefe und die Frage nach der Einheitlichkeit des 2. Korintherbriefs', *Zeitschrift für Neutestamentliche Wissenschaft* 95: 181–208.

Schmithals, W. (1971) *Gnosticism in Corinth: An Investigation of the Letters to the Corinthians*, tr. J. E. Steely. Nashville, Tenn.

(1972) *Paul and the Gnostics*, tr. J. E. Steely. Nashville, Tenn.

Schoon-Janßen, J. (2000) 'On the use of elements of ancient epistolography in 1 Thessalonians', in *The Thessalonians Debate: Methodological Discord or Methodological Synthesis?*, eds. K. P. Donfried and J. Beutler. Grand Rapids, Mich.: 179–93.

Schor, A.M. (2011) *Theodoret's People: Social Networks and Religious Conflict in Late Roman Syria*. Transformation of the Classical Heritage 48. Berkeley, Los Angeles and London.

Schwartz, E. (1914) *Konzilstudien*. Strasbourg.

(1936) 'Die Kanonessammlungen der alten Reichskirche', *Zeitschrift der Savigny-Stiftung für Rechtsgeschichte, Kanonistische Abteilung* 25: 1–114.

(ed.) (1927) *Codex Vaticanus gr. 1431. Eine antichalkedonische Sammlung aus der Zeit Kaiser Zenos*. Abhandlungen der Bayerischen Akademie der Wissenschaften, Philosophisch-philologische und historische Klasse, 32 vol. VI. Abhandlung. Munich.

(ed.) (1932–5) *Concilium universale Chalcedonense*, ACO 2 (6 vols.) Berlin and Leipzig.

Schwartz, J. (1961) *Les archives de Sarapion et de ses fils: Une exploitation agricole aux environs d'Hermoupolis Magna*. Cairo.

Scott, J. (2000) *Social Network Analysis: A Handbook*. London.

Seeck, O. (ed.) (1883) *Q. Aurelii Symmachi opera quae supersunt*. MGH AA2 VI/2. Berlin.

Sessa, K. (2012) *The Formation of Papal Authority in Late Antiquity: Roman Bishops and the Domestic Sphere*. Cambridge.

Sevenster, J. N. (1961) *Paul and Seneca*. Novum Testamentum Supplements 4. Leiden.

Shackleton Bailey, D. R. (ed.) (1965–71) *Cicero's Letters to Atticus* (7 vols.). Cambridge.

(ed.) (1977) *Cicero: Epistulae ad Familiares* (2 vols.). Cambridge.

(ed.) (1980) *Epistulae ad Quintum fratrem et M. Brutum*. Cambridge.

(ed.) (1987) *M. Tulli Ciceronis Epistulae ad Atticum* (2 vols.). Stuttgart.

(ed.) (1988) *M. Tulli Ciceronis Epistulae ad familiares, libri I–XVI*. Stuttgart.

(ed., tr.) (1912) *Cicero. Letters to Atticus 1–89*, LCL 7; *Letter to Atticus 90–165A*. LCL 8. London (repr. Cambridge, Mass. 2006).

Shaw, R. (2013) 'Textual disorder in the letters of St. Antony: An analysis and partial reconstruction. Part I: Disorder in the canon', *Downside Review* 131/462: 1–14; 'Part II: The likelihood of disorder: The letters in context', *Downside Review* 131/464: 59–68; 'Part III: Possibilities for reconstruction: A lost letter of St Antony?', *Downside Review* 131/464: 117–30.

Sillett, H. M. (1999) 'Culture of controversy: The Christological disputes of the early fifth century', PhD diss. University of California, Berkeley.

Silva-Tarouca, C. (1919) 'Beiträge zur Überlieferungsgeschichte der Papstbriefe des IV., V. u. VI. Jahrhunderts', *Zeitschrift für katholische Theologie* 43: 467–81, 657–92.

(1932) *Nuovi studi sulle antiche lettere dei papi*. Rome.

(ed.) (1934–5) *S. Leonis Magni, Epistulae contra Eutychis haeresim*, 2 parts. Rome.

(ed.) (1937) *Epistularum romanorum pontificium ad vicarios per Illyricum aliosque episcopos. Collectio Thessalonicensis*. Rome.

Silvas, A. M. (2008) *Macrina the Younger: Philosopher of God*. Turnhout.

(ed., tr.) (2005) *The Asketikon of St Basil the Great*. Oxford Early Christian Texts. Oxford.

(tr.) (2007) *Gregory of Nyssa: The Letters*. VCS 83. Leiden.

(ed.) (forthcoming) *The Letters of Basil of Caesarea*. Basilii Caesariensis Opera I.

Skeat, T. C. (1981) 'Two notes on papyrus', in *Scritti in onore di Orsolina Montevecchi*, eds. E. Bresciani. Bologna: 373–8.

(1990) 'Roll versus codex – a new approach?', *Zeitschrift für Papyrologie und Epigraphik* 84: 297–8.

(2004) *The Collected Biblical Writings of T. C. Skeat*, ed. J. K. Elliott. Leiden.

(ed.) (1964) *Papyri from Panopolis in the Chester Beatty Library.* Chester Beatty Monographs 10. Dublin.

Sotinel, C. (1992) 'Authorité pontificale et pouvoir impérial sous le règne de Justinien: Le pape Vigile', *Mélanges de l'École française de Rome* 104: 463–93.

(2000a) 'Pelagio I', in *Enciclopedia dei Papi*, vol. 1. Rome: 529–36.

(2000b) 'Vigilio', in *Enciclopedia dei Papi*, vol. 1. Rome: 512–28.

Spadavecchia, C. (1985) 'The rhetorical tradition in the letters of Theodoret of Cyrus', in *From Late Antiquity to Early Byzantium*, ed. V. Vavrínek. Prague: 249–52.

Stander, H. F. (2010) 'John Chrysostom on letters and letterwriting', *Scrinium* 6: 49–62.

Starr, R. J. (1987) 'The circulation of literary texts in the Roman world', *Classical Quarterly* 37: 213–23.

Stewart-Sykes, A. (1996) 'Ancient editors and copyists and modern partition theories: The case of the Corinthian correspondence', *Journal for the Study of the New Testament* 61: 53–64.

Stirewalt, M. L. (1993) *Studies in Ancient Greek Epistolography.* Atlanta, Ga.

(2003) *Paul, the Letter Writer.* Grand Rapids, Mich.

Stowers, S. K. (1986) *Letter Writing in Greco-Roman Antiquity.* Library of Early Christianity 5. Philadelphia, Pa.

(1987) Review of H. D. Betz, *2 Corinthians 8 and 9: A Commentary on Two Administrative Letters of the Apostle Paul*, *JBL* 106: 727–30.

Straw, C. (1988) *Gregory the Great: Perfection in Imperfection.* Berkeley and Los Angeles.

Stürner, W. (1969) 'Die Quellen der Fides Konstantins im Constitutum Constantini (§§ 3–51)', *Zeitschrift der Savigny-Stiftung für Rechtsgeschichte, Kanonistische Abteilung* 5: 64–206.

Taylor, J. (1975) 'The early papacy at work: Gelasius I (492–6)', *Journal of Religious History* 8: 317–32.

Teske, D. (tr.) (1997) *Gregor von Nyssa: Briefe.* Stuttgart.

Thiel, A. (ed.) (1867 [2004]) *Epistolae Romanorum Pontificum genuinae et quae ad eos scriptae sunt a S. Hilaro usque ad Pelagium II ex schedis clar. Petri Coustantii aliisque editis, adhibitis praestantissimis codicibus Italiae et Germaniae.* Braunsberg (repr. Hildesheim and Zürich, 2004).

Tiersch, C. (2002) *Johannes Chrysostomus in Konstantinopel (398–404). Weltsicht und Wirken eines Bischofs in der Hauptstadt des Oströmischen Reiches.* Studien und Texte zu Antike und Christentum 6. Tübingen.

Timbie, J. (2007) 'Non-canonical scriptural citation in Shenoute', in *Actes du huitième congrès international d'études coptes*, eds. N. Bosson and A. Boud'hors. Orientalia Lovaniensia Analecta 163. Leuven, Paris and Dudley, Mass: 625–34.

Tompkins, I. G. (1993) 'The relations between Theodoret of Cyrrhus and his city and its territory, with particular reference to the letters and *Historia Religiosa*', PhD diss. University of Oxford.

(1995) 'Problems of dating and pertinence in some letters of Theodoret of Cyrrhus', *Byzantion* 65: 176–95.

Torrance, I. R. (2011) *The Correspondence of Severus and Sergius. Texts from Christian Late Antiquity* 11. Piscataway, NJ.

(tr.) (1998) *Christology after Chalcedon: Severus of Antioch and Sergius the Monophysite.* Norwich.

Tóth, P. (2013) '"In volumine Longobardo". New light on the date and origin of the Latin translation of St. Antony's seven letters', *SP* vol. LXIV. Leuven: 47–58.

Towner, P. H. (2006) *The Letters to Timothy and Titus.* Grand Rapids, Mich.

Trapp, M. (2003) *Greek and Latin Letters: An Anthology.* Cambridge.

Trobisch, D. (1989) *Die Entstehung der Paulusbriefsammlung: Studien zu den Anfängen christlicher Publizistik.* Novum testamentum et orbis antiquus 10. Göttingen.

(1994) *Paul's Letter Collection: Tracing the Origins.* Minneapolis, Minn.

(2000) *The First Edition of the New Testament.* Oxford.

Turner, C. H. (1901) 'Chapters in the history of Latin manuscripts: II. A group of MSS of canons at Toulouse, Albi, and Paris', *JTS* 2: 266–73.

(1915–16) 'Arles and Rome: the first developments of canon law in Gaul', *JTS* 17: 236–47.

(1923) 'Introduction', in *La tradition manuscrite de la correspondance de saint Basile*, eds. M. Bessières and C. H. Turner. Oxford: 1–9.

(1928–9) 'Chapters in the history of Latin MSS of canons. IV. The Corbie MS (C), now Paris, lat. 12097', *JTS* 30: 225–36.

Ubaldi, P. (1901) 'La lettura CCXXXIII Πρὸς τὸν Ἀντιοχείας episc. dell'epistolario di S. Giovanni Crisostomo', *Bessarione* ser. 2, 6/1: 69–79.

Uhalde, K. (2007) *Expectations of Justice in the Age of Augustine.* Philadelphia, Pa.

Ullmann, W. (1981) *Gelasius I. (492–496): Das Papsttum an der Wende der Spätantike zum Mittelalter.* Päpste und Papsttum 18. Stuttgart.

Urbainczyk, T. (2002) *Theodoret of Cyrrhus: The Bishop and the Holy Man.* Ann Arbor, Mich.

Vandorpe, K. (2009) 'Archives and dossiers', in *The Oxford Handbook of Papyrology*, ed. R. S. Bagnall. Oxford: 216–55.

Veilleux, A. (1968) *La liturgie dans le cénobitisme pachômien au quatrième siècle.* Rome.

(tr.) (1980–2) *Pachomian Koinonia* (3 vols.). Kalamazoo, Mich.

Vielhauer, P. (1966) 'On the "Paulinism" in Acts', in *Studies in Luke-Acts*, eds. L. E. Keck and J. L. Martyn. Philadelphia, Pa: 33–50.

Vogel, F. (ed.) (1885) 'Vita Epiphanii', in *Magni Felicis Ennodi Opera.* MGA AA 7. Berlin: 84–109.

Vuolanto, V. (2012) 'A self-made living saint? Authority and the two families of Theodoret of Cyrrhus', in *Saintly Bishops and Bishops' Saints*, eds. J. Ott and T. Vedris. Zagreb: 49–66.

Waarden, J. A. van (2010) *Writing to Survive: A Commentary on Sidonius Apollinaris. Letters Book 7*, vol. 1: *The Episcopal Letters 1–11.* Late Antique History and Religion 2. Leuven, Paris and Walpole, Mass.

Wagner, M. M. (1948) 'A chapter in Byzantine epistolography: The letters of Theodoret of Cyrus', *Dumbarton Oaks Papers* 4: 119–81.

Wallraff, M. (2008) 'Tod im Exil: Reaktionen auf die Todesnachricht des Johannes Chrysostomos und Konstituierung einer "johannitischen" Opposition', in *Chrysostomosbilder in 1600 Jahren: Facetten der Wirkungsgeschichte eines Kirchenvaters*, eds. M. Wallraff and R. Brändle. Arbeiten zur Kirchengeschichte 105. Berlin and New York: 23–37.

(ed.) and Ricci, C. (tr.) (2007) *Oratio funebris in laudem sancti Iohannis Chrysostomi (Ps.-Martyrius Antiochenus, BHG 871, CPG 6517)*. Quaderni della Rivista di Bizantinistica 12. Spoleto.

Walsh, G. G. (tr.) (1947) 'The letters of St Ignatius of Antioch', in *Apostolic Fathers*, eds. F. Glimm, J. M. F. Marique and G. G. Walsh. Baltimore, Md: 87–127.

Wankenne, J. (1983) 'La correspondence de Consentius avec saint Augustin', in *Les lettres de saint Augustin découvertes par Johannes Divjak. Communications présentées au colloque des 20 et 21 Septembre 1982*. Paris: 225–42.

Wasserman, S. and Faust, K. (1994) *Social Network Analysis: Methods and Applications*. Cambridge.

Watt, W. S. and Shackleton Bailey, D. R. (eds.) (1968–71) *M. Tulli Ciceronis Epistulae* (3 vols.). Oxford.

Watts, D. (2003) *Six Degrees: The Science of a Connected Age*. New York.

Watts, E., Storin, B. and Sogno, C. (eds.) (forthcoming) *A Critical Introduction and Reference Guide to Letter Collections in Late Antiquity*. Berkeley and Los Angeles.

Watts, W. (tr.) (1996) *Augustine's Confessions Books I–VIII; Books IX–XII*, eds. T. E. Page and W. H. D. Rouse. LCL 26, 27. 2nd edn. Cambridge, Mass.

Weichert, V. (ed.) (1910) *Demetrii et Libanii qui feruntur Τυποι Επιστολικοι et Επιστολιμαιοι Χαρακτηρες*. Leipzig.

Welborn, L. L. (1996) 'Like broken pieces of a ring: 2 Cor. 1.1–2.13; 7.5–16 and ancient theories of literary unity', *NTS* 42: 559–83.

Wessel, S. (2004) *Cyril of Alexandria and the Nestorian Controversy: The Making of a Saint and of a Heretic*. Oxford.

(2008) *Leo the Great and the Spiritual Rebuilding of a Universal Rome*. VCS 93. Leiden and Boston.

White, J. L. (1986) *Light from Ancient Letters*. Foundations and Facets. Philadelphia, Pa.

(1988) 'Ancient Greek letters', in *Greco-Roman Literature and the New Testament. Selected Forms and Genres*, ed. D. E. Aune. Sources for Biblical Study 21. Atlanta, Ga: 85–105.

White, P. (2010) *Cicero in Letters: Epistolary Relations of the Late Republic*. Oxford.

Wickham, L. R. (1983) *Select Letters: Cyril of Alexandria*. Oxford Early Christian Texts. Oxford.

Williams, R. (2002) *Faith and Experience in Early Monasticism: New Perspectives on the Letters of Ammonas*. Akademische Reden und Kolloquien. Friedrich-Alexander-Universität Erlangen-Nürnberg 20. Erlangen-Nürnberg.

Winkler, G. (1985) 'An obscure chapter in Armenian church history (428–439)', *Revue des études arméniens* 19: 85–179.

Winlock, H. E., Crum, W. E. and Evelyn-White, H. G. (1926) *The Monastery of Epiphanius at Thebes* (2 vols.). New York.

Winstedt, E. O. (1906) 'The original text of one of St. Antony's letters', *JTS* 7/28: 540–5.

(ed.) (1904) *Corneli Nepotis vitae*. Oxford (repr. Oxford 1970).

Wipszycka, E. (2000) 'The Nag Hammadi library and the monks: A papyrologist's point of view', *Journal of Juristic Papyrology* 30: 179–91.

Wood, I. (1993) 'Letters and letter-collections from antiquity to the early Middle Ages: The prose works of Avitus of Vienne', in *The Culture of Christendom: Essays in Medieval History in Commemoration of Denis L. T. Bethell*, ed. M. A. Meyer. London and Rio Grande, OH: 29–43.

Wurm, H. (ed.) (1939a) 'Decretales selectae ex antiquissimis Romanorum pontificum epistulis decretalibus: Praemissa introductione et disquisitione critice editae', *Apollinaris* 12: 40–93.

(1939b) *Studien und Texte zur Dekretalensammlung des Dionysius Exiguus*. Kanonistische Studien und Texte 16. Bonn.

Young, F. M. (1983) *From Nicaea to Chalcedon*. London.

Zahn, T. (1975) *Geschichte des Neutestamentlichen Kanons*. Hildesheim.

Zelzer, M. (1980) 'Linien der Traditions und Editionsgeschichte der ambrosianischen Briefe am Beispiel des zehnten Briefbuches und den Briefen *extra collectionem*', *Anzeiger der Österreichischen Akademie der Wissenschaften. Phil.-hist. Klasse* 117: 207–30.

Zuntz, G. (1953) *The Text of the Epistles: A Disquisition upon the Corpus Paulinum*. The Schweich Lectures of the British Academy. London.

Index of people, places and things

Abgar, 8
Acacian schism, 25, 33, 220
Achaia, 39
Acts of the Apostles, 43, 44, 47, 51, 52, 53
Adana, 149
Addai, 8
administration, 120, 126, 207, 219
  papal, 214, 219
Adolia, 142
Aelian, 26
Aelius Theon, 10
Aemilia, 213
  bishops of, 213
Aeneas of Gaza, 26
Africa, 160, 201, 217, 218
agriculture, 216
Alexander II, 210
Alexandria, 24, 30, 33, 46, 83, 84, 90, 105,
    165, 166
  patriarch of, 23
  see of, 20, 141
Altar of Victory, 100, 110, 111
Ambrose of Milan, 6, 16, 97, 103, 104, 111, 210
  political activity, 110, 111, 112, 120
Ammonas, disciple of Antony, 16
Ammonas, monk, 68, 69, 70, 71, 72, 73, 74, 75,
    76, 77, 78, 79
Anastasia, 13
Anastasius, emperor, 24, 25
Anselm of Lucca, 211
anti-Chalcedonians, 20, 22, 29, 30,
    33, 90
anti-Johannites, 130, see John Chrysostom:
    opponents
Antioch, 33, 150, 152, 153
  bishops of, 110
  city of, 27, 136, 138, 145, 148, 150, 151, 152
  clergy of, 138, 142, 146
  deacon of, 143
  patriarch of, 20, 21, 28, 29, 30, 33, 90, 121, 130,
    147, 154

  presbyters of, 137, 142
  see of, 20, 22, 134, 136, 140, 144
Antony of Egypt, 16, 68, 69, 70, 71, 74, 75, 77,
    78, 79
  Life, 71
Anysius of Thessalonica, 142
Apelles, 92
Apollinarius, 121, 167, 168
Apollonius of Tyana, 26
Apollos, 40
apophthegm, 92
Apophthegmata Patrum, 92, see Sayings of the
    Desert Fathers
Arabic, 70, 74, 75
Arabissos, 144, 145
archive, 57, 144, 147, 169, 188
  of Asklepiades, 61
  of Euytchides, 60
  monastic, 69, 88, 89
  of Milan, 99
  papal, 33, 206, 207, 208, 209,
    210, 219
  papyrological, 60, 65, 80, 88
  of the strategus, 64
Arethas of Caesarea, 26
Arian controversy, 101, 108, 111, 120, 163,
    186, 211
aristocracy, 7
Arles, 19, 178, 179, 180, 181, 185, 189, 195, 196,
    208, 209, 217
  see of, 189, 208, 209, 220
Armenia, 134, 136, 143, 144, 145, 147,
    160, 165
Armenian, 9, 24, 73, 145, 165
Arsacius of Constantinople, 134
Arsenius, monk, 69, 92
Asclepiades, 61
Asia Minor, 39, 137
  elite, 138
Athanasius of Alexandria, 120
Atticus, 5, 12, 65, 186

Augustine of Hippo, 3, 7, 13, 14, 19, 23, 27, 30,
    108, 112, 196, 202, 204, 215
  conversion, 108
  letter packets, 23
  letters, 13, 32, 101
Augustus, 11
autobiography, 7, 101, 105, 112, 128
Avitus of Vienne, 18, 20

baptism, 101, 157, 159, 160
Basil of Caesarea, 12, 20, 26, 113, 114, 128
  archives, 119, 122, 123, 124
  Great Asketikon, 119
  letters, 14, 16, 101, 113, 114, 115, 116, 121, 122,
    123, 124, 126, 127, 128, 133
  Life, 114
Basil of Seleucia, 163, 164
Benedict I, 207
Besa, 71
biography, 7, 25, 30, 98, 99
bishops, 3, 7, 10, 11, 12, 15, 18, 20, 21, 24, 25, 27,
    101, 102, 103, 107, 134, 137, 139, 142, 148,
    153, 154, 160, 163, 165, 167, 168, 170, 175,
    176, 177, 178, 186, 188, 206, 208, 210,
    212, 213, 214, 215, 216, 218, 220
  neo-Nicene, 121
  Roman, *see* Rome, bishops of
  western, 110, 120
Boniface I of Rome, 186
Boniface of Mainz, 210

Caesarea, 13, 26, 27, 119, 120, 122, 123, 124, 135,
    138, 145, 149, 152
Caesarius of Arles, 32, 182, 200
Callinicum, 111
canon law, 10, 175, 179, 206, 211, 216, 220
canones urbicani, 178, 181, 182
canons, 8, 21, 39, 50, 86, 120, 126, 175, 177, 180,
    185, 187, 188
  Gallic, 179
  Greek, 180
Capua, 110
Caria
  bishops of, 142
Castus, 143
Celestine I, 17, 177, 178, 180, 181, 186, 187, 191,
    192, 201, 207
Cephas, 40
Chalcedon, 22
Chalcedonians, 26, 33
chancery, 119, 179
Childebert, 208, 213, 215, 217
Chion of Heraclea, 4, 8
Christophoria, 86
Chromatius of Aquileia, 138

Cicero, 3, 5, 6, 7, 11, 12, 19, 55, 56, 57, 58, 60, 65,
    80, 100, 102, 103
Cilicia, 149
Clement I, 14, 15, 40, 41, 45, 47, 210
Clement of Alexandria, 71
Clement, First Letter of, 40
clergy, 101, 134, 137, 138, 140, 142, 143, 144,
    146, 164, 170, 206, 213, 214, 215,
    216, 218, 219
Clermont, 6, 7, 19
collators, 8, 11, 113, 206, 211
Collectio Albigensis, 177, 178, 180
Collectio Avellana, 18, 25, 32, 210, 212, 216
Collectio Casiniensis, 166, 167
Collectio Coloniensis, 179, 180
Collectio Corbeiensis, 17, 175, 177, 178, 179, 180,
    181, 182, 183, 184, 187, 188, 189, 216
Collectio Dionysiana, 180, 216
Collectio Grimanica, 176
Collectio Laureschamensis, 182
Collectio Pithouensis, 17, 175, 177, 178, 180, 181,
    182, 183, 184, 187, 188, 216
Collectio Quesnelliana, 176
collections
  Gallic, 180
  Latin, 166
collectors of letters, 7, 16, 47, 162,
    165, 184
Colossae, 37, 39, 44
communities
  monastic, 93
Consentius, 31
Constantinople, 13, 22, 25, 33, 132, 135, 139, 140,
    143, 153, 162, 164, 165, 166, 186, 209,
    212, 213
  administration of, 137
  archives, 145
  bishops of, 148
  city of, 25, 136, 138, 144, 146, 148, 149, 150,
    151, 152
  clergy of, 137, 138, 142, 146
  Great Church of, 140
  laity, 137
  patriarch of, 25, 26
  presbyters of, 139
  priests of, 148
  see of, 133, 140, 141, 144
  urban prefect of, 106, 135
Constantius, 107, 133, 148, 150
Constantius II, emperor, 110
Constantius, bishop, 106
Constantius of Lyons, 19
Constantius, priest of Antioch, 23, 130, 132, 133,
    134, 136, 138, 143, 144, 146, 147
  letters, 144, 147

Coptic, 29, 30, 58, 59, 70, 74, 75, 82, 83, 84, 85, 86, 87, 91, 93
   Lives, 82
   papyri, 86
   parchment, 83
Copto-Arabic, 78
Corbie, 176, 180, 181, 182, 183, 184, 185, 187, 189
Corinth, 37, 38, 39, 40, 46, 48, 65, 66, 153
Cornelius Nepos, 65
Council of Aquileia, 97, 101, 104
Council of Capua, 101, 110
Council of Chalcedon, 26, 27, 28, 33, 155, 157, 163, 166, 179, 204, 212
Crates, 26
Cucusus, 13, 130, 133, 136, 138, 144, 145, 146
Cyriacus, 130, 136, 137, 143, 149, 150, 153
Cyril of Alexandria, 18, 22, 32, 154, 165, 168
Cyrrhus, 27

Dalmatia, 217
Damasus, 182, 186, 195, 202
Damian of Alexandria, 90
decretals, 7, 8, 15, 175, 180, 188, 211, 216
   pseudo-Isidorean, 211
Deir el-Bahri, 89
Delmaire, R., 16, 23, 129, 130, 131, 132, 135, 137, 138, 143, 153
Demetrius, 9, 10, 26, 142
Demetrius, pseudo, 12
Diogenes, 26
Dionysius Exiguus, 8
Dionysius of Antioch, 26

Egypt, 3, 16, 20, 22, 24, 29, 80, 81, 82, 83, 84, 87, 91, 104, 168
Elias the monk, 90, 91
embassy, 98, 106, 111
Ennodius of Pavia, 18, 22, 32
envoys, *see* embassy
Ephesus, 23, 27, 28, 37, 39, 42, 45, 46, 48, 60, 66, 155, 163, 165, 166, 170
Epiphanius, monastery, 89, 90, 93
epistolary networks, 27, 216
epistolography, 7, 14
   Graeco-Roman, 3, 4, 5
   monastic, 68, 80, 88
   sophistic, 156
estate management, 216, 217, *see also* property
estates
   imperial, 162
   papal, 209, 217, 219
Euripides, 4, 8
Eusebius of Samosata, 117, 120, 121
Eustathius the physician, 126
Eustathius of Sebasteia, 119, 121, 125

Eutyches, archimandrite of Constantinople, 163, 207
Eutychius, bishop of Constantinople, 217
Evagrius of Pontus, 69, 92
exile
   archives, 143
   consolation for, 13
   Gregory of Nyssa, 121, 124
   John Chrysostom, 23, 130, 133, 134, 135, 139, 142
   letters from, 13, 18, 133, 140, 141
   Olympias, 136
   Ovid, 4
   Severus of Antioch, 30
   Syrian bishops, 165

Faustinus, 149, 185, 186, 187, 188, 193, 202
Faustus of Riez, 202
Ferriolus of Uzès, 20
Firmus of Caesarea, 18, 22, 26, 28, 32
First World War, 114
florilegia, 78
   monastic, 70, 78
forgery, 8, 211
Frange, 88
Fronto, 5, 6, 7, 19
Fronton du Duc, 131, 132, 148
Fulgentius of Ruspe, 13

Galatia, 37
Galla Placidia, 14, 163
Gaudentius of Brescia, 153
Gaul, 175, 176, 177, 180, 185, 188, 208, 213, 217, 220
   bishops of, 189, 209, 213
Gelasius I, 10, 14, 206, 208, 210, 211, 212, 215, 216, 220
   canon law-collections, 216
George of Alexandria, 133
Georgian, 69, 70, 73
Gothic wars, 216, 217
Graeco-Roman
   empire, 3
   readers, 87
Greek, 8, 9, 11, 15, 58, 71, 77, 79, 82, 83, 93, 109, 114, 165, *see also* translation
   alphabet, 59
   Apophthegmata, 208
   Lives, 82, 91
   manuscripts, 73
   non-fictional letters, 7
   papyri, 86
   parchment, 59, 83, 85

Greek (*cont.*)
  terminology, 12
  translation from, 22, 24, 29, 70
  translation into, 58, 132
Gregory I, 10, 175, 182, 206, 207, 208, 209, 219,
  220
Gregory of Nazianzus, 18, 20, 117, 119, 121, 122,
  123, 124, 125, 179, 190
Gregory of Nyssa, 12, 113, 116, 121, 123, 124, 125
  archives, 124
  letters, 16

Heliodorus, 60
Heraclitus, 26
Hereleuva, 14
Herod Agrippa, 43
Hilary I, 195, 202
Hilary of Arles, 188, 189
Himerius of Tarragona, 181
History of the Monks of Egypt, 78, 92, 93
Homer, 161
homilies, 7, 14, 73, 78, 141
Honoratus of Marseille, 189
Honorius, 132
Hormisdas I, 13, 18, 19, 22, 25, 26, 31, 33, 177, 181,
  208, 210, 212
households, 6, 136, 147, 212, 216, 220

Ibas of Edessa, 167, 212
Ignatius of Antioch, 45, 47, 55, 80
Innocent I, 10, 14, 17, 129, 130, 132, 134, 137, 138,
  139, 140, 141, 142, 145, 177, 178, 180, 181,
  184, 186, 187, 188, 190, 191, 194, 195, 200,
  201, 202, 206, 207, 212
Irenaeus, bishop of Tyre, 103, 104, 105, 106, 107,
  160, 166, 167, 169
  exile, 166
Isidora, 61
Isidore of Pelusium, 26, 68, 69, 92
Iunius Brutus, 26

Jerome, 3, 7, 31, 58, 59, 66, 71, 79, 83, 84, 86, 87,
  93, 109, 225
Jerusalem, 43, 50, 149
Johannites, 134, 137, 144, 145, 147, *see also* John
  Chrysostom: supporters
John I, 177, 207
John III, 207, 208
John VIII, 210
John of Antioch, 18, 22, 24, 154, 164, 165, 166,
  167, 168
John Chrysostom, 13, 16, 22, 23, 25, 32, 97, 104, 129,
  130, 132, 133, 134, 135, 136, 137, 138, 139, 140,
  141, 142, 143, 144, 145, 146, 147, 148, 149
  archive, 143, 146

biography, 135
  exile, 13, 18, 23, 130, 133, 134, 135, 139, 140, 141,
    142, 143, 144, 145, 146, 147
  opponents, 137, 144, 145
  pseudo, 16, 129, 137, 144, 146, 147
  supporters, 134, 135, 136, 137, 145, 147
John the deacon, 204
John of Ephesus, 20, 24
John, *magister militum*, 214
John the monk, 92
John of Nola, 218
John, subdeacon, 208
John, *vicarianus*, 207
Jordanes, 220
Julian, emperor, 4, 11, 12, 26, 97
Juliana Anicia, 13, 153
Julius Titianus, 19
Julius Victor, 10, 11, 12
Justin I, emperor, 26
Justinian I, emperor, 23, 26, 29, 166, 212
Justus, bishop of Lyons, 104

Karteria, 13

labour, 31, 162, 216
laity, 34, 89, 137, 138, 140, 145, 147, 168, 178, 216
Laodicea, 38, 39, 135, 150, 152, 153, 193
Latin, 138, 139, 140, 165, 188, *see also* translation,
  Latin
  canon law, 179
  classics, 100
  competency, 138, 146, 183
  corpora, 206
  non-fictional letters, 7
  style, 100
  terminology, 12
  titles, 84
Lausiac History, 78
lay communities, 15
Leo I, 3, 10, 14, 17, 163, 177, 178, 179, 181, 184,
  185, 186, 188, 189, 192, 194, 196, 197, 198,
  200, 201, 202, 203, 213, 216
  canon law-collections, 216
  correspondence with Theodoret, 163
  discipline of clergy, 187, 215
  dispute with Hilary of Arles, 189
  interest in Gaul, 185, 188
  letter about Manichees, 185
  letter-collecting, 188
  letter-distribution, 176, 188, 189
  letters, 177, 185, 187, 206, 208
    on papal primacy, 212
  works, 176
Leo IV, 210
Leo of Catena, 209

Lérins, monastery, 217
letter-bearers, 12, 136, 214
letters
  administrative, 7
  of admonition, 7
  of advice, 7
  consolation, 7, 9, 10, 11, 13, 101, 120, 135, 136,
    140
  to Corinth, 40
  disciplinary, 7
  distribution, 3, 5, 135, 185
  documentary, 93
  episcopal, 15, 177
  festal, 24, 28, 90, 160
  friendship, 9, 13, 135, 137, 157, 160, 169, 170
  judgements, 7
  to Laodicea, 40
  organisation, 8, 16, 51
  papal, 8, 10, 13, 17, 175, 179, 182, 187, 189, 190,
    200, 206, 210, 211, 216
  pastoral, 7, 8, 9, 11, 24, 29, 32, 39, 103, 136,
    137, 139, 140
  Pauline, 40, *see also* Paul, apostle
  praise, 136, 137
Libanius, orator, 5, 11, 12, 26, 97, 104, 121, 160
Libanius, priest of Antioch, 136, 146
Libanius, pseudo, 10
Liber Pontificalis, 207, 209, 213, 218, 219
library, 6, 85, 87, 88, 89, 176, 188
  papal, 207, 209
Lyons, 108, 181

Macarius, monk, 69
  homily, 73, 78
Macedonia, 39, 153
  bishops of, 110
Macrina the Younger, 119
  Life, 124
Manichaeans, 85
Marcellinus, 150, 151, 152, 185, 186, 187, 193, 202, 220
Marcionite canon, 39, 46
Maximus, usurper, 98, 106, 111
Meletius of Antioch, 118, 121
Melleus the subdeacon, 219
Menander Rhetor, 10
Michael the Syrian, 21
Milan
  city of, 153
  see of, 24, 99, 106, 107, 108, 111, 140
monasticism, 81
  coenobitic, 82
  Melitian, 82
  Pachomian, 16
monks, 11, 21, 68, 75, 81, 82, 87, 89, 91, 93, 120,
  149, 151, 154, 165, 170, 217

Montfaucon, B. de, 131, 132, 148
Mopsuestia, 149, 165, 167
Muratorian canon, 39, 47

Narbonne
  bishops of, 186
Narses, general, 212, 213, 214, 218
Nestorius, 27, 165, 166, 167, 168, 207
Nicholas I, 209
Nish, 110
notaries, papal, 207, 209, 219

Olympias, 13, 23, 129, 130, 131, 132, 134, 135, 136,
  137, 138, 140, 141, 143, 145, 146, 148
Onesimus, 45
Origen of Alexandria, 71, 105, 106, 107, 109
Orontianus, 103, 104, 105, 106, 107
ostraca, 16, 69, 70, 80, 81, 83, 89, 90, 91, 93
Ovid, 4

Pachomian, 55, 59, 66, 84, 85, 87
Pachomius, 16, 55, 58, 59, 67, 68, 69, 81, 82, 83,
  84, 85, 86, 87, 91, 93
  Life of, 82, 91, 93
Palestine, 149
Palladius, 129, 130, 132, 141, 145, 147, 151, 154, 158
Paphnutius, 69
papyri, 16, 54, 55, 58, 59, 60, 61, 62, 64, 65, 67,
  69, 70, 80, 81, 83, 86, 88, 89, 91, 93
parchment, 50, 58, 59, 70, 83, 85, 91
Pastoral Epistles, *see* Timothy, Titus
Paul, apostle, 8, 9, 15, 22, 37, 49, 54, 56, 57, 60,
  65, 66, 80, 98
'Pauline involvement' theory, 51
'Paulusbild', 42, 43
Paul the Black, 20, 21, 22, 30
Paul of Edessa, 30
Paulinus, 196
Paulinus of Antioch, 182
Paulinus of Fossombrone, 214, 215
Paulinus of Nola, 3, 98, 105
Paulinus, priest, 97, 98, 99, 101
Pelagius I, 10, 17, 151, 166, 179, 206, 207, 208,
  209, 210, 211, 212, 213, 214, 215, 216, 217,
  218, 219, 220
Pelagius II, 204
Persians, 136, 159, 160
Phalaris, 26
Pharetrios of Caesarea, 13
Philemon, 37, 39, 43, 45, 46, 50
Philippi, 37, 39
Philo of Alexandria, 105, 106, 108, 109
Philostratus, sophist, 4, 26
Phoibammon, monastery, 89, 90, 93
Photius, 26

Pityus, 145
plague, 14, 102, 141, 212, 217
Pliny the Younger, 5, 6, 7, 19, 20, 80, 100, 102
Poemen, 92
poetry, 109, 161
Polycarp, 40, 45, 47, 80
poor, the, 3, 159, 162, 206, 216, 217, 218
Porphyrius of Antioch, 134
Porphyrius, bishop of Antioch, 134
poverty, *see* the poor
praetorian prefect, 207, 217, 218
primacy, 209, 220
  papal, 211, 212
prison, 22, 120, 136, 148
Procopius of Gaza, 26
property, 12, 22, 90, 98, 105, 142, 206, 216, 218, 220
  papal, 211, 212, 220, *see also* estates, papal
Prosper Tiro, 220
ps-Demetrius, 9
ps-Zachariah Scholasticus, 29

rhetoric
  Greek, 100
  Latin, 100
Rome, 4, 37, 46, 133, 140, 178, 180, 185, 186, 189,
    206, 211, 212, 213, 214, 215, 216, 217, 219
  bishops of, 3, 8, 11, 14, 15, 17, 25, 31, 33, 129,
      176, 189, 214, 218
  church of, 40
  city of, 46, 50, 61, 110, 153
  people of, 213, 216, 220
  see of, 138, 139, 140, 141, 210, 220
  senate, 100, 110
Rufinus of Aquileia, 15, 107, 109, 149, 152, 179,
    240
Rufus, bishop of Thessalonica, 183, 207
Ruricius of Limoges, 13

St Macarius, monastery, 70
Sanhedrin, 43
Sapaudus, bishop of Arles, 208, 209, 215, 217
Savile, H., 23, 131, 132, 148
Sayings of the Desert Fathers, 71, 92, 208
scrinium, *see* archive
  papal, 209
Scythopolis, 149
Seleucia, 13, 21, 163, 164
Seneca, 5, 6, 7, 8, 9, 10, 104
Sergius the Grammarian, 30
Severus of Antioch, 3, 12, 18, 19, 24, 26, 27, 29,
    30, 31, 32, 33, 90, 92, 150
Shenoute, 68, 69, 77, 79, 85, 86, 87, 90, 93
Sidonius Apollinaris, 3, 6, 7, 18, 19, 20, 26, 33
Silvanus, 9, 83
Silvanus (Silas), 48

Sinai, Mt, 70, 73
Siricius, 179, 181, 201, 204
Sofia, 110
Sozomen, 132, 139, 140, 145
Stephan VI, 210
Syagrius, bishop of Verona, 106
Symmachus I, 182, 195, 202, 204, 208
Symmachus, senator, 4, 6, 11, 19, 97, 100, 104,
    110, 111
Synesius of Cyrene, 3, 7, 14, 102
Synod
  Agde, 194, 200
  Antioch, 193
  Arles, 179, 193, 194, 200, 201
  Carthage, 193, 200
  Clermont, 200
  Constantinople, 135, 193, 196, 202
  Gangra, 177, 178, 180, 182, 184, 185, 190, 193
  Orange, 194, 200
  Orléans, 194, 202
  Riez, 194
  Rome, 200, 204
  Thélepte, 185, 186, 193, 201
  Turin, 193
  Vaison, 194, 200
  Valence, 193
Syria, 20, 22, 134, 137, 138, 144, 145, 149, 150, 151,
    152, 154, 157, 160, 165
  bishops of, 120
  clergy, 137
Syriac, 20, 21, 22, 24, 29, 30, 32, 70,
    73, 74, 166

Thebes, 88, 89
Themistocles, 4, 8
Theodora, 13, 136, 142, 148, 151
Theodore of Mopsuestia, 212
Theodoret of Cyrrhus, 3, 14, 16, 19, 24, 27, 28,
    30, 33, 141, 145, 154, 155, 156, 157, 158, 159,
    160, 161, 162, 163, 164, 165, 166, 167, 168,
    169, 170, 171, 212, 213, 215
  archive, 167
  exile, 155, 163, 166
Theodoric, 14, 25, 204, 211, 216
Theodosius I, emperor, 98, 101, 105, 111, 112, 124
Theodosius II, emperor, 14, 164, 165
Theodosius, patriarch of Alexandria, 21, 30
Theodotus, deacon, 146
Theophilus of Alexandria, 110, 134, 137, 141
Theophilus, presbyter at Constantinople, 143
Theophylact Simocatta, 26
Thessalonica, 101, 153
  bishop of, 101, 106, 189
  ecumenical synod at, 131
  first Christian community in, 9, 37, 39

Three Chapters controversy, 166, 167, 208, 212, 213, 214, 217, 219
Timothy, 8, 9, 37, 39, 41, 46, 47, 48, 50, 52
Titus, 8, 37, 41, 43, 50, 154, 155, 157, 168
translation, 86, 164, 167
   Arabic, 70
   Coptic, 93
   Georgian, 70, 71, 73
   Greek, 73, 93, 139, 140
   Latin, 17, 28, 70, 71, 82, 93, 114, 139, 140, 165, 208
      Jerome, 58, 66, 83, 84, 93
      Pelagius, 208
      Rufinus, 15, 107, 179
      Rusticus, 23, 167
   Syriac, 22, 29, 30, 32, 73, 166

Urban II, 210

Valentinian II, emperor, 100, 105, 106, 110, 111
Valentinian III, emperor, 14
Vannes, 200
Venerius of Milan, 138
Vetus Gallica, 181, 183
Victor, 42, 89
Vienne, 178, 208
   bishops of, 186
Vigilius, bishop of Rome, 177, 179, 208, 212, 213, 217
Vigilius of Trent, 140
Virgil, 100, 106, 110

White Monastery, 81, 87

Zeugma, 28, 152, 159
Zosimus, 17, 177, 181, 184, 186, 190, 201, 204

Index of biblical citations

Old Testament

Genesis 106
Gen. 18 161

Exodus 102
Ex. 30:11–13 102
Ex. 30:12–16 108

Deuteronomy
Deut. 21:16 103
Deut. 22:5 103
Deut. 32:39 103

Proverbs
Prov. 27:1 161

Jeremiah
Jer. 17:11 103

Haggai
Hag. 1:4 103

New Testament

Luke 43, 44, 47
Luke 1:3 44
Luke 1:4 44

John 45

Acts 43, 44, 47, 51, 52, 53
Acts 1:1 44
Acts 9:15–16 43
Acts 9:23–9 43
Acts 15:1–29 43
Acts 16:3 43
Acts 18:12–13 43
Acts 19:11–12 43
Acts 20:10 43
Acts 20:19 43
Acts 20:21 43
Acts 20: 27–9 43
Acts 21:17–19 43
Acts 21:17–26 43

Acts 22:30–23 :10 43
Acts 24:1–25 :12 43
Acts 25:23–26 :29 43

Romans 39, 40, 41, 43, 45, 50, 51, 107
Rom. 3:8 43, 50
Rom. 6:1–23 43
Rom. 7:6 43
Rom. 10:4 43
Rom. 12:1–2 43
Rom. 15:25–33 43
Rom. 16 39, 60

1 Corinthians 40, 45, 48, 50, 51
1 Cor. 1:1 48
1 Cor. 1:10–12 40
1 Cor. 1:10–17 43
1 Cor. 1:12 40
1 Cor. 1:17–31 49
1 Cor. 1:18–2 :16 43
1 Cor. 2:1–16 49
1 Cor. 5:9 37, 38, 43
1 Cor. 5:9–10 49
1 Cor. 9:1 50
1 Cor. 9:5 43
1 Cor. 9:20–1 43
1 Cor. 14:33b-36 38, 52
1 Cor. 15:8–11 43
1 Cor. 16:8 46
1 Cor. 16:19 46
1 Cor. 16:21 48
1 Cor. 16:21–4 48
2 Corinthians 37, 38, 40, 43, 45, 46, 49, 50, 51, 54, 55, 67
2 Cor. 1:1 48, 49, 51, 52
2 Cor. 2:4 37, 38
2 Cor. 3:1–6 43
2 Cor. 7:8 49
2 Cor. 8–9 55, 66
2 Cor. 9 67
2 Cor. 10:10 49

2 Cor. 10:10–11 98
2 Cor. 10:1–33 43
2 Cor. 11:16 49

Galatians 40, 43, 45, 50, 107
Gal. 1:1 37
Gal. 1:2 49, 51, 52
Gal. 1:10–12 50
Gal. 1:19 50
Gal. 2:1–14 43
Gal. 2:19 43
Gal. 3:1–5 43
Gal. 5:11 43, 50
Gal. 5:16–26 43
Gal. 5:18 43
Gal. 6:1 48

Ephesians 8, 37, 39, 40, 41, 42, 45,
    46, 50, 51
Eph. 1:1 42
Eph. 1:17–19 42
Eph. 2:13–18 42
Eph. 3:1 42
Eph. 3:14–19 42
Eph. 4:1 42
Eph. 4:7–16 42
Eph. 5:21–33 42
Eph. 6:10–17 42

Philippians 38, 39, 41, 43, 45, 49, 51
Phil. 1:1 48
Phil. 3:8 43

Colossians 8, 37, 39, 41, 42, 45
Col. 1:1 46, 48
Col. 1:23–5 42
Col. 4:6 37, 38
Col. 4:7–17 46
Col. 4:9 45
Col. 4:10 42
Col. 4:16 37, 49, 51, 52
Col. 4:18 46, 47, 48

1 Thessalonians 9, 39, 43, 51
1 Thess. 1:1 47, 48

1 Thess. 2:14–16 38, 52
1 Thess. 2:18 48
1 Thess. 4:13 37
1 Thess. 5:27 37, 39
2 Thessalonians 8, 37, 39, 51
2 Thess. 1:1 48
2 Thess. 2:2 37, 50
2 Thess. 2:15 49
2 Thess. 3:17 48

1 Timothy 8, 37, 41, 50, 51
1 Tim. 1:10–11 43
1 Tim. 1:2 47
1 Tim. 1:4 41
1 Tim. 1:11 43
1 Tim. 6:3 43
1 Tim. 6:11 43
1 Tim. 6:20 41
2 Timothy 8, 37, 41, 51, 52
2 Tim. 2:10–12 43
2 Tim. 2:16–18 37
2 Tim. 3:10 43
2 Tim. 4:13 50, 51, 53

Titus 8, 37, 41, 50, 51
Titus 1:1 43
Titus 1:3 43
Titus 2:2 43
Titus 2:12 43

Philemon 39, 43, 45, 46
Phlm. 1–2 37
Phlm. 10 45
Phlm. 19 48

Hebrews 37, 40, 51

1 Peter 39
2 Peter 8, 39, 42, 44, 47
2 Pet. 3:13 53
2 Pet. 3:16 43, 47, 53

1–2 John 39

Jude 39

Revelation 45